BUILDING TYPE BASICS FOR

transit facilities

BUILDING TYPE BASICS FOR

transit facilities

Stephen A. Kliment, Series Founder and Editor

KENNETH W. GRIFFIN

WILEY

JOHN WILEY & SONS, INC.

Library of Congress Cataloging-in-Publication Data:
Griffin, Kenneth.
  Building type basics for transit facilities / by Kenneth Griffin.
      p. cm.—(Building type basics)
Includes bibliographical references and index.
  ISBN 0-471-27339-2 (Cloth)
  1. Transportation buildings—Design and construction. 2. Terminals
(Transportation)—Designs and construction. I. Title. II. Building type
basics series.
  NA6290.G75 2004
  725'.3--dc22
                                        2003019194

Printed in the United States of America.
10 9 8 7 6 5 4 3 2 1

CONTENTS

CONTENTS

PREFACE

STEPHEN A. KLIMENT *Series Founder and Editor*

The first rail station in the United States was built in 1830 at Mount Clare, Baltimore, Maryland. As Kenneth Griffin points out in this book, "the new nineteenth-century steam-powered rail technology was immediately adopted by the rapidly industrializing nations and soon was the preferred method for moving raw materials and manufactured goods between factories, ports, and cities." "To win political support for the creation of new lines," adds Griffin, "the newly formed railroads offered passenger service, and thus began the construction of train terminals in most of the world's major cities.... Before long, the railroads were carrying European immigrants to the recently opened frontiers of the American West."

"The growth of the railroads meant not only the construction of passenger stations in the already developed cities of the eastern United States; it was instrumental also in forming the nuclei of the developing cities in the Midwest and West," Griffin emphasizes. By 1950, 40,000 passenger stations had been built in the United States. "Railroads have contributed immensely to the development of our world," in Griffin's estimation, "and have left a legacy of infrastructure and unique building forms that we continue to reuse and reshape."

Travel and transportation is the world's largest industry, and transit is a major government-funded activity. Over 500 U.S. public transit operators serve some 300 major urban areas, estimates Griffin, while another 5000 organizations furnish transit service to smaller cities and towns.

The dollars spent are significant. Some $7 billion in expenditures are apportioned each year to rail transit; $41 billion has been spent over the past six years under the Transportation Equity Act for the Twenty-First Century (TEA-21). New starts are rising in all parts of the country, including Puerto Rico, and rail extensions to major transit systems are planned in San Francisco, New York, and Philadelphia. Light rail systems are projected for Memphis, Dallas, Houston, and Raleigh. Buildings and infrastructure for commuter rail systems are slated for modernization in the northeast and the Chicago region.

Designing, adding to, or renovating the architecture to house these systems are major challenges because of the ingredients of movement, safety, and comfort that are unique to this building type. The design process for a typical station is complex and calls for the architect and engineer to work with many specialized disciplines.

In addition to surface-rail transit, chapters of this book are dedicated to transit stations at airports, cruise terminals, and intermodal facilities. Griffin focuses especially on such critical issues as urban planning and station area development, station types and configurations, engineering concerns, wayfinding, safety and security, and modernization.

This volume in the Wiley "Building Type Basics" series provides an overview of the entire planning process, and serves as a resource for professional staff at public transit agencies, architects, engineers and their consultants, urban designers, and transportation planners.

Building Type Basics for Transit Facilities, like the other volumes in the Wiley series, is not a coffee-table book lavish with color photography but meager in usable content. Instead, it contains hands-on information that architects and engineers and their clients and consultants require, especially in the crucial early phases of a project. Students at schools of architecture, engineering, planning, urban design, and landscape architecture will also find the volume useful, as a kind of Cliffs Notes to get a head start on an assigned studio problem.

Following the format of the other volumes in the series, *Transit Facilities* is tightly organized for ease of use. The volume responds to a set of twenty questions most commonly asked about a building type in the early phases of its design. The twenty questions include predesign (programming) guidelines, details of the project delivery process, design concerns unique to the building type, site planning, codes and ADA matters, energy and environmental challenges, engineering systems, lighting and acoustics pointers, signs and wayfinding, preservation and modernization issues, and cost and feasibility factors. For a listing of the twenty questions, see the endpapers at the front and back of this volume, which also serve as a quick index to these topics.

I hope you find this volume both helpful and inspiring.

ACKNOWLEDGMENTS

Special thanks to my wife, Nancy, for her support and tireless effort in helping me, and to my son Joe who patiently allowed me, while in his high school senior year, to pursue this endeavor. And to my sons Ken, Mike, and Dave for their continuous support.

This book could not have happened without the support of certain individuals who prepared the graphics to support the chapters and helped organize the general format. Special thanks go to Francisco Ruiz, Alfred Lau, Romy Alcasabas, Gus Courpas, Laura Musser-Frawley, Manny Ferro, and Nolen Strals for their efforts.

I wish to acknowledge the various transit agencies and architectural firms that permitted me to use their project photos.

CHAPTER 1
Special thanks to Paul Diez for his preparation of the Station Design Guidelines section and to Howard Gregson for his contribution to the System Technologies section. My appreciation goes to Frank Russo for his assistance on vehicle sizes and his review of the transit history section.

CHAPTER 2
Thanks to Diana Mendez and Sheldon Fialkoff for their collaboration on the chapter, and to Josh Sawislak for his thorough review.

CHAPTER 4
I would like to extend my gratitude to a close friend and collaborator on many transit projects, Martin Green. He was asked to create the examples to support the 12 planning steps to station design, as well as the NFPA 130 exiting analysis, and he performed the exercise extremely well, as I imagined he would.

CHAPTER 6
The General Design Considerations and Issues section is dedicated to two close friends who have influenced this book and enriched my life immensely, James Francomacaro and Wally DelaBarre. In addition to assisting with this chapter, they helped formulate the overall strategy for presenting a complex subject such as this. As always, I am in their debt.

The Vertical Circulation section received a thorough and detailed review by Lou Scurci, and I thank him.

Bruce Dandie prepared the Mechanical Considerations section, and a special note of appreciation goes to him.

ACKNOWLEDGMENTS

CHAPTER 7

Thanks to Matt Pollack for his preparation of this chapter.

CHAPTER 8

Thanks go to Catherine Houska of the Nickel Development Institute for her insightful recommendations on the use of stainless steel.

CHAPTER 9

I would like to extend my gratitude to Richard Carman. His dedication and his vast knowledge of acoustics have enriched the station planning profession and this chapter. Richard also acknowledges the efforts of Steven L. Wolfe for his in-depth review and suggestions for examples.

CHAPTER 10

Thanks to Domingo Gonzales and his assistant, A. C. Hickok, for their preparation of this chapter. They both wish to acknowledge Kathy Garcia for her hard work on the word processing and formatting.

CHAPTER 11

I would like to acknowledge Joseph Erhart and his firm for their tireless effort in writing this chapter.

CHAPTER 13

A very special thank you goes to Robert Davidson of the Port Authority of New York and New Jersey (PANYNJ) for sharing with us his knowledge of rail planning at airports. This chapter is dedicated to his assistants and the architects who collaborated with him in carrying out the detailed design of these many projects. Special thanks also go to Steve Plate of PANYNJ for his dedication to the construction of the Air-Train project and for giving me an insight into the complexities of building a rail system adjacent to an active airport.

CHAPTER 14

I would like to thank Richard Heidrich for being a talented architect and for his thorough and timely preparation of this chapter.

INTRODUCTION

Architectural history is rich in civic projects built for the common good of all citizens. Large engineering projects such as bridges and the older subway systems historically provided an architecture that offered more than strictly function. For instance, many of the older bridges were graced with sculptural pylons as symbolic gateways to the city. Much attention was devoted to highly detailed balustrades and hand-carved ornamentation. Utilitarian buildings such as train stations were highly refined and ornate works of civic architecture. The same civic commitment to quality architecture in the modern transit station is the focus of this book.

The interrelationship between the architectural design process and engineering design is critical. For most buildings architecture has the lead in setting the building form to serve the function, whereas the engineering team must have a high level of responsibility in site design, structural design, and the design of building services—that is, the mechanical and electrical equipment. Architects lead all development of concepts, building form, layout, and building functions. For transit stations the location, siting, and, to a large extent, station form are dictated by both architecture and engineering. This includes service requirements, site conditions, and operational requirements. This is especially true for the design of transit stations, which is typically driven by adjacent transit line profiles (depth, grades, curves, etc.), and the configuration of interfacing line structures such elements as tunnels, cut-and-cover boxes, shafts, and tracks.

Although engineering considerations have a greater influence on the design of transit stations than on most other buildings, good architectural design is essential, as is close cooperation between the architectural and engineering design groups. The concepts and design details controlled by architecture will always determine passenger convenience and comfort, developing ridership and public acceptance. Yet those design elements controlled by engineering—structural efficiency and cost-effectiveness, safe and efficient train operations, interior environmental conditions (temperature, humidity, air movement), fire safety, effective communications, reliability, durability, and maintainability—are usually either taken for granted by the public—or not understood. Architecturally well-conceived and well-designed transit stations will not only serve transportation functions for a reasonably long period, but are also appealing, convenient, efficient to use, and add significantly to the quality of urban areas.

The primary objectives of all urban transit systems are to encourage near-term and long-term transit ridership and to enhance urban development in line with public policy. The design of a transit system must serve these main objectives, as well as a number of others:

- Minimize physical and cost impacts on existing buildings and planned development.
- Minimize impacts during construction.
- Recognize such factors as geology, existing and planned utilities
- Show sensitivity to adjacent development (i.e., parks, hospitals, entertainment centers, major traffic arteries, and other urban features) likely to be affected by transit construction and operation.

This book is not intended to review the entire range of steps in the design of a modern rapid transit system, but rather to cite the critical steps. Some of the broad engineering assumptions determining station concepts are reviewed. Engineering design issues that affect station design are discussed, as well as the influence of engineering on the design of various station types.

Transit systems, including bus stations, are a major influence in our lives and have a direct impact on the cities and built environments in which we live. As a rule, a new transit station affects much larger numbers of people than a retail or office building. Architects must be more active in the overall transit planning process. This book is a start in that direction. By grasping the complex issues that contribute to the process of transit system and station design, the architect will be a stronger, better-informed participant, better positioned to influence the function and form of a station.

CHAPTER 1

PREDESIGN

HISTORY OF TRANSIT STATIONS

The history of railroad stations as a building form began in England in 1830 with the opening of the Liverpool and Manchester Railway. The first rail station, at Crown Street in Liverpool, is no longer in existence (Meeks 1975, pp. 26–27). The new steam-powered rail technology, created in the nineteenth century, was immediately adopted by the rapidly industrializing nations and was soon the preferred method for moving raw materials and manufactured goods between ports, factories, and cities. To gain the political support needed to create new lines and depots, the newly formed railroads offered passenger service, and thus began the construction of train terminals in most of the world's major cities. Steam-powered railroads were quick to expand in Europe and North America. Between 1828 and 1835 the Baltimore and Ohio's Old Main Line was constructed and became the first commercial railroad in the United States, connecting Baltimore with Ellicott City, Maryland. The first passenger rail station in the United States was built in 1830 at Mount Clare, Baltimore, Maryland.

Before long, the railroads were carrying newly arrived European immigrants to the recently opened frontiers of the American West. The growth of the railroads meant not only the construction of rail stations in the already developed cities in the eastern United States; it was instrumental also in forming the nuclei of the developing cities in the Midwest and West. Estimates are that more than 40,000 passenger stations were built in the United States in the next 120 years (Educational Facilities Laboratories 1974, p. 6). Similarly, railroads were forming in Europe, and new stations were generally located on the periphery of the historically defined older cities; they were, nonetheless, major social-economic forces that contributed to changes in the small towns and larger cities.

◀ The Ellicott City, Maryland, rail station which, was the terminus to the first commercial railway in the United States.

▲ Durand, Michigan. Early station design did not always keep pace with railroad construction, which often resulted in multisided terminals. (Photo: Educational Facility Laboratories, Reusing Railroad Stations.)

The volume of passengers traveling on railroads in the United States peaked in the mid-1940s with the wartime movement of military personnel. In the postwar United States, the automobile and the airplane, because of the flexibility and speed they offered, became the preferred modes of travel. It has been said that if the railroad owners of the early twentieth century were visionaries and truly in the transportation business, they would be the present-day airline owners.

Railroads have contributed immensely to the development of our world, and have left a legacy of infrastructure and unique building forms that we will continue to reuse and reshape for the transportation systems and intermodal transit centers of the future.

The Architecture of Railroad Stations

Initially, the major city train terminals were usually situated on the edges of the downtown business centers. Their entrance into the very core of the cities was restricted because of the fumes produced by the coal-burning locomotives and their deleterious effects on public health. The location of train terminals was also influenced by the opportunities to clear cities of slums resulting from the great demand for track space, as well as the city fathers' willingness to offer land. The newly formed train terminals developed into large-span cast iron and steel structures with roof openings to allow gases to escape and glass panels to let light in. As railroad travel increased, passenger services improved. No longer merely covered platforms, the stations developed into complex hubs that offered waiting rooms, baggage and mail handling, food service, and ticketing, similar in many respects to the modern airport terminal. Train terminals in the early 1900s were handling far greater numbers of passengers than today's average large city airport. Passengers and well wishers arrived at terminals by the thousands to board or meet arriving passengers on trains that were as frequent as several minutes apart, each carrying hundreds of passengers.

Many of the challenges presented by the functional requirements of stations encouraged the creation of innovative large public spaces, such as Grand Central Terminal and the former Pennsylvania Station in New York City and Union Station in Kansas City, Missouri (1910). The Kansas City station was designed to handle 350 trains a day, and during its peak in 1917, 218 trains per day stopped here. (Golay 2000, pp. 115–116). Structures like these had not been built since the great gothic cathedrals or the public arenas and baths of the Roman era. Prominent architects were employed to design the finest Beaux Arts and Classic Revival architectural styles of the times. Stations were being developed across the United States that embodied the spirit of the young New World.

Social change was happening throughout the country, and it was often reflected in the style of architecture chosen or, in many cases, inspired by its towns and communities. But while unique train station architecture was provided to attract customers to rival railroads competing for passenger business, basic principles of station planning were being consistently applied by the railroads. Standards of ser-

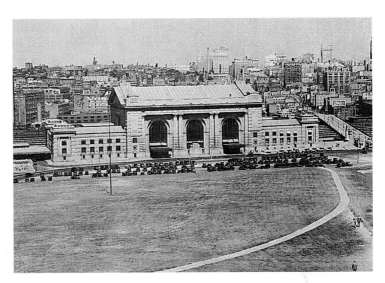

▲ Among U.S. stations, Union Station in Kansas City, Missouri, was second in size to Grand Central Terminal in New York City. It was built at a cost of $11 million in 1910 and had 16 through-passenger tracks. The station is currently a science center. This photo dates from the 1920s.

vice were being applied uniformly. Railroads wanted the passenger experience to be smooth and unencumbered.

In the early twentieth century two of America's greatest railroad terminals ever built were constructed in New York City, the nation's premier transportation center: The second Grand Central Terminal (1903–1913) and the Pennsylvania Station (1906–1910). Soon after Penn Station was built, author and railroad employee John Droege recognized that in the sprawling facility, which required passengers to cover long distances on foot, the walk was greatly enhanced by the spectacular physical setting. He described it as a "magnificent distance." Architect Charles F. McKim modeled the vast waiting room on the Roman baths of Caracalla. One hundred thousand people turned out on its opening day.

Stations in smaller towns and villages were the most self-assured and fully realized examples of eighteenth- and nineteenth-century American architecture. Many of these buildings still stand as the finest civic architecture achieved in their cities. It was a functional, practical architecture, embraced by communities and promoted by railroads, most of which were chiefly in the freight-hauling business but politically and economically placed in a position of public service.

The Evolution of Railroads

Today's transit systems evolved from the initial railroads and now accommodate the vast numbers of people who elect to commute to work via transit in lieu of an automobile. The popularity of transit is due to its reliability and affordability. In the following sections the evolution of railroads to other modes is discussed. It is the transfer of intercity transit to local travel, and the built infrastructure that it has left behind, that have provided us with much of the operating systems we have in place today.

Other forms of rail travel

While passenger railroads were busy connecting cities, other forms of fixed-rail service were being developed, such as streetcars, interurbans, commuter rail, and subways. Streetcar service grew in the mid-nineteenth century from horse-drawn wood carriages on fixed rails, to cable-pulled vehicles, and to eventually electric powered cars. Because of its compact size and flexibility, the system was never a driving force in defining the way in which older cities developed, but served more to provide fast, low-cost travel within the established street network.

An exception is the case of rail transportation in Los Angeles, California, beginning in 1873 with the first franchise issued by the city for a horse car line on Main Street from North Main and Alameda Streets to the city limits, now Jefferson and Main, a distance of about 3 miles. Over the next several years many more franchises were granted, which were ultimately consolidated into the Los Angeles Railway (LARY). Collis Huntington and his nephew Henry then acquired the LARY in 1898. Henry immediately proceeded to scrap the system, tearing out all cable car lines and the roadbed of the electrified lines, replacing them with new rails, ties, and cars. He also expanded the system, including new lines and car houses. He had also developed the Pacific Electric Railway Company (PE), extending service to new areas before selling the PE and other individual lines to the Southern Pacific Company in 1910.

Streetcars were a linking mechanism that provided riders a reliable connection between the inner city and the rail terminal. The technology was extremely popular until the mid-1950s, when it lost fa-

▼ *Union Station in Denver, Colorado: View from 17th Street looking toward the station in about 1905, with a welcome arch framing the entrance.*

vor with the encroaching reliance on the automobile and the development of extended suburbs. It never had a history of providing a fixed platform, canopy, or station structure but relied more on the existing streets and building canopies to offer shelter.

Electric interurban railways (interurbans)

Interurban systems were a popular form of rail travel that offered service between small towns and cities. They were developed principally in the midwest and were highly popular in the period between 1900 and 1930. Electric utility companies owned most of these lines. There were more than 500 miles of track existed in Texas alone, principally in the Dallas-Fort Worth area. The South Shore Line, a high-speed commuter railroad that connects Chicago with South Bend, is the last of this once vast network of electric railways. Competition from the steam railroads and the automobile drained ridership, and most systems went into bankruptcy. Bus services then captured their ridership. The interurbans operated on a time schedule with designated stations and low-level boarding platforms. Many of the station functions were consistent with inter-city rail stations, but there was less reliance on baggage and customer amenities.

Commuter rail

Commuter rail travel evolved as an extension of intercity railroad service, usually on the same tracks but operating between metropolitan and suburban areas. It had lower fares and offered monthly passes and was referred to as "regional rail" or "suburban rail." Most major cities in the world today have some form of commuter rail service. Within the United States the service was offered his-

▲ A modern version of the commuter rail station is the Virginia Railway Express system that serves Washington, D.C., from Manassas and Fredericksburg, Virginia. (Photo courtesy Robert Creamer.)

torically by the larger railroads, but not at competitive fares. This helped justify interurbans. With the reliance on automobiles and the spread of metropolitan areas, highways became congested and commuting by rail became time- and cost-effective for the average commuters looking for alternative means of getting to work. New rail companies were formed by public agencies and today have grown into some of the largest fixed-rail passenger carriers in the country, exceeded only by the older subway systems in cities such as New York, Boston, Philadelphia, and Chicago.

The characteristics of the commuter rail station are similar to those of the original steam-powered railroad stations, in that the architecture reflects an image the community is seeking to present. Much of the architecture draws from period styles.

Many of the older stations still have low boarding platforms, with "high-block" accessibility ramps at platform ends. Others are raising platforms to train car floor heights to meet the current accessibility requirements. Canopies are provided for weather protection, for support lighting, and for signing carriers. Electronic billboards and message centers keep riders informed of train departures and arrivals. Many of the stations provide adjacent automobile parking and are frequently served by bus feeder systems to encourage ridership. A number are equipped with bicycle lockers to attract commuters living within short travel distances.

Subways
In most major urban areas today the commute to work is from an outlying suburban area via a commuter railroad,

connecting to a subway system serving a densely populated urban area. It is in the stations of the subway systems where large numbers of passengers are accommodated due to the dense population and the reliable and frequent train service provided by the subway system.

London Underground

The London Underground is the oldest subway system in the world, the first section having been opened between Paddington and Farrington in 1863 by the Metropolitan Railway. Ever since the days of the coal-burning steam-locomotive-driven train, the system has continued its expansion: from electrification of the line, to tube line construction and conversion to automatic operation of the Victoria Line, to computer signaling and the driverless Docklands Light Railway. Today the Central Line has been modernized, the Jubilee Line Extension is complete, and new trains have been intro-

U.S. COMMUTER RAILROADS	
Baltimore, Md.	MTA, MARC
Boston, Mass.	MBTA
Burlington, Vt.	Champlain Flyer, VTA
Chicago, Ill.	METRA, NIRCIC, NIC
Dallas, Tex.	TRE
Los Angeles, Calif.	Metrolink, SCRRA
Miami, Fla.	Tri-Rail, TCCRA
New Haven, Conn.	Shore Line East
New York, N.Y.	LIRR, MNR, NJT, PATH
Philadelphia, Pa.	SEPTA
San Diego, Calif.	Coaster, NC
San Francisco, Calif.	Caltrain, PCJBP
San Jose, Calif.	ACE
Seattle, Wash.	Sound Transit, CPSRTA
Syracuse, N.Y.	On Track
Washington, D.C.	VRE

WORLD'S LARGEST SUBWAY SYSTEMS (BY RIDERSHIP)			
City	Year System Completed	Number of Riders (year)	Length (miles)
Moscow	1935	3.2 billion (1997)	212
Tokyo	1927	2.6 billion (1997/98)	174
Seoul	1974	1.4 billion (1993)	172
Mexico City	1969	1.4 billion (1996)	125
New York City	1904	1.3 billion (2001)	230
Paris	1900	1.2 billion (1998)	130
Osaka	1933	957 million (1997)	70
London	1863	866 million (1999)	257
Hong Kong	1979	790 million (1999)	50
St. Petersburg	1955	721 million (1996)	68

Sources: Jane's Urban Transport Systems, 2002–2003 edition, and individual subway websites.

duced on the older Northern Line (www.lurs.demon.co.uk). The London Underground started out (like most other late-nineteenth-century systems) as separate train lines transporting passengers in central London. The idea of putting trains underground resulted from the need to transport passengers from the main rail terminals into central London. Because of constraints such as the need to tunnel under buildings and overcrowding, the grand train lines could penetrate only the outskirts of London. In the beginning, any railway tunneling underground had to buy the buildings it passed under. The reason was that many believed that the underground digging undermined the foundations of buildings.

The Paris Metro

The Paris Metro opened in 1900, its first line (now the No. 1) running from Porte de Vincennes to Porte Maillot. Fulgence Bienvenue was the engineer in charge of construction; architect Hector Guimard designed the Art Nouveau entrances. The system has 130 miles of track and 15 lines. There are 368 stations (not including the Reseau Express Regional commuter rail stations), 87 of these being interchanges between lines. There are 3500 cars, which transport roughly 6 million passengers daily (www.paris.org/Metro).

The New York City subway

The New York City subway opened its initial (first of three lines) Interborough Rapid Transit (IRT) segment in 1904. Since then it has expanded to more than 230 miles of routes, more than 400 miles of single track, and 466 stations. The IRT operated from City Hall Loop north to Grand Central, west to Times Square, and north to Broadway and 145th Street.

The second line, the Brooklyn-Manhattan Transit (BMT) was steam powered before 1900. Routes were elevated, built into cuts, or underground, and electrified between 1900 and 1920. The third line, the Independent Subway System (IND), was built during the Depression between 1929 and 1940. Some extensions were built after World War II. The city took over operation of the BMT and the IRT in the early 1940s and merged with the IND into the present-day operating system. Today the New York City Transit (NYCT) subway system is part of the Metropolitan Transportation Authority of New York. Plans to extend the system along Second Avenue commenced with the design and construction of tunnel sections in the 1970s, and as of 2003 included the completion of the 8-mile line from 125th Street and Lexington Avenue to lower Manhattan's financial district (Korman, www.thejoekorner.quuxuum.org).

Other major cities in the United States, such as Philadelphia, Boston, and Newark, New Jersey, developed subway systems in the 1800s and early 1900s, which were significant forces in shaping the cities' growth and expansion.

Urban Mass Transportation in the United States

Although most countries have a long tradition of funding transportation projects, the United States did not begin in earnest until after World War II. The present-day network of mass transit systems evolved in response to competing interests for automobile roadways leading to growing suburbs and urban planners' desires to maintain the viability of cities. By international standards, urban mass transit in the United States is a work in progress, in terms of passengers carried by rail versus private automobile.

Heavy-rail transit

In the 1960s and 1970s many large metropolitan U.S. cities without a history of subways embarked on a program of design and construction of their first heavy-rail mass urban transit systems—Atlanta, Baltimore, Miami, San Francisco, and Washington, D.C. This effort was followed in the 1980s by construction of a street-running and underground light-rail system in Buffalo, New York; street and private right-of-way light-rail transit (LRT) lines in Portland, Oregon, and San Jose, California; and in the 1990s by the Los Angeles Metro and the San Juan, Puerto Rico, Tren Urbano heavy-rail projects. Canada and Mexico also joined in with construction of their mass transit systems in Montreal, Vancouver, and Mexico City. Toronto has an extremely efficient system dating back to the 1930s.

The new U.S. transit stations developed as part of their new mass transit systems form the background of much of the work presented in this book and reflect the rebirth of a hundred-year-old tradition of rail station planning. The basic principles of moving large numbers of passengers through public spaces, on and off platforms, quickly, safely, and effectively, are the basis of this discussion.

Other Transportation Technologies

Today's transportation industry encompasses many aspects of fixed guideway service, ranging from short trips on people movers between terminals at airports to long-haul journeys between cities on high-speed rail systems. In most cases the design trend and urban planning move-

◀ Federal Triangle Station, Washington, D.C., by Daniel, Mann, Johnson & Mendenhall. One of the first stations constructed in Washington Metro's heavy-rail transit system.

ment has been focused on connecting these various systems. This has led to the design of major intermodal terminals where many different technologies come together, presenting new challenges for architects and urban planners.

Automated people movers

The rapid growth of aviation terminals in the early 1970s introduced a fixed-guideway, fully automated technology consisting of small driverless vehicles connecting terminals and passenger parking. Automated people movers (APMs) have expanded into other areas of service such as inner cities (Miami and Detroit) and shopping centers. The system requires an exclusive right-of-way to separate it from any other form of transportation. Recent extensions of APMs are being made to interface it with other means of transit, such as the Newark, New Jersey, airport connection to the Amtrak Northeast Corridor. See Chapter

13, "Rail Stations at Airports," for a discussion of the new Newark station.

High-speed rail

Launched by the French in the 1970s, the modern high-speed rail (HSR) train is expanding rapidly in Europe, Asia, and, to a limited degree, in the United States. Reaching speeds of up to 300 km/h, it is the preferred means of travel within most major European cities, as evidenced by the success of the Train à Grande Vitesse (TGV) and Eurostar systems. Generally, the trains are fixed train sets, symmetric, and reversible, with locomotives, also called power units or power cars, at each end. They are powered by overhead electric catenaries and a single pantograph to the locomotive. High speeds are achievable because of the combination of the track curve radii and superelevation and the grade-separated trackways. The tracks are spaced farther apart to reduce the blast of two passing trains. The high-speed rail station is either a new station designed exclusively for a new rail system, as in the Taiwan HSR project, or an incorporation of the new line into an existing station, as in the Nagoya Station in Japan. The metro-like operation of HSRs has also slowly changed the approach to HSR station design. Although the conventional long-distance train lines are typically provided with waiting rooms and reservation services, not unlike the operation of an airport terminal, the operation of some of the high-capacity HSR systems has been more like a metro operation. Witness the Tokyo Main Station, where passengers can purchase their Shinkansen tickets from ticket vending machines (TVMs) and walk directly through fare gates onto the platform designated for the line for

▶ *Model of proposed Hsinchu Station in Taiwan on the high-speed rail line. Artech Inc. Architects in association with DMJM + Harris.*

◀ JR Central Station and Towers in Nagoya, Japan. Kohn Pederson Fox Associates PC, architects.

their destination and wait for the next train's arrival, usually within minutes. This type of operation obviously requires wide platforms, typically 35–40 ft, for most island platform stations. Design to accommodate passengers on a platform, like a platform for a metro system, requires careful planning in terms of circulation and egress.

Maglev

Considered by environmentalists to be the preferred means of moving large numbers of passengers between cities, because of its low noise levels, low use of electric power, and its low magnetic field emittence, maglev is still trying to get its first operational system in place. As a fairly new type of rail technology, high-speed maglev trains rely on an electromagnetic force for propulsion and braking functions. Typically utilizing aerial guideways, the vehicle locks itself onto the support structure through its operation. Able to reach speeds of 240–330 mph, it is a serious alternative system, like high-speed rail, to airline travel.

Light-rail transit

In the last quarter of the twentieth century, light-rail transit (LRT) experienced a significant revival in the United States, with many "new" systems being started, in most cases reinstating systems removed in the 1950s and 1960s. In some cases, even the same routes were used, such as the Los Angeles to Long Beach, California, "Blue Line." According to the American Public Transportation Association, there are currently 25 systems operating LRT (including historic trolleys) in the United States (see the table on page 12).

In other parts of the world, particularly Europe, the streetcar and street railways

U.S. LIGHT-RAIL TRANSIT AGENCIES					
City	**Agency**	**Directional Route Miles**	**Track Miles**	**Crossings**	**Stations**[1]
Baltimore, Md.	MTA, MDDOT	57.6	50.9	52	32
Boston, Mass.	MBTA	51	77.5	56	95
Buffalo, N.Y.	NFT Metro System	12.4	14.1	8	14
Cleveland, Ohio	GCRTA	30.8	33	22	34
Dallas, Tex.	DART	40.8	46.7	66	20
Dallas, Tex.	McKinney Avenue TA	2.8	2.8	NA	0
Denver, Colo.	RTD	28	28.5	34	20
Detroit, Mich.	Detroit Downtown Trolley	1.2	1.2	NA	0
Galveston, Tex.	Island Transit	4.9	4.9	57	3
Kenosha, Wis.	Kenosha Transit	1.9	1.9	14	1
Los Angeles, Calif.	LACMTA	82.4	85.7	77	36
Memphis, Tenn.	Memphis Area TA	5.8	6.1	40	28
New Orleans, La.	RTA of Orleans & Jefferson	16	13.7	124	9
Newark, N.J.	NJTC	22.1	24.9	16	23
Philadelphia, Pa.	SEPTA	69.3	171	1702	64
Pittsburg, Pa.	PA of Allegheny Co.	34.8	44.8	39	13
Portland, Ore.	City of Portland Street Car	4.8	4.8	NA	31
Portland, Ore.	TRIMET	64.9	71.9	111	47
Sacramento, Calif.	SRTD	40.7	39.4	90	29
St. Louis, Mo.	BiState Development Agency	34	36.2	12	18
Salt Lake City, Utah	UTA	29.6	29.6	46	16
San Diego, Calif.	San Diego Trolley	96.6	96.6	96	49
San Francisco, Calif.	MUNI	70	70	191	11
San Jose, Calif.	SCVTA	55.8	56.3	93	47
Seattle, Wash.	King County DOT	3.7	2.1	14	9

[1]*Many LRT lines have numerous stops in the street that do not meet the definition of a station.*
Source: *APTA website.*

retained their popularity throughout this period and were typically expanded and modernized over time. These systems were the major source of technological innovation and modernization as the systems adapted to growing populations and expansion of the urban areas. Vehicles went from single cars to articulated vehicles of 90 ft or more in length, incorporated the ability to train three or four cars, and adapted new control technology and grade separation. As a result of this evolution, the modern LRT system provides a very flexible operation, adaptable to almost any urban situation.

STATION DESIGN GUIDELINES

There are no generally accepted common standards for transit station design criteria. Comprehensive national or international standards do not exist. Typically, criteria are developed by individual transportation authorities and tailored for their use, based on their own experience, their operational and technological requirements, and information derived from building codes and industry groups like the National Fire Protection Association (NFPA) and the American Public Transit Association (APTA).

Design criteria for most elements of a transit station do, however, tend to fall within a relatively narrow range of values that represent a rough consensus for station design requirements. The data given here reflect a review of the criteria from many systems. Design criteria must continue to evolve. Therefore, any static criteria must be considered a baseline or starting point for a station design and should be evaluated in light of the specific application to which they will be applied. A successful design is a moving target. Design criteria must therefore be

a living body of knowledge that changes and adapts with time and circumstance.

The criteria contained herein are intended to provide the designer with the greatest possible flexibility while ensuring that the functional requirements, goals, and objectives of the station design are satisfied.

Station Site Considerations

Transit users are, by definition, pedestrians. Therefore, special attention must be paid to connecting a transit station to the surrounding pedestrian network. The simplest way of increasing the use of public transportation facilities is to establish an environment where pedestrian access is safe, convenient, and comfortable. Pedestrian facilities connecting the station to the surrounding pedestrian network include sidewalks, walkways, crosswalks, pedestrian bridges, ramps, and curb cuts.

Sidewalks are pedestrian facilities along streets. Sidewalks in residential areas should be of sufficient width for two people to walk abreast comfortably, or a minimum of 5 ft wide. Sidewalks directly leading to transit facilities (including bus stops) should be at least 6 ft wide. Sidewalks in commercial or urban areas must be considerably wider, based on projected patronage. Where sidewalks are not set back from the curb, additional space must be provided to act as a buffer between pedestrians and traffic and to allow for signs, light and signal poles, and other street obstructions (see the illustration on page 14).

Walkways are pedestrian facilities serving corridors not served by streets. Walkways may be designed as dual-use facilities to accommodate bicycle riders. Two-directional, dual-use facilities

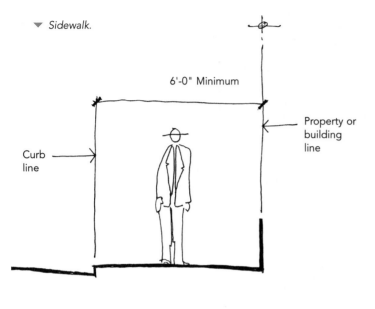

▽ *Sidewalk.*

6'-0" Minimum

Property or
building
line

Curb
line

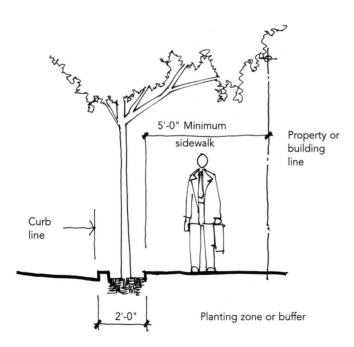

5'-0" Minimum
sidewalk

Property or
building
line

Curb
line

2'-0"

Planting zone or buffer

▲ *Sidewalk with planting zone or buffer.*

should be a minimum of 10 ft wide (see the illustration at right). Where site constraints or other factors restrict the width of a path, a width of 8 ft is permissible; however, pavement markings and signs may be necessary to avoid bicycle/pedestrian conflicts. Walkways intended only for pedestrians should be designed to the same criteria as sidewalks.

Crosswalks should be provided at all intersections along the primary pedestrian routes to transit facilities. Crosswalks should be as wide as the adjacent sidewalks or walkways and be clearly marked so as to be easily visible to auto traffic. Contrasting or textured paving may also be employed to clearly delineate a crosswalk from the roadway and provide a traffic calming effect. Crosswalks at high-volume or congested intersections should be signalized.

Pedestrian bridges should be designed as dual-use facilities to accommodate bicycle riders. Two-directional, dual-use facilities should be a preferred minimum of 10 ft wide; 8 ft wide where constrained, as noted earlier (see the illustration at right). Grades should not exceed 1:15 (6.66 percent) for pedestrian facilities. Grades exceeding 1:15 must meet code requirements for pedestrian ramps. Ramps may not exceed a slope of 1:12 (8.33 percent).

Auto Facilities

Provisions for automobiles at transit facilities include kiss-and-ride, park-and-ride, and parking areas. Kiss-and-ride facilities consist of short-term parking spaces located in close proximity to the station entrance, intended for passengers being dropped off or picked up by automobile. Kiss-and-ride facilities may be combined with taxi facilities, depending on the vol-

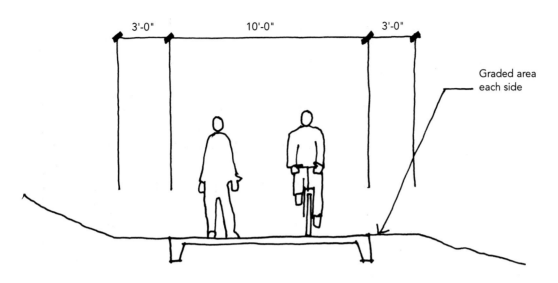

3'-0"   10'-0"   3'-0"

Graded area
each side

▲ *Shared-use walkway/bike path.*

▼ *Grade-separated shared-use
pedestrian/bike path.*

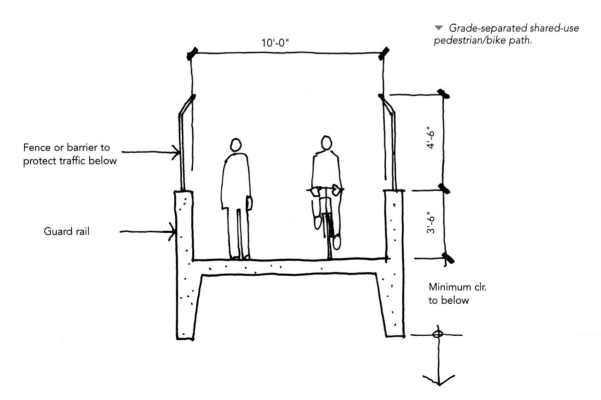

10'-0"

Fence or barrier to
protect traffic below

Guard rail

4'-6"

3'-6"

Minimum clr.
to below

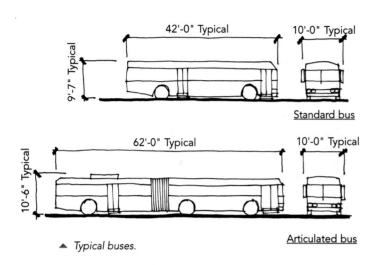

42'-0" Typical   10'-0" Typical

9'-7" Typical

Standard bus

62'-0" Typical   10'-0" Typical

10'-6" Typical

Articulated bus

▲ *Typical buses.*

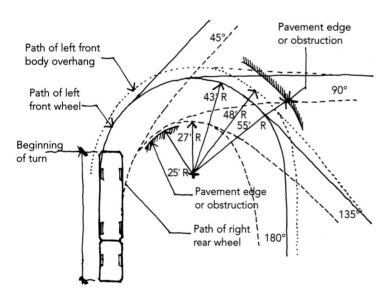

Path of left front
body overhang

Path of left
front wheel

Beginning
of turn

45°

Pavement edge
or obstruction

90°

43' R
48' R
55' R
27' R
25' R

Pavement edge
or obstruction

135°

Path of right
rear wheel   180°

▲ *Typical bus turning radii.*

ume of curbside service (drop-off and pick-up) anticipated at the station. High-volume stations usually function best with separate taxi facilities.

Park-and-ride facilities are intended for commuters who drive to the transit station; they provide all-day parking, usually for a fee. Park-and-ride facilities should be conveniently located relative to the station entrance but should be located beyond bus, shuttle bus, kiss-and-ride, and taxi facilities vying for the curb at the station entrance. Park-and-ride facilities may be configured as parking structures or surface lots, depending on site constraints, land acquisition, walking distances, and other factors.

Bus Facilities

Bus facilities serving transit stations range from single stops along adjacent streets serving one or two lines, to off-street depots serving multiple lines. A detailed description of bus facilities is beyond the scope of this book, but basic guidelines governing the configuration of bus facilities are included for planning purposes. Articulated buses can also be accommodated within these dimensions. The minimum clearance between the roadway and any overhead obstruction where buses operate should be 14 ft 6 in. Some vehicles operating on natural gas or other alternative fuels may require additional clearance overhead.

Bus stops on public streets must be planned as part of a comprehensive traffic engineering study. The curbside lane at a bus stop should be a minimum of 12 ft wide (14 ft preferred). Where the curbside lane is also used for parallel on-street parking, the minimum width should be 18 ft (20 ft preferred). Near-side bus stops—preceding an intersection in the direction of travel—should be at least 100 ft long, measured from the curbline of the intersecting street to the nearest on-street parking space. Far-side bus stops—following an intersection in the direction of travel—should be at least 80 ft long. Far-side bus stops following a turn at an intersection and mid-block stops should be at least 130 ft long. Stop lengths should be increased by 20 ft for articulated buses. Where it is anticipated that more than one bus may use a stop at the same time the stop length should be increased by 50 ft for each standard bus and 70 ft for each articulated bus.

Turnouts may be utilized at bus stops, depending on traffic conditions and site constraints. Bus turnouts are widened sections of the roadway designed for buses to pull out of the traffic stream. Although advantageous for general traffic, turnouts make it difficult for buses to reenter the general traffic lanes. Therefore, the use of turnouts should be contingent on an analysis of traffic characteristics, signalization, sight lines, and so forth. Turnouts should provide a minimum 50 ft long berth area at the bus stop (70 ft for articulated buses) and an approach and departure taper to the stop from the curb of the travel lane. The approach taper should be a minimum of 60 ft (80 ft preferred) and the departure taper should be a minimum of 40 ft (60 ft preferred). Turnouts should be a minimum of 10 ft deep (12 ft preferred), measured from the edge of the curb travel lane. Where it is anticipated that more than one bus may use a turnout stop at the same time, the length of the berth area should be increased by 50 ft for each standard bus and 70 ft for each articulated bus.

Sidewalks at bus stops should be a minimum of 10 ft wide (15 ft wide in urban and commercial areas). Shelters should be provided to protect waiting passengers from the weather. Where practicable, continuous shelter should be provided from the bus to adjoining transit facilities to allow weather-protected intermodal transfer.

Off-street bus stations may be designed using a variety of configurations. A "saw-toothed" bus bay (see the illustration on page 18) allows for an efficient use of space while facilitating vehicle operations, as the driver can pull into the bay, letting the front wheels of the bus touch the curb, and pull out by turning left without backing up. Saw-toothed stations may be side-loaded or designed with buses circulating clockwise around a center-loaded island. Center- and side-loaded bays may be combined, as illustrated. Pedestrian access to the bus bays must be designed to minimize conflicts with vehicle movement and ensure passenger comfort and safety, utilizing clearly delineated crosswalks, signals, and grade-separated crossings where necessary.

Bicycle Facilities

Bicycle use should be encouraged at public transit facilities, as it reduces traffic congestion, reduces pollution, increases the size of the station's catchment area, and increases transit ridership. Bicycle facilities at stations typically consist of bicycle racks and lockers. Bicycle racks are compact and inexpensive and suitable for short-term parking, or for long-term parking where crime and vandalism is not a problem. Bicycle lockers require much more space and expense, but provide secure, long-term parking. Both racks and lockers should be located close to the station entrance and protected from the

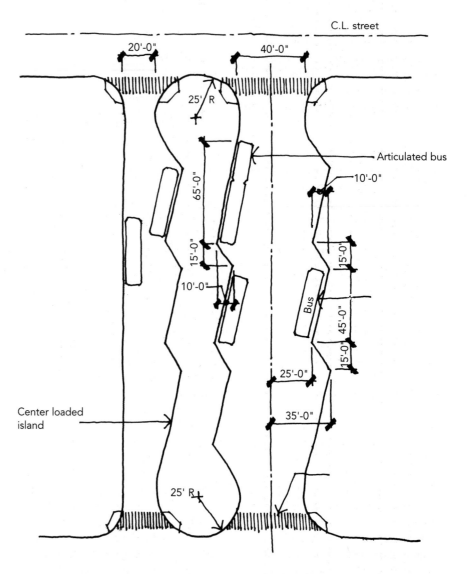

Off-street bus station.

weather if possible. Racks and lockers should be of a simple, low-maintenance design and constructed of durable, maintenance-free materials resistant to abuse and vandalism. Lockers in particular should be architecturally integrated in the station and/or site design. The quantity of bicycle racks and lockers should be de-

termined on the basis of station patronage and user characteristics and in coordination with local bicycle advocacy groups whenever possible.

Service Access

Station site design should provide access for transit staff and service vehicles to perform routine service and maintenance without interrupting normal station operations. Provisions should also be made for the periodic replacement of station equipment. Requirements for service access should be determined in coordination with the development of the station operations and maintenance plan.

Station Entrances

Station entrances provide the link between the station, the city, and the surrounding streets, and their design must reflect the distinct requirements of each. Entrances must provide convenient access for passengers and fit appropriately within the surrounding urban context and community.

Where space is a factor, as it is in most urban environments, station entrances should be positioned beyond the public way to preserve space for pedestrian circulation on the public sidewalks. To this end, entrances should be located within buildings and in public plazas where possible. Station entrances must be clearly visible from outside the station and positioned to be easily detected within the surrounding urban context. Station entrances should be positioned to take best advantage of the surrounding pedestrian network and be easily accessible to crosswalks, public plazas, and other pedestrian facilities. Entrances should also be positioned to provide convenient access to bus stops and other public transportation facilities. Entrances must be fully accessible and integrated with the accessible paths within the local pedestrian network.

A station entrance must be clearly recognizable as a part of the transit system—reflecting a consistent system

---

Factors Influencing the Design of Station Entrances

- The physical constraints of the surrounding structures and streets
- Adjacent land uses
- The availability and cost of real estate
- The surrounding pedestrian network and passenger catchment areas
- Accessibility
- Emergency egress
- Visibility
- Security and access control
- Accommodation of ancillary functions including ventilation and smoke exhaust
- Service and maintenance access

---

identity—and should reflect the architectural character of the surrounding neighborhood.

In general, fewer points of entry will result in simplified wayfinding for passengers, a more efficient station design, and more effective station access control and security. Access to the vertical circulation elements at an entry must be as direct as possible, and the required path of travel should be obvious to the passenger immediately upon entering the station. Vertical circulation elements at the entry must be protected from the weather to ensure passenger safety and comfort and to protect machinery (elevators, escalators) from the deleterious effects of the weather (water, ice, snow, salt, etc.).

Access control (gates, doors) must be provided at the station entrance to close the entrance for maintenance, emergencies, or during nonoperating hours. Consideration must be given to how the entrance will affect the surrounding environment when closed. Hidden niches, vestibules, and overhangs tend to attract undesirable activities in urban areas when the station is not in service, resulting in the trash accumulation, vandalism, and security concerns.

The station entrance size is largely determined by the number and size of the circulation elements (both vertical and horizontal) located within it. The projected patronage for the station, the required level of service, and emergency egress requirements determine the number of circulation elements. Stations with multiple entrances must be carefully evaluated to establish the number of passengers expected to use each entrance.

General dimensional criteria for station entrances are as follows:

- The minimum overhead clearance from the finish floor to a localized obstruction (e.g., a lighting fixture, sign, or structural element) should be 8 ft 6 in. (10 ft preferred) to prevent passengers from reaching the overhead element. The minimum overhead clearance at a ceiling or continuous structure should be 10 ft minimum (12 ft preferred) to allow for lighting, signage, and equipment below the ceiling. Obviously, architectural considerations (spatial proportions) are important in determining ceiling height.

- Sufficient space should be provided at the entry portal to accommodate normal queuing and meeting-and-greeting activities that typically occur at station entrances. Therefore, a minimum of 10 ft should be provided on the exterior of the station entrance

outside of the pedestrian flow on the public sidewalks.

- The width of the entry portal (or portals) must be determined by the projected number of passengers expected to use the entrance, the established level of service desired for the entry, and emergency egress requirements. Typically, a minimum width of 6–9 ft is maintained at entry portals serving low-demand stations, contingent on site-specific requirements.

- Weather protection at the entry must be designed to suit local weather conditions and other site-specific factors (e.g., climate, prevailing winds, topography, and adjacent structures). The goal is to ensure the comfort and safety of passengers using the station entrance. Particular consideration must be given to stairs and escalators because of the safety issues associated with them.

- Queuing and run-off requirements for vertical circulation devices and other equipment are addressed in a following section.

Equipment and furnishings located at station entrances vary greatly according to specific station configuration and use. Typical equipment at station entrances may include fare vending, collection, and control devices, passenger information displays, and customer service facilities.

Some systems allow or encourage commercial vending, concessions, and joint development in or adjacent to station entrances. In such cases the effect of these activities must be factored into the design of the station entrance. The design of these functions must be subordinate to the transit-related functions of the station.

Fare Control and Collection Areas

The station entrance typically leads to a fare control and collection area. Depending on the station's configuration and operational and site characteristics, the fare control and collection area may be located anywhere between the station entrance(s) and the platform. A single fare control and collection area may serve multiple entrances. The fare control and collection area is potentially the weakest link in the station's circulation system, as it is the point where passengers are required to make multiple decisions. Passengers must choose directions, purchase fares, interpret travel information, and orient themselves in a dynamic pedestrian environment. This often leads to a buildup of queuing at key choke points as passengers pause to orient themselves. Therefore, the design of the fare control and collection area must minimize cross flows and conflicting movements between arriving and departing passengers.

Different transit systems have different policies regarding fare control and collection and these policies have a significant impact on the design of transit facilities. Fare collection design and considerations are discussed in detail in Chapter 7; however, general dimensional criteria for fare collection areas are shown below. A minimum queuing distance of 12 ft should be provided at the face of the fare vending machines to allow passengers to wait in line, count money, verify purchases, and so forth.

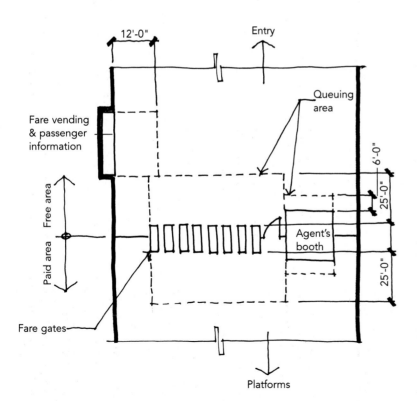

◀ *Fare control area.*

- Passenger information displays (system and neighborhood maps, electronic displays, etc.) should be placed outside the passenger flow between the station entrance and the fare gates, with a minimum queuing distance of 12 ft.
- A minimum queuing distance of 25 ft should be provided on both the free and paid sides of the fare barriers. This distance may be modified according to the projected passenger flows.
- A queuing area of 6–9 ft should be provided on the free and paid sides of the customer service kiosk (or agent's booth) in the area where employees are expected to communicate with the public.

As in the station entrance, the minimum overhead clearance from the finish floor to a localized obstruction (e.g., a lighting fixture, sign, or structural element) should be 8 ft 6 in. minimum (10 ft preferred) to prevent passengers from reaching the obstructing element. The minimum overhead clearance at a ceiling or continuous structure should be 10 ft minimum (12 ft preferred) to allow for lighting, signage, and equipment below the ceiling.

Platform Areas

The platform area is where passengers access trains. The platform area must facilitate multiple passenger circulation functions: circulation along the platform, boarding and alighting from trains, queuing at the platform edge while waiting for a train, queuing at vertical circulation elements, and waiting at benches or rest areas. Because of these complex and often conflicting circulation charac-

teristics, overcrowding on the platform may create uncomfortable or even potentially dangerous situations where passengers are crowded near the platform edge. Therefore, sizing station platforms is critical, and designers should err on the side of safety when determining the size of a station platform.

Platform length is determined by the length of the longest train anticipated for the station platform, plus any additional length required by train operations (e.g., an eight-car train with 75 ft long vehicles will require at least a 600 ft platform).

Platform width is typically determined by several factors:

- The width of any vertical circulation elements located within the length of the platform. A minimum clear distance to any obstruction (such as a vertical circulation element) from the platform edge typically includes the 2 ft wide platform safety edge, a clear passage for passengers circulating along the platform length (generally defined as sufficient space for a wheelchair and ambulatory passengers to comfortably pass one another), and a 1 ft buffer zone along the length of the obstruction. This minimum clear width varies between systems from approximately 7 ft 6 in. to more than 11 ft, with most U.S. systems being in the range of 8 to 10 ft (see the illustration at right).
- Station patronage and emergency exiting requirements.
- Additional space as determined by level of service requirements.

The total width of the platform is equal to the sum of these factors. See Chapter 4 for a detailed discussion of the process that establishes platform length and width.

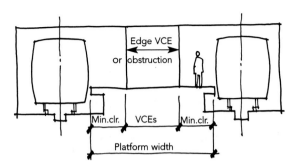

Cross-section, center platform

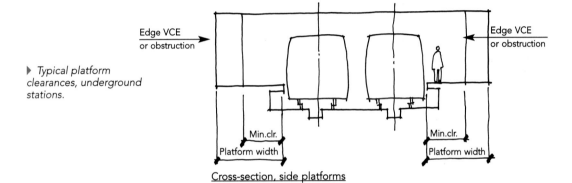

▶ *Typical platform clearances, underground stations.*

Cross-section, side platforms

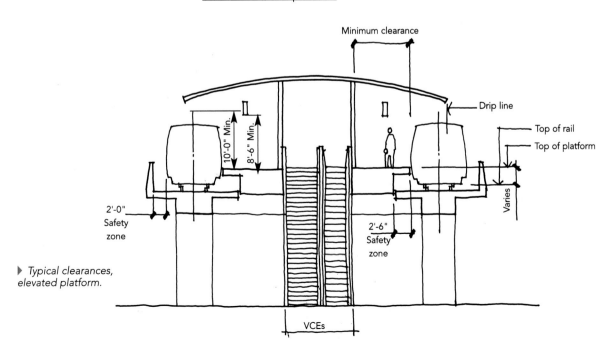

▶ *Typical clearances, elevated platform.*

▲ DelAmo station, Los Angeles Metro. Note the clearance between platform edge and all vertical obstructions.

The following principles should be applied to the design of station platforms:

- All elements of the platform area must support safe passenger circulation and access to the trains.

- The design of the platform must facilitate the clearing of the platform as soon as possible. Vertical circulation elements must be positioned to minimize the need for passengers to make decisions on the platform, causing them to hesitate and impede passenger circulation. Because platforms are typically crowded and subject to passenger surges and cross flows, pausing passengers can cause circulation problems for other patrons.

- Platform access points and vertical circulation elements should be situated to encourage balanced vehicle loading and unloading. Passengers tend to board vehicles near the points where vertical circulation elements intersect the platform.

- Visual obstructions should be minimized and alcoves or other hidden areas on the platform avoided for reasons of orientation, safety, and security.

- The platform areas should not contain any ancillary or nontransit functions (e.g., vending or concessions) that may obstruct, inhibit, or impede passenger circulation.

- The path of emergency egress along the platform must be clearly delineated and lead as directly as possible to an area of safety.

Platform height is typically measured from the top of the rail to the finish floor at the platform edge. Platform height is determined by the height of the transit vehicle's floor above the top of the rail. Typical platform heights are approximately 4 ft above the top of the rail depending on specific vehicle technologies. The platform edge must align with the vehicle floor to facilitate passengers' safe and comfortable boarding and alighting from the train. In the United States, the horizontal gap between the platform edge and the vehicle may not exceed 3 in., and the vertical alignment between the platform and vehicle floor must be within plus or minus ⅝ in. to comply with accessibility standards.

Most transit systems employ an under-platform safety area along the platform edge between the underside of the platform and the track bed, which provides emergency refuge for workers or others should a train enter the station unexpectedly.

The minimum overhead clearance from the finish floor to a localized obstruction (e.g., a lighting fixture, sign, or structural element) should be a minimum of 8 ft 6 in.

Overhead clearance

Platforms at elevated or at-grade stations require weather protection for passengers, vertical circulation elements, and equipment. At a minimum, vertical circulation elements must be protected from the weather by canopies. A portion of the platform's passenger waiting area should also be protected from the elements. Windscreens should be provided to block prevailing winter winds (see the photo on page 26).

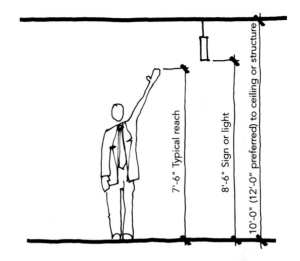

▲ Overhead clearance.

◀ Typical platform clearances.

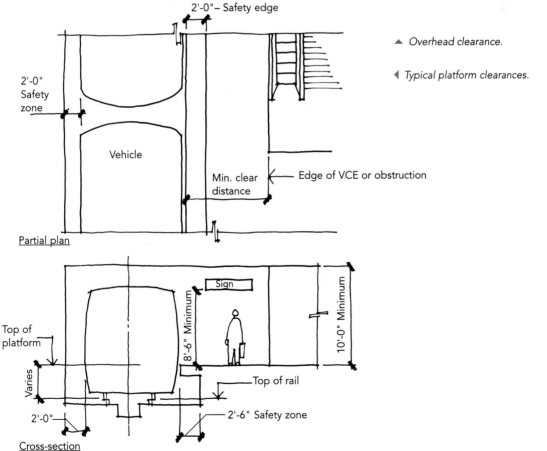

▲ *Windscreens on exposed platform at Old Court Road Station, Baltimore Metro. DMJM and Kaiser Engineers.*

Vertical Circulation Elements

Vertical circulation elements (VCEs) are the devices used to transport customers between different levels of a station. VCEs comprise elevators, escalators, and stairs (including emergency egress stairs). See "Vertical Circulation" in Chapter 6 for a detailed discussion of VCEs.

General Planning Principles

Utilize escalator/stair pairs: Wherever feasible, stairs and escalators should be provided side by side to facilitate a choice in vertical circulation, provide an economical alternative to escalators where the vertical rise between levels is less than 12 ft, and provide an alternate path to escalators that are being maintained or are otherwise out of service.

Modular planning and interchangeability: Stairs and escalators should be sized in modular units of width corresponding to the width of the escalator planned for use in the station (depending on the type and configuration of the escalator used). This unit represents the outer dimension of either a 48 in. wide escalator (nominal 40 in. wide at the tread) or a two-lane stair (60 in. between handrails). Structural, mechanical, and spatial provisions must be made during design to accommodate the future interchangeability of stairs and escalators in the original construction.

Provide adequate capacity (minimum number of VCEs): The minimum number of VCEs will be determined by the level of service, given the forecast peak passenger design loads or emergency exiting requirements, whichever is most stringent. Typically, a single upward escalator and stair pair will be considered the minimum vertical circulation unit at any point of vertical circulation.

Provide adequate space for queuing and run-off: Adequate queuing and run-off space should be provided for all public stairs and escalators. Each elevator should be provided with a queuing area to permit passengers disembarking the elevator to exit without interference from those waiting. The required queuing and run-off areas for vertical circulation elements should not overlap.

Right-hand circulation: VCEs shall be positioned to encourage right-hand circulation and minimize conflicting passenger movement and cross flows.

Public stairs

Public stairs are those intended for normal passenger circulation. Because of the safety hazards and energy expenditure associated with human locomotion on a stairway, designers must be particularly cognizant of the pedestrian behaviors and traffic patterns of transit stations and design stairs accordingly.

Application

- Stairs should be used as the primary mode of vertical circulation where the vertical rise between levels is less than 12 ft.

- Stairs should not be used as a means of normal public access (as distinguished from emergency egress) where the vertical rise between levels exceeds 36 ft.

Location

- Stairs should be located along the normal and direct path of passenger circulation and be visible and easily identifiable as a means of access to the levels they connect.

- Where feasible, stairs should be paired with escalators to facilitate efficient and economical passenger movement.

Width

- Wherever practicable, all stairs should be planned using a modular width corresponding to the applicable escalator module used in the station design, including installation and construction tolerances, and designed to be replaced with an escalator in the future.

- Where the use of an escalator module is not possible or appropriate, the minimum width of a stair should be 5 ft or as determined by passenger demand based on the level of service (LOS), standard or emergency egress requirements.

Queuing and run-off space

- Adequate queuing and run-off space must be provided at the top and bottom of all stairs. Where a stair is paired with an escalator, the queuing and run-off areas should coincide with those of the adjacent escalator. Where a stair is not adjacent to or does not align with an escalator, provide a minimum of queuing and run-off area equal to the width of the stair or 8 ft, whichever is greater.

Minimum headroom

- The minimum headroom over a stair, as measured perpendicular to the line of the tread nosing to the underside of the ceiling, structure, or overhead obstruction, should be 10 ft.

General considerations

- Provisions should be made to facilitate the maintenance and cleaning of the stair (e.g., the provision of runnels on either side of the stair tread to facilitate channeling water and debris down the stairs for cleaning).

- When a stair runs alongside an escalator, the angle of the stair nosing should be aligned with that of the escalator (at 30 degrees), at or below the line of the escalator treads, such that the top of the stair handrail will be at or below the height of the escalator balustrade. Where the floor-to-floor height of the stair may dictate multiple landings due to the long run of the stair, the designer may consider increasing the angle of individual flights and aligning the landings with the slope of the escalator (see the illustration on page 28).

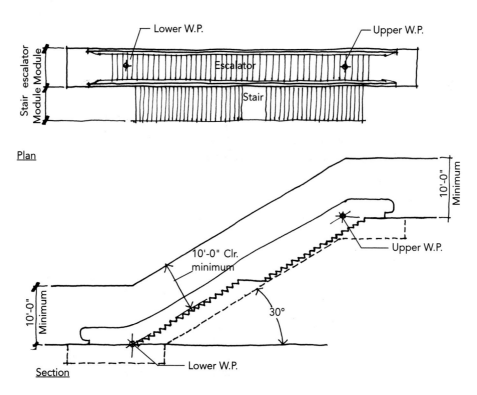

▲ Stairs and escalators.

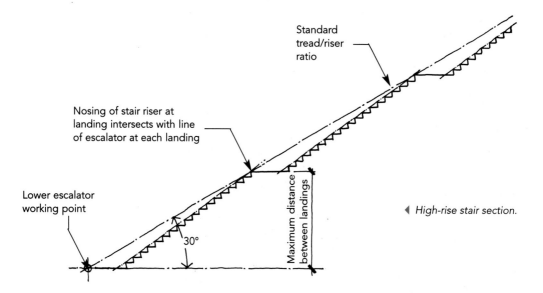

◀ High-rise stair section.

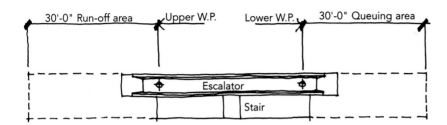

30'-0" Run-off area   Upper W.P.   Lower W.P.   30'-0" Queuing area

Escalator

Stair

◀ *Queuing and run-off areas for stairs and escalators.*

Emergency egress stairs

Stairs provided for emergency egress purposes should comply with the requirements of the applicable local codes and NFPA 130.

Escalators

Application
- Where the vertical rise between levels on the path of public circulation exceeds 12 ft, escalators should be used as the primary mode of vertical circulation.
- It is recommended that at least one path of vertical egress assisted by an escalator be provided from any point in the station as a passenger convenience and to assist the mobility impaired and passengers with baggage.

Location
- Escalators should be located along the normal and direct path of passenger circulation and be visible and easily identifiable as a means of access to the levels they connect.
- Where feasible, escalators should be paired with stairs to facilitate efficient and economical passenger movement.

Width
- All escalators should be at least two lanes, 48 in. wide nominally (40 in. wide at step).
- Escalators should be planned as modular interchangeable units, including installation and construction tolerances, to accommodate external drives (if required).

Queuing and run-off space
- Provide a minimum of 30 ft of queuing and run-off space, as measured from the upper and lower escalator working points, clear to any obstruction at the top and bottom of each escalator.
- Where escalators are located in sequence and there are no pedestrian cross flows or other obstructions to customer movement (e.g., at intermediate landings independent of intervening customer circulation elements), the required combined queuing and run-off space may be reduced by 25 percent.
- The width of the queuing and run-off space should correspond to the modular width of the escalator.

Minimum headroom

- The minimum headroom over an escalator, as measured perpendicular to the line of the tread nosings to the underside of the ceiling, structure, or overhead obstruction, should be 10 ft.

General considerations

- Consideration should be given to servicing and replacing escalators and escalator equipment during station operations. Escalators should be designed so that routine operations and maintenance can be easily performed without disrupting normal station operations. Provisions should be made for replacing the escalator treads, motors, trusses, drive mechanisms, and so forth, as required after the effective life of the escalator.

Public elevators

Elevators in modern transit systems are intended for the use of the general public, and access to elevators should be "self-service" and not restricted during normal operations. Whereas elevators are provided to comply with accessibility requirements, elevators in transit applications are also intended to provide an enhanced quality of general customer service, comfort, and convenience, as well as to assist people with impaired mobility and passengers with baggage or packages or who are otherwise burdened.

Application

It is recommended that elevators be placed to provide effective redundancy along the path from the station entrance to the platform to maintain accessibility in the event of breakdown or routine maintenance. Therefore:

- A minimum of two elevators should be provided, connecting the en-trance(s) and fare collection area(s) where entry and fare collection are on different levels. The elevator must connect the entry with the free, or unpaid, side of the fare array.
- A minimum of two elevators should be provided connecting the fare collection area(s) and the platform(s). The elevator must connect the paid side of the fare array with the platform.

Location

Street entry to fare collection area elevators.

The location of entrance elevators is based on a number of factors, which in turn are influenced by the physical constraints of the surrounding structures, streets, and utilities, adjacent land uses, local demographic characteristics, the availability and cost of property in the station area, and the configuration of the station. Given these constraints, the criteria for locating elevators are as follows:

- Elevators should be conveniently located for all customers and facilitate access for people who are mobility impaired or otherwise disabled.
- Elevators should be located to provide convenient access to bus stops and other modes of public transportation.
- Elevators should be located as closely as possible to other vertical circulation elements (stairs and escalators) in the station entrance, while allowing reasonable access and adjacency to the unpaid portion of the station control area.
- Visibility: Elevators should be located to provide service along the normal path of passenger travel and positioned to be easily identifiable to passengers with a minimum of signs. Elevators should be visible to security personnel,

station staff, and the general public for security and surveillance purposes. Shafts and cabs should be transparent to facilitate surveillance of the cab interior. Closed-circuit television (CCTV) coverage should be provided within the cabs and at all waiting areas.

- Pedestrian network: Elevators should be located to provide direct access to the local pedestrian network, including sidewalks, plazas, building entrances, circulation paths, and crosswalks. Elevators should be located so as not to obstruct pedestrian movement along the public way and sidewalks. In general, elevators—including landing and queuing areas—should not be located on sidewalks where space is a concern.

- Aesthetics: Elevators at street level should be located to minimize their visual impact on adjacent structures and should be designed to complement the surrounding urban context. The scale, materials, and form of elevator structures should harmonize with adjacent buildings and the surrounding streetscape.

Fare collection area to platform elevators

- Elevators should be conveniently located for all customers and facilitate access for those who are mobility impaired or otherwise disabled.

- Elevators should be located as closely as possible to the direct path of travel between entry and platform in order to minimize travel distances for those using them.

- Elevators should be located so as to be visible from the Station Service Center for surveillance purposes.

- Where feasible, elevators should be located in a consistent manner from station to station to facilitate customer wayfinding and orientation.

- Elevators should be located so as not to obstruct general passenger circulation or visually obscure other vertical circulation elements along the path from the fare collection area to the platform.

Size
Elevators should be of a minimum size to comply with the requirements of the Americans with Disabilities Act (ADA) and accommodate emergency services and emergency personnel with a stretcher. Consideration should also be given to local ridership characteristics in selecting elevator sizes (e.g., a high percentage of bicycle commuters or customers with baggage may dictate the selection of larger elevators).

- Minimum cab sizes for elevators as specified in the ADA are 51 in. deep by 80 in. wide, with a 36 in. wide door centered along the elevator's width, and 51 in. deep by 68 in. wide, with a 36 in. wide door located to one side along the elevator's width. In either case, the minimum distance from the back wall of the elevator to the door is 54 in.

Queuing space

- The elevator landing depth (the queuing and discharge space at the elevator door) should be a minimum clear distance to any obstruction equal to 1½ times the depth of the car or ten ft, whichever is greater, by the width of the elevator.

- Elevator landings should be

positioned so that the elevator queuing area does not impede general circulation, has adequate queuing space, and is not hidden from view.

- Queuing space should not overlap with queuing areas of other VCEs, fare gates, stairs, equipment, etc.
- Platform level elevators should not open in the direction of the platform edge.

General considerations

- Consideration should be given to servicing and replacing elevators and elevator equipment during station operations. Elevators should be designed so that routine operations and maintenance can be easily performed without disrupting normal station operations. Provisions should be made for replacing the elevator cab, motors, hydraulics, drive mechanisms, and so forth, as required after their effective life.
- Passageways connecting elevators to mezzanines, concourses, corridors, lobbies, and other public circulation areas should be less than 20 ft long, to comply with local codes and avoid creating a dead-end corridor.
- Elevators must comply with ADA requirements.

Ancillary Facilities

Ancillary and support facilities are the nonpublic areas that support and sustain transit operations. These facilities include the following:

- Transit personnel offices, lounges, and restrooms
- Maintenance and janitorial rooms
- Traction power facilities
- Communications rooms
- Station power and electrical rooms
- Heating, ventilating, and air-conditioning (HVAC) and mechanical rooms
- Storage facilities
- Public toilets

The design of ancillary and support facilities is contingent upon the functional requirements of the individual spaces and their locations. However, their design must be subordinate to the public transit–related functions of the station. Ancillary and support facilities should be provided with secure and restricted access to and from the station's public spaces. In general, access points to ancillary and support facilities should be consolidated to minimize security equipment, simplify access control, and minimize potential disruption of the public space.

After satisfying the obvious functional requirements and adjacencies, service access and utility routing constitute a determining factor in the design of ancillary and support facilities. Particular attention must be paid to the maintenance and replacement of equipment that is large and difficult to access or move. In general, ancillary and support facilities should be designed so that routine maintenance can be easily performed without disrupting normal station operations.

SYSTEM TECHNOLOGIES

Railway operating systems are all of the systems that actually enable a train to run along the tracks, process passengers through stations, and support the operations and maintenance staff in the performance of their duties. These systems include most, if not all, of the following:

- Vehicles
- Train control
- Power
- Communications
- Fare collection
- Mechanical and electrical systems
- Corrosion control

It can be seen from the very nature of these systems that they are, in fact, the very heart of the rail system, and how well they perform their functions will directly establish the perceived quality of the transit experience. Consequently, it is vitally important that these systems be accommodated and/or integrated, as necessary, into the station facilities and architectural design in a manner that enables them to perform at peak levels of effectiveness. Platforms must be the correct length to accommodate the longest train, as well as its stopping accuracy; otherwise, trains will be consistently delayed due to overrunning or underrunning the platforms. Sometimes trackside colored light signals must be placed at the ends of, or in the center of, a platform, and they must be visible to train operators as the train enters the platform.

Vehicles

The nature of rail vehicles varies considerably, depending on the purpose of the system. Rail systems can be broadly categorized in four main types: intercity railroad, commuter rail, heavy-rail transit, and light-rail transit. Some typical characteristics of the vehicles associated with these rail systems are discussed in the following paragraphs, but it must be remembered that these are typical. Rail transportation systems are sufficiently diverse that there is almost certainly an exception to every rule.

Intercity railroad

Not all trains in an intercity sytem stop at all stations and, consequently, trains often pass through stations at full speed, which may be up to 125 mph. Station platforms must be wide enough to allow passengers to stand sufficiently back from the platform edge so as not to be affected by the wind forces and not to feel threatened by passing trains. This is particularly important where stations are serving both intercity services and commuter services and a platform may be quite crowded with commuter passengers when an intercity train passes through.

Commuter rail

Commuter rail train services are designed primarily to carry passengers between city centers and suburbs or outlying towns, and most riders travel every business day. Trains may be made up of a locomotive and coaches or may consist of powered multiple units. Many systems utilizing locomotives and coaches are now using double-deck coaches, as the coach procurement cost per seat is less expensive than that of single-deck coaches.

Train lengths may be as short as two cars in lightly used areas or as long as ten cars on heavily used lines in peak periods. As with intercity trains, train operators manually control train speeds, and station platforms should accommodate a stopping accuracy of at least ±10 ft in addition to the maximum length of a train, including the locomotive. Not all trains stop at all stations and, consequently, trains often pass through stations at full speed, which may be up to 80 mph. Station platforms must be wide enough to allow passengers to stand sufficiently back from the platform edge so as not to be affected by the wind forces and not to feel threatened by passing trains. As noted earlier, this is particularly important where stations are serving both intercity services and commuter services.

Heavy-rail transit

Heavy-rail train services are generally designed to carry passengers within city areas and inner suburbs and to carry heavy passenger loads with frequent service, as close as 2-minute intervals in peak periods.

Train lengths may be as short as 150 ft in off-peak periods and as much as 600 ft on heavily used lines in peak periods. Train speed may be controlled manually by the train operators or automatically by a subsystem of the train control system, often called automatic train operation (ATO). Modern transit systems with ATO can provide a stopping accuracy of ±1 ft. However, allowances must be made to permit train speeds to be controlled manually on occasion. The distance between the ends of the train and the end doors is usually sufficient to accommodate train operator stopping accuracy. Trains normally stop at all platforms and will pass through platforms without stopping only during abnormal service conditions, usually with established speed restrictions.

Light-rail transit

Light-rail transit services are also generally designed to carry passengers within city areas and inner suburbs but are designed to carry lower passenger loads with less frequent service than heavy-rail systems.

Train lengths may be as short as a single 50 ft car or as long as 300 ft in peak periods. The train operators control train speed manually. The distance between the ends of the train and the end doors is usually sufficient to accommodate train operator stopping accuracy. Trains normally stop at all platforms and will pass through platforms without stopping only during abnormal service conditions, usually with established speed restrictions.

Train Control

Train control systems can vary significantly in technology according to the type of rail system and its age. However, certain features are almost always required, such as the following:

- Equipment room
- Wayside track
- Wayside equipment not attached to the track
- Cables

Power

Power requirements vary extensively according to the nature of the rail system. Diesel-powered railways require electrical power only for station services and support systems. Electric-powered railways also require electric traction power to operate the trains. Consequently, partial or all of the following elements of electrical power may be required:

- Power in-feed from the local electrical utility
- Station power system
- Traction power system

Electric-powered intercity and commuter rail systems

Typically, on electric-powered intercity and commuter rail systems, the traction

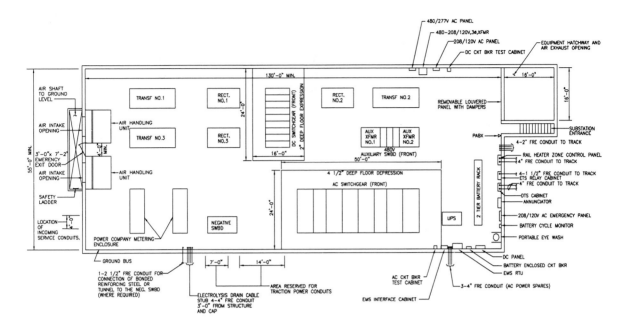

▲ *Typical underground substation.*

power system is completely independent of the station's electric power systems. In the electrical distribution rooms, panelboards will feed all the lighting and power circuits as well as the equipment rooms, such as communications, train control, elevators, escalators, and HVAC.

Heavy-rail transit

For heavy-rail transit systems, station power is usually supplied by two redundant medium-voltage feeders from the electric utility, either of which has the capacity to feed the entire station. The feeders come into a power substation, which may be a single space or two separate spaces, depending on the level of power security desired.

A heavy-rail train may draw up to 6000 amps when accelerating, and the cable feeders between the substation and track will require up to fifty-six 3-in.

conduits from each substation. They should be placed in a location away from the under platform safety zone as they run through the platform area.

Third rail current collection comes in a variety of designs. The simplest is what is called "top contact" because that's part of the rail upon which the pick-up shoe slides. Being the simplest it has drawbacks, not the least of which is that it is exposed to anyone or anything that might come into contact with it. It also suffers during bad weather, the smallest amount of ice or snow rendering top contact third rail systems almost unworkable unless expensive remedies are carried out. Side contact is not much better but at least it is less exposed. Bottom contact is best—you can cover effectively most of the rail and it is protected from the worst of cold weather.

(Cova 2002)

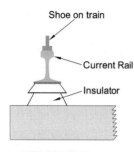

TOP CONTACT

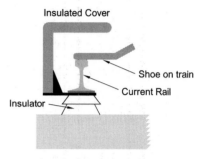

TOP CONTACT WITH COVER

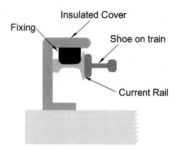

SIDE CONTACT

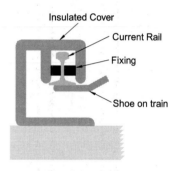

BOTTOM CONTACT

▶ *Types of DC third-rail collection systems. (Courtesy Electric Traction Power Supply.)*

Light-rail transit

Light-rail stations are usually quite simple surface structures, and a single low-voltage feeder from the electric utility usually supplies the station power. The electrical distribution requires no unusual features.

Traction power distribution is implemented by an overhead catenary system. Station designs must accommodate the required placement of poles and associated equipment to support the catenary wire. When placed in streets, the catenary system can have a significant impact on the streetscape, and every effort should be made to combine the support pole with other pole functions such as street lighting. See page 37 for a diagram of an overhead current supply system.

Communications

Communications systems vary widely according to the type of rail system. Some, such as a fiber-optic backbone, need only provisions for equipment and cables, whereas others, such as public address and CCTV, need to be carefully integrated into the station design. The following paragraphs discuss a number of systems that may be required and their design integration requirements. The actual systems required will depend on the specific project. However, a communications equipment room is typically required at each passenger station. This may be a masonry structure or a prefabricated metal bungalow and may be integrated into the station facilities. At underground stations, the room will have to be integrated into the station.

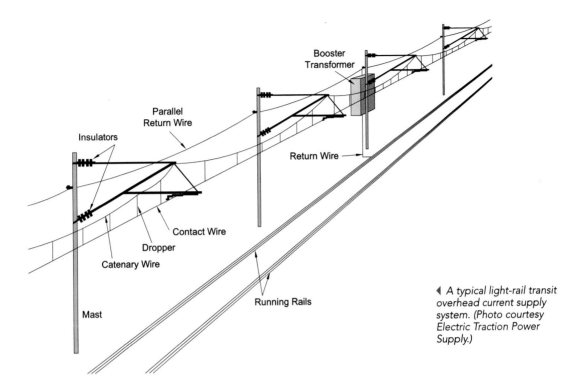

Booster
Transformer

Parallel
Return Wire

Insulators

Return Wire

Contact Wire

Dropper

Catenary Wire

Mast

Running Rails

◀ *A typical light-rail transit overhead current supply system. (Photo courtesy Electric Traction Power Supply.)*

Telephones

Telephones are provided throughout station areas and along the right-of-way for a variety of normal and emergency applications. Telephones are placed in staff accommodations and equipment rooms for use by operations and maintenance staff. Direct line (or automatic ringdown) telephones may be required in some of these locations where communications may be needed in unusual or emergency situations.

Public telephones are placed in various areas of a station for passenger convenience and should be located where users will not interfere with passenger movements into or out of a station.

Telephones for passenger assistance are placed throughout a station's public areas and may serve one or both of two fundamental functions: an emergency function whereby passengers may call for help in the event of an emergency and an assistance function whereby passengers may call for nonemergency assistance, such as travel directions or train service information. Telephones are given names such as "help point intercoms," "station emergency telephones," or "passenger assistance telephones" in different systems, but all perform the same basic functions.

Emergency telephones should be placed throughout the entrance, mezzanine, and platform areas and should be located not more than 200 ft apart. Assistance telephones should be concentrated in entrance areas, particularly adjacent to fare vending machines and on the platform. Emergency telephones should be clearly visible and contain concise instructions for use.

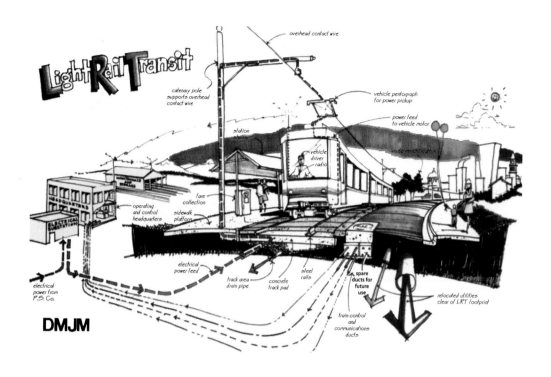

Light Rail Transit

overhead contact wire

catenary pole supports overhead contact wire

vehicle pantograph for power pickup

power feed to vehicle motor

station shelter

vehicle driver radio

node rectification

fare collection

operating and control headquarters

sidewalk platform

electrical power feed

electrical power from P.S. Co.

track area drain pipe

concrete track pad

steel rails

spare ducts for future use

relocated utilities clear of LRT footprint

train control and communications ducts

DMJM

▲ Architect's sketch showing system distribution along an LRT guideway. DMJM+Harris.

Radio

Radio systems are provided for the exclusive use of operations and maintenance personnel. In surface and aerial stations, special provisions for radio systems are not usually required. However, in underground facilities, all areas where radio coverage is required must be in line-of-sight of a radio antenna.

Underground radio antennae are of two basic types: 1) a leaky feeder radiating cable and 2) an individual, discrete antenna. Leaky feeder radiating antenna cables vary in diameter from less than 2 in. to more than 2 in. To support them, use hangers or brackets made of a nonmagnetic material and place a minimum of 4 in. from any structural element. If they are covered, the cover must be of a nonmagnetic material that will pass radio waves.

Individual antennae are less visually imposing than leaky feeder radiating ca-

bles and can be used in large open spaces such as stations built by the cut-and-cover method.

Information kiosks

Information kiosks may be provided in station entrance areas to provide information to passengers regarding the train service, general travel information, the location of public amenities in the vicinity of the station, and advertising for local businesses. These facilities are typically in the form of a computer terminal mounted in a cabinet and appear very similar to a bank's ATM machine. They should be located in areas where people using them will not interfere with passenger movement through the station.

Public address

Public address systems are an essential feature of all rail systems to provide information to passengers. To provide a consistent and adequate sound power level, with good audibility, cone-type speakers in back-boxes are preferred. However, in simple surface station structures, such as most light-rail stations and many commuter rail stations, this is not practical and horn-type speakers are used. Cone speakers in back-boxes offer greater opportunities to integrate the speakers with the station architecture so that they are hidden from view. This also serves to eliminate the possibility of vandalism.

The public address system should have good audio characteristics and should accommodate the full frequency range of the human voice from 85 Hz to 10 kHz. The hard finishes of a station often preferred for their long life and vandal resistance, such as tile, metal, and granite, create reverberations that destroy audio quality. An acoustic analysis is an essential part of the design of a modern underground station.

Variable message signs

The Americans with Disabilities Act mandates that any facility equipped with a public address system must also be equipped with a variable message sign system so that messages can be presented both audibly and visually. Signs with 4-in. characters are suitable for a reading range of up to 150 ft, and the quantity and placement of signs should be determined accordingly. Signs may be used for any combination of the following purposes and should be located accordingly:

- Train service advisory messages (may be controlled automatically by the train control system to advise passengers of the location and time of arrival of approaching trains)

- Emergency messages
- Directional messages (controlled by the direction of escalators and whether entrances are open or closed)
- Advertising messages
- General advisory messages
- Station open or closed messages
- Escalator "about to stop" messages

Although variable message signs are a communications system because of their technology, their functionality and placement should be developed as an integral part of the station signage design. The individual signs should be integrated into a common sign-holder system that also holds fixed signage.

Closed-circuit television

Traditionally, closed-circuit television (CCTV) systems have been installed in heavy rail transit stations and larger commuter rail and inter-city train stations to inform operating staff of the general status of the station. This function is particularly useful during serious crowding conditions as may occur during a train service disruption. These systems also provide a partial security function, but are not usually touted as having this purpose and very few rail operators have staff dedicated to watching the monitors at all times.

Cameras are usually placed above the platform level to observe the platform edges. These images may be viewed by control center operators for crowding, by station staff for general oversight, and by train staff in conjunction with the control of train doors. Control center operators, station staff, and security personnel may place cameras in other public areas of stations for general status oversight.

Since the terrorist acts of September 11, 2001, many train service operators are looking at ways to improve the general level of security in their facilities. One way to do this is to provide closed-circuit television surveillance of nonpublic spaces in stations such as ancillary area corridors, ancillary equipment rooms, emergency exit corridors, stairs and doors, and parking lots. The provision of closed-circuit television for security purposes should be implemented in conjunction with a security policy that clearly defines what the objectives are.

Cameras and lenses are enclosed in housings and should be placed so as to be beyond the reach of vandals. However, they must also be placed so that their field of view is not obstructed by structural, architectural, or other elements of the station.

Fire detection and alarm

The current NFPA fire codes require that passenger stations be equipped with means for detecting fires and issuing alarms. Some spaces are also required to have automatic sprinklers. Most ancillary spaces are either equipped with automatic sprinklers or with heat and smoke detectors. Public spaces, however, are more difficult to deal with. A smoke or heat detector typically covers an area of approximately 100 sq ft, and a large public station may well require about 500 sensors. This quantity, when multiplied by the number of stations, presents a major maintenance task that, if not conducted properly, can lead to improper performance and false alarms.

As an alternative to smoke and heat detectors, many systems rely on fire conditions in the public spaces being observed by a member of the staff or a passenger. Facilities for notification, such as emergency telephones or manual alarm stations, are then required.

Each station should also have an emergency management panel or an incident command center. This is a device where a responding fire department can establish its headquarters to manage the response. The command center should provide status information on the station's fire detection and alarm system, the ventilation system (if one is provided), and public address and telephone communications to the station and to the rail control center. It should be located in one of the station entrance areas, but not below ground level in an underground station.

Access control and intrusion alarm

Access control and intrusion alarm systems should be relatively invisible to the traveling public. All access routes between public and nonpublic spaces should be secured and alarmed for unauthorized access. This includes doors between public and nonpublic areas of stations, end-of-platform gates, and emergency exit doors and hatches that exit into public areas.

Mechanical and Electrical Systems

See "Mechanical Considerations" in Chapter 6 for a detailed discussion.

A station's mechanical and electrical systems include low-voltage power and lighting circuits, ventilation, air-conditioning, pumps, sprinklers and fire mains, and domestic plumbing. Most of these systems are primarily located in ancillary facilities.

Ventilation systems in underground stations require large spaces for fan rooms and air plenums, some of which must serve the public spaces. These ventilation systems usually require the largest allocation of ancillary space of all the supporting systems, and the ducts to the surface require large areas for air intake and exhaust.

Fire hydrants are required throughout the public areas of enclosed stations. Hydrants must be located so that no point is more than 100 ft from a hydrant. Hydrants are often located in emergency cabinets; such a cabinet hides the actual hydrant from public view and also contains an emergency telephone.

CHAPTER 2

URBAN PLANNING AND STATION AREA DEVELOPMENT

INTRODUCTION

The planning process is shaped by three primary influences: federal programs, state and local initiatives, and community involvement in the urban planning process. The role and characteristics of each station must be related to the distinct scales within the overall planning process—regionally, within a specific transportation corridor, and as an element in a local community. This chapter includes a three-part discussion of diverse planning issues and passenger ridership data that must be addressed to ensure that stations are well integrated into the host community and to fully realize opportunities for community enhancement:

- Urban Planning Process
- Ridership
- Station Area Development

URBAN PLANNING PROCESS

Three distinct forces drive the planning, development, and design of station facilities:

- The regulations and guidelines governing federal investment in rail transit facilities, administered by the Federal Transit Administration

◀ Example of a medium LRT station platform at Burlington, New Jersey, town center. FMG Architects; urban planners DMJM+Harris Architects. (Illustration by D. R. Becker, New Jersey Transit.)

- State and local programs affecting land use and development review, administered by local governments
- Insights provided by residents and business interests in adjacent communities

The influences of these factors on the design professionals are enormous. Yet more often than not, the architect is not fully involved in the early stages of project development when many of the overall project characteristics that ultimately influence station design are typically defined. As a consequence, the design architect often inherits a variety of conditions with little understanding of their basis, and even less of a sense of which of these are flexible and which are not. This section focuses on providing the designer with the overall progression of the typical project, the points at which decisions are made, and the opportunities for influence over design outcomes.

Federal Project Development Process

Consistent with the trends that evolved in the early 1900s, the Urban Mass Transportation Act of 1964 continued the tradition of placing responsibility for the construction of new rail transit systems on the public sector as opposed to private enterprise. Consequently, the design and delivery of transit stations is strongly influenced by a host of funding programs and guidance administered by the Federal Transit Administration (FTA). Housed within the U.S. Department of Transportation (USDOT), FTA has the lead responsibility for overseeing federal investment in public transportation infrastructure. FTA is particularly vigilant regarding the planning and de-

velopment of stations, given the profound impact the location and design of stations can have on the overall success of a rail line and the health and character of the community.

Federal planning regulations and guidance outline a multistep process to develop major capital investments for transit. The program covers a wide range of system technologies, including transit guideways, commuter rail, heavy-rail, light-rail, monorail, streetcar, and even rapid-transit bus systems. The process is intended to invite consideration of a broad range of values to be incorporated into facilities' design, as well as the perspectives of a wide range of constituencies. The major capital investment planning process is designed to provide an appropriate level of detail at each step in the project delivery process to support incremental decisions.

The FTA major capital investment process affords federal and local policy makers a cohesive framework for a balanced and reasoned approach to decision making, which ultimately reduces the risk of project delays and increased costs through broad public discussion. For the station architect, it is by its nature an exercise in compromise, with aesthetic and functional concerns competing across a wide range of transportation, social, economic, and environmental values. Consequently, it is important for the design professional to be familiar with the major phases of the federal process and the opportunities to affect decision making at each phase.

The major steps in the process are as follows:

- System planning
- Corridor study

- Preliminary engineering and environmental findings
- Final design and right-of-way acquisition
- Construction
- Operation

At each step, the definition of the project emerges at increasing levels of detail. At the same time, more detailed information on the project definition and design, effects on the human and natural environment, and commitments made both by public agencies and the private sector regarding station location develop. Because each successive step requires higher levels of financial commitment, and because the cost and schedule impacts of reversing or revisiting earlier decisions increase over time, the commitment to proceeding with the design should increase as the project proceeds. The basic provisions of each step are described in the following discussion in terms of their impact on project definition and design, environmental review, policy commitments, and roles and responsibilities.

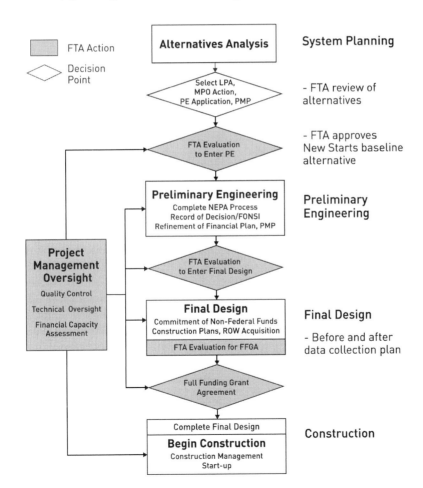

◀ Federal planning regulations outline a multistep process to develop major capital investments for transit.

System planning

The system planning phase typically lasts about one year, with the level of effort dependent on the size of the metropolitan area, the overall health of the transportation system, and the scope of the improvements. During this period the basic parameters governing the need for stations and their sizing, location, and distribution are established, but at a very gross concept level. For this reason, physical design professionals at this stage participate in a modest way, as transportation and regional planners typically lead the process with only limited attention to spatial issues. Architects and designers later in the planning process typically inherit these preliminary and gross-level location decisions made in systems planning. They are often difficult to change because they are included in locally adopted regional transportation plans and political consensus begins to build around them.

Project definition during system planning

This initial step in the project development process, project definition, is focused on regionwide transportation needs and an early assessment of the kinds of transportation improvements that may be appropriate for different travel corridors. Investment priorities are established for travel corridors in which major fixed-guideway, high-capacity transportation investments, requiring stations, are identified. The travel corridors that are ready to proceed to the next step are identified and defined and included in the Long-Range Transportation Plan for the region as part of the federal Metropolitan Area Planning process.

The Long-Range Transportation Plan, which is updated or prepared upon completion of system planning, includes preliminary definitions of the priority projects, including the general extent and location of facilities. This is the first step in establishing the overall project budget for the entire investment, including stations, based on the general order of magnitude and unit costs. As part of the Long-Range Transportation Plan adoption, public meetings are held to provide communities the much desired opportunity to affect the planning process.

System planning environmental review

The main focus of environmental review during system planning is on air quality and energy issues. This is because the Long-Range Transportation Plan, resulting from system planning, must be shown to conform to the requirements of the federal Clean Air Act. The number of stations, station spacing, and relationship of stations to the regional bus network all affect the conformity analysis and can be influenced by the outcome of the conformity analysis and vice versa, ultimately affecting the project definition included in the Long-Range Transportation Plan.

Other major environmental issues will be considered when corridors for potential transportation are identified. The analysis is based on very broad data and is typically limited to identifying and avoiding those critical environmental issues that are of such extraordinary magnitude that implementation of the project would be extremely costly, severely impeded, or even precluded. Social, economic, and environmental factors that can delay a project typically include large numbers of property displacements, wetlands and water resources, endangered species habitats, archaeological/historic resources, park-lands/open space, and toxic materials. Although environmental screening is sometimes an integral part of this step, the formal start of compliance with the National Environmental Policy Act (NEPA) is typically deferred until specific corridor improvements are better defined in later phases. Consequently, many of the physical environmental concerns that ultimately shape station planning and design are not addressed in detail until those later phases in which the station architect addresses them more fully.

Policy commitments at the system planning stage

Federal laws and policies require that the Long-Range Transportation Plan must be affordable within reasonably expected levels of funding for transportation improvements. The plan must be adopted by the designated metropolitan planning organization (MPO) and updated at regular intervals. In adopting the plan, the MPO identifies the level and sources of funding that are likely to be available for major transportation projects. Any project that receives federal funding must be included in a *conforming* and *financially constrained* adopted Long-Range Transportation Plan. A plan is "conforming" when it is found to meet the requirements of the Clean Air Act. A plan is considered to be "financially constrained" when the potential sources of funding for proposed improvements are available or reasonably foreseeable. These two yardsticks start to influence both the configuration and the costs allocated to stations as part of future project development. The design professionals subsequently charged with developing station concepts must be prepared to work within such constraints.

Corridor study

The second step in the project development process, corridor study, typically requires 1–2 years to complete. The corridor study involves the evaluation of alternatives and a preliminary environmental review for the potential projects identified in the financially constrained Long-Range Transportation Plan during system planning. The level of effort and duration are influenced by the following:

- Complexity of the transportation problems to be solved
- Characteristics of the corridors
- Number and types of alternatives being considered
- Level of controversy related to the potential transportation solutions

Because of these factors, budgets for completing a corridor study can vary greatly but typically range from 0.5 to 1.0 percent of the construction cost of the proposed improvements. The same factors influence the station location along a route, its final location within a community, its physical character and appearance, and how it operates and functions.

At this stage, stations are but one of a number of project elements under development. Competition for resources among the different project elements is therefore intense. Because of regulatory requirements protecting different resource areas (such as cultural or environmental assets), the budgets available for station development are often limited and do not progress much beyond conceptual planning at perhaps a 3 percent design level, consisting of a general program, gross footprint, and generalized site location. An exception to this level of

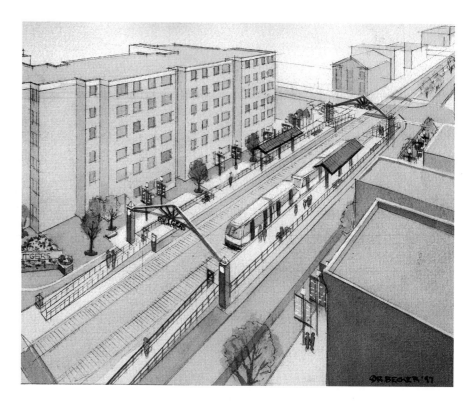

▶ Example of a side platform LRT station at Rutgers University in Camden, New Jersey. FMG Architects; urban planners DMJM+Harris Architects. (Illustration by D. R. Becker, New Jersey Transit.)

effort typically occurs if a station is in an area that evokes a high degree of community scrutiny or involves potential impacts to resources (such as a historic structure) that are potential "showstoppers." Under such circumstances, a higher level of design development effort is typically required. Nonetheless, the level of design rarely exceeds 10 percent at this stage, and then only in specific locations. An example of such additional design is a case in which a station needs to serve a location adjacent to a historically significant building and studies are necessary to demonstrate design compatibility.

Corridor study project definition

The next step in the project development process focuses on refining and evaluating a range of alternative transportation solutions to advance the concepts identified during the Long-Range Transportation Plan process. The product of a corridor study is the definition of a design concept and scope. The process addresses traffic congestion and accessibility to other communities within the metropolitan served by the proposed system. This outcome, known as a locally preferred alternative, defines the project that will be developed further to 3–10 percent of the complete final design and is carried forward to the next step in the project development process.

The project definition includes the mode or modes to be developed and the service levels to be provided, a general alignment route and preliminary identification of real estate acquisition, and coordination with existing major structures.

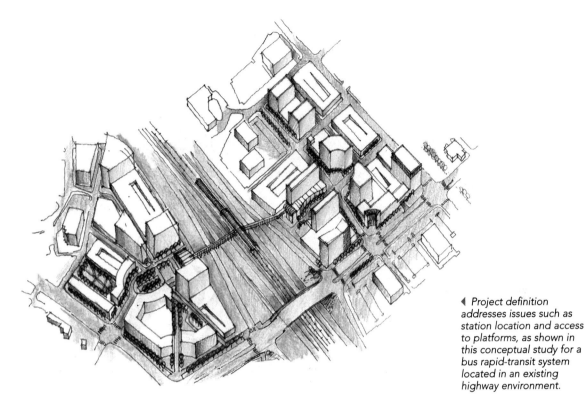

◀ *Project definition addresses issues such as station location and access to platforms, as shown in this conceptual study for a bus rapid-transit system located in an existing highway environment.*

Included at this stage is preliminary station location, as well as provisions for customer access and egress. Cost estimates are typically prepared with contingency levels of about 30 percent.

RIDERSHIP

Ridership forecasts are an important element in identifying and justifying transit service. The need for ridership information does not end with the identification of need, the selection of a particular alignment, or even the location of the station stops. The station architect needs this information to design each station. Ridership volumes and direction will influence the location and size of various elements of the station, such as entrances, fare collection and control areas, size and number of vertical circulation el-

ements (i.e., escalators, elevators, and stairs) within the stations, and at suburban stations, even ancillary elements such as need for and size of park-and-ride lots, drop-off areas, and bus interface facilities. It is important for the design team to understand that the development of the ridership forecasts is a highly specialized effort.

The development of such forecasts typically involves a regional transportation planning agency and/or the transit operator, usually using a computerized travel simulation model. Forecasts may be provided by the agency, or the agency may provide the basic travel data necessary for the design team to prepare the forecasts. There are several methods and models available and in current use to prepare these forecasts. Should the design team be assigned the preparation, a specialty consultant is usually retained as part of the team.

Ridership projections are prepared for a base or opening year and for a future or "forecast" year (typically 20 years beyond the opening year) so that architects and engineers can design a station that serves today's needs as well as those of the fully mature system. At the station design level, this information is specific to the particular area surrounding and served by the station and is incorporated into a process known as station area planning. Ridership information for this process includes the following:

- Origin and destination of passengers using an individual station

- Mode of arrival for passengers arriving at and leaving the station

- Volume of passengers (by day and peak hour)

Each of these elements is discussed in the following paragraphs to explain its contribution to the design of each transit station.

Origin and Destination Information

Passenger origin and destination information identifies where people come from or go to when entering or exiting the station. The information is important to the station designer in locating street entrances to the transit stations, especially for urban underground or elevated systems. In large cities, it indicates the side of the street on which an entrance can be located to minimize the need for people to cross the main roadway. It also helps to determine whether there should be entrances at the ends of the station or at its middle and helps to start determining the number of entrances.

Typically, major generators of activity around the station, such as office buildings, hospitals, or shopping areas, will determine the origin or destination of passengers. However, other factors, such as roadway and street configuration, will determine the pattern of how passengers arrive or leave the station. For example, major roadways with multiple lanes of traffic pose a potential obstacle to passengers, even with traffic control devices such as traffic signals and pedestrian crosswalks. Knowing where passengers are coming from or going to helps to minimize the need to cross the roadway by positioning the station entrance on the side that favors the majority of passengers. At times a simpler and possibly even more effective solution may be to create entrances on both sides of the roadway. If safety is not the issue, however, the cost of a second entrance, often measured in millions of dollars for construction and sometimes in increased impact because of increased private property takings, may dictate only one entrance.

In a similar vein, knowing the direction of travel to and from the station could, by splitting the location of the entrances, effectively provide two entrances. For instance, in locations such as Manhattan, station lengths are usually 800–1000 ft long and cover three or four city blocks in the north-south direction. Location of an entrance at either end of the station improves access to it for a greater distance and allows for the location of an entrance on either side of a major arterial roadway, which runs north and south, parallel to most of the subway lines.

Passenger Mode of Arrival/Departure

Although origin and destination information tells us from what direction passengers are coming, it does not tell us whether they are walking, transferring from another subway line, or arriving by bus or automobile. Whether a person walks, drives, rides a bicycle, is driven, or transfers from another form of public transit is another piece of information that is critical to the design of individual stations.

As an example, assume that the origin-destination information for an individual subway station indicates that 75 percent of all trips arrive from east of the subway station. Mode of arrival information indicates that two-thirds of the trips from the east are arriving by bus and the rest of the trips are walks to the station. Assume the subway station is located underground beneath a six-lane roadway with heavy traffic, including trucks and autos. The station is located at a four-lane cross street with two way traffic and heavy turning movements. A bus operates along the cross street in each direction, with far-side stops (west of the intersection westbound, east of the intersection eastbound).

Although the information indicates that the majority of the trips are from the east, suggesting an entrance location on the east side of the street, the mode of access indicates that most (two-thirds) of the passengers arrive by buses that stop on the west side of the street. Based on the additional information about the mode, the location of a station entrance on the west side of the street westbound and an entrance on the east side of the street eastbound would be better than a single entrance on either side of the street. In the case of a suburban or rural station, mode of access data will help determine how much parking is necessary, the importance and size of bus stop locations, and the size of vehicle drop-off and pick-up areas. In urban stations, the mode of access informs the designer as to whether a number of passengers are transferring from a nearby rail transit line or whether bus transfer represents a major portion of the passengers using the station. Both pieces of information will, depending on the numbers, influence the location and size of the street entrances to the underground subway station.

Although the example reveals the influence that bus-versus-walk arrival or departure modes may have, passengers transferring from or to a nearby subway line are equally important in the design of the station. In major cities with extensive transit systems, such as Washington, New York, or Chicago, passengers often use more than one subway line to reach their final destinations. In the case of a new subway line and new stations, the potential for transfers must be treated as another mode of arrival or departure from the station. There are circumstances, particularly where a new station or line intersects an existing line, in which such data are important for sizing facilities and determining a need for underground corridors providing direct access between stations for transferring passengers.

The influence the transferring volume may have on the ultimate design of the station depends on volume. For example, high transfer volume may favor more direct-access underground corridors, in addition to more vertical circulation elements, between the mezzanine and the platform at the new station than from the street to the mezzanine.

Passenger Volume

Ultimately, the number of passengers moving through the station determines the vertical circulation elements as well as the size of the platforms and fare control areas and other areas of the station. The sizing of the various station elements is based on the need to meet the peak loading requirements for each station that typically occur during the morning and evening commute times, normally the 2–3 hours in the morning and evening when most of the passengers access that station. Typically, the peak hour of the morning rush time is used to size the station facilities and the 15-minute peak of the peak hour is used to identify the critical surge volumes.

Depending on the individual station, the peak volumes and direction of traffic can become highly significant. A station located in a largely commercial/employment area has the vast majority of the peak-hour users moving in the same direction. In the morning peak hour, passengers are leaving the station, and entering in the evening. Based on this information, the number of vertical circulation elements (VCE) needed, including stairs, escalators, and elevators, is based on serving the peak direction.

However, in the case of a station serving both a residential (origin) and commercial/employment (destination) area, even though the total volume may not change, the inclusion of entering passengers at the same time could substantially increase the number of VCEs even if the directional volumes are not equal. To plan for this scenario, passenger peak volumes and the origin-destination information are applied to identify the type of usage the station will have.

Hence, ridership information is critical not only to justify location of a station but also, at the station design level, to help the station designers size underground mezzanines and platforms and

to identify the number of entrances and the locations and sizes of these entrances specific to the particular station.

Under this series of guidelines, stations must provide sufficient vertical circulation elements to accommodate the worst-case ridership condition for the station, using either the standard stairs and escalators or using them in conjunction with additional emergency egress stairways.

STATION AREA DEVELOPMENT
Principles of Station Area Development
Development plans

The establishment of all development plans, particularly those that are supportive of transit, requires the careful consideration of several interwoven layers of components, including the following:

- Land use considerations, such as types of uses, the arrangement of these uses, intensity, and design standards

- Infrastructure and public facilities planning, including utility service and capacity expansion, transportation, and other capital improvements

- Parks, open space, and community facilities planning

- Circulation and parking planning for various types of transportation, including pedestrian, bicycle, and bus

Development plans for the station areas should reflect sound market and economic analyses and incorporate the characteristics that are exhibited by successful transit station areas.

Characteristics of successful transit station areas
Studies of existing transit station areas have been conducted to determine which

characteristics encourage transit ridership and promote development that is supportive of transit.

Each proposed travel corridor can have different opportunities and constraints, built and natural environments, development potential, forecasted levels of ridership, and intermodal transit service. Therefore, each station area will require a different mix of land uses to respond to the needs of the surrounding community, existing development, and existing circulation patterns. In some station areas, for example, there are opportunities for new construction, whereas in others the potential for compact, mixed-use development lies with infill and redevelopment. Although the differences among the proposed station areas are many and the development plans for each may differ, the characteristics of successful transit station areas should be present in the design and development of each.

Principles of station area development

From a consideration of the characteristics of successful transit station areas, the following guiding principles have been derived: design for mixed and concentrated land use, provide adequate access and parking, and create an enhanced station area environment. These principles, which are highly interrelated, are intended to foster a sense of community, leverage private investment, and build system ridership. Through their application, development in the station areas is anticipated to shift away from auto-oriented, low-density land use patterns toward mixed-use, compact development that is oriented to the pedestrian, bicyclist, and transit user.

Mixed and concentrated land use
The design should concentrate a diversity of complementary uses within walking distance of the station that are well integrated, promote balanced levels of transit ridership throughout the day, create active and secure pedestrian environments, and reduce dependence on the automobile.

Adequate access and parking
Circulation patterns should be created that form a convenient, safe, and accessible network for all types of transportation, that interconnect the surrounding residential, commercial, and employment areas, and that provide direct connections to the stations. Parking facilities should be provided that balance the need to adequately serve transit and other uses with the need to reduce land consumption by parking.

Enhanced station area environment
A compact neighborhood environment should be created within the station area that is attractive, safe, and orderly. Public and private spaces should be organized to create an environment that invites pedestrian activity, and design elements should be incorporated that increase the comfort and security of these spaces.

The principles of transit-supportive development must be interpreted to fit the various circumstances of the pro-

TRANSIT STATION ACCESS OPTIONS	
Distance from Stations	**Typical Access Options**
Approx. 0.5 mile	Short walk, bike, or bus
Approx. 1 mile	Long walk, bike, or bus
Approx. 3 miles or more	Bike, bus, or park-and-ride

Transit Station Areas and Qualities That Make Them Successful

Mixed-Use Development

- Supports increased densities
- Integrates with surrounding development and neighborhoods
- Incorporates public and civic space
- Encourages walking and bicycling
- Integrates mutually compatible land uses
- Extends the hours of activity
- Enhances market and financial feasibility
- Improves security
- Balances ridership

Concentrated Development

- Supports increased densities and commercial traffic
- Consolidates trips
- Makes walking and biking convenient options
- Allows land uses to support one another
- Enhances the pedestrian environment and increases transit

Complementary Land Uses

- Makes the transit trip more convenient
- Supports financial feasibility
- Promotes day-night activity and increases security
- Makes the station area more interesting and lively
- Builds a community focal point through inclusion of civic components

Pleasant Pedestrian Environment

- Makes increased density more acceptable
- Encourages street activity and walking
- Ranks pedestrians over autos
- Includes sidewalks, paths, trees, benches, lighting, and usable public open space
- Enhances flow toward transit
- Provides a safe and secure walking experience
- Supports mixed-use development

Pleasant Bicycle Environment

- Promotes an alternative to driving
- Helps achieve concentrated development
- Makes bicycling easy, efficient, and safe
- Provides a low-cost, nonpolluting alternative to the auto

Good Station Access by All Modes of Transportation

- Improves transit accessibility and promotes use
- Emphasizes bicycling and walking over auto use
- Efficiently connects the station to surrounding areas
- Provides visual connections to the station
- Increases efficient transportation
- Links uses and activities
- Reduces development and operating costs

On-Street Parking

- Increases the safety of pedestrians by establishing a buffer between cars and pedestrians
- Provides convenient parking
- Reduces parking lot requirements
- Enhances retail access

Structured Parking

- Decreases the amount of land required for parking, thus increasing concentration
- Makes parking more convenient, closer to the buildings
- Improves the pedestrian environment
- Allows for project phasing through the conversion of surface lots to structured parking

posed station areas. Each station area should be expected to evolve over time as circumstances change, transit ridership increases, and regional growth occurs.

Definition of Station Planning Area

Planning area

Planning for transit-supportive development is primarily focused on the area that is within a reasonable walking distance of the transit stop or station. The perception of a reasonable walking distance varies according to such factors as the presence of interesting and diverse activities along the route, a sense of safety, natural or man-made barriers, and weather. Experience from some regions may indicate that most people will walk 5–15 minutes to get to or from a transit station; however, other studies show that up to 20 minutes of walking between home and the transit station is common.

This 5–15 minute walk corresponds to approximately ¼ to ½ mile. For distances greater than ½ mile, the proportion of people who will walk to transit rapidly decreases. However, beyond the walking distance to the transit station, other types of access may be available, including local bus, feeder bus, shuttles, park-and-ride, kiss-and-ride (drop-off), and bike-and-ride.

Depending on the types of access used and the quality of the station area environment, the areas from which primary ridership will be drawn (catchment areas) could extend to 4½ miles from the station. More compact urban station areas such as those in downtowns are likely to have smaller, more intensely developed catchment areas, whereas stations in suburban environments are likely to have even larger catchment areas. Bike-and-

ride catchment areas may increase where the physical characteristics and improvements are conducive to cycling.

Station planning area zones

Based on these distance factors, the station planning area consists of the following zones, which also reflect a gradient of land use intensity:

Core: The area extending to approximately ¼ mile from the rail station (approximately a 5-minute walk from the station).

Neighborhood or ring: The area approximately ¼–½ mile from the rail station (approximately a 10–15 minute walk from the station).

Support area: The size of the support area will vary, depending on the character of the development and natural features that surround each station. Some portions may be within a 20-minute walk of the station.

Density gradient

To support ridership and take advantage of the growth-focusing benefits of rail (and other fixed-guideway) transit, development in the station areas must evolve from the practice of large-parking-lot, auto-dependent, dispersed development toward a more concentrated, mixed-use, pedestrian-friendly pattern of development. Using the station planning area zones, a gradient of development intensity may be applied to the area surrounding each rail station as appropriate. The table at top of page 57 describes the levels of development intensity anticipated in each zone.

Station Area Classification System

The middle table on page 57 shows the range of residential and nonresidential

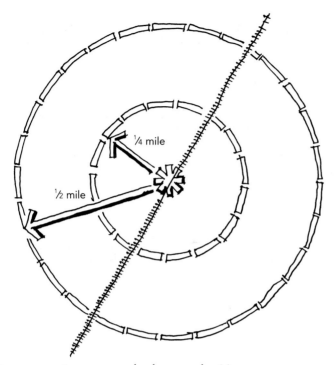

¼ mile

½ mile

▲ Station area planning zones.

development densities necessary to support transit. Within these ranges, station areas may support different levels of activity related to surrounding residential and nonresidential development, market, natural features, and other factors. For instance, in the Triangle Fixed Guideway Study (1995), from which a regional transit plan was developed, four levels of activity were identified to correspond with the types of station locations identified in three counties. The bottom table on page 57 includes the minimum development intensities for residential and nonresidential development surrounding the stations. Activity Level 1 was subsequently determined to be too low to support rail and other fixed-guideway transit.

The proposed locations and respective levels of activity for each of a travel corridor's rail stations should be selected because of its marketability and its capacity

to support more concentrated, transit-supportive future growth at varying levels of intensity.

In using these guidelines, it is important to look at the minimum densities and the specific locations at which they are proposed for implementation.

In addition to levels of activity, the station areas should be classified by the land use and transportation development pattern anticipated for each. Although the activity levels describe the station areas in terms of land use intensity, other characteristics such as the location, mixture of existing and future land uses, types of access, and development potential further differentiate each station area. Understanding the nature of each station area so that the principles of station area development may be applied appropriately is important. Based on the desired characteristics, the types of desired land uses, the transit service, and the development approach for each of the station areas, the following six station area types have been identified as examples with a station area classification system that could be appropriate for the kinds of stations likely to occur in many travel corridors:

- Urban mixed-use
- Urban specialty
- Town center
- Suburban employment
- Suburban residential
- Suburban mixed-use

The table on page 59 highlights the land uses associated with each of the six station types. To further define the mixtures of uses that are appropriate and desirable for each of the six station types, the table on pages 60–61 has been developed as a guide for determining which

GRADIENT OF LAND USE INTENSITY

Relative Level of Development Intensity

¼ mile radius	Higher density, mixed land use including office, retail, and service businesses, residential, and compatible community facilities
¼–½ mile radius	Medium density, mixed land use including office, retail, and service businesses, residential, and compatible community facilities
½–1½ mile radius	Development intensity is likely to vary, relative to the development that surrounds the overall station area. Mixed, medium-density land use may continue in support of the neighborhood/ring area, and lower-density development, including retail and service businesses serving larger markets, may occur.

INTENSITY OF LAND USE AND TRANSPORTATION RELATIONSHIP

Residential Use	Commercial Use	Transportation Compatibility
15+ units/acre	50+ employees/acre	Supports rail or other high-capacity service
7–14 units/acre	40+ employees/acre	Supports local bus service
1–6 units/acre	2+ employees/acre	Supports cars, carpools, and vanpools

Adapted with permission from New Jersey Transit.

MINIMUM HOUSING DENSITY AND FLOOR AREA RATIO BY STATION ACTIVITY LEVEL

ACTIVITY LEVEL	RESIDENTIAL GROSS DENSITY (units per acre)			NONRESIDENTIAL GROSS DENSITY (floor area ratio)		
	Core	Neighborhood	Range (0–½ mile)	Core	Neighborhood	Range (0–½ mile) (avg. empl/acre)
1*	10	4	10–4 (7)	0.3	0.15	.30–.15 (24)
2	15	7	15–7 (11)	0.5	0.20	.50–.20 (35)
3	22	10	22–10 (16)	0.7	0.25	.70–.25 (52)
4	45	15	45–15	1.0	0.30	1.0–.30 (113)

Activity Level 1 in the Triangle Fixed Guideway Study (TFGS) included residential and nonresidential densities too low for regional transit system station areas.

Source: *Triangle Transit Authority,* Triangle Fixed Guideway Study *(TFGS), Phase III Report. 1995.*

uses, when combined in mixed-use development, complement each other and create the environments that are necessary to support transit. Furthermore, the table identifies the zone(s) in which each land use might be located. The list of land uses given in the table is a partial list—many other uses may be acceptable. However, it is the site design and intensity of each acceptable use that will determine the appropriateness of each use. For this reason, the design guidelines that follow this section and the densities set forth in the tables on page 57 have been established to address these issues.

Application of the Principles

Principle 1: Mixed and concentrated land use

Concentrate a diversity of complementary uses within walking distance of the station that are well-integrated, promote balanced levels of ridership throughout the day, create active and secure pedestrian environments, and reduce dependence on the automobile.

Transit-supportive, mixed-use development brings together a variety of complementary land uses that are within convenient walking distance of one another and concentrated at densities that

▲ *Bus access directly in front of entrance to Washington, D.C., Metro College Park Station. DMJM+Harris.*

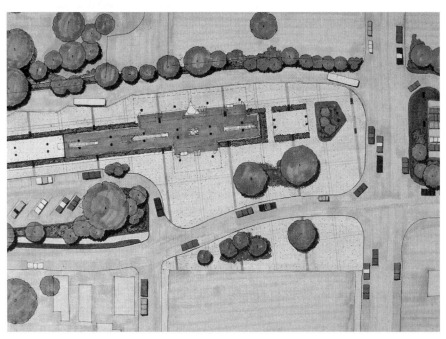

▶ *Pedestrian access at street level leads to aerial platform. Miami, Florida, Metro Culmer Station. DMJM+Harris.*

STATION AREA CLASSIFICATION AND ASSOCIATED LAND USES

CLASSIFICATION	STATION AREA FEATURES		
	Distinctive Characteristics	Examples of Desired Land Uses	Transit Service*
Urban mixed-use	Mixed and multiple land use, employment and retail center, cultural/civic activity, government center, high density (residential and nonresidential), predominantly structured, parking and some surface parking, grid streets, 3+ story buildings	High-density commercial, office, and residential, mixed-use buildings, cultural and civic facilities, hotels and conference centers, restaurants and services, government offices	Regional rail Intracity bus Express bus Feeder bus Local bus Shuttle Taxis
Specialty urban	Thematic land use (university, hospital, etc.) mixed and multiple land use, employment center, mid to high density (residential and nonresidential), structured or surface parking, grid or modified grid streets	Institutional and office uses, hospitals, clinics, research and development facilities, mid- to high-density housing, educational facilities, retail restaurants and services, university-related cultural facilities	Regional rail Express bus Feeder bus Local bus Shuttle Taxis Park-and-ride
Town center	Mixed and multiple land use, employment center, "main street" commercial, mid-density (residential and nonresidential), structured or surface parking, grid or modified grid streets	Retail (facing the street), mid-density, housing and office, mixed-use buildings, town square, restaurants and services, some government offices, entertainment	Regional rail Local bus
Suburban employment	Employment center, mid- and high-density (residential and nonresidential), structured or surface parking, interconnected streets	Mid- and high-density office and housing, research and development facilities, light industry, restaurants and services, accessory retail	Regional rail Local bus Shuttle Park-and-ride
Suburban residential	Mix of attached and detached housing, neighborhood business, mid-density (residential and nonresidential), surface parking, interconnected streets	Mid-density office and housing, neighborhood retail, services and restaurants	Regional rail Local bus Park-and-ride
Suburban mixed-use	Mixed and multiple land use, employment and retail center, mid- and high density (residential and nonresidential), structured or surface parking, interconnected streets	Mixed-use buildings, retail and office, mid- and high density housing, civic spaces, entertainment	Regional rail Local bus Shuttle Park-and-ride

Will vary with actual location; may include other types of transit in future phases.

LAND USE/STATION AREA COMPATIBILITY MATRIX

STATION AREA TYPES

Land Uses	Urban Mixed-Use C	R	S	Specialty Urban C	R	S	Town Center C	R	S	Suburban Employment C	R	S	Suburban Residential C	R	S	Suburban Mixed-Use C	R	S
High-density office	—			—						—						—		
Mid-density office		—			—			—			—		—	Δ			—	
Moderate-density office				Δ		Δ	Δ				Δ		Δ					
Medical office	Δ	Δ		—	Δ		Δ						Δ			Δ		
Local services	—	—	—	—	Δ	Δ	—	Δ		Δ	Δ		Δ			Δ	Δ	
Hospital		Δ		—												Δ		
Hotels/motels	—	Δ		—	Δ		—	Δ		—			—			—		
Movie theaters		Δ	Δ	Δ	Δ		Δ	Δ					Δ			Δ		
Restaurants		—	Δ		—	Δ	—	Δ		—	Δ		—				—	Δ
Local shopping	—	Δ		—	Δ		—			—			—					
Regional shopping	Δ													Δ				Δ
Neighborhood/convenience retail		—	—	Δ	Δ	Δ	Δ	Δ		Δ	Δ		—	—	Δ	Δ	Δ	
Gym/health club	Δ	Δ	Δ	Δ	Δ		Δ	Δ		Δ	Δ		Δ			Δ	Δ	
High-density residential	—	—		—			—									—		
Mid-density residential	—	—			—	Δ	—	—	Δ	—	—	Δ	—	—	Δ	—	—	Δ
Low-density residential														Δ				
Urban park	—	—			—	Δ	—	Δ		—	Δ		—				—	Δ
Regional park		Δ			Δ			Δ			Δ			Δ				Δ
Cultural facilities	—	Δ					—									Δ		

	Urban Mixed-Use			Specialty Urban			Town Center			Suburban Employment			Suburban Residential			Suburban Mixed-Use		
	C	R	S	C	R	S	C	R	S	C	R	S	C	R	S	C	R	S
Land Uses																		
Public agencies/ community uses	_			_			_			_			_			_		
Child day care	Δ	Δ	Δ	Δ	Δ	Δ	Δ	Δ		Δ			Δ			Δ		
Colleges/universities			Δ	_					Δ			Δ			Δ			Δ
Major government agencies	Δ						_											
Schools and other institutions			Δ			Δ			Δ			Δ			Δ			Δ
Research and development				_	Δ	Δ				_	Δ	Δ						
Light industry/ manufacturing			Δ			Δ			Δ	Δ	Δ						Δ	Δ
Auto repair and service			Δ			Δ			Δ			Δ			Δ			Δ

_ Essential use   Δ Desirable use   C Core   R Ring   S Support area

generate high levels of pedestrian activity and transit use. The term *mixed-use* refers to the combination of multiple uses in a single building or development project, either horizontally or vertically, or to a mixture of single-use buildings or small developments in a highly organized walkable area. Buildings should be contiguous or grouped, removing the need for long walks between buildings and adjacent development. Safe, direct, and convenient connections between the varied uses are essential.

Principle 2: Adequate access and parking

Create circulation patterns that form a convenient, safe, and accessible network for all types of transportation, interconnecting the surrounding residential, commercial, and employment areas and providing direct connections to the rail station. Provide parking facilities that balance the need to adequately support transit and other uses with the need to reduce the consumption of land and other resources by parking.

In a successful station area, the competing demands of pedestrians, bicyclists, autos, buses, and trains must be comfortably blended. Accommodating these different transportation needs in a manner that promotes the use of the rail service and future fixed-guideway system and supports nearby business and housing is a difficult and important design consideration. In general, the priority of station access should be (1) pedestrians and bicyclists, (2) trains and buses, and (3) automobiles. Even though many transit riders may arrive by car, they will all be pedestrians at some point. Ease-of-access issues must also be addressed. For example, if a station is designed with limited parking to encourage people to access the station by walking and bicycling, it is important to ensure that there are adequate sidewalks and secure facilities for bicycle storage. It is also critical to look at secondary issues, such as whether limiting parking at the station will only push commuters to park in the surrounding neighborhoods, creating a conflict with local residents.

Principle 3: Enhanced station area environment

Create a compact neighborhood environment within the station area that is attractive, safe, and orderly. Organize public and private spaces to create an environment that invites pedestrian activity and incorporates design elements that increase the comfort and security of these spaces.

The various elements of the station area environment can be combined to create interest and visual order. They can help transit users to become oriented and to comprehend the size and character of the station area. The character or theme of the station area may be further reinforced through the use of elements of continuity, which may include unique signage, planting, lighting, artwork, street furnishings, banners, and other improvements. Through the establishment of comfortable surroundings and a clearly discernible system of pedestrian and bicycle routes, people are increasingly willing to walk longer distances and travel farther on bicycles.

CHAPTER 3

STATION TYPES AND CONFIGURATIONS

Most modern transit systems use many of the station configurations described in this chapter to varying degrees. It is not uncommon to have all three station types—aerial, at-grade, and underground—in any particular city served by mass transit. A key determinant as to which station configuration to use, along with a particular type of train and power technology, is made early in the design process and hinges on these principal factors:

- The numbers of passengers anticipated to be carried
- Cost
- Physical constraints defined by the related infrastructure
- Social-economic benefits

Many of these issues are addressed in greater detail in Chapters 2 and 6.

STATION DEFINED BY TRAIN AND POWER FEATURES

At this stage in the planning process the technology most likely has been defined, and the designer must become familiar with the characteristics of the station's program.

Heavy-Rail Transit

Typical Characteristics

Headway: as frequent as 2 minutes

Car length: maximum 75 ft; platform lengths: even car lengths up to 700 ft

Passengers on fully loaded car: average 160 standing

Station types: aerial, at-grade, and underground

Platform heights: average 3 ft 8½ in. above top of rail

Power: third rail (United States); catenaries in some countries

Guideway: grade separated

Light-Rail Transit

Typical Characteristics

Headway: as frequent as 5 minutes

Car length: 90 ft average; platform lengths: single car lengths up to 300 ft

Passengers on fully loaded car: average 150 standing

Station types: at-grade, aerial, and underground

Platform heights: 1 ft 8 in. above top of rail for low-floor vehicles

Street boarding without continuous platforms requires an ADA-approved elevated portion of the platform at select boarding locations.

Power: electric overhead contact system

Guideway: allows street running with automobile traffic

Commuter Rail

Typical Characteristics

Headway: as frequent as 4 minutes

Car length: average 85 ft; platform lengths: up to 12 car lengths plus locomotive

Passengers on fully loaded car:

Single level: 110 (85 ft car) to 125 (92 ft car); average 120 standing

Bi-Level: 135–140 average (MARC, VRE, Sounder); maximum is 175 (MBTA) standing

Station types: at-grade, aerial, and underground

Platform heights: average 3 ft 8½ in. above top of rail

Power: third rail, diesel, or electric locomotive (OCS), diesel or electric motorized units (OCS)

Guideway: grade separated in urban areas, street running in outlying areas.

Intercity Rail

Typical Characteristics

Headway: as frequent as 30 minutes

Car length: average 85 ft; platform lengths: up to 16 car lengths plus locomotive

Passengers on fully loaded car: Amtrak intercity single-level varies by class:

business class: 60

Metroliner: 60–66–68

coach seating: 74–88 (all seated)

Station types: at-grade, aerial, and underground

Platform heights: average 3 ft 8½ in. above top of rail

Power: diesel or electric locomotive (OCS)

Guideway: grade separated in urban areas, street running in outlying areas

STATION DEFINED BY PHYSICAL CHARACTERISTICS

The three basic station types described here are applicable to most of today's system technologies. Most systems, except light-rail transit (LRT), require grade-separated fixed-guideway or signalized track crossings. The following overview

▼ *Platform lengths for each of the four major rail transit systems*

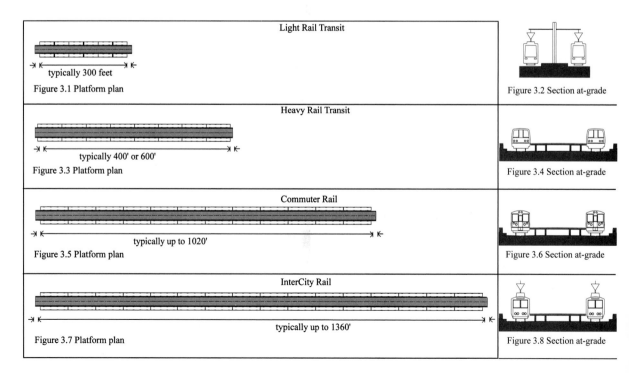

Light Rail Transit

typically 300 feet

Figure 3.1 Platform plan

Figure 3.2 Section at-grade

Heavy Rail Transit

typically 400' or 600'

Figure 3.3 Platform plan

Figure 3.4 Section at-grade

Commuter Rail

typically up to 1020'

Figure 3.5 Platform plan

Figure 3.6 Section at-grade

InterCity Rail

typically up to 1360'

Figure 3.7 Platform plan

Figure 3.8 Section at-grade

of types (and subgroupings) will help the designer better understand their uses and limitations.

Aerial

Elevated guideway

Design elements

- Dependent on vertical circulation elements.
- Fare collection and entry at street level or mezzanine.
- Requires canopy over platform.

Application

- Relevant to system using an aerial guideway structure.
- Support piers must be compatible with ground constraints.
- Must maintain adequate clearances above street level.

Architectural implications

- Strong visual and physical impact in urban running.

- Guideway structure and canopy help define the form and image of the station.
- Passengers and vertical circulation elements may be exposed to weather.

At-Grade

Ground or street running

Design elements

- Not dependent on vertical circulation, provided that track crossings are permitted.
- Fare collection and entry at street level or requires mezzanine when track crossing is not permitted.
- Requires canopy over platform.

Application

- Consistent with highway median or railroad right-of-way.
- Requires pedestrian bridge or tunnel.
- Works best in low-volume passenger systems where track crossing is permitted.

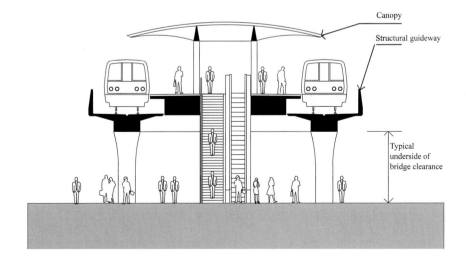

◄ *Elevated guideways.*

Architectural implications

- Significant visual and physical impact in urban running.
- Canopy and wind shelters help define the form and image of the station.
- Requires passenger protection against vehicles and noise when running in a highway median.

Retained fill

The designation *retained fill* typically refers to a station that is constructed on top of an embankment or an earth mound that is either an existing earth structure or a new earth structure that has been determined to be less costly to construct than an aerial structure.

Design elements

- Dependent on vertical circulation.
- Fare collection and entry at street level.
- Requires canopy over platform.

Application

- Typically located in an existing railroad embankment.

- Track raised above grade to a level where an aerial guideway is not cost-effective or practical.
- Passenger access from both sides may result in narrow concourse and therefore be perceived as a tunnel.

Architectural implications

- Inappropriate as a new system in an urban running because of the strong visual barrier created as a result of the earth embankment.
- Track supported on retaining wall or sloped berm presents an opportunity for wall treatment or the use of land-scaping to soften the visual impact.
- A significant horizontal image is presented by berm, platform, and canopy.

Open cut

Design elements

- Dependent on vertical circulation unless grade change permits ramp access to platforms.

▼ *Ground or street running.*

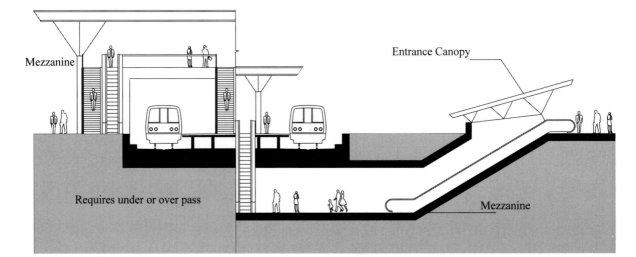

Mezzanine

Requires under or over pass

Entrance Canopy

Mezzanine

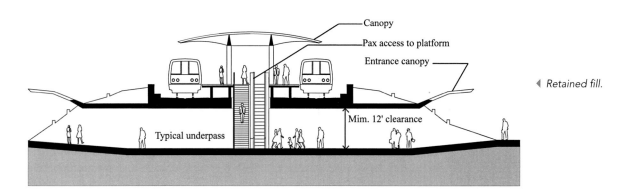

Canopy

Pax access to platform

Entrance canopy

◀ *Retained fill.*

Mim. 12' clearance

Typical underpass

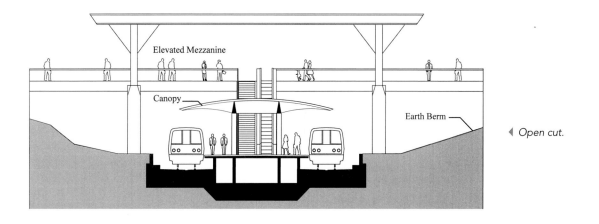

Elevated Mezzanine

Canopy

Earth Berm

◀ *Open cut.*

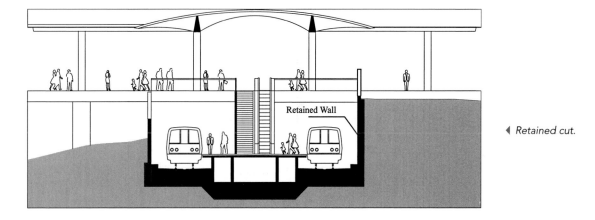

Retained Wall

◀ *Retained cut.*

- Fare collection and entry at street level or mezzanine above platform.
- Requires canopy over platform.

Application

- Less costly than underground configuration.
- Inappropriate for urban running (unless within an existing right-of-way) because of large amount of land required and the negative effect it creates with the depressed setting.

Architectural implications

- Less conspicuous than at-grade or aerial structure
- Sloped berm presents an opportunity for wall treatment or landscaped surfaces.
- Maintains sense of openness, natural lighting, and implied feeling of security.

Retained cut

Typically refers to a station that is built into the earth, where the platform is located below grade and retaining walls hold the adjacent earth back.

Design elements

- Dependent on vertical circulation.
- Fare collection and entry at street level or mezzanine above platform.
- Requires canopy over platform.

Application

- Less costly than underground configuration.
- Inappropriate for urban running unless within an existing right-of-way.
- Allows limited right-of-way width, provided that retaining walls are utilized.

Architectural implications

- Same as for open-cut stations.
- Reduces noise and vibration impacts in residential and other sensitive locations such as hospitals.

Underground

Cut-and-cover

Design elements

- Dependent on vertical circulation.
- Fare collection and entry at street level or mezzanine above platform.
- Mechanical ventilation and artificial lighting required.

Application

- Typically located in earth below street right-of-way.
- Implemented when aerial or street running is not effective.
- Conducive to urban running and dense areas.
- Works best when alignment is directional with street grid.

Architectural implications

- Least visual and physical impact in urban environment.
- Requires life safety systems and emergency exiting provisions.
- Requires acoustical control.
- Street-level entrances become major visual focus points.
- Requires waterproof construction.
- Access permitted on both sides of street.
- Facilitates strong expression of structure and helps define station character.
- Interior structure protects architectural features from weather.

Mined

Mined typically refers to a station built in rock or geology that is suitable for restraining sufficiently to construct a vaultlike roof. Several construction techniques are used in response to the geology and are covered in greater detail in Chapter 6, "Engineering Considerations."

Design elements

- Dependent on vertical circulation.
- Entry at street level; fare collection typically on mezzanine within cavern.

- Mechanical ventilation and artificial lighting required.

Application

- Used where soil conditions and surface restrictions encourage mined construction.
- Typically requires cut-and-cover shafts at station ends to house vent fans and provide access for tunnel-boring machines.
- Conducive to running in dense urban areas.

▼ *Underground cut-and-cover deep.*

▼▼ *Underground cut-and-cover shallow.*

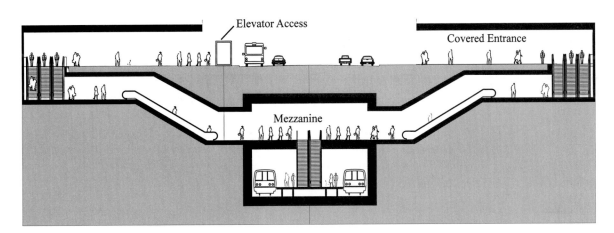

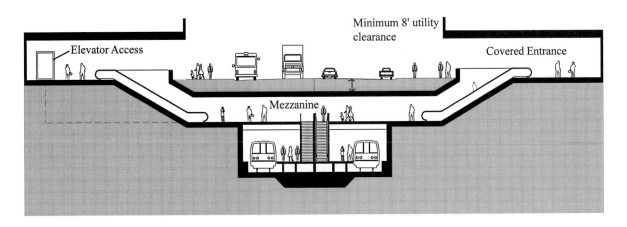

- Permits horizontal alignment without regard to street grid, provided that surface access is obtainable.
- Enables tunneling to run under existing buildings, provided that geotechnical and easement criteria are satisfied.

Architectural implications

- Similar to those of cut-and-cover stations.
- Arched configuration has less cross-sectional area in which to run mechanical and electrical services.
- Interior columns offer no structural benefit—preferred architectural criterion is to have column-free platforms.

Stacked

Stacked typically refers to a station in which two levels of track and platforms are constructed one over the other. It generally means that the platforms are parallel to each other; however, many are built that are perpendicular to each other.

Design elements

- Similar to those of mined stations.

Application

- Similar to mined and cut-and-cover stations.
- Typically used in terminal or transfer stations.

Architectural implications

- Similar to those of mined and cut-and-cover stations.
- Noise and vibration from overhead train is a significant issue.
- When the mezzanine location is at an intermediate level (below the upper platform), it can create a tall vertical rise for vertical circulation and result in longer travel time.
- When the mezzanine location is above the upper platform, it requires vertical circulation to penetrate the upper platform to access the lower. This may deprive the upper platform of

▼ *Underground mined (typically deep).*

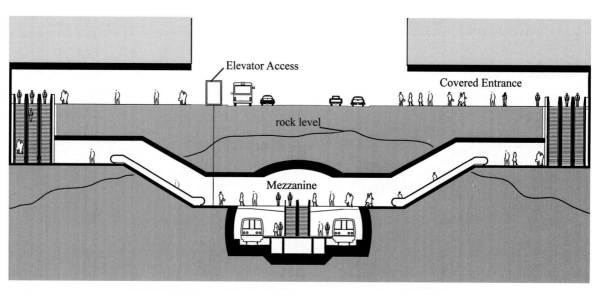

circulation space needed to move passengers effectively. May cause the upper platform to be wider than the lower platform.

- Emergency exiting from the upper platform may require downward movement of passengers to access the mezzanine.

Binocular

The designation *binocular* typically refers to underground stations that are built as individual tubes serving single tracks and platforms with connecting pedestrian passageways.

Design elements

- Similar to those of mined stations.

Application

- Similar to mined stations.
- Utilized when mining techniques or geotechnical constraints limit the mined cavern size.
- Mezzanine is typically located above caverns with suitable soil separation.

- Distance between caverns is determined by tunnel diameter and geology.
- Typically deep stations.

Architectural implications

- Small platform caverns, resulting in confined space and image.
- Typically uses cross passages connecting platforms and vertical circulation elements.
- Most difficult to make safe; requires significant closed-circuit television (CCTV) coverage.
- Has all the disadvantages of a side platform station.

PLATFORM CONFIGURATIONS

Each station type is readily configured as a center or side platform station. Selecting the appropriate configuration to meet a project's needs is discussed in greater detail in Chapters 4 and 6. The tables on pages 73 and 74 provide the advantages and disadvantages of each. In usual prac-

▼ *Stacked.*

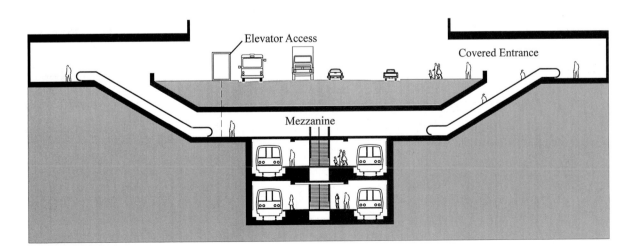

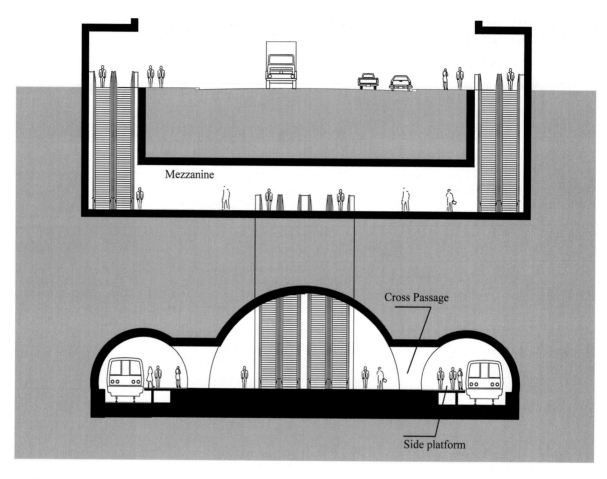

Mezzanine

Cross Passage

Side platform

▲ *Binocular.*

tice a center platform is preferred over a side platform for reasons of improved passenger circulation, lower station cost, and improved safety, as all passengers are on the same platform and thereby providing self-policing. Infrastructure constraints such as tunneling under existing buildings in an underground alignment may be prohibitive and reduce the number of the choices as to platform type. For instance, constraints generated as a result of the track spacing between center platforms will be greater than side platforms; therefore, the guideway (tunnel or aerial) has a wider spacing and consequently a

greater station structure width. It also has a greater potential to influence the adjacent buildings or roadways in which it is running, potentially causing significant added cost needed to acquire property. This issue is covered in greater detail in Chapter 6, "Engineering Considerations."

MEZZANINE CONFIGURATIONS
The term *mezzanine* is used to describe the public area space of a station, which is, in effect, an intermediate space for passenger transition. Another use of mezzanine space is as a nonpublic or ancillary space. Although the station may require a

CENTER PLATFORMS

Advantages

- Platform width may be less than combined width of side platforms, and resulting station may be smaller and less expensive.
- Center concourse (mezzanine) width can be less than combined concourses for side platforms.
- Allow wider spacing between tracks to accommodate track crossovers.
- The total number of vertical circulation devices required may be fewer than for side platforms when direction of peak loads is taken into account.
- Require fewer elevators to the platform.
- May better accommodate surge loads (bulk queuing).
- When a single concourse (mezzanine) is provided, the need to cross oncoming traffic to reach vertical circulation may be reduced.
- Passengers who board the wrong train may change directions without changing levels.
- Provide more flexibility for layout of service areas at platform ends.
- Provide more phasing flexibility for maintenance and repairs.
- Shared access to platform provides more options for pedestrian movement.
- Potential to locate attendant at a single point with access to all trains in off-peak times.

Disadvantages

- Because of wider spacing between track centers (wider alignment), the cost of line work may be greater than for side platform station.
- Limited ability to add vertical circulation, so optimal vertical circulation should be determined at the start of design, including attention to NFPA 130 platform evacuation requirements.
- Options for elevator placement are more limited; for example, locating elevators midway in the length of the platform may decrease capacity handling at the location where it is most needed.
- Linear queuing for vertical circulation must mix with less flexible bulk queuing for boarding that may extend laterally across the platform. In effect, detraining passengers may have to compete with entraining passengers in the area along the length of the platform, which coincides with the queuing space for vertical circulation.
- May limit full use of available concourse area, inasmuch as vertical circulation should be centered on the platform.
- Physically wide vertical circulation (needed to handle loading on two platforms) may restrict visual sight lines, such as concealing the fact that a stair farther down the platform is available and less crowded than a closer, overcrowded device.
- Emergency exit layout may be restricted, and exiting passengers may have to cross tracks.
- Out-of-service vertical circulation may create more disruption of pedestrian flow, because linear queuing may have to backtrack through bulk queuing from two platform edges. In effect, if the escalator is out of service, then passengers must navigate through the passengers waiting for the next train
- Visually impaired passengers may perceive side platform stations as being less dangerous for use because a continuous sidewall is available for location reference.

SIDE PLATFORMS	
Advantages	**Disadvantages**
• Greater station capacity handling because more vertical circulation devices can be provided. Side platforms can also better accommodate long-term ridership changes, such as increases in the number of reverse commuters. • Can better accommodate linear queuing by reducing the need to mix with bulk queuing. • Can be designed so that future platform widening is possible. • Can be designed so that visual cues and signage are simpler. • May have greater emergency exit capacity. • Potential flexibility of station operation, because it may be possible to provide part-time attendant on off-peak side. • In an underground station, where insufficient depth below grade is available for placement of a mezzanine above the platform, the side platform configuration is more adaptable to access from a platform-level mezzanine. • More amenable to locating concessions such as newsstands so they do not hamper capacity handling and queuing. • More wall area available for advertising; easier access to advertising.	• Greater cost, due to wider station and more vertical circulation devices. • Prone to reduced capacity handling if passengers do not make decisions about direction and transfer before reaching the platform. • May handle fewer people under surge loading. • May be less flexible when repairs to platform area are needed, because of the narrower width of each platform. • While on the concourse level, patrons need to select appropriate platform to avoid backtracking and delay. • Minimally sized platforms that meet requirements under NFPA 130 will be larger than a single minimally sized center platform. • Surveillance of vertical circulation may require more cameras and/or station attendants. • Side platform stations with no central or common concourse may require attendants in two locations at least part of the time.

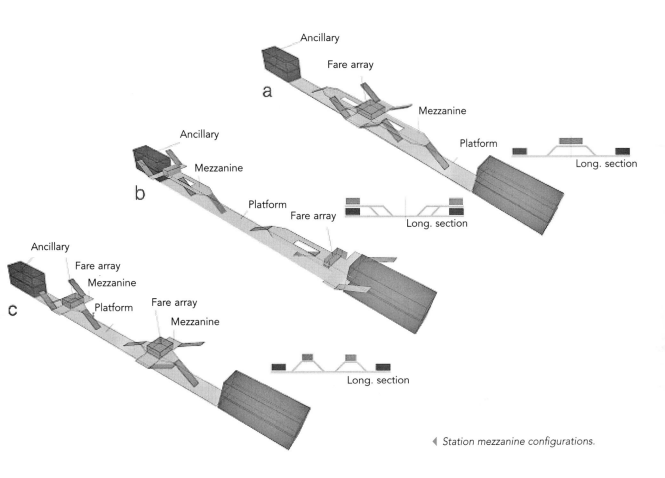

Ancillary
Fare array

a

Mezzanine

Platform

Long. section

Ancillary

Mezzanine

b

Platform
Fare array

Long. section

Ancillary

Fare array

Mezzanine

Platform

c

Fare array

Mezzanine

Long. section

◀ *Station mezzanine configurations.*

public mezzanine zone, it is also good practice to use this level for station operations and mechanical support functions. For instance, diagram *b* in the illustration above shows mezzanines at the ends of the station. The space on a mezzanine or between mezzanines is also a potential location for mechanical support space.

Mezzanines are frequently provided to enable passengers to access platforms from horizontal walking areas (street), using vertical movement whenever a direct access (street to platform) is not permitted or the fare collection system re-

quires movement through a fare barrier (see the discussion of fare collection systems in Chapter 7). A mezzanine can also serve as a location for a station agent business center or security control, as well as a transition space for deep underground or tall aerial platform stations where the principal means of movement are escalators and stairs and heights are limited (see "Vertical Circulation" in Chapter 6). Most mezzanines are used for transition from horizontal to vertical, purchasing a ticket, and moving through a fare collection turnstile. Factors that influence mezzanine location include number of entrances to be served, passenger volume, platform length, and the National Fire Protection Association (NFPA) Standard 130 exiting requirement for passengers to be off the platform in 4 minutes. The configurations shown depict mezzanine locations in relation to the platform. Stations with long platforms (450 ft or longer) may require at least two mezzanines to collect the vertical circulation passenger flow off the platform. In the case of large-passenger-volume stations, a continuous mezzanine may be required to allow frequent spacing of stairs, escalators, and elevators to meet the passenger entraining/detraining loads or satisfy code exiting demand.

PROGRAM ELEMENTS
Passenger Circulation
In all transportation-related public spaces, the primary goal of circulation systems is to move passengers efficiently to their destinations. Whether in an airport concourse, a ferry terminal, a bus station, or a transit station, the governing principles are the same, namely, to:

- Minimize travel distances
- Minimize the number of horizontal and vertical transitions
- Make the circulation corridor direct
- Separate opposite passenger flows when possible

The circulation system is defined initially by the station type (aerial, at-grade, or underground) and, second, by the fare collection/ticketing system. Chapter 4 discusses the planning process for sizing circulation corridors and vertical devices. The basic passenger flow diagrams are as shown, according to the fare collection system employed.

Station with fare barriers
Transit systems usually require passengers to access their system by paying a fare. This is collected in a series of turnstiles, which together with gates and other elements constitute a fare barrier.

▼ Station flow diagram with fare control.

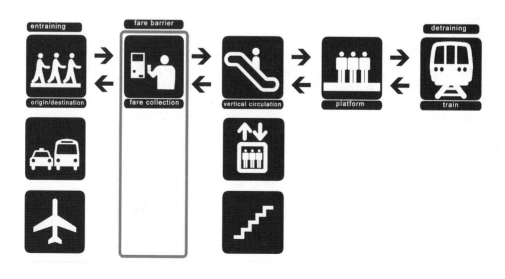

In most heavy-rail transit systems, the passenger typically enters the station from a street, parking area, or building or transfers from another intermodal route and moves vertically to a mezzanine space. The passenger then purchases a ticket, moves through the fare barrier system, and then to the platform via vertical circulation elements.

Station with ticketing and waiting

Stations with ticketing and waiting features are typically used in intercity or commuter railroad stations. The passenger enters the station, purchases a ticket at a designated window, moves to a designated waiting area, and then moves to the platform after the track location has been announced.

Station with ticket vending or honor-based fare collection

Stations that rely on ticket vending or honor-based fare collection are frequently used in light-rail transit systems. The passenger purchases a ticket from a vending machine and proceeds directly to the platform.

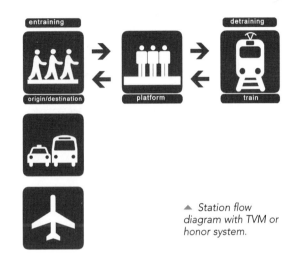

▲ Station flow diagram with TVM or honor system.

▼ Station flow diagram with ticket sales and waiting area.

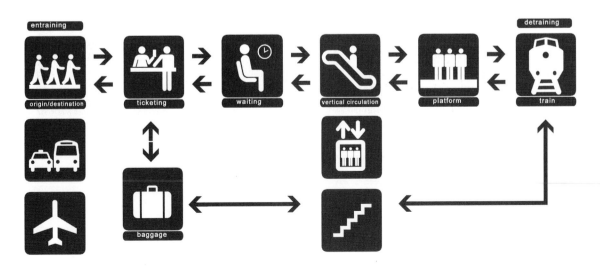

ANCILLARY SPACE PROGRAM

Function	Location	Required Area (sq ft)
Station Electrical Services		
Electrical distribution	Mezzanine	2 x 900
Collector bus room		2 x 420
Uninterruptible power supply (UPS) and battery room	"	2 x 260
Tunnel lighting	Track	2 x 80
Traction Power		
Control room (electrical)	Mezzanine	200
Power room 1	"	2000
Power room 2	"	2600
Power room 3	"	4000
Signals		
Signal room interlocking	Platform	1200
Signal room noninterlocking	"	320
Station Operations		
Station CTA	Mezzanine	100
Station dry storage	"	100
Station chemical storage	"	100
Refuse storage room	Platform	100
Scrubber (floor)	"	100
Scrubber (floor)	Mezzanine	100
Station Exhaust		
OTE-UPE No. 1	Platform/mezzanine	1200
OTE-UPE No. 2	"	1200
Station Ventilation		
Chiller room No. 1	Mezzanine	2600
Chiller room No. 2	"	2600
Tunnel Ventilation		
Tunnel ventilation room No 1	Mezzanine	4900
Tunnel ventilation room No 2	"	4900
Vent blast shaft No. 1	"	2000
Vent blast shaft No. 2	"	2000
Plumbing and Fire Protection		
Ejector room 1	Track	300
Ejector room 2	"	300
Pump room	Platform	240
Sprinkler valve	Mezzanine	120

Function	Location	Required Area (sq ft)
Plumbing and Fire Protection (continued)		
Toilet—unisex	"	2 x 40
Toilet, public—men	"	90
Toilet, public—women	"	90
Maintenance		
Ladders, lifts storage	Mezzanine	200
Lamps and ballast	"	200
Porters' supply and equipment	"	100
Communications		
Communication room	Mezzanine	800
Public telephone equipment	"	100
Commercial wireless telephone	"	100
Security & Control		
Station service center 1	Mezzanine	120
Station service center 2	"	120
Station emergency management panel	"	100
Concessions (if required)		

Ancillary Spaces

Both the specific system technology used and the station type influences the extent and type of ancillary spaces used in transit stations. Generally, street running and aerial stations use less space to support the operation of the station or the system technology then does an underground station. This is principally due to the demands placed on the underground station for an environmentally safe air conditioning system, requiring smoke exhaust systems for both the station and the tunnel, and space to accommodate traction power equipment and the station's other electrical needs. Several new high-speed rail stations, particularly terminal stations, are being designed as aerial configurations, offering the passenger an environmentally controlled facility. In this case the station ancillary spaces are similar to those in an underground environment. The following list identifies several types of support spaces, according to station type.

Aerial and at-grade stations in HRT and LRT

- Train control and communications
- Toilet facilities
- Traction power
- Escalator and elevator machine rooms

Aerial and at-grade stations in railroads (commuter, inter-city, HSR)

- Train dispatching
- Baggage handling

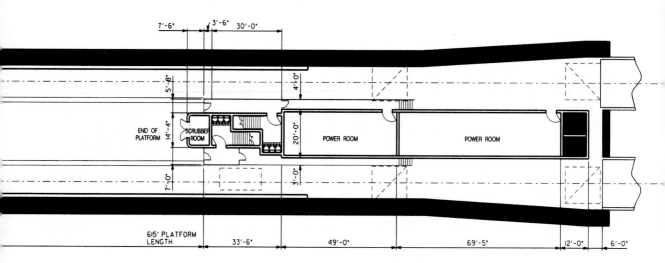

▲ *Platform plan.*

- Crew quarters
- Ticket dispensing
- Concessions
- Toilet facilities
- Escalator and elevator machine rooms

Underground Stations

- Tunnel ventilation fan rooms
- Traction power substations

- Station ventilation
- Overtrack and underplatform exhaust fan rooms
- Electrical distribution
- Communications
- Track drainage sump pumps
- Sewage pumping stations
- Emergency stairs

DESIGN CONCERNS AND PROCESS

This chapter focuses on the specific design process and addresses overall design goals and principles, as well as design steps to follow in sizing public circulation spaces. It offers guidance on defining the overall station, including the ancillary spaces.

Many transit agencies have their own goals and corporate objectives, which include a policy on the architecture of their stations. This chapter is offered to help guide a specific station design and bring consensus among designers and transit authorities.

Designers are encouraged to use imagination and skill in achieving the best solutions. Stations should exceed the defined technical standards and requirements. Creative use of systemwide components can help establish a station's uniqueness. Designers are expected to balance *elements of continuity* versus *elements of variability* to provide systemwide assurance to the passenger. The use of standard design elements such as lighting and signage make for consistent passenger comfort and orientation. The creative expression of structure and major design elements such as walls, platform finishes, and railings allow the designer to create architecture that reflects local values and identity.

DESIGN CONCERNS
Concern for Context

Designers are encouraged to create station designs that reflect the location and express the goals of the community. A new station form may play an important part in the urban nucleus and have an impact on the urban fabric, property development, and the communities the transit system serves.

▲ Baltimore, Maryland, Metro's State Center Station used strong expression of structure as a major architectural theme. R. Reynolds Architect.

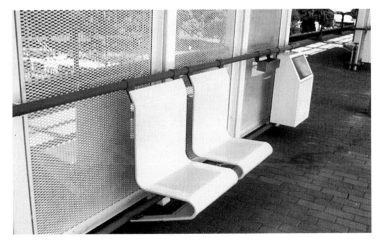

▼ The initial Vancouver, British Columbia, SkyTrain transit system stations used furniture, trash containers, railings, and windscreens as design elements of continuity. DMJM+Harris.

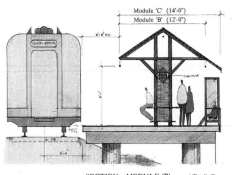

Module 'C' (14'-0")
Module 'B' (12'-0")

SECTION - MODULE 'B'   1/2" = 1' - 0"

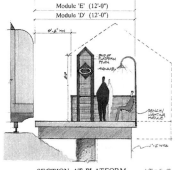

Module 'E' (12'-0")
Module 'D' (12'-0")

SECTION AT PLATFORM   1/2" = 1' - 0"

▶ *A modular approach to planning platform canopy and shelter locations was used in the Virginia Railway Express planning process. DMJM+Harris.*

SIDE ELEVATION

Module 'A'

SECTION - MODULE 'A'

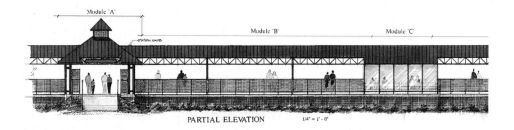

Module 'A'   Module 'B'   Module 'C'

PARTIAL ELEVATION   1/4" = 1' - 0"

Customer-Friendly Connections

A primary goal of all transit systems is to create a seamless journey between different systems and modes of travel. Connections to other stations should be direct and effortless. Minimum variations in vertical transitions are best. Give special thought to connections be-

tween adjoining transit systems that may require separate fare collection control. Minimizing travel distances between systems is crucial, as is concern for passengers carrying luggage. Clear passenger information displays help support transfer at multiple locations along a route.

▶▶ *The London Jubilee Line station is an excellent example of clarity in circulation. (Photo courtesy Alfred Lau.)*

Safety and Ease of Use

Station designers must understand the physical attributes of the passengers and plan the station accordingly. Many stations serve a high volume of older passengers or people with disabilities (such as those near hospitals, schools, or senior-citizen housing), which may require unique design solutions. Stations providing passengers with access to airports or railroads require methods for dealing with luggage and for sizing elevators. Carrying luggage on escalators is discouraged within the United States, thereby placing extra loads on elevators. Once designers fully understand the needs of passengers, they must plan the entire route accordingly. The route typically begins at a drop-off by taxi or arrival by another mode of travel and works its way through the station, through ticketing services, and ultimately to the platform. The entire path must be adaptable to passengers with disabilities as well as those who may be unique to the particular station setting, such as an airport. Safety and ease of use must be continuous along the entire path.

Clarity of Circulation and Orientation

Station designers should achieve clarity in the travel path and orient the passenger in relation to the station and surrounding areas.

STATION PLANNING PROCESS

In designing a new station, several basic steps are required for underground, at-grade, and aerial stations. An underground station is the most complex design because of the geotechnical and other engineering influences on the track and tunneling. These are described in detail in Chapter 6.

Efficient Passenger Movement

Efficient passenger movement must incorporate:

- Natural orientation to the surrounding area
- Design of vertical circulation elements to meet demand and maintenance requirements
- Adequate queuing in front of all vertical circulation elements (stairs, elevators, escalators)
- No overlap of queues
- No reverse changes in direction, whenever possible
- No cross flows
- An orderly hierarchy of decision points, so that procedures needed to be followed when using the station, such as purchasing a ticket or reaching the correct platform, are readily apparent

Design

Overall design should:

- Develop an overall expression, based on function, combined with simplicity of form.

- Develop an expression of structure.

- Create a balance between station context and elements of continuity (defined as physical elements that have a systemwide reference).

- Develop elements of continuity as standard planning devices, such as structural grids, and use modular components whenever practical.

- Use natural light and multivolume spaces to enhance the passenger experience and orientation.

- Use timeless, natural materials (such as granite), monumental in appearance, long in performance, and readily maintainable.

- Integrate all building services, systems, lighting, and graphics into the architecture.

- Create an acoustically acceptable environment.

- Create a design that supports station maintenance.

- Avoid fads and short-lived styles in architecture. Instead, strive for an architecture that will support the 100-year life of the station.

The initial step of locating a station is defined in Chapter 2. The architect defines the general location of the station platform and the access from and to the community the station is to serve. Marrying the two can be a major challenge. Working both at the platform and the street levels, a series of studies must establish precisely the location of the final platform position and the location of the entrances. The process typically consists of the following 12 steps (using the underground station as an example):

1. Determine the passenger peak 15-minute ridership (entering and exiting).

2. Determine the peak ridership, both detraining and entraining, at each train headway (usually in minutes).

3. Size the platform length (based on maximum train length).

4. Size the platform width (center or side).

5. Determine the passenger ridership, both directions, based on catchment area input.

6. Locate and size all vertical circulation elements (VCEs).

7. Determine the mezzanine type and location, such as: centered over platform length; located at one-quarter points; or at platform ends.

8. Size the mezzanine or concourse level (if implemented) to handle passenger flow, both directions.

9. Size the fare collection system (if any) to handle passenger flow in both directions.

10. Locate entrances at street level, based on the station area planning process.

11. Locate vertical circulation elements to handle passenger flow to/from the street.

12. Perform an exiting analysis using National Fire Protection Association (NFPA) 130 Standards to demonstrate compliance (see details, page 100).

These steps require design studies to ensure that the primary goals of the station are met, namely, to configure the public areas, circulation routes, and vertical circulation elements to handle the passenger flow. Because passengers are both arriving and departing from the station, all elements along the pathway must recognize this two-way passenger movement.

Planning Steps

The 12 steps, discussed in detail in the following pages, are recommended to develop the basic public circulation areas for an underground station. They apply similarly to other station types.

The steps include examples demonstrating the design implications. The passenger flow calculations are supported with the NFPA 130 calculations for exiting compliance.

The planning steps demonstrate how the station is sized in an actual situation. Although every station has its unique conditions (policy, passenger flow speed, etc.), the information described here is a tool to be used. More important, it needs to be adjusted to the conditions of a particular locale. For this example, the design assumptions are as follows:

- The station is part of a heavy-rail transit system.

- Assume 75 ft vehicles with practical capacity (not crush capacity) of 175 persons per car.

- Assume six-car trains with practical capacity of 1050 persons per train.

- Headway is two minutes in both directions.

- Total peak hour ridership is 22,000 people: 15,000 peak direction, 7,000 nonpeak direction.

Assume the following station characteristics and projected patron service established in the Environmental Impact Study:

- A center platform station in a new system serving northbound (NB) and southbound (SB) trains arriving at 2-minute headways.

- Double end-loaded intermediate mezzanine with controlled fare system serving entrances at two street intersections.

- Projected morning peak-hour station ridership of 3200 passengers, with 1370 arrivals and 1830 departures.

- Approximately 26 percent depart station from northbound trains, 74 percent from southbound trains.

- Approximately 33 percent arrive from northbound trains, 67 percent from southbound trains.

Step 1. Determine the passenger peak 15-minute ridership (passenger movements at the station). Chapter 2 describes the process for establishing the peak 15-minute period when the station is busiest. For existing transit systems, where actual patronage data are available, statistical methods can be used for calculating ridership. For new transit systems, the projected peak hour passenger load is divided by 4 and multiplied by the system surge factor to arrive at the average number of passengers using the station during the peak 15-minute period in each direction. The system surge factor is a distribution curve correction and can be varied for a particular system if suffi-

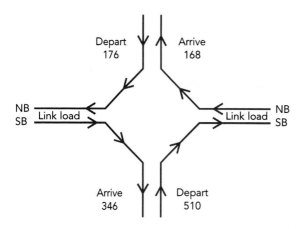

Depart 176   Arrive 168

NB SB   Link load   NB SB   Link load

Arrive 346   Depart 510

▲ *Morning peak 15-minute flow diagram.*

cient data are available for verification. Where data are not available, 1.5 is a reliable factor to use.

Example: Assume a surge factor of 1.5. The 15-minute figures corresponding to the hourly rates in step 1 are as follows:

Projected A.M. peak 15-minute ridership = 3200 (peak hour) ÷ 4 × 1.5 = 1200 patrons

Departures = 1830 ÷ 4 × 1.5 ≈ 686 patrons, Arrivals = 1370 ÷ 4 × 1.5 ≈ 514 patrons

Step 2. Determine the peak ridership, both entraining and detraining, at each train headway, in each direction.

With the peak 15-minute passenger ridership data in hand, the designer needs to know the passenger count when distributed according to percentages arriving and departing. This information is typically provided through the system planning process (see Chapter 2) or dynamic simulation modeling (defined in this chapter). Take these numbers and divide by the headway spacing in minutes to arrive at the passengers situated on the platform when the train arrives, and passengers detraining in any period as related to the headway spacing.

Example: Using the percentages from EIS for northbound and southbound trains from the station model assumptions and the arrivals and departures from Step 1, we arrive at a station flow diagram. See the illustration at left.

Northbound 15-minute arrivals = 0.327 × 514 ≈ 168

Southbound 15-minute arrivals = 0.673 × 514 ≈ 346

Northbound 15-minute departures = 0.256 × 686 ≈ 176

Southbound 15-minute departures = 0.743 × 686 ≈ 510

Determining the entraining load at platform. The passengers waiting at a platform for a train at the time of its arrival can be determined by using the numbers of departing passengers for that train during the 15-minute peak number determined earlier. This number is divided by 15 to obtain the rate per minute and multiplied by the headway to equal the waiting passengers at the train arrival (this is equivalent to dividing by the numbers of trains arriving in 15 minutes). For this prototype the results are as follows:

Northbound = 176 ÷ 15 × 2-minute headway ≈ 24 waiting passengers

Southbound = 510 ÷ 15 × 2-minute headway = 68 waiting passengers

For an island platform, trains from both directions must be considered. If trains arrive on the opposite tracks at the same time, the total would be the sum of northbound and southbound passengers.

Total waiting passengers = 68 southbound + 24 northbound = 92

The probability of trains arriving simultaneously, however, is generally small and relates to the dwell time of a train at the station as compared with the headway between train arrivals. Assuming in this example a dwell time of 30 seconds, the probability is 25 percent.

30 ÷ 120 seconds = 0.25

A basis for determining typical loading is to take the larger number of passengers (southbound in the example) and add 25 percent of the northbound, as follows:

Total waiting passengers = 68 southbound + 0.25 × 24 northbound = 74

This does not necessarily tell the number of passengers within the station. For instance, in heavily trafficked stations with 1.5-minute headways, there could be a 6-minute travel time to platform, which would mean that there would be four times (6 divided by 1.5) the headway passengers moving within the station during any 1.5-minute headway period. This information provides the total passengers on the platform and the passengers detraining during train headways.

Example: Determine the detraining load to platform. Using the 15-minute peak period northbound and southbound passenger arrivals, the passengers detraining onto the platform can be determined by using the method for determining the entraining passengers:

Northbound = 170 ÷ 15 × 2-minute headway ≈ 23 entraining passengers

Southbound = 344 ÷ 15 × 2-minute headway ≈ 46 waiting passengers

As discussed earlier, the probability of two trains arriving together in this prototype is 25 percent. A reasonable assumption is that the separation would be on the order of 1.75 minutes. If, as in the prototype, the criterion for clearing the platform were 30 seconds, the platform circulation would be designed to handle the larger of the detraining loads.

Step 3. Size the platform length. The maximum train length and the distance required to position the train precisely along the platform edge determine the platform length. Exact positioning distances are affected by such factors as the train operation controls—for example, automated stopping or driverless vehicles, which may provide a tighter tolerance for stopping than a driver-operated vehicle. Other factors influence the length, such as platform edge doors, the use of the ends of the platform for vertical circulation, and access to ancillary spaces in nonpublic areas. Generally, passenger queuing spaces while accessing vertical circulation elements (VCEs) should be exclusive of the platform waiting or circulation space so that passengers on the first and last cars of the train can entrain and detrain without overlapping with the circulation required for the VCEs. A preferred station configuration is to have all tracks running straight through the station and parallel to one another. This allows straight and rectangular platform shapes and avoids curved platforms that result in varying distances from the platform edge to vertical obstructions.

See "System Technologies" in Chapter 1 and Chapter 3, "Station Types and Configurations," for detailed discussions on various train types and lengths and platform configurations.

Example: In the station prototype cited in previous steps, assume:

- Six 75 ft cars, totaling 450 ft

- No edge doors

- Train control technology that allows stopping within the distance of the end of the platform and the first and last car doors

The prototype platform length shown in the examples is 450 ft.

Step 4. Size the platform width. Sizing the platform width requires establishing basic platform width conditions and then solving Steps 5 and 6 before confirming that the final width can accommodate the vertical circulation from platform to mezzanine.

Check for other factors that will influence platform width. As discussed in Chapter 6, particularly in underground stations, track and tunnel spacing leading into a platform area will have certain minimum centerline-to-centerline of track dimensions. For instance, tunnel-boring machines commonly create a 22 ft diameter bore to establish a tunnel liner for a train to pass through. Quite often the closest spacing between these bores is equal to a bore diameter (because of geotechnical considerations). This results in a track centerline spacing of 44 ft as it passes through the station. When the vehicle width and edge clearances are deducted, the result may be a predetermined platform width of 34 ft.

DOMESTIC AND INTERNATIONAL RAIL TRANSIT CENTER PLATFORM WIDTHS					
System	Station Type Use	Total Platform Width	Platform Edge to Side Wall or VCE	Tactile Edge to Side Wall or VCE	VCE across Platform Width
Proposed Second Avenue subway, New York	Heavy-rail transit, high patronage	28' or 29'4"	7'6" or 8'2"	5'6" or 6'2"	2
Los Angeles Metro	Heavy-rail transit, high patronage	32'0"	8'8"	6'8"	2
WMATA Metro	Heavy-rail transit, high patronage	30'0"	9'3"	7'3"	2
San Juan, P.R. Tren Urbano	Heavy-rail transit, high patronage	27'11"	7'6"	5'6"	2
Baltimore Metro	Heavy-rail transit, medium patronage	26'4"	7'6"	5'6"	2
New Jersey Transit	Commuter rail, high patronage	Varies	8'5"	6'0"	Varies
Boston Red Line	Heavy-rail transit, medium patronage	Varies	8'0" preferred 6'0" minimum	—	Varies
South Korea	High-speed intercity rail	32'10"	—	—	Varies
Taiwan	High-speed intercity rail	29'6"	8'2"	—	—
Proposed East Side access, New York	Commuter rail, high patronage	28'0"	7'10"	5'7"	2

The platform width and the track center-line spacing are somewhat flexible in that the track alignment has some leeway in narrowing the spacing in the distance between the platform edge and the tunnel portal. Once the minimum width, based on alignment, is established, the architect can proceed to confirm that the platform width can accommodate the passengers and all vertical circulation elements.

Example:

- Assume that the geology for the prototype station allows closer spacing and the minimum spacing, based on tunneling, is fixed at 30 ft.

- Proceed to additional tests as described in the next section.

Determine distance from platform edge to vertical obstruction. The distance from the platform edge assumes that an ADA tactile strip of 24 in. is required and is not considered a walking surface. In other countries this dimension will vary. ADA requires a 3 ft zone for wheelchair movement (exclusive of the tactile strip) and a 5 ft circle for the wheelchair (inclusive of the tactile strip) to change direction and enter the train vehicle. This establishes 5 ft as the minimum clearance per ADA standards.

Example:

- Check this restraint in the prototype station.

- Assume a 5' × 7' platform elevator with width allowance for a shaft, bi-parting doors, and enclosure equal to 2'8". Total width is 7'8" minimum 2 × 5' + 7'8" = 17'8", < 30'.

- Assume an escalator stair pair requires 5'8" escalation + 5'0" stair + 1'0" guardrails = 11'8" + 10' = 21'8", < 30'.

- The minimum wheelchair turning radius does not govern.

Although many transit design criteria have used 7 ft 6 in. as a guideline clearance dimension, the current recommendation is to increase this to a minimum of 8 ft 8 in. Surveys of major international transit systems (see table on page 88) show this to be a more universally accepted criterion.

Example:

- Assume 2 × 7'6" clearance =15'0" plus elevator @ 7' = 22'0", < 30'

- Assume 2 × 7'6" clearance =15'0" plus stair/escalator @ 11'8" = 26'8", < 30'

- Assume 2 × 8'8" clearance =17'4" plus elevator @ 7' = 24'8" < 30'

- Assume 2 × 8'8" clearance =17'4" plus stair/escalator @ 11'8" = 29'0" < 30'

The principal focus for the architect is to establish a satisfactory clearance that allows passengers to move safely and effectively along the platform length under varying conditions. The two primary conditions are: (1) for passengers moving to position themselves along the platform before a train arrives., the concern is to not make the strip so narrow that a passenger could fall off a platform edge, and (2) when the train arrives, there must be sufficient space to allow passengers to detrain and entrain simultaneously during the peak 15-minute period. In high-passenger-volume stations the actual width may need to be determined by dynamic computer modeling based on specific criteria of passenger movements tied to the characteristics of the vehicle, headway, entraining/detraining passenger demand, and passenger tolerances.

Another major determinant is the NFPA 130, 2-5.3 requirement that establishes the number and capacity of exits. The zone between the platform edge and each sidewall is considered a corridor and must be a minimum of 5 ft 8 in. wide. When computing egress capacity, deduct 1 ft from each sidewall and 1 ft 6 in. from the platform edge. This results in a minimum of 3 ft 2 in. for the effective egress width required to access the end of platform emergency stair. For general planning purposes, the platform width will be two platform edge clearance widths (8'8" × 2 = 17'4") plus the width of the widest obstruction, usually the vertical circulation elements. Advance to Steps 5 and 6 to determine the widest vertical circulation element.

Example:

- This results in a platform width of 2 × 8'2" = 16'4" + stair and escalator @ 11'8" = 28'0", < 30'

The 30 ft requirement for tunneling separation overrides all other requirements and therefore establishes the platform width in the prototype.

Confirm passenger circulation area capacity. Having determined the platform length (Step 3) and the width, the architect next needs to confirm that the area of the platform is sufficient to accommodate all passengers, per headway, during the peak 15-minute period. Multiplying the platform length times the width and subtracting the footprint area for all noncirculation spaces establishes the circulation area. Divide the remaining area by 10 sq ft per person (level of service "C" as defined by Fruin). This number must be greater than the headway passenger load during the 15-minute peak period. The headway passenger load should consist of those passengers detraining from one train plus the passengers waiting to board both trains. The load from the next arriving train is not considered because it is assumed that the vertical circulation ele-

ments are sized to transport all passengers off the platform before the next train arrives. The premise of level of service "C" is that passengers can comfortably stand on a platform while other passengers are allowed to move freely through them to access VCEs or to entrain.

Example: Test the prototype station platform area for safe accommodation of passengers. The preceding tests have established that 30 ft is the minimum platform width, based on tunneling considerations.

- Platform length × width = 450' × 30' = 13,500 sq ft
- Two stair/escalator footprints = 11'8" × 24' with 30' queuing zone = 1,260 sq ft
- Two elevator footprints @ 7' × 10' with 5' waiting area = 210 sq ft
- Net platform area = 12,030 sq ft
- Worse-case scenario, with trains on both tracks arriving simultaneously = 90 passengers detraining, 69 persons waiting = 159 passengers at platform
- Net area per person = 12,030 sq ft ÷ 159 > 10 sq ft per person

Conclusion: The 30 ft wide platform dictated by tunneling considerations passes all tests for platform circulation and waiting space for passengers and will be the width for the prototype station in subsequent steps.

Step 5. Determine passenger ridership, both directions, based on catchment area input. The architect must next determine the destination and origin of all passengers using the station. This subject is addressed in Chapter 2, under "Ridership," and is information generally available through the system planning process. Of the total number of passengers using the station during the maximum headway, in a 15-minute period, knowing the percentage of passengers favoring a particular entrance (if more than one is being considered) will enable the architect to determine which way the VCEs will have to face to serve the entrances. This is particularly crucial in stations having long platforms, heavy ridership, and multiple entrances. Passengers will want to ride in a car on the train that delivers them at a platform location with the shortest walking distance to the street exit. Knowing their destinations and planning VCE locations is critical at this stage of design development.

Example: The prototype station with two pairs of stair/escalators from the platform could serve a single entrance or multiple entrances by locating and orienting the platform circulation elements:

- The first consideration is to space the VCEs uniformly along the platform. In the prototype station the landings would be at quarter points.

- The orientation would generally be directed toward the center platform for a mezzanine serving a single-entrance station.

Orientation of the VCEs in a two-mezzanine station may be mixed (as illustrated in the prototype example) based on the distance between the mezzanine fare arrays.

Step 6. Locate and size all vertical circulation elements (VCEs).
This is one of the most sensitive design stages. Sizing the VCEs to handle the maximum headway passenger load, in both directions, on and off the platform, will maintain the platform unencumbered and safe. In

this step it is important to know the features and limitations of VCEs as described in Chapter 6, "Vertical Circulation," and Chapter 1, "Station Design Criteria."

Policy will determine: (1) using escalators versus stairs for moving passengers and (2) manually redirecting escalator direction between times of peak hour usage. For instance, an authority may require escalator capacity sufficient to handle passenger movement in both directions, thereby not requiring a station agent to leave his or her position to reverse escalators between A.M. and P.M. peak flow changes. In deep stations all primary up and down traffic should be by escalators. Expecting passengers to climb great distances (greater than 20–22 ft) by stairs is not good practice. Consistent with international practice, escalators should serve passengers on all vertical rises greater than 16 ft.

- Size all vertical circulation elements so that the passengers are off the platform within a specified time. In transit systems with close headways and large passenger loads it is reasonable to expect that trains will not arrive within 45 seconds of one another, thus allowing a reasonable time frame to guide the design of the VCEs. This means that the passenger loading is not based on the combination of two trains arriving simultaneously.

- Assume that a nominal 48-in. escalator carries 70 passengers per minute, based on 100 ft per minute escalator speed.

- Assume that a nominal 60-in. stair carries 52.5 passengers per minute based on one-way traffic and a lane width of 30 in. and 26.25 passengers/lane/minute capacity.

- Assume passengers' walking travel time on the platform at 200 ft per minute. The total travel time is based on the station platform geometry and the measured distance from the most remote train vehicle door to the nearest vertical circulation element.

- The platform circulation route is broken down into sequential horizontal and vertical segments and then tabulated.

- The circulation route for the reverse passenger flow must also be defined for the vertical segment and then tabulated.

- The combination of the two tabulations will provide the maximum number of passengers traveling vertically on circulation elements.

- The total number of vertical circulation elements must then be placed horizontally along the platform length at a distance not to exceed 150 ft (calculated at a walking speed of 200 fpm $\times$ 45 seconds = 150 ft).

- The vertical circulation elements must be sized and located as required to satisfy the Step 5 requirement. That calls for the VCEs to serve the areas at street level, based on the percentage split of passengers heading in different directions or to different entrances.

Example: Using the previous station prototype, next determine the number and size of vertical circulation elements required to move passengers to and from the platform during the peak minute. The service requirements for the platform VCEs are the combined detraining and entraining loads, as described in the following paragraphs.

Assume the scenario indicated in the peak hour A.M. flow diagram with 2-minute headways. The peak 15-minute flow can be derived from the hour by dividing by 4 and multiplying by the peaking factor (1.5 in the prototype case), resulting in the flow diagram on page 93.

Detraining. In a typical station, the number of passengers leaving each train during the peak 15 minutes is virtually consistent and can be determined by dividing the 15-minute detraining load by 15 and multiplying by the headway. In the prototype station, this operation results in the flow diagram on page 93.

- 15-minute arriving (detraining) NB passengers 15 ÷ 2 = 22 passengers per minute (PPM)

- 15-minute arriving (detraining) SB passengers 15 ÷ 2 = 68 PPM

- 15-minute departing (entraining) NB passengers 15 ÷ 2 = 23 PPM

- 15-minute departing (entraining) SB passengers 15 ÷ 2 = 46 PPM

The total arriving passengers when two trains arrive at the same time is the combined flow:

SB 68 + NB 22 = 90 PPM

As discussed in Step 2, the average flow adds 25 percent of the lesser to the larger flow:

SB 68 + .25 $\times$ 22 ≈ 72

Entraining. The number of passengers entering the station can assumed to be uniform during the peak 15 minutes, and the PPM moving to platforms can be determined by dividing the peak 15-minute flow into minutes. (As discussed in Step 2, the number of people waiting at the platform will depend on the waiting period between trains, but the *flow* to the platform is independent of train operations.)

Entraining: 23 NB + 46 SB = 69 total

The combined VCE service requirements are the SB detraining plus the total entraining flow:

90 PPM + 69 PPM = 159 PPM

Using the established performance criteria for escalators (use 75 PPM for 100 ft per minute [FPM] operation) and for stairs (typically 10 PPM per ft of stair width for flow in two directions with a minimum travel lane of 22 in.), the requirements for stairs and escalators can be determined. Assuming that at least two 5 ft wide stairs would be provided to serve the platform regardless of service requirements, and assuming a maximum desirable platform queue time of 1 minute, a matrix can be constructed.

Note that for stairs, the minimum width would be the two 5 ft wide stairs as discussed in the preceding paragraph.

Three case studies are analyzed and illustrated:

Case 1. Provide four escalators (two each direction) and two 6 ft wide stairs to the mezzanine. This allows reasonable distribution along the platform and reasonable performance when an escalator is out of service. All vertical travel in the up direction can be by escalator. This is the preferred arrangement where the vertical rise is less than 20 ft.

- Assume that two escalators and half the stair capacity serve the detraining passengers. Total capacity = 2 × 75 + 50 = 200 PPM.

- Assume travel to VCE landings = 75 ft; travel time = 75 ÷ 200 ≈ 0.38 minutes.

- Detraining passengers ÷ VCE capacity = 72 ÷ 200 = 0.36 minutes.

- Travel time of .38 minutes > VCE rate < 2-minute headways.

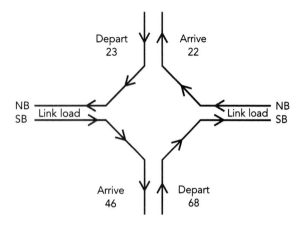

▲ Morning peak headway flow diagram.

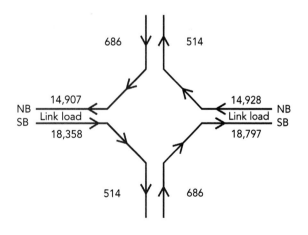

▲ Morning peak hour flow diagram.

- Travel time > VCE rate, therefore there will be no queues at stairs or escalators

Case 2. Provide four 8 ft wide stairs to mezzanine. This also satisfies circulation requirements, allows good distribution along the platform, and is acceptable when the vertical rise is less than 15 ft. In stations with low patronage, elevators can serve a reasonable percentage of passengers. Most modern systems establish an operating policy that requires all levels of the station to be served by escalators serving passenger movement in the exiting direction.

- Assume one-half of four 8 ft wide stairs serve the detraining passengers. Total capacity = 4 × 10 × 4 = 160 PPM.
- Assume travel to VCE landings = 75 ft; travel time = 75 ÷ 200 ≈ 0.38 minutes.
- Detraining passengers ÷ VCE capacity = 72 ÷ 160 = 0.45 minutes.
- 0.45 minute exit time < 2-minute headways.

- Travel time < exit time; queue time will be very short; 0.45 minutes – 0.38 minutes = 0.07 minutes.

Case 3. Provide escalators paired with stairs. This illustrates a circulation arrangement for a system operating eight car trains totaling 450 ft. This arrangement also includes four escalators. The two stairs are double-wide, or as wide as possible without impacting platform width. The arrangement has stair and escalator in pairs. The advantage of the alternate arrangement is that the distribution of escalators is more uniform. The circulation times of Case 3 arrangements are virtually the same as for Case 1.

Step 7. Determine mezzanine type and location. Most underground stations have mezzanines that can be grouped in one of the following types according to location above the platform (see also the illustration on page 75):

Center loaded. One mezzanine located centrally over the platform at midpoint

▼ *Three case studies for determining vertical circulation requirements of a platform.*

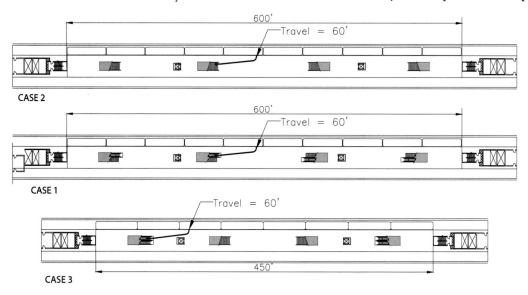

CASE 2

CASE 1

CASE 3

along its length. This configuration lends itself to a single station entrance.

End loaded. Two mezzanines located over the platform at the extreme ends of the station. This configuration lends itself to serving widely spaced street entrances. It may require an additional station agent at the fare control area.

Quarter-point loaded. Two mezzanines located over the platform at quarter points from the platform ends. This too may require another station agent. The primary advantage to this configuration is that the travel distance from the most remote point on platform is one-quarter the platform length, whereas for the other two it is one-half the platform length.

Determiniation of the appropriate mezzanine configuration is based on many factors, such as the following:

- The need for a fixed fare control system or an honor system. This will, in effect, determine whether the mezzanine is divided between free and paid areas.

- Criteria for employing single or multiple station agents. The cost to the transit operator of employing more than a single agent at a station must be a factor in determining which mezzanine configuration is the most appropriate. If, in effect, a *center-loaded* configuration satisfies the functional criteria of a station, then the cost to employ additional personnel over the life of the station can be significant.

- Opportunity for street entrances at single or multiple locations, as determined by Step 5.

- Opportunity to use mezzanine space for ancillary functions.

- For reasons of safety and security, quick access to the platform.

- NFPA 130 requirement for a "point of safety" as part of the 4- and 6-minute exit time restrictions.

- ADA minimum requirements and transit agency policy aimed at increased elevator service.

Example: For the prototype station, assume there are two remote entrances with fixed fare barriers separating paid and free areas. Each fare area is to be controlled by an agent during peak hours. The secondary entrance is to be closed during off-peak or late-night operation. Assume a vertical rise between the platform and the mezzanine and between the mezzanine and the street, as indicated in the illustration on page 96.

As determined in the preceding steps, the total entraining and detraining flow is 159 PPM. Assume the service rate of the (reversible) fare gates is 30 PPM. In calculating the number of gates, the flow rate is typically doubled to allow for future growth and equipment downtime for servicing. As indicated in Step 9 following, the number of gates required in both directions for both entrances is therefore $2 \times 159 \div 30 = 10.6$, say 11 gates total. Assume that in the two-entrance prototype station, 66 percent of passengers use the north entrance. The number of gates required will be $159 \times 0.66 \div 15 = 7$ gates.

Step 8. Size mezzanine to handle passenger flow. Once the mezzanine configuration has been determined, circulation studies are performed to size the public area floor space to handle the passenger loads. Waiting is rare on the mezzanine level (in a HRT station), so passenger

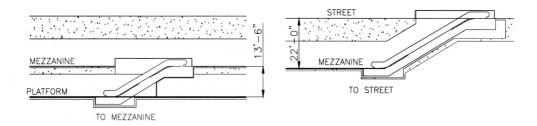

▲ Prototype station, with vertical dimensions of 13'6" (platform to mezzanine) and 22'0" (mezzanine to street).

▼ Prototype station with a two-entrance configuration.

movement is essentially free-flowing in both directions. Allow for queuing in front of all vertical circulation zones. Avoid overlapping of queues, and design circulation corridors so that they do not impede passengers moving onto or off VCEs.

Example: In the prototype station illustrated in the previous step, a 30 ft space between the escalator work point and any obstruction is allowed at each end of all of the reversible escalators. This space must not overlap with the queue space required for the elevator, fare machines, or fare gates. Criteria for transit systems with fare arrays establish queue space on each side of the fare gates, typically 20 ft.

Step 9. Size fare collection system. Fare collection systems are discussed in detail in Chapter 7, "Special Equipment." The criteria for use and passenger flow rates generally are specific to each system. Design of the fare collection equipment includes turnstiles, emergency gates, handicapped gates, fare vending equipment, and station agent control booths (referred to as the fare array). At a minimum, fare array turnstiles should be provided in sufficient numbers to meet the capacity, in persons per minute, of VCEs (or other sources of traffic) feeding the fare array in both directions.

Design capacities for turnstiles are based on the peak 15-minute period vol-

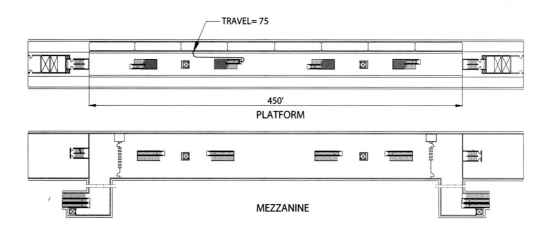

ume. That number is then doubled for design purposes to allow for growth and equipment downtime for servicing. The one-way capacity of a turnstile (for this example) is considered 30 passengers per minute. Where two-way operations are assumed, capacity is reduced by 20 percent to 24 passengers per minute as a result of exiting and entering passengers using the same device.

Example: In the prototype station illustrated in Step 7, the fare gates are assumed to be reversible, so that each gate is dedicated to either the entering or exiting direction.

One-way passenger flow calculations separate entering and exiting passenger volumes. Each direction is analyzed for morning and evening peak 15-minute periods, and the inbound and outbound devices are tabulated. The maximum number of turnstiles for the two periods determines the minimum requirements. A similar calculation can be performed based on two-way capacity of the turnstile devices; however, the requirements based on one-way flow are generally lower than those for two-way flow.

In this step of the station sizing process, the percentage of passengers using a particular mezzanine (Step 5) has been determined and the quantities of VCEs and the passenger flow rates (Step 6) have been defined. As a rule of thumb, one-way flow capacity of a turnstile at 30 passengers per minute (PPM) and two turnstiles processing 60 PPM is roughly equivalent to an escalator and/or a 60 in. wide stair at 70 PPM. Therefore, two turnstiles for each escalator/stair unit (on both sides of the fare array), plus a 35 percent increase for the 52 versus 70 PPM differential between the devices, meets the actual demand. The architect

▲ *Old Secretariat Station in the Delhi, India, Metro, integrated into an urban park. Faber-Maunsel Corporation.*

is advised to double the quantity of devices to accommodate future growth.

Step 10. Locate entrances. Keep in mind that in many instances the station entrance must be determined early and the entire design process performed in reverse. For instance, for an underground station in a dense urban area, the factors affecting entrance location and character are complex and subject to many influences. Entrances in such cases are critical and should be evaluated and defined early. Minor modifications in track profile and station structure location may be possible, thus avoiding difficult changes later or lower-quality entrances faced with the lack of satisfactory space or the physical restrictions of an existing building.

Chapter 2, "Urban Planning and Station Area Development," describes the overall planning process; the EIS for a specific project defines preferred locations for entrance areas or proximity to street intersections. In this step the station entrance design and location must be determined. The relevant factors include the following:

- Availability of real estate, property costs, and political implications of acquiring property
- Proximity to high-density land uses and potential trip generators
- Historic buildings and their landmarked status
- Ease of intermodal transfer, including bus routes and LRT.
- Existing open land use, particularly sidewalks, plazas, and parks
- Pedestrian network and access to destinations
- Use consistent with EIS process
- Community and public input
- Zoning and easement restrictions

Existing land use patterns will directly affect the station design in terms of morning and evening use. For instance, large residential areas will account for the majority of passengers entering the station in the morning peak hours. In effect, it is a commuter station with passengers leaving the area to go to work and returning in the evening. Conversely, large areas of commercial property will account for the station passengers exiting to places of employment. Some institutional land uses will have a moderating impact on passenger flow. A hospital will generate shift-change traffic for its employees while generating off-hour ridership based on patient visiting hours.

▼ Locating entrances in existing urban areas is often a challenge, resulting in underground passageways, as in this view of a Delhi, India, station. Faber-Maunsel Corporation.

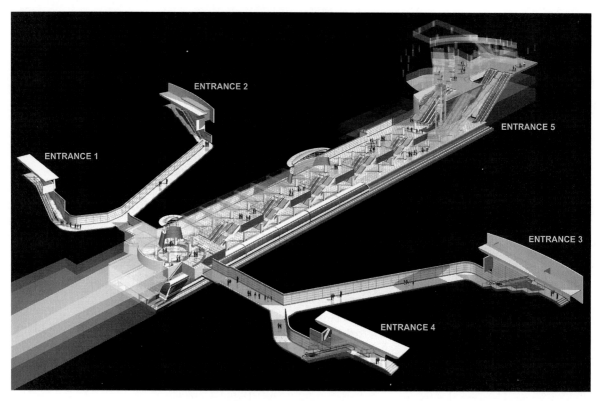

Establish station entrance program requirements. The actual physical entrance size is determined in Step 11, based on volume demand and the percentage split of passengers using the entrances. Additional design considerations that factor in the actual entrance type, location, and features are as follows (see also the illustration at left):

- Distance between entrance and mezzanine and the NFPA 130 requirement for a maximum 6-minute exit travel time from platform to point of safety

- Policy on several entrances serving multiple locations versus international practice of fewer but larger entrances

- Need to serve both sides of heavily trafficked roadways

- Policy on elevator access consistent with each entrance or minimum numbers per ADA requirements

- Provisions for fire department access in emergencies

- Weather protection

- Station identity and visibility

- Future development around entrance

- Relationship of station entrance to urban fabric; should be sympathetic to scale and character of surrounding structures

- Sidewalk congestion

- Safety and security, ease of surveillance, no obstacles or hidden spaces

- Art, signage, and lighting

- Cost, phasing, and constructability

Step 11. Locate vertical circulation elements to street. Exiting passengers move through the station at a mostly uniform rate of flow based on the carrying capacity of VCEs and the processing rate of the fare turnstiles. Long travel distances will tend to attenuate the passenger flow. The upward capacity of the vertical circulation from mezzanine to street must match the upward capacity from platform to mezzanine.

Example: In a multiple entrance station the number of escalators from the platform serving each mezzanine is based on the maximum A.M. or P.M. flow, and stairs will serve the flow in the reverse direction (if the vertical distance is within the limits set by the transit system criteria). The vertical travel distance between mezzanine and street, however, may require escalators in both directions.

Therefore, the same number of VCEs as established in Step 6 should be used. What may increase (but never decrease) this number is the policy on providing redundant escalators to provide for the evenutality that a unit is out of service.

Example: In most transit systems the criteria establish the use of escalators based on the vertical rise between landings. The assumptions in the prototype station are that stairs will generally serve the movements down to the platform (the prototype arrangement allows the station agent options for operating the escalators according to need). The rise between mezzanine and street will require two escalators operating from mezzanine to street and either a stair or an escalator for movements from street to mezzanine. If the rise from mezzanine to street is extreme (60–100 ft, for example) an additional backup escalator should be considered. For the modest rise in the prototype, passengers could negotiate the stair between mezzanine and street if one of the escalators were out of service. The minimum in the prototype example (depending on the passengers service goals set in the station criteria) is two escalators and a stair at each entrance.

Good planning practice is to provide a minimum of three VCEs serving primary entrances so that one stair and two escalators are provided (up to 36 ft rise) from mezzanine to street. This may end up exceeding basic passenger flow needs, particularly in stations with lower passenger volumes.

Step 12. Perform an NFPA 130 analysis. The next step is to determine compliance with accepted or mandated code requirements for station exiting. The standard, adopted by many jurisdictions in the United States, is NFPA 130, *Standard for Fixed Guideway Transit and Passenger Rail Systems.* Appendix C of the standard, although not part of the requirement, is included as an informational tool to assist architects and others in uniformly interpreting the standard in actual practice. The standard has been revised over the years and is likely to undergo further adjustments to meet the needs of the transit industry.

The procedure chosen in this book is to recognize the significance of the standard and recommend that it be followed regardless of its status in a particular jurisdiction. See the NFPA 130 calculations as applied to the station example. The example compares the size of VCEs needed to meet the passenger volume with the sizing of the station per the

NFPA 130 method. See page 103 for an example of calculating egress using NFPA 130.

LEVELS OF SERVICE AND PLANNING CRITERIA
Levels of Service (LOS)
John J. Fruin studied pedestrian behavior in the early 1970s and published a book, *Pedestrian Planning and Design.* It is considered the standard for planning passenger movement through public areas, particularly transit environments. References to his criteria and interpretation of a level of service are cited extensively in this book and accepted universally as the basis for planning. Yet even Fruin cautions in his book, "The ideas expressed therein should be tempered by recognized engineering practices, guidelines, codes and standards."

Planning Criteria
Stations should be planned to provide the level of service for use in the 15-minute peak period for the forecasted ridership.

Forecasts of ridership show that the it is usually greater in the A.M. peak period than in the P.M. period. Consequently, use the greater of the two as the greatest demand. Stations should generally be planned to accommodate the average flow per minute over the peak 15-minute period of the most stringent A.M. or P.M. condition. In high-volume, close-headway stations (as used in the preceding example), averaging the 15-minute passenger load over the 1-minute period will not satisfy the greater demand to unload the platform in the 45-second example used. Specific station passenger load conditions must be accounted for, or as an alternative policy, defined so that they

LEVEL OF SERVICE (LOS)		
Area	**Level of Service (LOS)***	**Quantitative Measure**
Open concourses or mezzanines	LOS C standing	10 sq ft per person
Passageways		
One-way	LOS D	15 passengers per minute per ft perwidth
Two-way	LOS C	12 passengers per minute per ft per width
Stairs		
One-way	LOS D	10.5 passengers per minute per ft per width
Two-way	LOS C	8.4 passengers per minute per ft per width
Escalators	—	70 passengers per minute per nominal 48 in. unit per 100 fpm speed
Platforms	LOS C standing	10 sq ft per person
Walking speed	Through LOS C standing passengers	200 ft per minute

*See Fruin, 1971.

will allow for lower levels of service (greater congestion or longer queues) during certain peak period conditions. This is a significant issue because it has a direct bearing on the numbers of vertical circulation elements required and the associated cost of installing and operating them.

In the table above, the areas for standing on the concourses, mezzanines, and platform are the net areas available after deducting the requirements for fixed elements such as rooms, benches, VCEs, columns, queuing for VCEs, and so forth and any inefficient spaces that the moving passenger clearly will not use.

Computer Simulation Modeling of Passenger Flow
Many of the larger transit agencies and transportation planners have been using computer simulation to analyze such concerns as:

- Train schedule changes
- Fare collection changes
- Platform congestion
- Ticket sales and queuing
- Transfers to new modes

There are several computer simulation software programs that are readily adaptable to the station planning process, including emergency egress analysis. These programs develop a microscopic simulation model to determine the characteristics of passenger flows and are based on specific station layouts, passenger habits in a geographic area, and performance of VCEs specific to the area and devices.

Step 1 *Determine maximum train loading and planned headway from the rail operations plan. Determine link load information from rail operations data and peak hour entraining and detraining patronage data from the EIS or MIS projections. Except for a terminal station, the passenger movements in each directions must be determined. This information is provided in the spread sheet calculation following.*

Station:	Prototype
Calculation	NFPA 130
Date	▮▮▮▮▮▮▮
Passenger Forecasts	Ultimate Year
Platform Type	Island

		Station Data	
	Train /Direction	To Station	Exit Station
Peak Hour Link Loads	NB	14907	14928
	SB	18358	18797
		Entering	Exiting
Station Loads	NB	469	448
	SB	1361	922
		Minutes	Trains/15Min
Headway	NB	2	7.5
	SB	2	7.5

This can be illustrated in a station flow diagram

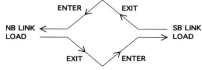

Modified Failure Period	1
Assumed Peaking Factor=	1.5
Failure Period [=Greater of 2 x headway or 12 Min.]	
Inbound Failure Period=	12 Min.
Outbound Failure Period=	12 Min.

0.65 K=AM to PM Conversion factor

Occupant Load Calculation
PEAK 15 MINUTE LOADS [=PEAK HR. LOAD X PEAKING FACTOR / 4]

		AM Peak		PM Peak (=K*AM)	
		Enter Station	Leave Station	Enter Station	Leave Station
Link Loads	NB	5590	5598	3634	3639
	SB	6884	7049	4475	4582
Station Loads	NB	176	168	114	109
	SB	510	346	332	225

Peak Direction	SB	SB

Step 2. Based on the 15 minute loads arriving at the station, compare calculated train loads from the peak direction with the maximum train loading.

Calculated Train Load [=PEAK 15 MIN LINK LOAD / (# Trains Per 15 Min) or Maximum Train Loading]
[PEAK DIR X 2; OFF-PEAK DIR. X 1]

Calculated Train Loading = NB	1	745	484
Calculated Train Loading = SB	2	1836	1193
Maximum Train Loading = 6 cars x 175		1050	
Total		1795	1677

Note: The calculated peak direction train load cannot be accommodated, therefore the maximum Train Loading is used.

Peak Entraining Load
[Peak Dir. = Peak 15 Min. Ent. Load / 15 Min. x Max (2 x Headway or 12 Min.)
OFF-PEAK DIR. = PEAK 15 MIN. ENT. LOAD/ (15 MIN./HEADWAY)]

NB	23
SB	408
TOTAL	431

TOTAL OCCUPANT LOAD [= CALCULATED TRAIN LOAD + PEAK ENTRAINING LOAD

TOTAL	2226

Step 3. Determine the combined exit capacity of stairs and escalators from the platform(s) based on the width and allowable rate in people per minute (ppm) for each type. Check the percentages of escalators and emergency stair rates compared to the total rate. This may not exceed 50% in either case.

Element	Direction	No. Units	Usable	Width	p/m	=ppm
Platform to Concourse						
Stairs	Up	4	4	72	1.59	458
	Down	0	0	0	1.82	0
			Width:	288		458
Emergency Stairs	Up	2	2	88	1.59	280
	Down	0	0	88	1.82	0
			Width:	176		280
Escalators**	Up	4	3	48	1.59	229
	Down	0	0	48	1.82	0
			Width:	144		229
			Usable Width:	144		229
			Platform Exit Capacity			967
			Percent Escalator Width			24%
			Percent Emergency Stair Width			29%

Step 4. Calculate exit capacity for the vertical circulation to the concourse level and to street. Determine the exit capacity of fare barriers (unless the fare system is barrier free).

Through Fare Barriers						
Turnstiles		0		1	40	0
Fare Gates		11		1	50	550
Service Gates		0		0	0	0
Emergency Gates		4		48	2.27	435.84
						985.84
Concourse to Grade						
Stairs	Up	2	2	60	1.59	190.8
	Down	0	0	60	1.82	0
			Width:	120		190.8
Emergency Stairs	Up	2	2	44	1.59	139.92
	Down	0	0	0	1.82	0
			Width:	88		139.92
Escalators***	Up	4	3	48	1.59	228.96
	Down	0	0	48	1.82	0
			Width:	144		228.96
			Usable Width:	144		228.96
			Concourse Exit Capacity			559.68
			Percent Escalator Width			41%

Step 5. Determine travel time on stairs (or stopped escalators) and walking time at each level while traveling from the furthest train door to the street exit.

Travel Time for Longest Egress Route		Ft	fpm	Minutes
Walking on Platform	T1	75	200	0.375
Vertical Rise Platform to Concourse Rise	T2	13.5	50	0.27
Walking on Concourse -	T3	185	200	0.925
Vertical Rise Concourse to Grade	T4	22	50	0.44
Grade	T5	35	200	0.175
T(total time)				2.185

Step 6. Perform NFPA 130 test number 1: Evacuate platform occupant load from most remote point on platform in 4 minutes or less.

		AM PEAK PERIOD		PM PEAK PERIOD	
Platform Occupant Load	2226				
Platform Exit Capacity	967				
W1=Platform Occupant Load/Platform Exit Capacity		2.3	Minutes	1.73	Minutes

Step 7. Perform NFPA 130 test number 2: Evacuate platform occupant load to a point of safety from the most remote point on the platform in 6 minutes or less

		AM PEAK PERIOD		PM PEAK PERIOD	
Wp(waiting time at platform exits) = W1-T1		1.925	Minutes	1.355	Minutes
Concourse Occupant Load	1381.66				
Waiting at Fare Barriers = W2-W1					
W2=Concourse Load/Fare Barrier Cap		1.4	Minutes	1.4	Minutes
Wf=Waiting Time at the Fare Gates					
Wf=W2-W1		0	Minutes	0	Minutes
Wc=[W3-max(W2 or W1)]					
W3=Concourse occupant load / concourse exit capacity		2.47	Minutes	2.47	Minutes
Wc=Waiting Time on the Concourse		0.17	Minutes	0.17	Minutes
Total=Walking Time + Waiting Time					
Total=T+Wp+Wf+Wc		4.28	Minutes	3.71	Minutes

Approach

Data are collected by the agency or planner that model the characteristics of passengers, such as walking time, habits while on escalators (whether walking or standing still), fare turnstile processing rates, and the like. An object-oriented simulation model based on input data and station layout is developed and later validated and calibrated by performing different case studies. The aim is to detect congestion and predict the point in time when passengers will no longer wait for an elevator or escalator and begin looking for alternative routes.

Expected results

The model is a tool to validate the design and help in visualizing and quantifying the effects of a station layout on passenger flows. It helps the architect understand the congestion points, long walking distances, and possible impacts of transferring passengers from other modes or connections. This allows the designer to optimize the layout for peak performance. For instance, modeling may reveal the levels of service and suggest studies to increase these levels, and corresponding levels of comfort, to improve the service.

Defining Overall Structure

A primary goal in planning an underground station is to determine its volume—in effect, the length, width, and height of the structure. Determining the width is straightforward: After having determined the platform width, based on the preceding steps, the designer adds the width of the train plus the safety clearances to the walls and any architectural finishes required.

To establish the overall length requires planning also for nonpublic ancillary functions, such as traction power, electrical distribution rooms, signals, communications, mechanical ventilation, tunnel ventilation, and so forth. This is done through the creation of a functional program.

Developing a Program

The functional program is developed on the basis of input from the engineering disciplines and from operational personnel familiar with the transit systems' operations, maintenance, and security requirements.

Station layouts are prepared using both the program and the passenger functional diagrams to create the basic station concept. This process calls for agreement by all team members.

See the table in Chapter 3, "Ancillary Space Program" on page 78, for an example of typical spaces, location, and area requirements for an underground station.

PROCUREMENT
Design-Bid-Build

The method of procuring the construction of transit and other transportation systems has a significant impact on the design process by the design team. Until recently, procurement in the United States has followed the conventional design-bid-build method. With that approach, the owner, usually a public agency, prepares the final design drawings and specifications with in-house staff or through the use of a team of design consultants. After the design is complete to the owner's satisfaction, the design plans and specifications are advertised for bid. Prospective contractors prepare bids based on these final design documents and submit sealed bids. The bids are then opened in public, and a tentative award is made on the basis of the lowest qualified bid. Assuming that the contractor has met all contract conditions after review by the owner, a contract will be awarded and a Notice to Proceed is issued. The owner also provides construction management, again with in-house staff or through a team of consultants. Thus, the owner maintains full control of all aspects of the project throughout the program.

Design-Build

The design-build process differs from the more conventional approach in that the owner prepares, again with in-house staff or consultants, the design of all system elements to a preliminary level adequate to clearly define the intent and desired quality of the finished project. The owner also prepares a set of detailed procurement documents that include the preliminary drawings, performance specifications, any relevant survey or other data collected by the owner during preliminary design, and a set of very detailed contract conditions. Prospective contractors form a team, including design capability, and develop the design for all project elements to a level of confidence that allows the contractor to prepare a "firm fixed price" bid to accomplish the project, complete in all respects, as requested in the solicitation.

Following award of the contract, the design-build team completes all final design and details in accordance with the requirements and criteria specified in the bid documents. The final design by the contractor's team is expected to achieve much closer design coordination between the contractor and the final designer. This cooperative approach is intended to allow the contractor to introduce innovation into the design, directly related to the means and methods considered in the construction project, and at the same time to reduce disputes.

Although it is not the intent here to discuss the pros and cons of the procurement processes, it should be noted that proponents of the design-build approach expect that the assignment of responsibility to the contractor and the resulting innovation will contribute to reductions in cost and scheduling. In any event, in either procurement method, the design issues to be addressed are the same.

CHAPTER 5
LIFE SAFETY, CODES, AND ADA

This chapter discusses the principal elements of the various standards and codes that require a station to be safe during an emergency and affect the station design to make it a readily accessible public space.

LIFE SAFETY
Background

The definition of a transit station by the various codes as a building type was not clear until the National Fire Protection Association (NFPA) issued in the early 1980s the NFPA 130, which is known as the *Standard for Fixed Guideway Transit and Passenger Rail Systems.* Until that time stations were designed to meet local codes and guided by certain known code compliance safeguards such as fireproof construction, Class A finishes, and prudent analysis of egress needs to ensure that passengers exited within a reasonable time. NFPA 101 was often followed as a standard for exiting analysis.

Typically, during the early design stages of a new transit system, the transit agency and its consultants form a Fire/Life Safety Committee, made up of representatives from state and local fire departments and fire marshals' offices. The committee is charged with providing specific opinions, code interpretations, and rulings as to how the station should comply with state and local codes. Whereas most transit stations fall into one of the three broad definitions as an aerial, at-grade, or underground configuration, it is the underground that is the greatest challenge to the designer in terms of creating a fireproof station that is readily evacuated in an emergency.

Among the most important and effective measures in fire prevention are to minimize or eliminate the presence of combustible material in the design and to remove the causes of ignition such as extreme temperatures, electrical arcing, and similar conditions. Strategically located smoke and heat detectors are important elements for early detection and, if necessary, evacuation. Other critical elements include special communication linkages to the station control center, the operations central control, and the emergency management panel so that fire detection signals can be promptly identified and communicated to operating and fire-fighting personnel.

Emergency evacuation routes are located and sized in accordance with specific formulas and procedures stipulated by NFPA 130. Emergency routes are usually located at the ends of the station and are well marked, incorporate emergency battery-powered lighting in the event of power failure, and are under a slight positive pressure to exclude smoke. Requirements of the Americans with Disabilities Act (ADA) are for specific areas of refuge with voice communications to the station control center for use by patrons with disabilities.

Fire suppression facilities are designed to serve the fire-fighting plans prescribed by the local fire authority. Such facilities normally include a dedicated phone system linking the emergency management panel at the surface with various communication points in the subway areas and valve pits at the surface to control the flow of water to the dry standpipes and deluge system.

Authority Having Jurisdiction

Architects deal with a myriad of code-related issues on a regular basis for all buildings that they design. Determining the authority having jurisdiction (AHJ) is the first step in determining which codes are applicable. Quite often the design of a station, however, will fall into one of two unfamiliar categories, characterized as follow:

- The local AHJ has no experience with NFPA 130 or is experienced with the standard, but it has not been adopted locally. In this case, obtaining an official opinion as to what code to follow, and held to be accountable for, is crucial. It may require gaining the transit agency's cooperation and concurrence and, in some cases, approval, according to an ordinance by the local jurisdiction.
- The station is part of a railroad or major subway system that does its own code compliance certification. In this instance, code requirements are usually clearly established. The system may typically adopt a model building code such as the new International Building Code, along with the NFPA 130, and enforce these codes itself.

Establishing All Applicable Codes

In working with the AHJ and the transit authority, several codes, standards, and guidelines are relevant to a station design and may include the following:

- State Building Code
- City Building Code
- NFPA 130, *Standard for Fixed Guideway Transit and Passenger Rail Systems*
- NFPA 72, *National Fire Alarm Code*
- NFPA 70, *National Electrical Code*
- NFPA 101, *Life Safety Code*
- Authority design guidelines

Fire/Life Safety Strategy

Early stages of a project should focus on developing a fire/life safety strategy for addressing all key aspects of a project, which includes defining design criteria for issues such as:

- Egress (emergency evacuation). For instance, signage that must react to various evacuation routes cannot be just a static signage system. The current and long-term concerns for potential terrorist activity require a much more comprehensive and flexible emergency evacuation information system.
- Smoke compartmenting.
- Fire protection of the structural systems.
- Smoke management.
- Detection and alarm systems.
- Fire suppression systems.
- Fire department access and emergency response procedures.
- Fire department equipment location.
- Emergency lighting and power. Signage needs must be evaluated and be an integral part of an emergency power system.
- Fire safety management.
- Materials' flame spread, fire rating, and combustibility.

The overall approach adopted during the development of a fire/life safety strategy is based on adherence to the principles described in the aforementioned applicable codes. The following is an overview of the elements of a fire/life safety strategy for an underground station configuration.

Design of fire scenarios

Develop principal fire scenarios for a range of conditions. Address the fire location (passenger train, trash, concessions), maximum fire size (measured in mBtu/hr), and heat release rate and fire growth curves to demonstrate the time period in which the peak heat release is attained.

Means of egress

Provide sufficient exiting capacity in the number of stairs and escalators so that passengers can evacuate to a point of safety in accordance with code requirements. In the case of NFPA 130 the requirements are:

- Four minutes to clear the platform
- Six minutes to reach a place of safety

As an alternative to satisfying the egress times, an engineering analysis to demonstrate a tenable environment along the egress route may be developed and presented to the AHJ. In deeper underground, or higher aerial, stations the mezzanine may be used as the point of safety, per NFPA 130.

Provide protected stairs in an underground configuration to allow for:

- Egress from adjacent tunnels.

Consider signage requirements.

- Development of an alternative route for passengers to evacuate the platform that will bypass the mezzanine and exit directly to street. Recognize the need for a dynamic signage or display system to inform public.

- Development of an alternative route from a mezzanine space in the event of a fire.

- The provision of an area of rescue assistance for people with impaired mobility.* The Americans with Disabilities Act (ADA) requires one wheelchair space for every 200 occupants.

Smoke management

Develop alternative smoke ventilation systems to include the following:

- End-of-platform tunnel ventilation fans
- Fans used to maintain critical velocity in the tunnel sections during a fire
- Over- and under-platform vehicle area exhaust systems
- Station ventilation system designed for smoke management
- Combustible storage areas (concessions, for instance) provided with smoke control system

Fire management

- Station structure and materials are to be in accordance with NFPA 130.
- Interior finishes are to be limited to Class A.

---

*An area of rescue assistance is an area that has direct access to an exit, where people who are unable to use stairs may remain temporarily in safety to await further instructions or assistance in an emergency evacuation.

- All combustible loads are to be separated from potential fire hazards and sources.
- All storage and concession areas are to include a fire suppression system.
- Smoke and fire detection system monitoring is to be both central to the system and local to the station.
- Station agent functions are to be coordinated in accordance with operational policy, as discussed in Chapter 16.

Fire detection and alarm

- Automatic and manual emergency alarm reporting devices located on platform
- Closed-circuit television (CCTV) cameras throughout the station to provide remote monitoring and assistance during an emergency
- Fire department to be automatically notified
- Automatic detection systems provided in all nonpublic areas
- Automatic heat and smoke detection in all ventilation duct systems
- Voice alarm public address system
- ADA-compliant horns and strobe lights to assist/alert people who are hearing or visually impaired, as well as any nonnative-language-speaking passengers, such as at an international airport station.

Fire suppression

- Manual dry standpipes.
- Hose connections must be consistent with local fire department standards.
- Fire extinguishers are to be at key locations.

- A manual undercar deluge system is to be provided along the tracks in the stations.
- Automatic sprinkler systems are to be provided in storage areas, concessions, trash rooms, and the steel truss portion of escalators where there is one primary entry to a station.
- Sprinkler systems are not typically provided in public areas of a station.

Control of fire spread (compartmenting)

- A minimum of 3-hour fire-rated construction to separate all transit public areas from nontransit occupancies.
- A minimum of 2-hour fire-rated construction between adjacencies, as defined in NFPA 130, 2-2.3.2, "Ancillary Spaces."
- Recommended Type 1 construction throughout.
- All doors in rated walls to be rated consistent with wall rating and remain closed with rated automatic door closers and latch sets.

Impact on adjoining areas

- Station entrances accessed through other buildings are to have a 3-hour separation between the transit and nontransit structures and be compliant with the code requirements for the nontransit structure.
- Ventilation air and tunnel ventilation openings should be designed to prevent station air intake and exhaust to be contaminated with each other. Provide a safe distance apart, depending on code, wind patterns, and engineering principles.
- Station areas that connect to areas of other stations (as in an intermodal or

transfer station) are to have fire separation capabilities for emergency conditions.

- There is a need to have comprehensive location and orientation maps for the transit passengers. Maps should reflect station entrances that are accessed through other buildings and station areas that connect to areas of other stations. Maps should be oriented to the station architecture so that a person can clearly relate the built environment to the presented map.

Fire-fighting facilities

- Lessons learned from the September 11, 2001, destruction of the World Trade Center prove that a fire department's radio equipment must be capable of working within a station. Coordinate this need with the overall communications system. For the future, it is important to plan for functional, operational, and circulation changes in security inspection, the wayfinding process, and evacuation.

- Provide fire department connections and standpipes at each station entrance and at emergency stair egress points.

- Coordinate the fire management emergency panel with the design of the primary station entrance.

Emergency lighting and signage

- Provide emergency lighting throughout the station at a minimum illumination level of 1.0 foot candles (10 lux) with 5.0 footcandles (53.8 lux) at exits. Coordinate with the requirements specified in Chapter 10, "Lighting," and specific code requirements.

- The emergency signage system is to enable clear guidance through the use of audible and visual media sources to assist all passengers in their safe

movement while exiting the station in an emergency. See Chapter 11, "Wayfinding."

Emergency power

Provide a backup power supply system to be used should an incident affect the primary power supply and hence the fire/life safety critical systems. All emergency static and dynamic signage must be backed up on the emergency power system.

Occupancy

In nontransit occupancies the model building codes group their intended uses into several classifications based on potential numbers of people using each type and the potential capacity for storing combustibles. Based on this classification, a building's fire rating and height and area restrictions are determined. In the NFPA 130 definition of a station, occupancy is a transient space, with passengers occupying the building long enough to wait for the next arriving train. All nontransit functions such as concessions are to be treated in accordance with NFPA 101, Life Safety Code, as appropriate for the class of occupancy.

Construction Type

All new stations, per NFPA 130, are to be of not less than Type 1 or Type 2 construction, or combinations of the two, as defined by NFPA 220, *Standard on Types of Building Construction.*

Interior Finishes

Interior finish materials should be limited to Class A.

Codes and the ADA

The Americans with Disabilities Act

(ADA) 4.3.10, "Egress," requires accessible routes serving any accessible space or element to also serve as a means of egress for emergencies or connect to an accessible area of rescue assistance. One wheelchair space is required for every 200 passengers. With a typical emergency station loading, at say 3000 passengers, it would require 15 spaces on the platform.

CALCULATING OCCUPANT LOAD EXIT CAPACITY

See Chapter 4 for the 12-step station design procedure wherein the example provided is analyzed for compliance with NFPA 130.

AMERICANS WITH DISABILITIES ACT (ADA)

This section discusses how to meet ADA requirements in a transportation facility. It follows the typical passenger through the station and points out the pitfalls that cause many stations to fail an ADA review.

The September 1994 publication by the U.S. Architectural and Transportation Barriers Compliance Board (Access Board) entitled *Americans with Disabilities Act: Accessibility Guidelines for Buildings and Facilities, Transportation Facilities, and Transportation Vehicles* is frequently referred to by section and paragraph numbers in the following sections. This publication is the primary source of guideline information for the design of all proposed stations.

ADA Guidelines are not the only standards related to design for accessibility, nor are the ADA Guidelines necessarily the most stringent. This review is intended to identify the key accessibility compliance issues related to a typical transit station pro-

ject. It is not intended to be a comprehensive code review for all requirements for the design of the transit station. It is the responsibility of the architect to be certain that the final design complies with all applicable codes and requirements.

In addition to providing a transit station that is accessible to the general public, the transit authority is also an employer. The architect must inquire of the transit authority which of the administrative, operational, and maintenance tasks within the station may be performed by individuals with specific physical abilities. Those portions of the station used exclusively by these employees (such as maintenance and operations) may be exempt from some of the accessibility requirements of the ADA Guidelines because of a job description that requires them to be mobile. Seek guidance in these matters from the transit authority and the Access Board.

Accessibility Design Goals

The following are minimum requirements for ADA compliance, along with cost saving opportunities to exceed those minimum standards and achieve full compliance with the spirit of the law, which is nondiscrimination. To achieve this goal and evaluate proposed design standards and specific design solutions, the following principles may be followed:

- First, design without physical barriers and provide for the total integration of individuals with disabilities and able-bodied persons. Do not include a barrier in the design unless it is absolutely essential.

  Example: Rather than introducing a typical curb between roads and walkways, examine alternatives such as providing wheel stops, bollards, change of paving material, and other appropriate design features to separate vehicles and pedestrians without creating the barrier of a curb that must be overcome with the use of curb ramps.

- Second, if barriers are unavoidable because of technical, programmatic, site-related, or financial constraints, provide access by the use of low-tech, no-maintenance means. Solve the problem in the simplest and least expensive manner.

Example: When designing a raised transit platform, if possible, provide access by the use of a sloped sidewalk (1:20 maximum slope) that will be used by all passengers, rather than a ramp (1:12 maximum slope along with continuous handrails and guardrails on each side, 5 ft landing at top and bottom, etc.) and a stair.

- Third, if special devices are required, they should be usable by a disabled individual without assistance.

Example: If a lift or elevator is essential to provide access to a platform on another level, the equipment should be located and operable so that no assistance is required.

Arrival/Departure from the Transit Station

The sequence of events surrounding the arrival and the departure at a transit station must ensure accessibility of all components. The process must be clearly signed to address accessibility for all users.

▲ *Visually impaired passengers require wayfinding systems that will guide them through all spaces, including large mezzanines, as in this London Underground Jubilee Line station. (Photo courtesy Alfred Lau.)*

Parking
Any parking must comply with the following standards:

Location [4.6.2]*
Accessible parking spaces must be located on the shortest accessible route of travel from the parking area to an accessible entrance.

Quantity [4.1.2(5)]
The number of accessible parking spaces to be provided must comply with the minimum standards included in the ADA Guidelines or in local planning and zoning requirements, whichever is greatest.

Size [4.6.3]
Accessible parking spaces must be at least 96 in. wide and of the length specified by the local zoning requirements.

---

*Numbers in brackets, such as [4.6.2], refer to sections of the ADA Guidelines.

Configuration [4.6.3]

Parking access aisles must be part of an accessible route to the facility. Two accessible parking spaces may share a common access aisle. An access aisle must be at least 60 in. wide.

Van accessibility [4.1.2(5) b]

An access aisle must serve one in every eight accessible spaces, but not less than one, at least 96 in. wide and designated as "van accessible."

Passenger loading zones [4.6.6]

An accessible passenger-loading zone must be provided at each station. This loading zone must comply with the ADA Guidelines and include an access aisle at least 60 in. wide and 20 ft long adjacent and parallel to the vehicle pull-up space.

Accessible Route between Arrival/Departure Point and Platform

Provide at least one accessible route complying with ADA Guidelines [4.3], within the boundary of the site, from public transportation stops, accessible parking spaces, passenger loading zones, and public streets or sidewalks, to an accessible entrance to the station. Be sure to design the site without any barriers [4.1.2(1)].

Location of route [4.3.2(1)]

Try to make the primary public access route to the station the accessible route.

Crossing tracks [10.3.1(13)]

If tracks must be crossed to reach the boarding platform, the route surface must comply with the guidelines regarding the flush travel surface, the permitted gap at the rails, and the requirements for detectable warning strips [4.29.5]. Best is

to avoid the necessity of crossing tracks.

Detectable warnings at hazardous vehicular areas [4.29.5]

If a walk crosses or adjoins a vehicular way, and curbs, railings, or other elements between the pedestrian areas and vehicular areas do not separate the walking surfaces, the boundary between the areas must be defined by a continuous warning strip, 36 in. wide, complying with 4.29.2.

Width of the route [4.3.3]

The minimum clear width of an accessible route must be 36 in. except where a person in a wheelchair must make a turn around an obstruction.

As an element of site design for a station, all walkways must be at least 6 ft wide to allow for passing space for passengers and required exiting width from the platform. Specific guidelines and code requirements related to this issue are discussed further in other chapters.

Passing space [4.3.4]

If an accessible route has less than a 60 in. clear width, then passing spaces at least 60 in. by 60 in. must be located at intervals not to exceed 200 ft. A T-intersection of two walks is an acceptable passing place.

Headroom [4.4.2]

All circulation spaces must have at least 80 in. minimum of clear headroom. If the vertical clearance of an area adjoining an accessible route is reduced to less than 80 in., a barrier to warn blind or visually impaired persons must be provided.

Ground and floor surface textures [4.5.1]

Paving surfaces along the accessible

routes and on the station platform, including walks, ramps, stairs, and curb ramps, must be stable, firm, and slip resistant and comply with 4.5. Recognizing that safe walking demands a stable and regular surface, it is therefore necessary that walking surfaces should have a static coefficient of friction, as defined in the American Society of Testing and Materials (ASTM) Standard C1028, of 0.6 on an accessible route and 0.8 on ramps, sloping sidewalks, and stairs.

Slope/cross slope [4.3.7]

An accessible route with a running slope greater than 1:20 is defined as a ramp and must comply with 4.8. Nowhere may the cross slope of an accessible route exceed 1:50.

Slope of grade adjacent to walkway

Where the unpaved grade adjacent to an accessible route slopes away from the walkway at a rate exceeding the maximum allowable for a ramp (1:12), incorporate an appropriate warning device into the walkway. Among the choices for acceptable warning devices are a 4 in. high curb, a 36 in. high rail with a cane detection rail located lower than 27 in., a 24 in. wide textured warning strip complying with 4.29.2, or a 24 in. wide strip of planted materials at a 1:20 maximum slope before the steeper slope begins. Where the adjacent grade has to exceed a slope of 1:2 and the vertical distance of the grade change is less than 30 in., a 36 in. guardrail must be provided. Where the vertical distance of the grade change is 30 in. or greater, provide a 42 in. guardrail.

Changes in level [4.3.8]

Changes in level along an accessible route must comply with 4.5.2. If an accessible route has changes in level greater than ½ in., then a sloped sidewalk, curb ramp, ramp, elevator, or platform lift needs to be provided to comply with 4.3.7, 4.7, 4.8, 4.10, or 4.11, respectively.

Where possible, accomplish changes in level with sloped sidewalks rather than ramps. If that is not possible, use ramps rather than elevators or other mechanical means. When providing ramps, stairs should also be included, as some individuals with particular disabilities may find the use of stairs preferable to ramps [A4.8.1].

Platform Requirements

Most stations have an elevated platform for access to the transit vehicles. Platforms must be safe and convenient.

Access to the platform

An accessible means of egress is as important as access for all individuals to a transit platform, in case of an emergency.

Sloping sidewalks [4.3.7]

Sloping sidewalks are preferred over ramps because they serve all, are easily

▼ The New Orleans, Louisiana, Riverfront trolley system uses ramps within a canopy to access the floor of the trolley. DMJM+Harris.

▲ Use of ramps to manage changes in elevation are preferred over elevators, particularly in outlying areas with low patronage. Seen here is a Virginia Railway Express station. DMJM+Harris. (Photo: Robert Creamer.)

used, they should be included as an alternative means of access for-able bodied individuals as well as a choice for some disabled individuals (such as those on crutches) who may prefer steps to ramps [A4.8.1]. Stairs must comply with the provisions of 4.9.

Elevators [4.10]

Whenever the vertical travel distances exceed a reasonable distance to travel by ramp, elevators may be necessary. To be considered an accessible means of egress, an elevator must comply with the governing building codes related to emergency power and other egress provisions.

Platform lifts (wheelchair lifts)

Platform lifts in lieu of an elevator or ramp are not permitted unless specific conditions are met, which are described in 4.1.3(5). Care should be taken in selecting lifts, as some are not equally suitable for use by both wheelchair users and semi-ambulatory individuals [A4.11.2]. Moreover, the building codes may not permit a platform lift to serve as part of an accessible means of egress.

Width of access/egress

All forms of access/egress to and from the platform must be a minimum of 6 ft wide to conform to the exiting requirements of NFPA 130 for ramps of more than 4 percent slope [2.5.3].

Width of platform

The platform is part of the accessible route within a site and must comply with the ADA Guidelines regarding the minimum width and passing space requirements [4.3.3 and 4.3.4]. The platform must have a 24 in. wide detectable warning strip running the length of the

used, and do not require handrails and landings. Depending on the site conditions, they may also not require guardrails and curbs. At a maximum allowable slope of 1:20, and assuming a vertical rise of 24 in. to the platform, the horizontal length of the sloping sidewalk will be a minimum of 40 ft.

Ramps [4.8]

Any walkway slope exceeding 1:20 is defined as a ramp and may not exceed a slope of 1:12. A ramp must comply with all of the requirements of 4.8 and applicable building codes related to handrails, landings, and guardrails. To gain access to a 24 in. high platform, at minimum a ramp of 24 ft is required. A level landing at least 5 ft long is required at each end of the ramp, bringing the total length to a minimum of 34 ft. When a vertical rise exceeds 30 in., an intermediate landing is required.

Stairs [4.9]

Although stairs are not considered to be part of an accessible route [4.3.8], in instances where sloped sidewalks cannot be platform; a 36 in. wide accessible route running the length of the platform; passing spaces of at least 60 in. × 60 in. at reasonable intervals; and 48 in. deep wheelchair accessible seating areas at reasonable intervals adjacent to fixed seating areas. This results in a minimum clear platform width of 9 ft (plus space for columns, guardrails, windscreens, etc.) to comply with the ADA Guidelines. Other requirements and guidelines may require a greater platform width.

Length of platform

The ADA Guidelines state that transit stations may not be designed to require disabled individuals to board or alight from a vehicle at a location other than those used by the general public. The length of the raised platform must allow all entry points to the transit vehicles to be accessible from the platform [10.3.1(10)].

Platform edge conditions

The open edge of the platform adjacent to the track must have a detectable warning strip that complies with ADA Guidelines [10.3.1(8) and 4.29.2]. To serve as a warning device and a means of channeling pedestrian movement, all other platform edges must be protected by windscreens, guardrails, or handrails which include a cane detection device, such as a rail, at a maximum height of 27 in. for visually impaired individuals [A4.4.1].

Handrails

The design of all handrails must comply with the ADA Guideline provisions included in section 4.26.

Transfer to and from a transit vehicle

The vertical height of the platform must

be coordinated so that it is within plus or minus ⅝ in. of the floor height of the vehicles under normal loading conditions [10.3.1(9)]. The horizontal gap between the platform and a vehicle, when it is at rest, must be no more than 3 in. [10.3.1(9)]. Platform design must be coordinated with the vehicle's ADA criteria and specifications to achieve these standards.

Ticketing and Other Equipment

Modern transit systems make extensive use of self-service ticketing and fare verification equipment. This equipment must be convenient and available for use by all transit patrons. Access to the equipment must be provided for both front and side approaches for individuals in wheelchairs. Equipment for use by the general public must be located and designed to comply with the most restrictive criteria (generally the requirements for a front approach).

Ticket machines

Location [10.3.1(1)].

Fare vending or other ticketing areas, and

▲ *A paver accent strip behind a detectable warning strip is an additional feature that helps to visually contrast the edge conditions.*

fare collection areas, must be located to minimize travel distance for disabled persons.

Quantity [10.3.1(7)]

At least one accessible piece of equipment must be provided and located conveniently for all users of the platform.

Clearances and configuration [10.3.1(7) and 4.34]

Automatic fare vending, collection, and adjustment systems must comply with the requirements for automated teller machines [4.34] as well as the specific requirements for transportation facilities [10.3.1(7)]. This includes a clear floor area and reach ranges, controls, and equipment for persons with vision impairments. A 48 in. × 48 in. clear floor area will be required to comply with the requirement that equipment be accessible for both a front and a side approach for an individual in a wheelchair.

Telephones
Location [4.31].

If public telephones are provided, at least one accessible unit must be located adjacent to an accessible route and must be in compliance with the following accessibility requirements.

Quantity [4.1.3 (17)]

If provided, accessible public phones must be in the quantity described by the table in this section of the ADA Guidelines. For the typical station, one accessible phone is sufficient.

Clearances [4.31]

Accessible public telephones must comply with the clear floor area, mounting height and protruding object criteria de-

scribed in 4.31.2, 4.31.3, and 4.31.4, respectively. A 48 in. × 48 in. clear floor area will be required to comply with the requirement that equipment be accessible for both a front and a side approach for an individual in a wheelchair.

Special conditions [4.31 and 10.3.1(12)]

All accessible public telephones must comply with the requirements for hearing aid and volume control, push-button controls, cord length, telephone book availability, and text telephones as described in 4.31.5–9 and 10.3.1(12).

Passenger Information Systems

Passenger information systems include signage, public address systems, graphics, maps, emergency alarms, and any other means of conveying necessary information to the systems' users. All such systems should be treated uniformly at all stations and must be accessible to all system users. All signs must conform to the system standards and with the requirements of the ADA Guidelines. See Chapter 11, "Wayfinding."

General information
Lettering height, proportion, contrast, and other specifics [4.30 and A4.30]

The ADA Guidelines contain a substantial number of highly specific criteria for the design and installation of signage for individuals who are visually impaired. The architect is advised to refer to these appropriate sources when designing and specifying the signage for a rail station. Also see Chapter 11, "Wayfinding."

General location of signs [10.3.1(4) and (6)]

Signage must be placed in uniform locations within the total transit system so that information is easy for all users to find.

Many disabilities include limitations in the movement of the person's head and reduced peripheral vision. Thus, signage positioned perpendicular to and within 30 degrees to either side of the centerline of the path of travel is easiest to notice [A4.30.1].

Station entrance signs [10.3.1(4)]
At least one sign at each entrance identifying the station must comply with the requirements for raised and brailled characters and pictograms [4.30.4] and for accessible mounting location and height [4.30.6]. When a station has no defined entrance, the accessible signage must be placed in a central location.

Station identification signs [10.3.1(5)]
Station identification signs must be placed along the platform so as to be seen from the transit vehicles, in compliance with this guideline. The guideline also stipulates that identification signs must be located on both sides of the vehicle. The height of signs is dependent on the height of the windows of the vehicles and must be coordinated with the specific vehicle for the system.

A minimum of one sign identifying the specific station and complying with the requirements for raised and brailled characters and pictograms and for accessible mounting location and height [4.30.4 and 4.30.6] must be provided in a uniform location on each platform or boarding area [10.3.1(6)].

Maps
Where maps or other graphic materials are provided, tactile maps or prerecorded instructions and information should be provided for people who are visually impaired [A4.30.1].

Stations, routes, or destinations served [10.3.1(6)]
System identification maps, providing a list of all stations, routes, or destinations served by the station, and located on the platform, must comply with 4.30.1, 4.30.2, 4.30.3, and 4.30.5.

Emergency information
Audible and visual alarms, where provided, must comply with the relevant criteria [4.28 and A4.28].

Public address system
Where public address systems are used to convey information to the general public, provide a means of conveying the same or equivalent information to persons with hearing loss or who are deaf [10.3.1(14)]. This should include a stand-alone visual paging system that is integrated into the total information system, architecture, and interior environment.

Seating and Other Furniture
Depending on the system's timetable, passengers may spend a lot of time waiting for the transit vehicles or to be picked up by a bus or automobile. The waiting areas and the incidental site furnishings, such as fixed seating and trash receptacles, must meet the requirements of all passengers.

Waiting areas
Location [4.1.3(18)]

Seating areas for people in wheelchairs must be provided adjacent to an accessible path of travel and must be an integral part of the fixed seating plan, providing choices comparable to those for the general public [4.33.3]. Furthermore, the locations should provide a direct view of the arriving transit vehicles and convenient access to the transit vehicle entrances. Locations should be based on a thorough wayfinding analysis and evaluation (see Chapter 11), including elements such as art, advertising, furnishings, fixtures, visual clutter, lighting, audio, directories, maps, fire response, sprinklers, security cameras, structural barriers, and the total comprehensive signage program.

Quantity [4.1.3(18)]

At least 5 percent, but not less than one, of the fixed or built-in seating areas must comply with 4.32.

Size [4.2.4(1)]

Clear floor area must comply with 4.2.4(1), 30 in. × 48 in. minimum.

Other concerns

Fixed seating areas should recognize the needs of semi-ambulatory passengers, such as those who use walkers or crutches, as well as those in wheelchairs. Although the ADA Guidelines do not specifically address this need, if the height of some fixed seating (at least 5 percent but not less than one seat) is 18–19 in. above the platform, this will be an advantage to some of these individuals, who may have difficulty in using lower seating. A solution may be to provide fixed seating that is all mounted at 18 in. above the platform.

Trash receptacles

See Chapter 12, "Safety and Security," for a discussion of trash receptacles.

Location [4.3.2(2)]

Locate trash receptacles so that they are accessible from at least one accessible path of travel. Many people with mobility impairments have a reduced travel range and speed, so these elements should be placed close to an accessible entrance, seating areas, ticket machines, and other such elements used by all individuals

Configuration [4.2]

All accessible elements within a facility should comply with the limitations described in section 4.2 and should be usable from a front or side approach via wheelchair. In addition, consideration should be given to the ease of operation by individuals with limited use of one or both of their hands, as well as those who are visually impaired.

Lighting

In general, the ADA Guidelines provide little direction regarding levels of illumination. The only guidance for transit facilities is that illumination levels in the areas where signage is located must be uniform and must minimize glare on signs. In addition, lighting along circulation routes shall be of a type and configuration to provide uniform illumination [10.3.1(11)].

Illumination levels on sign surfaces are recommended to be in the 100–300 lux range (10–30 footcandles) on the vertical surface of a sign face and located so the illumination level of the sign is no less than ambient light or a visible bright lighting source behind or in front of the sign [A4.30.8]. Coordinate ADA lighting with the guidelines presented in Chapter 10, "Lighting," and Chapter 11, "Wayfinding."

CHAPTER 6

ENGINEERING CONSIDERATIONS

GENERAL DESIGN CONSIDERATIONS AND ISSUES

Engineering considerations are influenced by a number of factors, primarily the system characteristics, the alignment configuration (at-grade, aerial, or subway), and the physical and geotechnical features and characteristics of the area in which the system will be constructed. This discussion is not intended to cover all design problems that will be encountered in transit station design, but rather to clearly demonstrate the need to consider both architecture and engineering to achieve a balanced solution that will result in a successful, high-quality transit station. This chapter focuses on the modern vehicle systems and describes some of the characteristics that significantly influence the design of the tracks and their supporting structure (the "guideway"), stations, and their use in various situations.

Urban Systems

The first two urban systems considered here, light-rail transit and heavy-rail transit, are typically used in situations that involve moving large volumes of passengers quickly and efficiently in large, dense urban areas.

Light-rail transit (LRT)

It is the ability to operate at grade in urban streets together with vehicular traffic that most clearly defines the difference between LRT and other forms of urban rail transit. It is the characteristic that requires:

- Overhead contact for traction power
- Shorter trains, essentially to fit between intersections

- Track- or street-level boarding/alighting
- Short-radius curve capability to negotiate turns at street intersections

LRT may operate on either exclusive or nonexclusive rights-of-way. Station spacing may range from ¼ mile to 1 mile or more, depending on the density of the area being served, and in street operation stops may be even more frequent and identified only by painted islands that do not fit the definition of stations. In those on-street stops, handicapped access can be provided by on-vehicle lifts or, where space permits, by raised blocks at one end of the stop.

Heavy-rail transit (HRT)

HRT is typically characterized by larger and wider cars, higher operating speed capability (up to 80 mph), and third rail power pick-up (in U.S. systems). These characteristics, particularly the third rail power pick-up, require an exclusive right-of-way and complete separation from pedestrian and vehicular traffic (referred to as *grade separation*), which in turn allows the higher speeds and longer trains. Stations may be spaced as close as ¼ mile in dense urban areas, but in more suburban areas typically use ½ to 1 mile spacing to take advantage of the higher speed. Stations also have high-level platforms, extensive vertical circulation systems, and significant requirements for ancillary spaces needed by the more sophisticated vehicle operating systems.

Automated guideway transit (AGT)

AGT, or people movers, are more appropriate in smaller areas and are typically

▲ Grade-separated heavy-rail transit relies on an aerial guideway structure in suburban areas.

rail typically uses traditional locomotive power, either diesel or electric, pulling multicar trains.

High-speed rail (HSR)

High-speed rail is a long-haul intercity rail system designed to be competitive with air travel over distances of 300–500 miles. As such, the station spacing is wide, typically with one station in each city served (except in the largest cities), and the alignment is fully grade separated and in an exclusive right-of-way. High-speed rail systems are in service in Japan and Europe, but although several areas in the United States are in various stages of planning, no such system is in place here. The Northeast Corridor between Washington, D.C., and New York City, where speeds of up to 150 mph may be observed on some sections, has the only rail system in the United States that currently approaches high-speed rail service.

Configuration and Cost

Either LRT or HRT systems may be operated at-grade, overhead, or in a subway. For either system, the at-grade configuration is much less expensive, with costs ranging from $10–$20 million per alignment mile and $200,000–$1,000,000 per LRT station (depending on construction difficulty and system technology). The Government Accounting Office (GAO) prepared a report presenting a bus rapid transit and LRT comparison in response to congressional requests. That report, published in September 2001, provided a cost history for 13 new LRT systems built in the United States between 1980 and 2000. Total costs, adjusted for the year 2000, ranged from $12.72 million per mile in Sacramento, California, to $118.83 million in Buffa-

used in airports, amusement parks, and, in a few cases, such as Miami and Detroit, as circulators in central business districts. The AGT systems typically use smaller vehicles, traveling at lower speeds at close headways (spacing between trains or vehicles) on fully grade-separated guideways with closely spaced stations.

Power

All of these three urban system types are usually propelled by electric power collected from either overhead wire (catenary-type systems) or a trackside power distribution rail at track level (third rail) providing traction power. It is worth noting from an engineering perspective, however, that at least one new U.S. system (Southern New Jersey LRT) is using diesel-powered motorized units (DMU) to save the cost of the overhead contact system.

Intercity Rail Systems

Commuter rail

Although a few systems have some motorized units (MUs) with motors on at least two axles of every car, commuter lo, New York. (Note that the Buffalo system included significant underground construction, whereas Sacramento and most other LRT systems use extensive at-grade construction). The 13 systems included 309.7 miles at a combined cost of $10,774.58 million, or an average cost per mile of $34.79 million. Subway costs, at the other extreme, can run up to $100 million or more per alignment mile, with station costs of up to $50 million or more per station, again depending on construction difficulty. Costs for elevated systems generally fall between these extremes.

However, in the case of LRT, the right-of-way (ROW) does not have to be exclusive, as it does with HRT. The requirement for an exclusive ROW for HRT results from:

- The use of third rail power supply typical in U.S. systems
- The fact that HRT is usually at least partially, if not fully, automated
- Operation at higher speeds (up to 80 mph)
- The use of much longer trains (up to 6 or 8 cars and up to 600 ft in length)

Under these restrictions, the most advantageous at-grade application for HRT is in the median of freeways or expressways where the requirement to grade separate the highway simplifies both ROW acquisition and construction of the transit system. In addition, it creates a true "transportation" corridor to realize maximum utilization of the ROW to move people. It does, however, introduce some special requirements for passenger access to the platforms, requiring either bridges over or tunnels under the highway lanes from both sides of the highway. Stations located in freeway medians also typically incorporate extensive park-and-ride and/or bus transfer facilities to encourage and facilitate mode change. LRT, on the other hand, is much more flexible, able to operate on nonexclusive ROWs even in mixed traffic on existing streets (at significant penalty in travel speeds) while still offering the opportunity for grade separation where possible. It therefore has significant cost advantages where at-grade operation is possible for significant percentages of the system or route.

These advantages quickly diminish, as illustrated by the Buffalo, New York, cost per mile cited earlier, where grade separation, either by overhead or subway configuration, is used because the basic structure cost is a much greater percentage of total system cost and is relatively independent of system technology. The design and construction difficulty increases geometrically as the system progresses from an at-grade, through an overhead, to an underground configuration.

Track

Track design, for either LRT or HRT is typically provided by a specialist or specialty firm familiar with and experienced in the unique requirements of the various switches, operational and emergency crossover, guardrails, track fasteners, and other elements of track design and operation. In the United States, virtually all rail transit systems use continuously welded rail (CWR), with conventional "T" rail. In at-grade applications, the most common track construction is *tie on ballast,* whereby the rails are fastened to a wood or concrete tie bedded in crushed rock (ballast) on a prepared subgrade. In subways or on elevated structures, rail may also be installed by *direct fixation,* using a spring clip bolted directly to a resilient pad under the rail to absorb vibrations and reduce noise transmission, which in turn is bolted to the concrete structure.

A special condition is found in LRT applications when the rails are installed at-grade in a street and transit operations will involve mixed traffic. In that case, the top of the rails must be flush with the pavement and a groove provided for the flange of the train wheel.

Stray Current and Corrosion Control

Direct current (DC) electrical systems typically used in rail transit normally use the running rails for the return path to complete the circuit to the traction power substation for the propulsion power. In any such DC system, electricity tends to "leak" from the running rail (the return path) to the adjacent ground or structure. That leakage is picked up by metallic conductors (reinforcing steel, underground pipes, etc.) and then travels along the conductor as a "stray current" to the end. At that point, it leaves the conductor and corrodes the metallic structure. The designer responsible for the engineering design of stations and other transit structures must be aware of the issue and ensure that proper mitigation measures are incorporated in all elements of the design.

At-Grade Alignments
HRT stations

Rail transit operation using the HRT mode requires an exclusive ROW and is most appropriate where such ROW already exists. Examples include freeways and grade-separated expressways where

the transit can be installed in the median. Existing railroad alignments also offer at-grade opportunities where the ROW is grade separated. Although the line sections are easily accommodated in most such ROWs, the stations present a more serious issue because of the width required for platforms, passenger amenities, and vertical circulation. In addition, pedestrian bridges or tunnels leading to a mezzanine either over or under the platform must be provided. (See the illustration on page 66.)

Engineering considerations for such a median station relate primarily to ensuring that:

- Space is available to develop the station with adequate clearances for fences, traffic barriers, and similar provisions to ensure that highway traffic cannot enter the rail ROW.

- Appropriate provisions are included to accommodate intermodal transfer for buses and autos delivering or receiving passengers at the station area (see Chapters 2 and 3).

- Traffic engineering and street design incorporates signals, signal timing, turn lanes, pedestrian cycles, and similar provisions to facilitate movement to and from the station area by buses, autos, and pedestrians.

- Station and station area design is fully coordinated with and approved by the city, county, state, and/or federal agency with responsibility for the freeway or expressway or, in the case of joint use with railroads, the railroad company.

- Provisions for access by emergency vehicles meet all cognizant authorities' requirements and conditions.

LRT stations

LRT operations are much more flexible in that they do not require exclusivity but can operate at-grade in streets in mixed traffic as well as in grade-separated ROWs. Although mixed traffic operations are often necessary, where possible the guideway should be located in an ROW, such as a street median, that allows dedicated but not grade-separated alignments. Eliminating the conflicts with shared traffic improves both the speed and safety of the service. In any case, that operational flexibility, combined with normally much shorter trains, barrier free fare collection (see Chapter 7), low platform capability, and manually controlled trains, makes an at-grade configuration much more appealing for LRT and also makes station design more flexible. At-grade LRT has been employed in many urban areas, both in the United States and overseas, and is more adaptable to the urban environment than the HRT mode for several reasons:

- Power supply is overhead from a catenary system, which allows both crossing and parallel vehicular and pedestrian traffic.

- LRT can easily employ low curbside boarding with accessibility requirements met by on-vehicle lifts, thus eliminating the need for high platforms.

- LRT usually operates with short train lengths that will fit within city blocks and will not block intersections when stopped at stations.

- The problem of inadequate street space necessary for LRT tracks can usually be solved by creating guideway corridors in wide urban streets, if

▲ LRT station at 14th and Stout Streets in Denver. DMJM+Harris.

▼ LRT station low platform with wheelchair-access boarding provided by "high blocks" or ramps to an elevated boarding platform.

▲ *LRT station with canopy to provide system identity and protection for passengers.*

Another at-grade condition applicable to LRT is the "transit mall," whereby vehicular traffic other than transit is removed entirely or restricted to varying degrees. Examples of areas using this configuration include Portland, Oregon; San Jose, California; and Long Beach, California, among others. Each such application is unique and requires the cooperative efforts of the urban planner, urban designer, architect, and engineer, particularly the traffic engineer, for successful implementation. Although the "mall" configuration involves the alignment segments as well, it affords an excellent opportunity for more extensive station treatment. Typical treatment can include unique lighting, more elaborate station design and street furniture, more extensive landscaping, and special hardscape treatment to define the mall. Engineering concerns in a mall application will include those already described: fitting into the street, utility relocation, traffic, structural design, and pedestrian circulation. Engineering design services may be expanded to include the services required for lighting, irrigation, and other support systems that are identified and designed in cooperation with the other team members to suit the unique project requirements.

A significant engineering issue, also applicable to any track alignment in the street, is relocation of utilities. Typically, many utility systems, including sewer, water, telephone, and the like, are located in the street and must be relocated to be outside the guideway to permit access for service and repair of the utilities without interrupting transit service. Utilities crossing the alignment may be sleeved under the guideway. In all cases involving metallic conduits, the requirements

they exist, or by creating vehicle-free malls for guideways. Using a "couplet," with one-way operation on each of two paralleling streets, is another way to incorporate LRT in an area of narrower streets.

In an in-street operation, LRT stations are most often located at street intersections and are very similar to bus stops, with "platforms" defined by curbs or even painted lines. In these station types, engineering considerations are minimal, consisting primarily of "fitting" the station area into the available street width.

In off-street locations and in dedicated ROWs, platform canopies are recommended to provide some system identity and a measure of passenger protection. In such cases, the engineer supports the architect to provide structural design and any mechanical or electrical service needed, as well as civil and traffic engineering for utility relocation. Pedestrian access is typically at the street intersection via the crosswalk, and intermodal access is usually by simple bus stops at curbside.

for corrosion protection, as directed by the corrosion engineer or the owning utility, must be provided.

Aerial or Elevated Alignments

Either rail transit mode, LRT or HRT, may be operated in an aerial or elevated configuration, and the engineering considerations are similar in each case. However, it must be noted that the significant cost and flexibility differentials associated with LRT in the at-grade configuration are quickly reduced when the system becomes grade separated. Aside from longer stations required to accommodate the six- to eight-car trains typical of HRT, other conditions are similar for both systems. Although it is more common with LRT, either system can operate with the less costly and more space-efficient barrier-free fare collection systems: The Metro Red Line of Los Angeles and the Metro of San Juan, Puerto Rico, are examples.

In the case of grade-separated alignments there is a direct relationship between the horizontal and vertical alignment of the line segment and the station in terms of:

- Height above grade
- Width and clearances
- Platform arrangement
- Supporting column placement and foundations
- Passenger access and vertical circulation
- Station elements such as pedestrian bridges and mezzanines

Height above grade

The type of ROW that the aerial alignment is in or crossing governs clearance under the structural beams of the guideway and the stations. In the United

▼ Architectural models are a good technique to study relationship between structural guideway and station elements.

▲ Vancouver, British Columbia, SkyTrains' linear-induction-motor–driven LRT vehicles on an elevated guideway approaching a station. Guideways require emergency walkways and railings. DMJM+Harris.

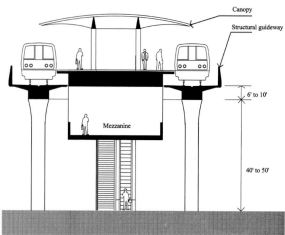

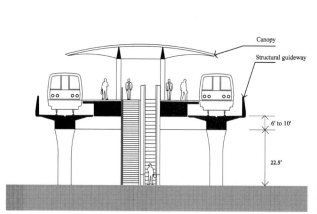

Study model for an APM guideway. Note clearance above highway may apply to beam on pier.

the range of 6 to 10 ft, depending on the span, the top of the running rail is about 25–30 ft above grade on tangent line segments. Where stations are involved in similar conditions, the requirement for bridges and a mezzanine to allow passengers to access the platforms from either side of the station will add 15–20 ft to the total height above grade, or about the fourth or fifth floor level of adjacent buildings. Although placing the mezzanine and access passages underground can reduce the overall height, the construction disruption and total cost are increased significantly.

There are, however, circumstances in which an elevated alignment may be preferable. Such opportunities recognize the major cost differential between elevated and subway configurations and include stations located off-street in private ROWs combined with joint development that integrates the station into office and/or high-density residential complexes. This allows the mezzanine to be located at grade with direct passenger access to the platforms from ground-level

States, for systems located in a public street, for example, a minimum clear dimension of at least 14 ft is necessary (actual clearance will be as required by the cognizant municipal or state authority), whereas location in or crossing an interstate highway (U.S.) will require a minimum clearance of 16.5 ft. Many state utility commissions establish 22.5 ft clearance above any railroad. Because the depth of a typical guideway beam is in

Guideway clearance.

128

plazas or from the integrated buildings. Another opportunity exists where urban streets or freeways have a median that is too narrow to support an at-grade system but will allow columns protected by traffic barriers. In that case, the station will represent a joint use of the public ROW and promote a "transportation corridor" concept in the urban area.

Width and clearances

Major factors affecting the width of an elevated station include the following:

- The vehicle width at the sill or floor level

- The dynamic envelope (the cross-sectional outline of the vehicle that defines the space necessary to allow for sway and lateral movement of the cars)

- The platform width, including space for vertical circulation

- The platform arrangement, either side or center

Among these factors, the most significant difference from station to station is the platform arrangement with the center platform station being narrower. The center platform station is also more efficient in terms of vertical circulation, inasmuch as one set of escalators and elevators serves both travel directions. See the tables on pages 73 and 74 for a comparison of center and side platform stations.

The platform arrangement also affects the guideway design leading to and from the station site. A typical alignment structure for an elevated guideway is a single box beam carrying both directional tracks. In a side platform station, this structure can be carried through the sta-

tion and the platforms and other station features built around the guideway. However, for a center platform station, the tracks must be spread by the width of the platform and required clearances, resulting in a split guideway for some distance on both ends of the station, thus requiring additional columns, foundations, and ROW width leading to the station area.

▲ *A guideway structure should be aesthetically sensitive to its setting as in the initial Vancouver SkyTrain system.*

▼ *Typical elevated guideway.*

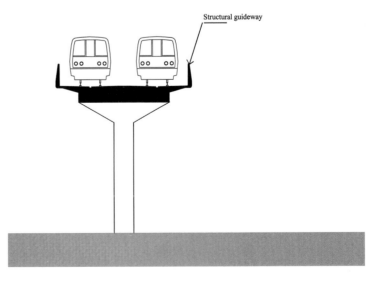

Structural guideway

Station elements

In many instances the enclosed public areas of the stations are climate controlled, particularly where climate conditions may be more extreme. Climate control is typically applied to mezzanines, pedestrian bridges or tunnels, and other closed spaces and can include heating, cooling, and/or simple ventilation, as appropriate to the climate at the station location. It is not usually provided at open platforms, except for a canopy over all or part of the platform to provide some sun and rain protection. Transparent windscreens and radiant heating may be distributed along the covered portions of the platform in cold climates. Other platform furniture and amenities include informational signs and annunciations, limited seating, a station identification pylon and system map, and platform lighting. These station features are generally the responsibility of the station architect, and the engineering design team—structural, mechanical and electrical—coordinate their work to support the architectural requirements.

Platform edge doors

Platform edge doors (PEDs), also referred to as train screens, are similar to elevator doors and are located at the edge of the platform to coincide with the operation and location of the doors on the transit vehicle when it is stopped at the station. They have been used in a few instances in European systems for many years. In the United States, platform doors are typically used on "people mover" systems and, in recent years, have been suggested for some mass transit systems. Arguments in favor of the use of PEDs include improved safety, preventing patrons from jumping or falling into the guideway, and the ability to permit climate control at the platform. However, these advantages come at a significant capital and operating cost, because a station may require as many as 30 to 40 doors for each directional side of the platform.

Subway Alignments

As discussed earlier, underground alignments are almost always employed in the center city portions of an HRT transit system. The long trains of six to eight cars, high platform, third-rail traction power (typical in U.S. systems), and at least partially automated operation preclude the use of at-grade configurations in dense urban centers. Elevated guideways and stations for either HRT or LRT are also usually not acceptable in modern systems in downtown areas, as they are noisy, block light and air, adversely impact adjacent buildings, interfere with cityscape views, and require supporting columns in the streets. While still providing a fully grade-separated alignment, the subway configuration avoids these issues.

The greatest disadvantage to the subway configuration is capital cost. Anoth-

▼ *Plan elevated guideway/center platform.*

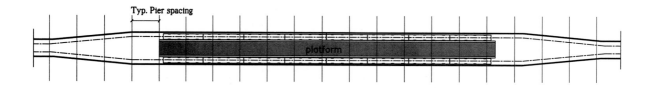

er disadvantage of subway alignments is greater adverse impacts during construction. These construction impacts are caused by the necessity to excavate through and under streets, move or support utilities, protect building foundations, and sometimes modify buildings at the surface level to provide for station entrances. Construction impacts also include the risk of building and pavement subsidence caused by underground excavation. Although good planning and good design can mitigate these disadvantages, they cannot be totally avoided.

Excavation considerations

The issues of alignment, both horizontal and vertical, that affect stations are more closely interrelated and have a greater impact on cost in the construction of subway than for any other configuration. Therefore, although the focus of this book is the design of stations, rather than the guideway segments that connect them, it is important to recognize the significant characteristics of transit structures on either side of the stations that influence station design.

The character of the line structures as they abut the station can greatly affect the station layout and the interrelationships of the station interior volumes. An example is centerline-to-centerline track spacing. A double-track, single or double box cut-and-cover subway results in the narrowest track arrangement (typically about 14 ft center to center) and can best be coupled with a side platform station, allowing the tracks to retain the narrow spacing through the station. The tunneled subway with side-by-side driven tunnels is the widest, requiring track centers 30–40 ft apart, and can best be coupled with a center platform

station. Such factors as station entrance locations and number of entrances, space required at station ends for emergency exiting and ventilation, and space for electric power substations and for crossovers either ahead of or behind the platform can all affect station size.

Where a shallow profile in the range of 40–60 ft is practical and possible, both line (guideway) structures and stations are usually designed as cut-and-cover boxes. Although the cut-and-cover method can be used for deep line structures and station boxes, other methods are available that may result in reduced cost and disruption and must therefore

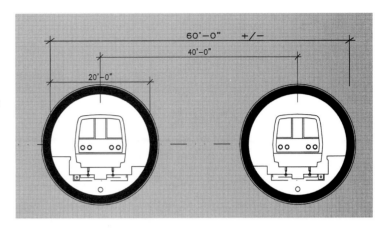

▲ *Typical side-by-side driven tunnel configuration.*

▼ *Typical shallow subway concrete structure.*

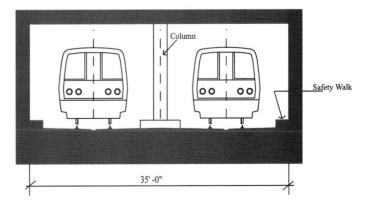

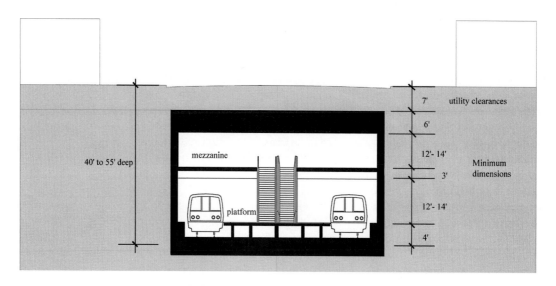

40' to 55' deep

mezzanine

platform

7' utility clearances

6'

12'- 14'

3'

Minimum dimensions

12'- 14'

4'

▲ *Typical shallow station structural clearances.*

also be considered.

The guideways for shallow subway profiles are usually double reinforced concrete boxes, about 35 ft wide, with a single track and safety walk on each side. Shallow subway stations are usually designed as reinforced concrete boxes in the range of 56–58 ft wide, using center platforms, and in the range of 40–55 ft deep, depending on whether a mezzanine is employed. Excavation support systems for cut-and-cover line structures and stations are typically soldier pile and lagging, with horizontal ground pressure resisted by either cross bracing or tiebacks. Sometimes, however, special geologic conditions and/or special adjacent foundation conditions require the use of alternative ground support methods (e.g., slurry or other types of diaphragm walls) to minimize ground movement and/or exclude groundwater.

Soils

Although there is a wide range of classifications used in soil mechanics to describe soils, those encountered in excavation can generally be defined by two general

classes, rock and soft ground. "Rock" can be defined as any consolidated material with a compressive strength of 250 lb per square inch (psi) or more.

Everything else is "soft ground," which includes sand, clay, silt, and mixtures of these types of soils and may contain groundwater. In terms of hardness, soft ground can range from soft sand through stiff clays to various shales that are very hard but can be "ripped" with excavating machines without blasting.

Soft ground may also include boulders and rock fragments that require special consideration when planning and selecting excavation methods. In effect, the term *soft ground* applies to all underground materials except competent or weathered rock. Each of these conditions imposes specific requirements on the excavating machines and equipment that must be evaluated for each project.

Where both rock and soft ground are encountered at the same time at the excavation face in tunnel construction, it is called a "mixed face tunnel." This is a very difficult condition, because progress through the rock is much slower than through the soft ground portion, which is normally in the upper portion of the face. In that case, the soft ground portion may tend to cave and expose the top of the tunnel ahead of the shield. Extreme caution must be exercised during construction to avoid such an occurrence; this may include the use of support boards, chemical or cement grout, or other methods to hold the soft ground portion of the face in place while the rock is excavated. The designer should avoid this condition, if at all possible, during design by changing the profile so that it is either entirely in the rock or in the soft ground.

Geotechnical considerations

An accurate assessment of the geology and corresponding structural and construction solutions are critical for subway design. Small inaccuracies in determining the character of the soils and the groundwater—and how they will act and react during construction—can have a great influence on program cost, schedule, and ultimate quality of completed facilities.

For this reason, special attention and adequate time and budget must be devoted to assessing the geology and developing adequate geotechnical data in the design process. A detailed and comprehensive boring and testing program is essential to determine soil types; horizontal and vertical boundaries of various soil masses; and soil characteristics, including density, moisture content, cohesion, grain size, gradation, and probable deformation under loads. Determinations of groundwater levels, groundwater variations, and perched water tables, if they exist, are mandatory. Pump tests to assess soil porosity, transmissibility, and layering are essential to determine the ability to dewater during excavation, the effects that groundwater removal and migration will have on the construction process, and the potential subsidence affecting adjacent existing structures.

A Geotechnical Data Report (GDR) is usually prepared for rapid-transit projects to present detailed soil and groundwater boring and laboratory data to prospective bidders. A Geotechnical Design Summary Report (GDSR) is usually prepared for prospective bidders to present judgments concerning the ways in which soils will act and react during underground construction. The GDSR is prepared by the owner's engineer for the conventional design-bid-build procurement process, but it is usually prepared by the design-builder's engineer in the design-build procurement process. (In some jurisdictions the GDSR is called a Geotechnical Basis Report, GBR.)

Ventilation

Special attention to the design of ventilation facilities for subways is important to meet the need for adequate fresh air and provide for comfortable temperatures and humidity under varying weather conditions. Ventilation design for subways and subway stations must also deal with the piston effects of train movements in tunnels on both air quality and air movement in stations. It must ensure and satisfy the need for fresh air moving in specific directions to provide for safety in evacuating patrons and fighting fires in underground spaces. See "Mechanical Considerations" in this chapter (page 163) for a more thorough discussion of ventilation.

Waterproofing

The most important aspect of waterproofing underground structures is prevention of leakage through the basic structure. The second most important is to channel any water that does get into the station box to drains as quickly and unobtrusively as possible. To achieve effective waterproofing, various membranes are applied to the excavated surfaces, both walls and invert slab, prior to placing the interior structural walls and the final invert slab. Waterproofing membranes are typically thick plastics such as polyvinylchloride (PVC), high-density polyethylene (HDPE), or similar impervious material. Joints and seams are typically heat welded to form a continuous membrane. In addition, waterstops at all base slab, wall, and roof joints should be provided.

Other waterproofing methods include the use of bentonite panels placed against the excavated surface before placing the concrete. The bentonite liquefies upon contact with water, and the resulting soft slurry penetrates the pores and hairline cracks in the structure to prevent the passage of water. In instances of highly saturated ground with high head against the structure, a grout curtain between the wet soil and the back surface of the structural wall may be used.

The small amounts of water that leak through the waterproofing and enter the

station box can be collected by carefully detailed drips, drain channels, and catch basins and led to the undertrack drainage system and ultimately to the pump stations. This collection system works well if the architectural finish includes a cavity wall or inner architectural shell. Where the basic structural wall is exposed as the finished surface, any leakage through the wall will cause unsightly staining.

Careful detailing of the station roof structure and waterproofing is necessary to effectively minimize leaks due to percolating rainwater or water from leaky utilities. The use of membranes, bentonite panels, and/or hot mastic on the top of the slab is a typical means of waterproofing roof structures. Pitching the roof slabs to the edge, or to a drain combined with a thin gravel blanket, to facilitate movement of water to the edge or drain can also remove standing water above the roof slab.

Drainage and utilities

Underground tunnels and stations must include drainage facilities to accommodate storm water inflow from vents, shafts, and entrances, as well as groundwater intrusion. Despite the best effort to exclude water through design and construction methods, water inflow is inevitable and must be collected and pumped out. A pipe of about 12 in. diameter laid in the invert paving, with periodic catch basins at track level typically provides drainage in tunnels. Water is conducted through the track drain to a low point, preferably at a station or vent structure to facilitate servicing and maintenance. In cases where a low point is unavoidable between stations or vents, a pump station is required. Station drainage is handled in a similar manner,

▼ *Typical track drain detail. Good practice is to slope entire station 0.3% ± to facilitate drainage.*

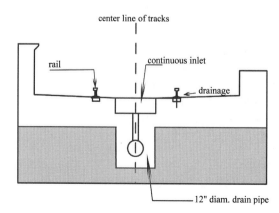

center line of tracks

rail

continuous inlet

drainage

12" diam. drain pipe

with water being conducted to a sump or pump station at the station invert level and then pumped to a suitable municipal storm drainage system. Where sanitary sewage from restrooms in the station is included, separate pumping and ejection systems are required. Pump station design must also include appropriate environmental controls, such as grit and oil separators and similar features required by responsible agencies or municipal departments. The engineering team must estimate the total inflow from all sources and then work with the station architect to locate and size the pump stations and other necessary facilities within the station box.

Other utilities to be provided may include domestic water, sanitary sewer, and various communication and power services to support the operating systems. Domestic water is generally required at all stations to service janitorial and cleaning requirements, and sanitary sewer connections will depend on whether toilet facilities are provided and the number of fixture units involved. The need and location for the various utilities must be coordinated with the station architect and systems engineering requirements.

Clearance Requirements

There are several factors that influence the clearance requirements at stations and on the guideway structures. Each type of system—people mover, transit, or commuter rail—will impose specific clearance requirements set by the regulating agency as well as the operating property. The designer must ensure complete familiarity and understanding of the specific requirements as dictated by the system technology, the operating condi-

tions, and by the agency/operator. Issues such as combined freight and passenger operations on commuter rail lines or express or skip-stop operations on rail transit will introduce specific requirements both for station design clearances and for the structural design, particularly for subway stations where air movement and pressure resulting from the piston effect must be considered. However, in any system or operating scenario, one element is common in the determination of clearances: the dynamic envelope.

Dynamic envelope

The dynamic envelope is unique to each system and vehicle design and is provided by the vehicle builder. It represents a worst-case condition, taking into account all construction tolerances, failure conditions such as a broken or deflated spring, and the sway roll or yaw of the vehicle under operating conditions. The dynamic outline is the extreme outside of the envelope created by the sum of these variables and is presented in both graphic and tabular form. In regard to designing a station, the dynamic outline is a critical factor in locating the platform as well as any signs or informational material mounted on the walls of the train room. Although the dynamic outline is important in all applications, it is particularly important in subways where various items such as emergency walkways, standpipes, cables, and signal equipment are typically hung on the walls of the tunnel. Signals and, at crossover locations, switch machines placed along the guideway must be considered when establishing the size of the tunnels and station entrances, and in all cases must recognize the dynamic envelope of the particular vehicle system used.

135

Effects of curvature

In addition to the dynamic outline, the effects of curvature must be taken into account when setting clearances. As a vehicle passes through a curve, the midpoint of the vehicle is offset from the centerline toward the center of the curve (mid overhang), and the ends are offset away from the center (end overhang). The degree of offset is a function of the wheelbase (distance between truck centers), vehicle length, vehicle width, and curve radius and superelevation, all related to the dynamic outline. In the case of tunnel design, the track position within the tunnel envelope is varied to account for the overhang conditions.

Platform clearances

In station design, the most critical clearance issue is platform location relative to the track centerline. Although the most favorable condition is placement of the station on a tangent location whenever possible, there are times when placement on a curve is necessary. That condition is most likely to occur on commuter rail lines where very long platforms are required and/or where infill stations are added to an existing transit line. In designing new transit lines, the designer should place a station on a curve only as a last resort. As indicated, the factors determining the overhang values are the wheelbase, vehicle width at the sill, vehicle length, and curve radius.

For ease of design calculations, many existing systems have established simplified equations for clearance measures that reflect the particular vehicle in use. For example, the "New York City Transit (NYCT) system" has developed the center and end excess values for a 75 ft car as follows:

Center excess (CE) (in inches) = 4374 ÷ R

End excess (EE) (in inches) = 2945 ÷ R

Where R is the radius of the curve in feet

Americans with Disabilities Act requirements

The maximum gap between the platform edge and the sill at the vehicle door is established by the Americans with Disabilities Act (ADA), which states:

In stations covered by this section [10.3.1(9)], rail-to-platform height in new stations shall be coordinated with the floor height of new vehicles so that the vertical difference, measured when the vehicle is at rest, is within plus or minus 5/8 inch under normal passenger load conditions. For rapid rail, light rail, commuter rails, high speed rail, and intercity rail systems in new stations, the horizontal gap, measured when the new vehicle is at rest, shall be no greater than 3 inches. For slow moving automated guideway "people mover" transit systems, the gap in new stations shall be no greater than 1 inch.

Platform on the outside of a curve

If a platform is on the outside or "high" side of a curve, the centerline of the car will pull away from the platform edge by the center excess (CE) of the car. The doors nearest the centerline of the car will likewise move a proportional amount toward the center of the curve, away from the platform edge. In contrast, the corners of the car will move toward the platform edge by the end excess (EE) of the car, and the end doors will move a proportional amount. Both of these will have an impact on the clearance between the sill plate of the car and the platform edge.

Design standards require the designer to increase the minimum distance between the centerline of the track and the platform edge by the amount of end excess in order to maintain equipment clearance through the platform for the corners of the car. This adds to the platform gap at the door locations.

Platform on the inside of a curve

When a platform is on the inside or "low" side of a curve, the ends of the car move away from the platform and the longitudinal centerline of the car moves toward the platform edge. The NYCT MW-1 vehicle, for instance, requires that the distance between the track centerline and the platform edge be increased by the center excess to ensure equipment clearance through the platform for the center of the car. The platform gaps at the end doors are not adversely affected by the curvature; however, the platform gap at the doors nearest to the center of the car exceeds the ADA-required maximum. A curve of radius not less then 4200 ft should be used in this case to maintain the 3 in. maximum ADA platform gap.

The preceding calculations assume that there is no superelevation on the curves. The basic recommendation is to use platforms that are on tangent. To provide platform gaps within the ADA maximums, each instance of platforms in a curve must be carefully reviewed and their curvature adjusted as necessary.

Operational Impacts

Operational features can influence design significantly. For example, express or skip-stop operations, where used, result in trains running through stations at speed, causing air currents at the station that can be significant, particularly in subways. In subways, as the train approaches the station, it pushes a large volume of air ahead of it, producing a positive pressure entering the station. Similarly as it leaves the station, it pulls air after it producing a negative pressure in the station. Although these pressure cycles are relatively brief, they can cause significant damage to architectural finishes such as ceiling and wall panels, signs, lighting, and graphic elements if not properly accounted for in the structural design of connections, panel thickness, and other structural elements. The actual positive and negative pressures to be experienced are a function of the train speed approaching and leaving the station, the size of the tunnels, the station volume, and the effectiveness of the ventilation system, particularly the major vent shafts at the ends of the station for tunnel ventilation (sometimes referred to as "blast shafts"). The determination of these pressures requires specialized experience and computer models (see the earlier discussion of ventilation).

Structural Issues

Structural design considerations for at-grade and elevated structures are similar to those encountered in the design of public buildings of similar dimensions, except for the unique dynamic loading that can result from train movements into and out of a station. Starting and stopping a fully loaded train imposes significant reaction loads along the line of the tracks, particularly on elevated structures. Other loads, including wind loads, seismic loading, snow loading, and similar design load conditions, must be determined according to the specific site and location conditions, much as for any public building, and according to appropriate building codes.

The structural design of subway structures is primarily a function of the geotechnical conditions encountered at each station site and the depth and physical dimensions of the station. Soil pressures as a function of depth, soil type, and presence of groundwater are determined by the various geotechnical studies conducted as a basis of design. Particular care must be given to the junction of the tunnel structure and the outer end walls of the station to ensure a watertight joint. Similar attention must be given to other penetrations of the basic box structure, such as entrances, vent and other shafts, and utility conduits (see the previous discussion of waterproofing).

In cases involving a new start, particularly with a new agency or operator, the design team may be required to develop the design criteria that recognize the system characteristics and operating conditions. Once established, the criteria will govern the design of all structures to the maximum extent possible.

Design codes, manuals, and specifications

In addition to the design criteria set by the agency or owner, there are local codes and regulations that apply specific requirements to the design of structures and stations. In general, all design criteria will have been developed to comply with such requirements unless modifications or updates have been made. For example, seismic codes may be updated as a result of recent experience or research. In such cases, the criteria and codes must be brought into agreement. In addition,

codes and regulations are usually incorporated into the criteria by reference, and general design issues explicitly covered may be intentionally omitted from the criteria to avoid future conflicts as changes occur.

Therefore, any design condition not covered by the design criteria must comply with applicable municipal, county, state, and federal regulations and codes. For design of facilities outside the United States, the designer must become familiar with all appropriate local codes, regulations, and requirements and incorporate them into the criteria. Where these do not exist, it is suggested that the U.S. codes and requirements can provide a model.

Other design criteria and guidelines

Various governmental, quasi-governmental, and private institutes and agencies have prepared design criteria and guidelines for many issues and items not specifically covered by building codes. These criteria and guidelines are often included in the design criteria for transportation facilities by reference.

Design loads and forces

Transit structures, including stations, are subjected to a wide range of loads and forces, including erection loads. (See the sidebar on page 139.)

Construction materials

The basic structural material in underground stations is cast-in-place reinforced concrete. In some instances, for example, where the New Austrian tunneling method (NATM) is used to develop the basic station volume, reinforced shotcrete (concrete sprayed under pressure over reinforcing steel) is used to construct the primary structural walls. In

Design Loads and Forces

For loads to be included in design, include:

- Dead load (DL). Actual weight of the structure, including all permanent equipment, construction, and features.
- Live load (LL). Any nonpermanent load, including machinery, equipment, stored material, persons, transit vehicles, vertical circulation and other moving objects, construction and maintenance loads.
- Impact or dynamic effect of the live load (I). Static equivalent of the dynamic loads resulting from the vertical acceleration of the live loads.
- Centrifugal force (CF). On curves, a percentage of the transit loading per track, without impact, calculated as a function of speed and applied horizontally a set distance above the top of the low rail.
- Rolling force (RF). A percentage of the transit loading per track applied downward on one rail and upward on the other, on all tracks.
- Longitudinal force (LF). Forces resulting from trains braking and accelerating. A force equal to a set percentage of the transit loading applied longitudinally a set distance above the top of the rail. Consideration must be given to combinations of accelerating and decelerating forces where more than one track occurs.
- Horizontal earth pressure (E). The horizontal force applied to retaining structures, determined in concert with the soils engineer from geotechnical studies and including allowances for hydrostatic pressure and consideration of surcharge loads.
- Hydrostatic pressure and buoyancy (B). These forces must be determined and considered whenever the presence of groundwater is indicated. These forces are particularly critical in the case of tunnels and subway stations where buoyancy and uplift must be counteracted by the weight of the structure and backfill plus a safety factor. The designer must consider the construction sequence to ensure adequate safety against flotation during all phases of construction.
- Thermal forces (T). Thermal forces are important in the design of aerial (elevated) guideways and stations. They must be determined for concrete, steel, and composite structures and must be considered in the design of rails and fasteners. The forces are a function of the range of temperatures that can be expected in the local design area and the construction material. Provisions must be made for transverse and longitudinal forces in the rail due to temperature variations and are applied in a horizontal plane at the top of the low rail. Transverse forces occur at curves as a function of curve radius, and longitudinal forces per structure per rail are a function of the clamping force of the rail fasteners and the average length of two adjacent spans.
- Wind and seismic loads. Wind and seismic loads must be determined for the specific area where the system will be built. Wind loads are based on a specific design velocity and shape factor, and seismic loads are determined as a percentage of total loads according to the requirements for the particular seismic zone. Both loads must be considered as acting on the structure and also on the trains operating on the tracks and are applied horizontally, acting through the center of gravity. In the case of the train (the live load), the load is applied as acting as concentrated loads at the axle locations in a plane a set distance above the low rail and normal to the tracks.
- Other loads. Each design location must be considered for other loads unique to the area. These can include ice and snow loads in northern climes, stream flow and scour at columns and foundations in streambeds or flood areas, ice pressure on columns, and similar load types. The designer must determine the applicability and values for any such loads.

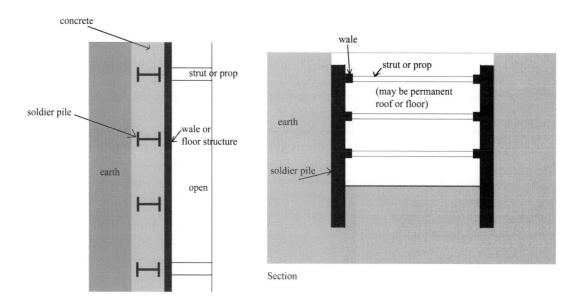

▲ SPTC used as the final perimeter wall.

the case of a soldier pile tremie concrete (SPTC) wall system, the inner structure may use structural steel beams and columns to support the various station elements, essentially a structural steel building inside a concrete shell. This approach was used in the Shot Tower/Marketplace Station in Baltimore. There is greater freedom of choice in selecting the basic structural material for elevated and at-grade stations, and both steel and reinforced concrete are common. This is an area in which the interaction between architect and engineer must consider the station context (area character, climate, adjacent development, and similar factors), and the maintenance requirements with steel construction may be a significant factor in the choice. Durability, ease of maintenance, and life-cycle costs are important issues in selecting finish materials. Materials such as granite, stainless steel, ceramic tile, and surface coats may be more expensive initially but can produce significant savings in maintenance and replacement cost.

Structural Engineering and Architectural Relationships

For the design of most buildings the architectural discipline leads the design, with the various engineering disciplines providing support. Typically, the architect will analyze the function to be served and develops the layout and spatial requirements to serve the function. The architect also establishes the building form, the criteria for the interior spaces, and the building's relationship to the surrounding environment. The engineer then develops the civil, structural, mechanical, electrical, and systems designs within the context of that concept. For the design of transit facilities and stations, the engineering issues usually play a more important role in defining most of the significant elements that influence the development of the concept. Such issues may include:

- General locations
- Relationship to the guideway
- Constraints (such as street width) on height, width, and length

- Site access and layout
- Structures supporting elevated guideways or defining underground stations

Therefore, although the architect typically leads the station design effort, the emphasis should be on a design team involving all disciplines in the formation of concepts.

The level of design control by the architect varies according to the station configuration (at-grade, aerial, or subway). For at-grade stations, once the location has been set, the architect generally assumes design leadership, much as is the case for other buildings. However, for elevated and subway stations the engineering discipline has increasingly important responsibility, particularly for subway stations. For above-grade stations, the profile and alignment of the guideway is directly influenced by the height above grade and the platform relationship to line structures on either side of the station.

For aerial stations, the structural engineer and the architect, together, address the alternatives that will have important influences on the guideway and station form, cost, and the at-grade environment. One of the most important is the support for the above grade station structure and its relationship to the above-grade guideway in the station area. The two most often used alternatives are a guideway structure through the station area that supports only the guideway, with the station supported independently—versus a structure through the station area that supports both the guideway and the station.

In the first alternative the line structure through the station area is similar or identical to the line structures on either side of the station, and the station is supported on its own columns and, in effect,

wraps around the line structure. This type of structure typically involves three lines of columns, a center column supporting the guideway and a line of columns under each side of the platform structure. This configuration is normally not used where the alignment is in a public ROW, such as a street or freeway.

The second alternative can involve either a single or double row of columns, depending on the platform arrangement. The single-line arrangement would likely be limited to a side platform, whereby the trains can be carried directly above the columns rather than at the ends of a cantilever crossbeam. Moreover, where a single-column support is considered, the use of steel for the station structure should be considered because of the potential weight savings. In that case, the guideway through the station area may still be concrete with steel structure for the platforms and station enclosure supported from bolted connections at the crossbeams atop each column. In the case of a station with an elevated center platform that requires the spreading of the tracks, resulting in two columns approaching the station, the column lines can be extended through the station and the center platform supported between them.

The structural concepts adopted for the elevated line structures throughout the system can affect station design. Those most widely used in new transit systems use concrete, although steel structures are often used for special conditions such as spans in excess of 100 ft. The most widely used concrete structures for transit guideways are the following:

- Poured-in-place concrete
- Precast concrete beams
- Segmental concrete

All of these concepts can be adapted to both single-track and double-track schemes. Moreover, all of the concepts can be adapted to a single- or double-support column. The depths of the guideway beams usually vary from 6 to 10 ft, depending on the spans and other load conditions. The poured-in-place concept is obviously constructed in the field with forms supported on the ground below. This concept has been used less frequently in recent years because of the efficiency inherent in the other two concepts.

The precast beam concept employs beams of varying lengths and similar cross section, constructed in off-site casting yards, then carried to the site and erected by cranes. The segmental concrete concept employs relatively short precast segments of the same length and identical cross section. They are cast off-site, carried to the site, and erected, usually, by a traveling crane on the guideway. The load-carrying capability (resistance to bending) is provided by post-tensioned cables inside the beam segments.

The decision to carry the general line structure concept through the station area or to discontinue the line structure at the station and provide a special support for the station obviously strongly influences the form of the station and its structural components. The use of the line structure continuing through the station, with the station structure supported from the line structure, has a desirable unifying effect. Conversely, a separately supported station structure can adapt to special site conditions and may have cost advantages.

For underground stations, the general defining factors include location, depth, width, length, and the expected construction methods. A number of nonar-

chitectural considerations are critical to this definition, such as the following:

- Tunnel profile on either side of the station
- Subway configuration (tunnel or cut-and-cover box) that influences the selection of side or center platforms
- Geologic conditions
- Operational issues (e.g., crossovers)
- Character of existing urban development and foundations
- Existing underground utilities and other existing features (e.g., rivers, underground highways, and existing subways)

These conditions will determine the depth of the station box, its width and the approximate length. The depth of the subway tunnels, the geology of the site, and the character of the existing surface development are the most important factors in determining the structural character of the underground chamber and the method of construction, as described in earlier sections of this chapter. Once the geotechnical and structural engineers establish the character of the station box and the method of construction, the architect must ensure:

- Adequate length and volume to accommodate both public and nonpublic spaces, emergency exiting, and ventilation
- Number of and concepts for entrances and their relationship to surface development and urban planning policies
- Adequate space for station wall and roof finishes and waterproofing
- Adequate space for vertical circulation facilities
- Possibility for introduction of full or partial mezzanines

There are several structural considerations that can be addressed at this point in a subway station concept development that can have significant effects on the character and quality of the completed station. The architectural team has an important role in these assessments, as discussed in the following paragraphs:

In the cut-and-cover concept the choice of the structural concept for support of excavation can affect the space available for station finishes and the usability of the space with respect to watertightness. For instance, the use of an SPTC wall excavation support system, as opposed to a plain slurry diaphragm wall with a second reinforced concrete structure built inside can have an important effect on usable station width. SPTC walls are much thinner than those provided in the double structure method. This is especially important for stations built in narrow street rights-of-way.

In the cut-and-cover concept the height of the ultimate station box, as compared with the depth of backfill, can affect spaces for mezzanines and ancillary equipment. The volume of the box and the height of the roof can also greatly affect the aesthetics of the station interior. Although the introduction of a mezzanine may seem to be a costly choice, its use as a horizontal strut often has a great advantage in reducing costs and structural requirements for station sidewalls. The choice of the structural roof system can impact the architectural quality of a station. Well-crafted structural concrete roof structures can be left exposed and illuminated, with positive architectural results. Roof structures composed largely of steel trusses usually need a hung ceiling.

Mined stations are constructed horizontally below grade and facing directly into the soil. They present some unique challenges that must be addressed jointly by the structural engineering and architectural disciplines. Mined stations are almost always constructed with an arched cross section. In addition, they require a shaft at each end, between which the mined arch is constructed. At an early stage of development the architect needs to determine the adequacy of space for mezzanines, if required, and space for ventilation ducts, and conduits for communications and lighting must test the concept. Mined stations always require an inner structure for an architectural finish. The architect and structural engineer together must consider various alternatives for structural adequacy and spatial sufficiency, as well as methods for attaching architectural finishes and lighting and communication elements.

VERTICAL CIRCULATION

Escalators and elevators are the workhorses for moving passengers safely and quickly through underground and elevated stations.

Much of the architect's level of involvement depends on whether the design is a single unit replacement, as in a station retrofit, a new station within an existing system, or a new station within a new rail system where multiple stations will occur. Some decisions are within reach of the architect; others are the responsibility of the transit authority. The design process for vertical circulation consists of the following:

- Determining the needs for vertical circulation elements (VCEs)
- Designing the proper installation
- Specifying and procuring the appropriate equipment

- Managing the correct maintenance plan
- Educating the public on the safe use of the VCEs

Stairs too are a significant component of any carefully thought-out passenger circulation plan. They are critical, reliable elements in the plan. Working in tandem with escalators and elevators, they provide the balance inherent in a reliable system.

Vertical circulation, although an international planning issue, is local in terms of codes, people's behavior, maintenance and operations, and funding. The architect must become aware of the demands of their location, then adapt designs to those conditions. For instance, the speed of an escalator varies considerably according to country. Although high speeds (120 to 180 ft per minute, fpm) seem to

▼ *Graphics are used to explain safety concerns to escalator users in the London Underground's Paddington Station. Photo: Alfred Lau.*

work well in many Asian and European countries, the practice in the United States is to slow them down (90, 100, or 125 fpm), prior to the release of the 2000 edition of the American Society of Mechanical Engineers (ASME) A17.1.1 Code. This version of the code allows a maximum of only 100 fpm, further emphasizing the code committee's view that an escalator with a lower speed greatly reduces the possibility of accidents.

Escalators

Escalators are available in several widths; the typical 40 in. unit is designed to handle at least 3000 people per hour. In a typical building, if open 10 hours per day, an average escalator could handle 30,000 people. Normally, there are not that many people, but even if each escalator carried only 3000 people per day, it would approximate 1 million riders per year. There are at least 30,000 escalators in the United States, which amounts to more than 38.5 billion riders per year. This means that the escalator industry in the United States could potentially move the entire U.S. population every two days. That is a higher frequency than achieved by the entire airline industry (Elevator Escalator Safety Foundation, 2002).

Escalators are the most effective mechanical devices for moving large numbers of people quickly between levels in a station. The expected life cycle of the transit-duty escalator is 30–35 years.

Escalators should be treated as a primary means of vertical circulation and should be provided wherever a vertical rise on the path of public circulation exceeds 16 ft. Escalators should be grouped in pairs with stairs to facilitate reverse movements during peak flows, continued circulation during breakdowns, and routine maintenance. Escalators should be reversible to accommodate A.M. and P.M. peak flows as required. For transit applications, escalators should be 48 in. wide nominal (40 in. wide at step). They should be planned as modular, interchangeable units and coordinated with stair widths for future installations, as noted earlier.

Provide 30 ft of queuing and floor space, measured from the upper and lower escalator working points, clear to any obstruction. Where escalators are located in sequence and there are no pedestrian cross flows or other obstructions to passenger movement (e.g., at intermediate landings independent of intervening passenger circulation elements), the required queuing and run-off space may be reduced by 25 percent. The minimum headroom, measured perpendicular from the nosing of the escalator tread, should be 10 ft. Provide an arm's length (3'–3' 6") clearance from the escalator handrail to any adjacent wall (or other surface) to discourage passengers from touching adjacent surfaces.

Escalators must be protected from the weather to safeguard the mechanical equipment and ensure passenger comfort and safety.

Consideration should be given to routine maintenance and replacement of escalators and escalator equipment. Escalators should be designed so that routine operations and maintenance can be easily performed without disrupting normal station operations. Provisions should be made for replacing the escalator treads, motors, trusses, drive mechanisms, and so forth, as required after their effective life.

Sizes

Escalators come in three nominal widths: 24, 32, and 40 in. The vertical rise of an escalator is basically unlimited, up to approximately 150 ft. However, a vertical rise below 16 ft should be avoided; instead, rely on stairs. The actual planned width dimensions of escalators should be near 5' 9" for low and medium rises and 5' 10" for high rises. Units employing external drives may require greater widths. Widths of up to 6' 6", dependent on rise and step loading, are not uncommon. Consult with the manufacturer and closely review the standards of the transit authority, if available.

Types

Escalators are available in two basic types: commercial and heavy-duty (HD) transit. Several manufacturers now offer the heavy-duty type. In addition, escalators are available as solid metal balustrade or glass types. Although solid balustrades are usable in all locations, it is recommended that glass be used in platform-to-mezzanine configurations in underground stations. There is an architectural benefit due to visual transparency. Glass also offers a wider clear inside escalator width and may be beneficial particularly in stations where passengers are carrying luggage. Glass is also more cost-effective, but requires stocking replacement glass in sizes needed to fit all conditions.

Incline

Escalators in the United States are manufactured to a standard 30-degree incline. Asian and European countries use similar angles, but escalators there are also manufactured to other angles, such as $22\frac{1}{2}$ degrees.

▶▶ *Short rise stairs are a cost effective and reliable alternative to escalators on short rises. Baltimore Metro Shot Tower Station, DKP Joint Venture.*

Speed and passenger-carrying capacity

Escalator speed in the United States is established by code, which must be adhered to. The common speeds and their potential for carrying passengers are as follows:

90 fpm—up to 60 passengers per minute

100 fpm—up to 70 passengers per minute

120 fpm*—up to 80 passengers per minute

Although many manufacturers report great passenger-handling capacity for their escalators, the best practice is to be conservative in estimating potential passenger movement. Many factors, such as escalator downtime for activation of safety devices, equipment failure, vandalism, scheduled repairs, and so forth, affect their capacity to carry passengers. For instance, in stations where the typical passenger is over the age of 50 or very young, has various degrees of mobility impairment, or is dealing with simultaneous hand, foot, and eye coordination, the units should be run at 90 fpm.

Cost

See the table on page 148 for an approximate construction cost estimate for escalators. The estimate is in 2002 US dollars and includes the cost of the unit delivered and installed, including the contractor's overhead and profit. These amounts are for general planning and budgeting purposes and vary depending on location, specification features, and bidding climate.

Escalator types according to rise

Escalators and escalator wellways can be divided into the following classes, based on the vertical rise between working points:

Low—rise of 20 ft or less

Moderate—rise of more than 20–60 ft

High—rise of more than 60 ft

Flat steps

The following minimum number of flat steps at the top and bottom of each escalator should be provided:

Low—2 steps

Moderate—3 steps

High—4 steps

Safety features

An escalator has a multitude of safety devices that bring it to a reasonably smooth stop. Codes define this stopping distance parameter at a constant 3 ft/sec^2, with the stopping distance dependent on the escalator's speed. Although the average passenger is aware only of the emergency stop button located at the top and bottom, right side, on the upper radius of the handrail newel, there are approximately 11 other safety devices.

Codes

All escalators in the United States are manufactured and installed to be in compliance with the American National Standards Institute (ANSI) *Safety Code for Elevators and Escalators,* ASME A17.1.1. Although all the states use ASME A17.1.1, they do not use as a standard the most recent version of that code, the 2000 amended edition. Some states still use the

---

*100 fpm is maximum speed permitted by ASME A17.1, 2000 edition; however, some states permit higher speeds up to a maximum of 125 fpm because they have not yet adopted the recent 2000 amended edition.

1976 and 1987 amended versions, so it is imperative to establish the year of the governing code. NFPA 130, *Standard for Fixed Guideway Transit and Passenger Rail Systems,* determines passenger egress. It limits the number of escalators that can be counted toward the required exit width. Generally, it restricts the designer's calculation so that no more then one-half of the exiting requirements, minus one escalator unit, can be escalators. It is important to be familiar with the latest edition of the code (applicable to the local jurisdiction), because this standard is in NFPA committee and may be revised. For escalators to function in the proper exiting direction, they must be controlled by the station agent. See "Controls, Operation, and Maintenance" on page 149.

The American Public Transportation Association's (APTA) *Heavy-Duty Escalator Draft Guidelines* (November 2001), is expected to be adopted soon and will provide an escalator tailored to transit needs and may exceed most code requirements.

Lighting

See Chapter 10 for specific guidelines for illuminating elements of an escalator-stair bank. Although even distribution of light levels along the length of these elements is important, the critical stage of approaching an escalator-stair bank and taking the first step is when many accidents occur. For this reason the top and bottom "transition" zones are critical and should be more brightly illuminated than the surrounding floor surfaces. Although lights can be installed in one or both sides of an escalator, the majority of transit authorities do not select this option because it becomes an object of constant maintenance and vandalism.

Description of operation

SAFETY DEVICES

The safety devices (1-12 below) bring the escalator to a smooth stop under full load, and lock out starting devices until the fault condition is cleared. A fault indication panel is provided for the safety devices to assist in troubleshooting. The controller circuit can be reset by the key stations only when fault conditions are cleared.

- ❑ Emergency stop button (1)
- ❑ Handrail inlet monitors (2)
- ❑ Combplate impact device (3)
- ❑ Broken step-chain switch (4)

- ❑ Speed monitors (5)
- ❑ Brake adjust & release monitors (6)
- ❑ Step-sag monitor (7)
- ❑ Step-lift monitor (8)
- ❑ Missing step monitor (9)
- ❑ Broken handrail monitor (10)
- ❑ Handrail speed monitor (11)
- ❑ Skirt monitor (12)
- ❑ Step band lock (13)
- ❑ Controller main switch (14)
- ❑ Key start switch (15)
  80-G04 (11/99)

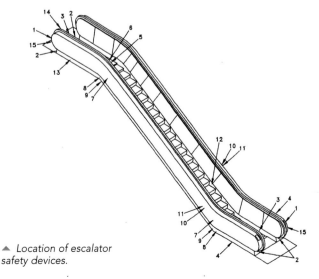

▲ Location of escalator safety devices.

ESCALATOR UNIT PRICE SUMMARY*			
	Escalator Vertical Rise (ft)	Price per Foot of Rise ($)	Escalator Unit Price ($)
Low Rise	12.0	21,000	252,000
	14.0	21,000	294,000
	16.0	21,000	336,000
	18.0	21,000	378,000
Mid-Rise	20.0	18,000	360,000
	22.0	18,000	396,000
	24.0	18,000	432,000
	26.0	18,000	468,000
	28.0	18,000	504,000
	30.0	18,000	540,000
	32.0	18,000	576,000
	34.0	18,000	612,000
	36.0	18,000	648,000
	38.0	18,000	684,000
	40.0	18,000	720,000
	42.0	18,000	756,000
	44.0	18,000	792,000
	46.0	18,000	828,000
	48.0	18,000	864,000
High Rise	50.0	15,000	750,000
	52.0	15,000	780,000
	54.0	15,000	810,000
	56.0	15,000	840,000
	58.0	15,000	870,000
	60.0	15,000	900,000
	62.0	15,000	930,000
	64.0	15,000	960,000
	66.0	15,000	990,000
	68.0	15,000	1,020,000
	70.0	15,000	1,050,000
	72.0	15,000	1,080,000
	74.0	15,000	1,110,000
	76.0	15,000	1,140,000

*Heavy-duty transit escalators
Note: Unit price includes overheat and profit.

Manufacturing Costs	Low Rise	Mid-Rise	High Rise
Labor (20%)	$4,200	$3,600	$3,000
Material (45%)	9,450	8,100	6,750
Installation Cost	7,350	6,300	5,250
Labor (35%)	21,000	18,000	15,000

Weather protection

Critical to the integrity of an escalator is overhead weather protection, particularly in the colder climates subject to snow and hail and the use of deicing salts. Consider enclosing escalators with four walls and a roof enclosure. Canopies are required by A17.1. It is considered good design practice to have the distance from the working point to the limit of side and roof closure equal to the queuing distance and a minimum of 20 ft. If there is a remote machine room at the same location, roof coverage should be added over the greatest dimension to ensure a watertight room. Provide natural or mechanical ventilation to compensate for heat buildup during warmer weather.

Queuing distances.

See "Station Design Guidelines" in Chapter 1, which describe the minimum distances for locating an escalator in a primary circulation path. Many variables (escalator speed, number of flat steps, etc.) affect the actual distance to be used in determining the safe queuing distance required. It is more important to provide the total number of escalators needed than just the proper queuing distance. If, for instance, a passenger flow analysis de-

termines that three escalators are needed to move passengers off a platform in 45 seconds and only two escalators are provided, chances are that passengers will have an increased waiting time and, furthermore, by the time the next train arrives, it could add more passengers to the platform, resulting in a potentially unsafe condition.

Controls, operations, and maintenance

The provision of service and preventive maintenance schedules is usually specified in the manufacturer's operation and maintenance manual. This manual includes charts that list all items to be checked on the escalator, categorized as "Every Visit," including the service brake, drive station, drive motor, return station, automatic oiler, step band, steps, skirts, comb segments, and handrail guides.

Remote stopping

Automatic controls for escalator operation are not permitted in the United States. In Europe, escalators provided with visual or closed-circuit television (CCTV) observation can be controlled remotely. In U.S. systems, action is required on the part of the station agent to reverse direction between peak passenger

▲ Roof coverage over escalators is crucial to maintaining escalators in good working condition. Currently required by A17.1 Code. John Hopkins Hospital Station on Baltimore Metro. DKP Joint Venture.

Control and indication at station control center

Station control centers should be equipped with controls to enable the station agent, during an emergency, to stop all inbound-traveling escalators. A visual display of escalator status should be provided at the station control center. The functions shown should be as follows:

- Direction of travel

- Out-of-service indication

- Indication that the escalator has stopped because of the activation of a safety device

Design

Certain planning procedures for dimensional sizing should be followed in designing an escalator wellway and pits, allowing a minimum of three manufacturers of heavy-duty units to bid. A transit escalator can have either a 32 in. or 40 in. clear step width. A 24 in. escalator cannot be used in new stations or additions because it does not comply with the ADA requirement for a 32 in. minimum. A 40 in. clear step escalator is normally preferred, because it allows two lanes of passenger flow, but the sizing selection must be closely coordinated with the NFPA 130 *Egress Analysis* to avoid overcrowding of established egress paths. The steps for obtaining adequate escalator dimensions are as follows:

- Obtain heavy-duty dimension product data sheets.

- Make a comparison chart of all the critical dimensions.

- Select the largest dimension from each category, and use this string of dimensions for planning the wellway and pits.

conditions or in emergencies. This requires the agent to leave his or her post. In high-volume passenger stations provisions should be made to have additional staff perform the daily change in reversing the direction of escalators. The agent can also restart a unit that has been stopped by the emergency stop button.

Storage space

In stations with large passenger volumes that include many escalators, adequate storage space with access from the street must be provided to accommodate parts and tools for maintenance of the escalators. In underground stations, an equipment/parts delivery path should be determined to ensure that heavy replacement parts have sufficient access to the storage area and between vertical levels. Parts and tools should never be transported down an escalator. Designated service or freight elevators should be designed to carry heavy replacement parts.

- Make sure the overall dimension reflects whether the controller is within the top pit or remote and that the proper number of flat steps, dependent on rise, is used.

- Escalator rises exceeding 16–18 ft normally require an intermediate support, and to avoid including this support for rises up to 19–20 ft, some manufacturers provide truss stiffeners, which adds another 8–12 in. to the rough opening.

Circulation

In countries where pedestrian movements are the same as their automobile traffic movements, right-handed in the case of the United States, place escalators so that the passenger, when facing a vertical ascent, will have at his or her right side an available escalator. In the event that the first right-hand escalator is out of service, the priority for escalator service remains with the passenger ascending; therefore, the next escalator in line is provided (reversed if necessary) to that person. Thus, looking at a typical bank of two escalators and a stair, the arrangement will place the elements as a person faces them from the lower level from right to left: escalator, escalator, and stair.

Vertical rise

Where the vertical rise between levels does not exceed 36 ft, two reversible escalators and a stair should be provided. The calculation of normal service capacity is based on one escalator operating in each direction. When one escalator is out of service, the stair should serve the descending patronage. In situations where peak-minute patronage demand does not exceed the escalator patronage flow capacity, a single escalator and two stairs may be provided; however, stairs should be designed for future replacement by an escalator.

Where the vertical rise between levels exceeds 36 ft, a third escalator should be provided to serve as backup for both up and down escalators. A stair (if required by NFPA 130) should provide emergency exiting capacity only and should not count in the calculation of normal service. The stair should not be in the basic vertical circulation element bank, but designed as a separate nonpublic emergency egress stair.

▲ Scissor arrangement of escalators is an effective means in which to deliver passengers along the length of the platform. Charles Center Station, Baltimore Metro. RTKL Architects. DMJM+Kaiser JV.

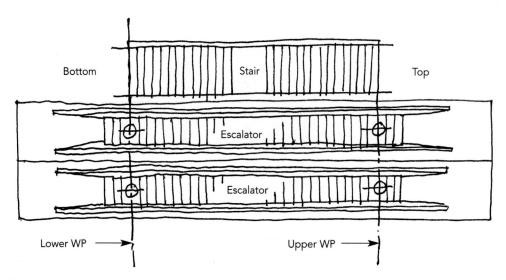

Bottom · Stair · Top

Escalator

Escalator

Lower WP · Upper WP

▲ *Plan of basic stair/escalator arrangement (right hand circulation).*

Several major transit authorities are currently revising their planning criteria for escalators to require that the maximum vertical rise for any installation does not exceed 30 ft. This means that deep-rise installations will be subdivided to include landings. The advantage is that in the event of an escalator failure, the passenger can take an alternate escalator at a landing. The disadvantage is that by subdividing the escalator rise, there is an increase in the passenger's chance of falling, because of the additional transfer level; the number of escalators, thereby increasing the failure rate; the number of units requiring maintenance; equipment cost; and construction cost. When two escalators are placed directly in line with one another, the code requires an interlock so that when one escalator is shut down the other automatically stops. This is done to eliminate a safety hazard due to passengers not having the service of the first escalator, causing them to move to another unit or crowd onto a mezzanine.

Other concerns

- 30-degree slope of escalator and adjacent stair with floors level and on slope (see the sketches at right)
- Redundancy—stair/escalator/escalator
- Weather protection
- Circulation issues/queuing
- Motor and control mechanism

The drive motor and drive mechanism can be located within the truss zone in the upper landing space or in a remote room below the upper landing, as classified by the following escalator types:

Low-rise escalators. The drive mechanism and motor can be located within the truss.

Medium and high-rise escalators. The drive mechanism and motor can be located either in the truss space at the upper landing or in a separate machine room.

Several well-established major transit agencies in the United States, Asia, and Europe believe that remote machine

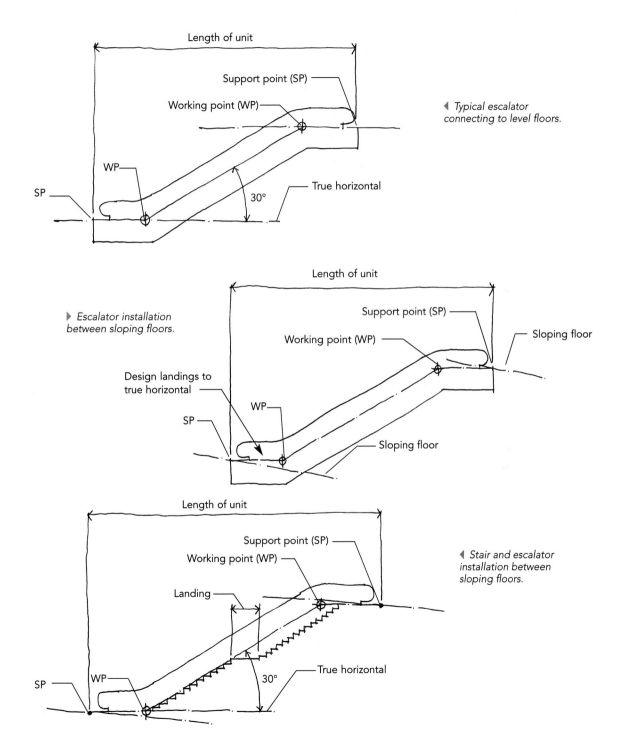

Length of unit

Support point (SP)

Working point (WP)

WP

SP

30°

True horizontal

◀ *Typical escalator connecting to level floors.*

Length of unit

▶ *Escalator installation between sloping floors.*

Support point (SP)

Working point (WP)

Sloping floor

Design landings to true horizontal

WP

SP

Sloping floor

Length of unit

Support point (SP)

Working point (WP)

Landing

WP

SP

30°

True horizontal

◀ *Stair and escalator installation between sloping floors.*

153

Escalator Specifications Summary

- Truss. Structural steel construction, hot-dip galvanized, AWS certified welding, and galvanized drip pans. The deflection of the loaded truss must not exceed one-thousandth (1/1000) of the free supporting distance of not less than 50 ft under full static load, including live load of 320 lb per 40 in. step and 256 lb per 32 in. step, instead of the 1/750 commercial grade requirement per ASME A17.1.
- Step chains. Precision roller chains, matched sets, not less than 4" rollers with sealed bearings, automatic lubricator, and tension carriage with dual springs.
- Steps. Certified for 674 lb loading, not less than 4 in. rollers with sealed bearings, spring clamp attachment to step chain shafts, die-cast aluminum with demarcation.
- Step loading. 320 lb per step, instead of A17.1 requirement of 192 lb for a 40 in. clear step width.
- Balustrade. All Type 316 stainless steel (see Chapter 8, "Materials and Finishes") or safety glass, skirt safety brushes, aluminum landing plates, running direction lights.
- Handrail. Indoor/outdoor type, traction-drive sheave, return roller guides, newel rollers/wheels.
- Drive machines. Acoustically quiet worm or helical gearbox, braking-code deceleration/stop distance, totally enclosed fan-cooled motors.
- Control features. Programmable logic controller (PLC), soft start, inspection speed, maintenance control station, National Electrical Manufacturers Association (NEMA) 3R or 4.

rooms for all escalators are vital to long-term maintenance and reliability. Escalator machine room sizes vary with the manufacturer. Basic planning suggests an allowance of 9 ft vertical height, 15 ft depth from support point to wall (away from the truss), and a width of 4 ft in addition to the escalator unit dimension. Access to a remote machine room requires either a floor access door located over the machine room (within the limits of the escalator) or a remote stair. Access doors located in the floor cause the greatest amount of concern for safety to passengers while the door is open for use. In multiple banks of escalators a remote stair, out of the main passenger flow path, is recommended. The following are major points for comparing internal- and external-drive machine rooms:

Advantages to external drive

- Allows passenger flow when the unit is having select types of maintenance work performed within the machine room—unit may be out of service or operating.
- Improved accessibility to equipment during maintenance or replacement.
- Reduced long-term operating costs.

Disadvantages

- Machine rooms may significantly reduce the circulation space on a platform if the distance from platform to mezzanine is shallow.
- The floor access hatch to the machine room requires space to one side of the escalator.
- Increased initial construction costs.

Specifications

Several manufacturers are producing heavy-duty transit escalators. The best resource for specifying these units is the American Public Transportation Association (APTA). Stringent requirements are established, as summarized in the sidebar at left.

Procurement

The goal is to procure high-quality heavy-duty transit-type escalators, procure them from the same manufacturer, and have consistent parts and uniform maintenance procedures to help ensure a long service life.

Scenarios that may affect a station design

Option 1. Procure each escalator with the station contract. If the project is a new stand-alone or a retrofit stand-alone station contract, the designer has little influence over system-wide equipment consistency. Work with the transit agency and design/specify a unit that is of the highest affordable quality and consistent with the previously described escalator features. This may also be an opportunity to establish a new system-wide high quality standard for future escalators.

Option 2. Procure all escalators in a single contract (lump sum or unit price), and furnish-install on future station contracts. In this scenario, all units are purchased with a single contract and delivered to stations as the construction schedule dictates. The escalator manufacturer is made responsible for designing, fabricating, installing, and maintaining all units over the duration of the construction period. The most vulnerable stage of an escalator installation is after the unit is installed but the system or station is still being completed.

Elevators

Like escalators, elevators have developed a reputation in the transit industry as a source of maintenance problems. This is due to a history of using basic commercial-quality equipment and not providing for the heavy use, exposure to weather, and high abuse to which many transit stations are subjected.

Basic data

Hydraulic elevator systems consist of a machine room, a car, doors, a controller, an in-ground plunger or holeless jacks, rails, and a pump unit as their main components. The rack and pinion elevator was developed in the 1960s and until recently was used strictly for the construction industry. Its basic system components are similar to those of the hydraulic elevator, except for the plunger or jack and the pump unit and car rails.

Sizes

Car interiors should be designed using minimum sizes/configurations complying with ADA requirements as a base to accommodate individuals who are physically disabled, while increasing the car size dependent on the expected traffic use: Most states have their own elevator codes or modifications of ASME A17.1 and their own design standards for accessibility. Therefore, thorough code documentation is necessary to establish the car size. The following sizes are per ADA requirements:

- Two-speed entry car door requires a minimum 4'3"D × 5'8"W car, 2000 lb capacity.
- Center-opening car door requires a minimum 4'3"D × 6'8"W car, 2500 lb capacity.

- Two-speed entry elongated hospital car door requires a minimum 6'8"D × 4'6"W car, 3000 lb capacity

Car interiors may also be designed for use in emergency medical service (EMS) and in some cases as necessary per the local governing code. The car sizes shown to accommodate ADA do not include sizing for a gurney. Good station planning suggests that gurney-sized car interiors be used in underground or tall aerial stations where the landing distance exceeds two levels of travel or 36 ft.

When considering a gurney-sized car the following figures are helpful in determining minimum car sizes:

- Figure B, below, illustrates for center opening doors the minimal car size that allows an EMT gurney.

- Figure C, below right, illustrates for two-speed slide doors the minimal car size that allows an EMT gurney.

- Figure A illustrates for two-speed elongated hospital car doors the minimal car size that allows an EMT gurney.

Door sizes

Doors should be designed to accommodate wide pieces of equipment in addition to wheelchairs (minimum 36 in.). Although ASME A17.1.1 requires a minimum height of 6'8", other station criteria must be considered, which may include

▼Typical elevator car sizes that allow an EMT gurney.

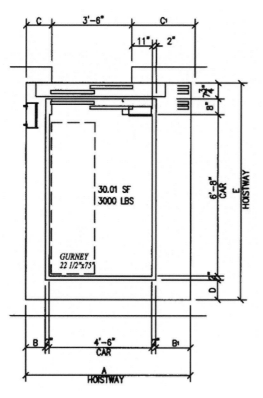

Figure A

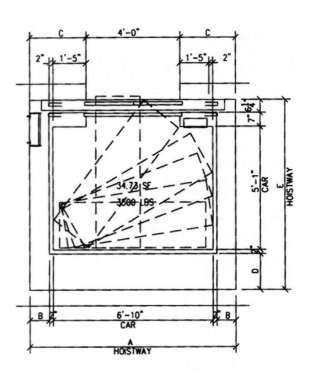

Figure B

the handling of tall objects such as cleaning equipment and telescopic lifts (requiring a minimum door height of 90 in.).

Types

Hydraulic elevator. A powered elevator in which the energy is applied, by means of a liquid under pressure, in a hydraulic jack. Hydraulic elevator types include in-ground plungers; the holeless elevator is offered in a selection of one- or two-stage jacks and a roped hydro. The selection of hydraulic type is governed by the total travel distance.

In-ground plunger. Has a travel limitation of approximately 50 ft, but which, when used in a transit application, should not exceed 40 ft. The 40 ft limitation is a guideline established by APTA in its *Heavy-Duty Guidelines,* which is expected to be released to the public at the end of 2003.

Holeless hydraulic. As a rule of thumb, a holeless one-stage jack travels 14 ft, a two-stage jack travels up to 22 ft, and a roped hydro must be used for travel distances greater than 22 ft up to 90 ft.

Roped hydraulic. A power elevator in which the energy is applied by a roped hydraulic driving machine.

Rack and pinion. A power elevator, with or without a counterweight, that is supported, raised, and lowered by a motor or motors that drive a pinion or pinions on a stationary rack mounted in the hoistway.

Speed and passenger carrying capacity

Hydraulic elevator speeds range from 90 fpm to 150 fpm. Although a higher speed of 200 fpm is available, it is not recommended for transit use. Speeds of this magnitude should be accomplished with a traction or rack-and-pinion type elevator. The APTA *Heavy-Duty Elevator Guideline Specification* (near the end of its draft version, with a probable public release at the end of 2003) recommends a speed of 100 fpm for travels up to 40 ft. Capacities range from 1,500 lb to 10,000 lb and up for hydraulic elevators. The higher capacities are achieved by use of multiple in-ground cylinders or multiple jacks for a holeless application.

The rack-and-pinion drive machine maximum speed is approximately 330 fpm with a capacity of 8,000 lb.

Safety features

The primary safety features that passengers are aware of include emergency communication, an alarm bell, safety rays on the door(s), firefighters' service, and emergency power. Those safety features behind the scenes include an overspeed

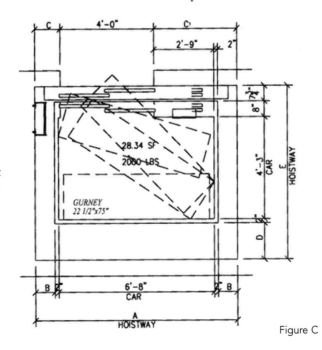

Figure C

device for in-ground or holeless one- and two-stage jacks, pipe rupture valves, a governor overspeed device for roped hydraulic elevators, and slack rope devices that stop the elevator when activated.

Codes

The majority of all states have accepted the national code of ASME A17.1, *Safety Code for Elevators and Escalators*. The designer must be aware that the most recent code is not necessarily the edition in effect, as this varies from state to state. Although a state may adopt a specific year of the ASME A17.1, it usually incorporates that state's version of modifications to that code. The reason a state is so selective in adopting a specific year of edition is its impact on existing equipment, and new editions may not allow a project to comply with the more stringent code. Although new construction could comply, it would not be to the state's advantage to have two codes. Therefore, the designer must be familiar with the most recent edition of the code.

Passenger security issues

- Glazing of the car and hoistway at all levels served by the elevator
- CCTV coverage of the car and at landings
- Emergency communication phones in the car connecting to the station control center

Elevators as a means of evacuation

Historically, elevators have always been designed per code to shut down to the public with the activation of the fire alarm system in the elevator machine room, lobby, and hoistway that initiates the operation of firefighters' service. In some codes it states that where a power outage occurs it requires an evacuation for individuals with impaired mobility and the code allows the use of an elevator as a means of evacuation. Many state and national codes now accept the use of elevators during an evacuation when the building is required to have an "accessible means of egress."

Lighting

Code requires a minimum illumination of 5 footcandles (fc) at the elevator floor level, whereas some transit authorities have a 25 fc requirement. The higher level is better suited for making a passenger feel more comfortable in terms of security and better for addressing the reading/operation of the car opening panel (COP). Lighting placement is best when it is recessed in the ceiling and has a vandal-resistant lens. The selection of lighting that has a long life is necessary to minimize maintenance.

ADA issues

Section 4 of ADA provides minimum guidelines on car sizes for cars with center-opening and two-speed slide doors; on placement, height, and identification criteria for car and hall fixtures; on communication; and on door sizes. The COP requirement for height consists of a minimum of 35 in. and a maximum of 48 in. (not 54 in.) for the operating/signal buttons, and their identification must be in braille and alphanumeric characters to the left of the buttons and floor descriptions, when necessary, to the right of the buttons. The maximum height of car buttons shown in ADA regulations is 54 in., but this was overruled by a court decision in the Little People of America discrimination suit. The ADA regulations in Section 10 are specific for transit facilities and must also be used in conjunction with Section 4. As with the elevator code, they must also be used with the requirements of the local governing authority for accessibility.

Queuing distances

Elevator planning of the queuing area for elevators relies on experience of past installations, which suggests that the transfer area directly in front of a one- or two-car bank, with elevators adjacent to each other, should not be less than 1.5 times the car interior depth; if the cars are opposite each other, the separation should be 2.0 times the car interior depth. In transit facilities, the transfer area should be generous to accommodate the passenger flows and the possibly higher concentration of baby strollers and passengers with impaired mobility. The transfer area in low-rise applications is likely not to have a high volume of passengers, because it is generally quicker to take the stairs or escalator to the upper level so a minimum queuing space is recommended. Applications that have a higher rise (20 ft or more) require close consideration of passengers exiting a car and those waiting for an elevator; an ellipse area of 7 sq ft per person is adequate for planning the queuing space. The higher-rise elevators generally have a larger capacity, anticipating that a higher density of passengers will use this means of transportation because it is convenient, more direct, and without interruptions.

Transparency of car and hoistway

If the governing authority adopts NFPA 130, it generally allows the use of glass in the hoistway and car, providing the passengers with a better sense of security with the car's transparency. The use of glass also eliminates the solidness of the hoistway, allowing greater transparency across the platforms.

Controls, operations, and maintenance

See also the discussion in regard to escalators under "Controls, Operations, and Maintenance" on page 149.

Control and indication at station control center

A station control center should be equipped with a global or per-station public address (PA) system, reaching each car for emergency notifications. A visual display of elevator status should be provided at the station control.

Fire deptartment use

All elevators should be designed with firefighters' service. Depending on which version of the A17.1 Code is used, those traveling more than 25 ft require this service; the 2000 version of A17.1, for instance, requires all elevators to have this feature. Firefighters' service consists of Phase 1 and Phase 2 operation. Phase 1 operation consists of the elevator(s) being automatically recalled to the designated main level without stopping at any hall or car dispatch requests, automatically unlocking any car or hall security lockout feature, opening the car's doors and shutting it down. The *main* designated level is the level at which the firefighters would enter the station in response to a fire alarm.

Phase 2 operation is in effect when the firefighters arrive at the station and enter a car already in Phase 1 and use their firefighters' key in the COP to travel to any floor.

Design

The construction of new transit stations or additions to stations having elevators allows greater flexibility in designing the car size and selecting the elevator type to fit the requirements of the application, than retrofitting a new elevator in an existing station. New elevators placed within an existing station generally include limitations to the design due to associated costs as a result of structural modifications to construct the hoistway. Therefore, the best location for an elevator is not always possible because of some form of existing limitation. It is good practice to have sufficient knowledge of the elevator code to ensure that hoistway projections and recesses, machine room equipment clearances, and equipment access conform to code requirements. When adequate funding is available, the designer should strategically place the elevator for maximum utilization. Prioritizing the design steps includes determining the capacity (gurney accessibility, desired movement of anticipated number of people) and selecting the elevator type, based on design requirements and equipment capabilities.

Location

Most transit authorities have been reluctant to provide more than one elevator from street level to mezzanine or platform levels because of cost, maintenance, and security concerns.

All stations (aerial or underground) should have at least two elevators providing vertical access between each two levels of a station. This is to ensure redundancy, so that in the event of equipment failure or scheduled repair there is a backup elevator. For instance, an aerial station with an intermediate mezzanine (used for fare collection) should have two elevators connecting the street level to the free area of the mezzanine and two independent elevators connecting the paid area of the mezzanine to the platform level. In the event that there is an entrance at both ends of the station, one elevator to the street and one to the platform would serve each entrance. Whenever possible, elevators should be placed contiguous with the main stair-escalator banks so that entrances are in the primary circulation path and readily identifiable.

Several transit authorities have policies regarding the location of escalators on platforms in close visual proximity to the train conductor. If the conductor is positioned in the center of the train, then the elevators should be positioned accordingly. Lacking any predetermined criteria for placing them on the platform, the guideline should be to locate them at one-quarter points along the platform length so that the handicapped travel distance is minimized to one-quarter of the platform length. In the event of an end-loaded platform, the elevators should be near the main stair-escalator bank.

If elevators land at a mezzanine level with a fare collection system and a station agent's booth, then the location of the elevators should be in visual proximity to the agent's booth to ensure the safety and security of the passengers.

Weather protection

Elevators that have landings at street level without cover should have their own canopies that project out from the hoistway face, over the door, a minimum of 6 ft. with and a width of 8 ft. This provides protection from the rain for those waiting and a transitioning dry zone for those leaving a car in rainy weather.

Snow melting provisions are also necessary. A snow melting system should be incorporated into the sidewalk areas in front of the elevator hoistway door at exterior landings in cold weather climates. This system should be a minimum of 8 ft wide and extend to the nearest street curb, or at least 20 ft. A door threshold heater enhances door operation and minimizes downtime.

Hoistways

In deep underground stations having landing stops greater than 36 ft, an emergency access door allows firefighters to remove stranded passengers, as required by A17.1. This requires an independent stair or an adjacent elevator sharing the same hoistway, which is very costly. Factor this into the design, particularly if the subsurface is rock and the cost to construct an enlarged shaft may greatly influence the decision regarding numbers of elevators to be used and their location.

Machine rooms

Locating and determining the minimum size of an elevator machine room may be the biggest challenge in designing an elevator system. The best choice is usually to locate it on the mezzanine level or in an ancillary area. In the case of hydraulic elevators, the best location for the machine room is adjacent to the hoistway; when a remote machine room is required, its remoteness should be kept at a minimum so that equipment efficiency and operation will not be sacrificed.

Specifications

Generally, the transit authority requires the designer to use its master specification as the design base, relying on the designer's edit to meet the project conditions;

equipment changes can be allowed if a waiver is issued by the transit authority. With an available master specification, the designer has a good foundation on which to develop the bid document. It becomes more of a challenge to the designer when there is no standard specification by the transit authority. The master elevator specifications' accurate description of what is required for the elevator system and its components generally requires the installed products to be of the highest quality. The expected release of the APTA *Heavy-Duty Elevator Specification Guidelines* (low-rise applications) will provide those transit authorities already having a master specification an opportunity to update, and those not having a master an opportunity to adopt a base for their own master specifications.

Procurement

See "Procurement," in regard to escalators, on page 155.

Stairs

Public stairs

Because of the safety hazards and energy expenditure associated with people moving on a stairway, designers must be particularly cognizant of the pedestrian behaviors and traffic patterns of passengers on stairways in transit stations. The following factors should be considered in the design of public stairs:

- Public stairs should be located so as to be visible and easily identifiable as a means of access to the levels they connect.

- Adequate queuing and runoff space must be provided at the top and bottom of all stairs. Public stairs should have a minimum 30 ft clear distance (same as for an escalator) to any ob-

Open risers are encouraged to maintain visual transparency and improve safety. London Jubilee Line. Photo: Alfred Lau.

the stair. Runnels along the stair sides should be used to facilitate cleaning and drainage.

- Stair elements (riser, tread, and railing configurations) should be designed to assist human locomotion, particularly for persons with impaired mobility.

Stairs can be used as the primary mode of vertical circulation where the vertical rise between levels is less than 16 ft. Stairs are recommended as the primary mode for the downward movement of passengers where the vertical rise between levels is less than 20 ft. Stairs should not be used as a means of normal public access (as distinguished from emergency egress) where the vertical rise between levels discourages normal use by healthy passengers.

Wherever practicable, all public stairs should be planned using a standard modular width, including installation and construction tolerances, and designed to facilitate possible replacement with an escalator in the future. To achieve this requires designing the stair using a modular stringer with bolted connections at the same points where an escalator would normally be supported. All clearances around the stair should be equal to those of a finished escalator installation. This requirement also extends to the escalator machine rooms. The machine room space should be designed for the event when all stairs in a vertical circulation bank are converted, so that machinery, motors, chains, and so forth, have the required clearances and transitioning to an escalator does not require major structural conversions. Where stairs are planned alongside escalators, or planned for replacement with escalators in the future, they should be designed so that the slope of the stair

struction at the top and bottom of the stairs.

- Provide a minimum clear distance of 10 ft measured perpendicular from the nosing of the stair tread to any overhead obstruction for headroom along the stairway.

- Where stairs are planned alongside escalators, use the most stringent clearances, depending on which unit is the most forward (typically the escalator).

- The stairway must be well lit.

- Provisions should be made to facilitate the maintenance and cleaning of matches the 30-degree slope of an escalator. Where the floor-to-floor height of the stair may create problems in plan due to the long run of the stair, the designer may consider increasing the angle of individual flights and aligning the landings with the slope of the escalator.

Basic data

The reader is directed to "Station Design Guidelines" in Chapter 1 for additional data on stair planning.

Sizes

Public stairs should be a nominal 60 in. wide (between handrails), with actual stair width compatible with an escalator unit (5 ft 9 in.).

Emergency exit stairs

- Provided from each platform end (side and center platform)
- Quantity and size determined on the basis of NFPA 130 exiting analysis
- Preferred configuration: scissor type, two per platform end

MECHANICAL CONSIDERATIONS

The modern underground railway system has a number of mechanical elements, both passive and active, to improve the comfort and safety of passengers. In the United States, the National Fire Protection Association (NFPA), in *Standard NFPA 130, Standard for Fixed Guideway Transit and Passenger Rail Systems,* documents life safety criteria. This standard has generally been adopted worldwide, with minor variations to accommodate local practice.

Elements to improve the comfort and safety of passengers include the following:

- Piston relief shafts
- Fan systems for smoke control

- Fan systems to provide adequate fresh air and improve the station environment.

▲ *Deep rise stairs are to be considered as back-up devices only to escalators when out-of-service.*

Piston Relief Shafts

As a train passes through a tunnel, it pushes a mass of air ahead of it. This mass of air is caused by the effect of the train moving through a limited area, namely, the tunnel itself. To balance the pressures generated, a similar column of air is induced behind the train. This effect is similar to that of a piston moving in a cylinder and is referred to as the *piston effect.* The amount of the piston effect is principally related to the blockage ratio (the cross-sectional area of the train relative to the cross-sectional area of the tunnel) and the speed of the train.

As a train approaches a station, the piston effect can cause high air velocities at platform level, which may result in unsafe conditions for any passengers standing near the platform edge and can cause aural discomfort due to the effect of the passage of the induced pressure wave. If the pressure wave is not mitigated, it will then create airflows through the mezzanine levels and entranceways that will cause dust and dirt to flow through the station. Historically, many methods have been tried to relieve the piston effect, including the use of numerous sidewalk gratings and mid-tunnel shafts. The current approach, and the most effective, is to construct piston relief shafts from the running tunnels to the surface close to the station box at each end of the station. As the train approaches the piston relief shaft, air flows through the shaft, thereby reducing the size of the pressure wave in front of the train to the extent that it has minimal effect at the station. Similarly, after the train passes the piston relief shaft, air is pulled back into the tunnel system. This action has the effect of exchanging air with the surface and assists in keeping the tunnel environment ac-

ceptable as well as relieving the piston effect pressures.

It is possible to increase these effects by combining the shafts. It is generally restricted to tunnels that are very close to the surface so that the length of shaft is very small. Conversely, for deep tunnels, it is normal to have one shaft for each tunnel tube. Obviously, space allocation must be made where the shafts penetrate the surface.

Smoke Control in Tunnels

There are a number of different types of fire that can occur in the tunnels of subway systems. These are train fires, fires resulting from trash on the tracks, and fires caused by maintenance activity along the tracks. Modern subways systems are constructed with tunnel ventilation systems to manage the smoke from these types of fires to maximize the safety of passengers and rail staff. As the tunnels are restricted by nature, the smoke management systems are configured as push-pull systems. This means that a fan plant is required at each end of each station to protect the intervening tunnel section. The size of the fan plant is predicated on the maximum fire size and a concept known as critical velocity. With a fire in a tunnel, smoke can flow in both directions, depending on the buoyancy effects. To prevent such flow, a sufficient volume of air at the appropriate pressure is introduced into the tunnel to balance the buoyancy forces and force the smoke to flow in one direction only. This provides a clear route for passengers to escape in a smoke-free environment in the opposite direction to the airflow. The velocity at which the airflow balances the buoyancy forces for any given tunnel section is the *critical velocity*.

▼ *General arrangement of piston relief shafts for a two-track system.*

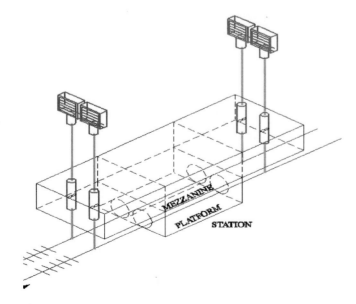

As the tunnel ventilation fan plants are generally located at the ends of the stations, it is normal for them to be connected to the piston relief shafts to minimize the number of connections required to the surface. This arrangement means that space for the fan plant plus inlet and outlet plenums must be allocated in the station box. Moreover, because the fans are required for life safety reasons, system redundancy is usually provided. This allows for a possibility that one fan in a fan plant may be out of service at the time of an incident, or one fan plant may fail because of the location of the fire or the temperatures encountered during a fire.

With the installation of tunnel ventilation fans, it is possible to ventilate tunnels mechanically. This means that if the tunnel environment becomes unacceptable from either an air quality or temperature, the fans can be operated to provide air from the surface. In some subway systems, this feature may be required, particularly where the cars are air-conditioned or where congested operation (train stoppages in the tunnel system because of directions from the signaling system) occurs. In the case of air conditioned cars, the air-conditioner has a set point at which it automatically stops functioning. Therefore, the system must be kept ventilated so that discrete hot spots are not allowed to build up.

Smoke Control at a Station

Fires in the passenger areas of a station can occur as the result of a train on fire at the station, a trash fire, or a fire in a concession booth. The size of the fire and the amount of smoke generated in these events vary greatly; however, the method of managing the smoke to provide a safe environment for passengers

and staff is the same for all such events.

NFPA 130 lists various permissible levels for a tenable environment, such as air temperature, carbon monoxide content, smoke obscuration levels, and heat flux. In addition, NFPA 130 requires that all passengers be able to escape from the platform level within 4 minutes and escape from the station to a point of safety within 6 minutes. The combination of these requirements, together with the fire size, determines the design and arrangement of the smoke management system.

For stations with low passenger volumes it may be possible to operate the tunnel ventilation system in such a way that a tenable environment is provided

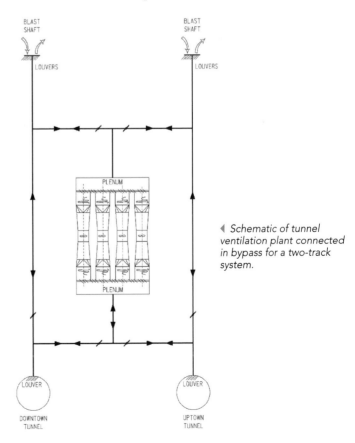

◀ Schematic of tunnel ventilation plant connected in bypass for a two-track system.

when it is required. Alternately, this may be achieved with the addition of smoke boards, a more specialized fan system, or a combination of both. As the station population increases, or the station geometry gets more complex, it may become more problematic to achieve a satisfactory solution with a simple fan system. In these instances, particularly for a train fire at platform level, an over track exhaust (OTE) system may be required. An OTE is simply an exhaust duct running above the trackway with exhaust inlets over the train. A fan system connected to an OTE can provide localized exhaust and is an efficient solution. An additional benefit of the OTE is that it may also be operated during normal operation to remove heat from the train's air conditioners directly from the source. Of course, where OTEs are provided for this reason, they can also be used for fire events.

Comfort Ventilation

Comfort ventilation systems are provided to improve the environment for the passengers. Depending on the environment and the design requirements, comfort ventilation can range from simply ensuring that the piston relief shafts exchange air with the outdoor ambient temperature efficiently, having mechanical ventilation for certain periods of the year, or providing a tempered air system or a fully air-conditioned station.

Where cooling is introduced into the station area, such as with air-conditioned or air-tempered stations, consideration should be given to providing platform edge doors (PEDs). PEDs perform the function of separating the running tracks from the station environment. In general, there are two kinds of PEDs: partial platform edge doors and full-height platform edge doors.

A partial PED extends from the platform surface to a height approximately level with the train roof. PEDs of this kind provide passenger security and partial improvement in terms of noise and dust transfer into the station. Unfortunately, they have little effect in terms of heat load and station cooling load, as the tunnel and station environments are still connected above the PEDs.

A full-height PED extends all the way to the platform ceiling and creates a barrier between the platform and the track, acting as a seal to the train piston effect. This prevents conditioned station air from being lost to the tunnel, as well as the transfer of hot tunnel air and particulates into the station, thus reducing the load on the station ventilation and air-conditioning system.

Fire-Suppression Systems

Because of the large area to be covered, fire-suppression systems in station environments are usually limited. Throughout the platform and mezzanine areas these are generally limited to hose reel systems and dry standpipes. A specialized system that may be employed in station areas is the undercar deluge system. This is a manually activated system consisting of a series of deluge valves laid along the track within the station to spray water vertically upward toward the underside of the car. The reason for providing an undercar deluge system is that as a consequence of the close tolerance between a rail car, the platform, and the side wall, it is difficult for firefighters to get access to the seat of the fire when it is located beneath the floor of a rail car. To date, however, no undercar deluge system has been operated to fight a fire, and its implementation is limited to a small number of rail systems.

CHAPTER 7
SPECIAL EQUIPMENT

FARE COLLECTION

Fare collection equipment in a transit station creates two conflicting demands on the station architecture. First, the equipment layout has to accommodate bidirectional traffic, as busy stations in peak periods have large numbers of passengers entering and exiting. Second, there must be enough equipment to meet demand, and it cannot be placed so that it interrupts passenger flows into and out of the station.

This chapter describes the fare collection system, the concept of open and closed fare collection, and the fare collection equipment to be used. It also shows how to determine the amount of equipment, how to place it, and the typical procurement process. See "Station Design Guidelines" in Chapter 1 for fare collection information regarding dimensional clearances, queuing distances, and so forth.

Fare Collection Basics

As part of the development of a fare collection system, a transit agency will make decisions regarding fare pricing strategy, fare media, and fare media value.

Fare pricing strategy

The fare pricing strategy determines what differential, if any, will be charged to passengers for transit trips with different characteristics.

Flat-fare system. A single standard (flat) fare is charged for every journey, independent of time of day or distance traveled.

Distance-based fare system. The fare charged varies according to the distance traveled.

Time-based fare system. The fare charged varies by the time of day and/or day of the week.

Market-based fare system. The fare rewards frequent users of a transit system through reduced rates for the purchase of large-volume trip increments, (e.g., ten-trip tickets or monthly passes).

Fare media

Fare media are the means of exchange by which the passenger pays to enter the transit system.

Cash. The simplest form of payment. Usually collected at the start of the journey. Best suited to a flat fare system.

Tokens. Serve as a substitute for cash. Best suited to a flat fare system.

Paper tickets. a receipt for a prepaid fare that provides authority to travel. One-way and round-trip tickets are the most common, but multiride tickets and passes, in various forms, are offered by many transit systems. Introduces a means of accounting for fares.

Magnetic farecards. Data are written to and read from farecards using fixed equipment in fare barriers. This represents the first level of automated fare medium. The *write* capability allows for origins and destinations, time of day of travel, and date of travel to be encoded on the ticket at the time of entry into the system. Based on this information, a fare system that deducts from a stored value card, based on certain conditions such as distance traveled, time of day traveled, or day traveled, can be implemented.

America, is largely confined to commuter and light-rail systems, inasmuch as crowded, frequently stopping heavy-rail systems do not lend themselves to verification of payment by inspectors.

Rapid transit systems are commonly designed as closed fare collection systems; that is, access to the property is controlled with the use of some form of barrier that separates the station into paid and unpaid zones. The barrier to access is usually in the form of a turnstile or gate, which also functions as the point of payment verification. The fare barriers are typically released by inserting fare media into the barriers. No verification is required for exiting passengers in a flat (single) fare system. In a distance-based system, passengers' fare media must be checked at both the start and the end of each journey. In this instance, the barriers are used to verify entry and exit.

Fare Collection Equipment

A transit system's fare collection system may consist of one or more of the following types of equipment:

- Fare vending machines
- Add-fare machines
- Fare barriers
- Ticketing office

Fare vending machines

Fare vending machines issue fare media (e.g., tokens, tickets or, smart cards) to passengers. The fare vending machines can be as small as a pay phone or as large as a soda machine. The size of the fare vending machine depends on its vending amenities. The simplest machines sell a single type of medium, such as a one-way ticket or a token, and accept a single type of payment, such as coins/bills or a credit card.

▲ *A full range of ticket vending machines are available to support the various fare media used.*

Smart card. A credit-card-sized device in which a microchip is embedded. A smart card can be encoded with significantly more data than magnetically encoded farecards. Smart cards are appropriate when the amount of data required to implement the transit system fare policy is greater than can be held on a magnetically encoded ticket

Designing a Station for Fare Collection—Open versus Closed

A fare collection system is either *open* or *closed*.

An open fare collection system (also known as barrier-free) has no form of barrier control and relies on the passenger holding proof of payment for the duration of his or her trip. The proof of payment is usually in the form of a ticket or pass. Proof of payment, in North

More complex fare vending machines have multilingual touch screens (with audio for patrons with disabilities) to identify options for passengers. These machines can provide multiple sizes and types of fare media and allow multiple payment options (e.g., coins, bills, credit cards, and debit cards). Processing coins is space-intensive, as a large internal volume is needed to collect coins and provide change.

Add-fare machines are usually required in distance-based fare systems. In the event that a passenger exceeds the distance allowed by his or her fare medium value, the add-fare machine allows the passenger to add monetary value to the fare medium so that the passenger can exit. The size of the add-fare machine usually matches the size of the transit system's fare vending machines.

Fare barriers
Fare barriers are used in a closed transit system to validate the passenger's fare before the trip. The barriers are fitted with a coin/token acceptor, a ticket reader, or a smart card reader. Fare barriers are arranged into arrays (i.e., rows) that act as a boundary to the patron's passage onto the station platform. In many systems the barriers are operable in either direction, thus reducing their numbers.

Standard fare barriers are configured as turnstiles or as gates. Turnstiles are traditionally less complex and less expensive, but passenger throughput is slower than through a gate because there is physical contact between a turnstile and the passenger, whereas a gate swings open to allow unobstructed passage.

Accessible barriers must be provided at every station for passengers with disabilities, carrying large packages/suitcases, or with small children. These barriers are wider than a standard barrier and accept the fare media at a lower position suitable for use by a wheelchair-bound patron.

Ticketing office
Many transit agencies provide a ticketing office at locations with high ridership or at popular tourist stations. These offices typically sell an agency's entire spectrum of fare media, and usually accept all forms of payment. The ticketing office provides an opportunity to create an attractive architectural element near the station entry. Proper placement and viewing distance allows ticketing offices to contribute to security design. Ticketing office staff act as more than salespersons; they provide customer service and security assistance as well.

Other equipment
Beyond the visible fare equipment, a station designer needs to plan for electrical

▼ A fare barrier is usually configured with turnstiles or gates. Many configurations are available to suit system needs and passenger flow requirements.

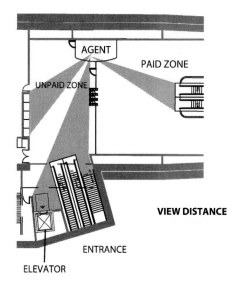

VIEW DISTANCE

ENTRANCE

ELEVATOR

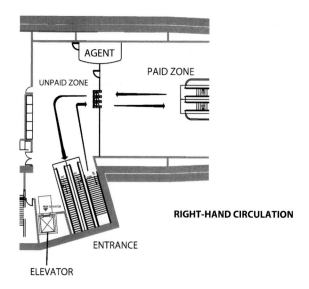

RIGHT-HAND CIRCULATION

ENTRANCE

ELEVATOR

▲ Examples of a typical station fare collection area. Plan at left demonstrates viewing area from agent's booth. Plan at right shows passenger circulation path.

power, communications, and data conduit needs, and must place these unobtrusively throughout the station. In many fare collection systems, a station computer provides controls and indications for the local fare collection equipment. The station computer is linked to a centrally located master processor, sending equipment status, sales data, and alarms. When credit or debit purchases are allowed, the station computer may interface with a central computer connected to a clearinghouse.

Equipment Quantity

How much equipment is needed depends primarily on the ridership projections (see Chapter 2). When calculating equipment quantities, always be conservative. In many cases, ridership projections are too low, and the riding public tends to have little patience with long queuing, especially in a new station.

Quantity of fare vending machines

When projecting the quantity of fare vending machines needed, the station planner will have to determine more than simple ridership numbers. The planner should also determine the percentage of patrons who require a fare medium on any given day, because patrons who purchase multiride fare media do not purchase a ride every day. The planner should try to determine the percentage of patrons who will use cash, credit, and debit. Cash purchases are faster than credit purchases, which are faster than debit purchases. There should never be fewer than two machines, inasmuch as the failure of one will leave a station with no provision for fare sales.

Fewer add-fare machines are needed than fare vending machines. The planner must obtain data on the percentage of users requiring additional fare. For a rough guess, estimate one add-fare machine for every four fare vending machines. As with the fare vending machines, never place a single machine, because a failure will disable the system.

Quantity of barriers

A barrier that is required to check (and return) a ticket is slower than a coin-based or free exit barrier. A good starting point for estimating fare barrier quantity is 24 patrons per minute through a bidirectional turnstile, and 30 patrons per minute for a bidirectional swing-type gate. Never place a single barrier at an entry/exit point. As a rule of thumb, try to place no fewer than one ADA-compliant barrier and two regular barriers.

Fare Equipment Placement

Poorly placed equipment can impede passenger flow into and out of a station, and may have safety (evacuation) implications. When placing the fare equipment, always remember that a transit station must accommodate both fixed and free-flowing activities without conflict or obstruction.

Fare vending machines

Fare vending machines must be placed in areas that are well lit and readily accessible. A well-lit area is required to give the customers a sense of security during a period in which they are exposing their purses, wallets, cash, cards, and the like. Providing a readily accessible area entails designing a single route, thus "forcing" passengers to pass the equipment on their way to the station platform. Typically, fare vending machines are placed near the station entrance and grouped together to prevent unnecessary queuing at a single machine. (See the figure showing a typical fare array layout on page 21.)

Equally important, the fare vending machines must be placed to allow queuing for purchase and yet ensure that these queues will not interfere with the main flow of passengers. In addition to purchase space, passengers may require standing space prior to reentering the main flow.

When different types of fare machines are used (e.g., exact change, no bills, no credit/debit, or credit/debit only), the machines should be clearly identified as to their restrictions, at a height that can be viewed at a distance before choosing a machine to patronize.

For convenience and reduced queuing, fare machines should always be located near system maps and fare purchase instructions. In general, fare equipment should be located away from public telephones to afford patrons privacy at both places.

Provide maintenance access when placing cash-handling equipment. In many cases, the agency needs to bring money carts to the machines to transport heavy cash containers. All machines, not just ADA machines, should be reachable by a cart without crossing obstacles, such as steps.

Fare barriers

Barriers should be located to prevent queuing problems. Avoid placing a barrier array entry point too near the exit from a vertical circulation element, as this may result in a safety hazard. Also avoid placing the barrier array too close to fare vending machines, which can result in queue overlap and confusion.

Passengers entering and exiting the transit station naturally flow in a right-hand direction (assuming U.S. configuration). As a rule of thumb, signage should encourage a right-hand flow through the barriers. Center gates are typically bidirectional and switched throughout the day, depending on the dominant traffic flow.

Accessible barriers are typically placed at one end of a barrier array. If the barrier array is attached to a ticketing or information kiosk, the accessible barriers are placed on the end nearest the kiosk. Place elevators near the accessible barriers to prevent a counter flow across the normal traffic flow.

Add-fare machines

Add-fare machines typically have little queuing and are usually placed fairly close to the exit fare barriers. As with the fare vending machines, access must be provided for money carts.

Ticketing office

Ticketing offices typically have a much slower throughput than a vending machine because of the human contact that encourages conversation and explanations. As such, a ticket office can develop a queue, but channeling the line can reduce the space taken up by the queue. Ticketing offices should be located to allow staff to see barriers and vending equipment. Many agencies try to locate the office to provide oversight of both paid and unpaid areas.

Ancillary security equipment

For unstaffed stations, security equipment such as video cameras and intercoms are typically placed throughout the station space. Video cameras are aimed to observe and record station entry, fare purchase, barrier use, and station platform areas. Intercoms are located at the fare vending machines for customer service and security purposes.

Typical Fare Collection Development Life Cycle

When designing a transit station within an existing transit line, most of the decisions regarding fare collection have already been made, and the designer must make use of the existing parameters. When a transit line is being designed in its entirety, however, designers need to understand the life cycle of a fare collection system in order to understand and encourage timely fare collection decisions before they impact the design of the station. The major phases of the fare collection development life cycle are as follows:

- Policy
- Preliminary design
- Specification
- Procurement
- Installation
- Commissioning

When scanning the following sections, know that there may be unforeseeable delays such as agency reluctance to make decisions, budget problems, political change, or changing priorities. Larger fare collection systems will also require more time.

Policy

The policy phase involves the transit agency and (usually) consultants, as they determine how their fare system will take shape. At a minimum, the agency should decide whether the fare system will be open or closed and what the fare pricing strategy will be.

This phase varies greatly in length; depending on the aggressiveness of the agency, this phase may be as short as six months or as long as five years. Some agencies, faced with an upcoming capital project and no solid fare policy, will move forward but try to keep the design as open as possible to allow the decision point to be delayed as long as possible.

This usually drives up the costs of both the design work and the procurement. Fare policy should be in place before moving into preliminary design.

Preliminary design

The preliminary design phase involves the transit agency and (usually) consultants, as they determine (1) the functional requirements of the equipment and (2) the criteria to be used to integrate the fare collection system into the station architecture and other areas of the agency (e.g., operations, maintenance, finance). The resulting criteria can usually be expressed in five pages. During this phase, the agency should obtain a preliminary estimate that outlines both capital and operations/maintenance costs. This phase should take six months to a year.

Specification

The specification phase involves the transit agency and (usually) consultants, as they ready bid documents for the fare collection suppliers. Depending on the type of procurement, the level of specification will vary. For a turnkey (design-build) procurement, the agency may choose to release little more than the preliminary design documents. For a more traditional procurement, an agency may require a contract bid set that approaches 100 percent design, including exact equipment quantities, cable runs, data messages, and power requirements. By this phase, final life cycle estimates should be in place. Based on the level of detail, the agency's review/approval requirements, and whether the policy phase has truly concluded, the specification phase can take between six months and two years.

Procurement

For this discussion procurement refers to the contracting method the transit authority uses to purcahse the fare collection. The procurement phase involves a design portion (6 months to 1 year), and a manufacturing and software customization portion (approximately 6 months to 1 year). Following completion of manufacturing, the typical procurement includes requirements for a factory-testing demonstration prior to delivery to site.

It is important to note that many transit agencies make a fare collection system the last procurement in their capital project, under the assumption that fare collection is merely an equipment solicitation with very little risk involved. This is a dangerous assumption. Fare collection procurements can be difficult and litigious, fraught with delays and rework caused both by a supplier's inability to meet the specifications and an agency's unwillingness to stick with its original decisions. Never allow a fare collection procurement to be released too late in the capital procurement phase.

Installation

The length of the installation phase varies, depending on the amount of equipment to be installed. Assume that most of the electrical infrastructure has been placed by a previous contractor, allowing the fare collection installer to simply place equipment and install the cable. A fare collection installer will typically be competing for station space with the station finish and electrical-mechanical contractors (power; communications; heating, ventilating, and air-conditioning [HVAC], etc.). Conflict between these contractors can adversely affect the ability to reach designated milestones, and access issues should be addressed in the contract documents.

A particular issue that needs to be addressed early is the means and space to deliver the fare equipment, especially the larger items, which may not easily fit down stairs or escalators. In a particular contract, space constraints forced delivery of fare equipment to the platforms via light-rail vehicles. Careful thought during the design phase can reduce the possibility of expensive problems during installation.

Commissioning

In the commissioning phase, fare equipment is tested for function. Every function of the equipment is executed, and the equipment is stressed to maximum levels to ensure proper operation. The length of this phase varies, depending on the amount of equipment to be installed, but should not exceed 1 week per station. Upon completion of commissioning, the fare collection equipment is deemed ready for revenue service.

MATERIALS AND FINISHES

The decision to use a particular material or finish touches on the most basic of issues in station design. It is driven by the architecture being created, which is influenced by the expression of form and texture and the use of light and color, and tempered by pragmatic considerations such as affordability, performance, and long-term maintenance.

Transit stations are public spaces subject to intensive and sometimes abusive use, exposure to the weather, and water attack, particularly in an underground configuration. Limited annual operating funds quite often restrict quality maintenance in many systems. Good policy is to build less station area, when possible, and to use higher-performing materials and design the station to encourage ease of maintenance. This chapter provides an overview of the process of evaluating a station's anticipated use, frequency of service, and exposure to weathering elements and how to determine the appropriate materials and finishes.

GENERAL DESIGN PRINCIPLES

All finishes should be extremely durable, hard wearing, and easily maintained, have good colorfast properties, and be readily replaceable. Interior wall and ceiling finishes should be tested in accordance with American Society for Testing and Materials (ASTM) standard E 84 and must be Class A, noncombustible, with flame spread of 0–25; smoke developed index of 0–450; and totally fire resistant. Products that can emit harmful gases, smoke, or dust particles must not be used.

If stainless steel is used, the specific type must be identified and compliance with the appropriate ASTM specifications is required. Generally, Type 304, 304L, 316, or 316L is specified. The "L" designation signifies low carbon, and this type should be used in welding sections heavier than about 0.25 in. (6 mm). The choice is determined by the application's exposure to corrosive pollution, urine, and/or coastal and deicing salts.

Metal designs should avoid creating small, tight crevices that can accumulate corrosive compounds, because they can be sites for corrosion. Tight crevices should ideally be removed by welding the components, but sealant may also be used. The serviceable life of the finish should be consistent with the expected life of the station, normally in the 100-year range. It is reasonable to plan for a mid-life station overhaul or a 50-year life span for finishes. This is contingent upon the actual use and placement of the finish. High-service areas, such as floors in front of a fare array, will require more highly wear resistant finishes than adjacent floor areas.

Specify finishes with proven maintenance techniques and procedures. Build into the station design provisions that will encourage the station operators to readily maintain surfaces. For instance, floor surfaces requiring the use of cleaning machines also require adequate vertical transportation of such machines to access all floor areas.

Building services, such as conduit, piping, and ductwork, located behind walls or above ceilings are generally to be avoided. Where this is not possible, incorporate durable access panels into the finish system. Hinged panels are preferred over removable panels to ensure their long-term reliability. Careful attention should be devoted to details in access panel design to ensure that an installation is consistent with the expected long-term performance of the wall or ceiling system. Locate services requiring access away from main circulation routes.

Light reflectance values for floors, walls, and ceilings should be coordinated with the lighting designer early in the design. Consideration is to be given to maintenance policy and factors such as brake dust that will influence how long light reflectance values are maintained. Brake dust is less likely to accumulate on or cause staining of smooth surfaces.

Finishes, lighting, and signage elements (including support systems) should be designed to resist the following influences when appropriate: exterior wind pressures, air pressure variations caused by train movement through stations (recognizing that some trains may not stop at a specific station and that therefore pressures may be exceedingly high), seismic forces, and vibrations due to trains. The design of these elements requires input from a structural engineer.

Floors

If movement can be expected, expansion joints should be provided in floor finish and structural systems. In floor systems exposed to weather and/or freezing temperatures, careful thought should be given to surface wear and water drainage to ensure that the installation remains serviceable. Expansion joint infill materials in floors are subjected to extreme wear due to ultraviolet light degradation, foot traffic, deicing salts, and abuse from objects such as umbrella tips.

The design of the finish expansion joint should be coordinated with the structural expansion joint to ensure that all movement between elements is anticipated and transferred adequately. Quite

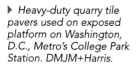

▶ Heavy-duty quarry tile pavers used on exposed platform on Washington, D.C., Metro's College Park Station. DMJM+Harris.

often a slight misalignment causes finishes to bridge the structural joint, and therefore shear cracking occurs in the finish surface immediately parallel to the finish expansion joint.

Select floor materials that are consistent through the body of the product to ensure that appearance is not sacrificed to wearability. Materials such as granite and porcelain tile are preferred. Specify extremely low moisture absorption rates, in the range of less than 0.5 percent. Stainless steel floor plate is being used for transit flooring and stair applications in Europe.

High-wear areas of floors, such as at fare turnstiles and at the tops and bottoms of stairs, should be protected with highly resistant materials such as granite.

Floors in traction power substations will require dielectric epoxy coatings, typically over a concrete slab, with material turned up 4 in. at walls. Similarly, battery rooms will require acid-resistant floor coatings.

The general floor finish for all public areas should be nonslip, hard-wearing, and nonstainable.

The static coefficient of friction for different floor areas should meet the minimum requirements of ADA, that is, 0.6 on walking surfaces and 0.8 on ramps, sloping sidewalks, and stairs.

Specify concrete floor finishes to receive a floor hardener and an antidusting curing agent or sealer.

Walls

Columns on platforms and in mezzanines are discouraged as a general rule. If they are to be used, consider high-impact and wear-resistant cladding or applied finishes.

Structures that are susceptible to water seepage or leakage, such as in an underground station, are best maintained

over the 100-year life if wall finishes are used that stand a short distance from the structure and are planned with water leakage as a consideration in selecting materials and support systems. The use of freestanding walls, readily demountable or that afford ready access for maintenance and inspection, is encouraged. Design water collection systems at each floor level with provisions for accessing drain covers and cleanouts.

▼ Stainless steel checkerplate flooring used in London Jubilee Line Station. (Photo: Alfred Lau.)

▲ Porcelain floor tile can add light color and contribute to an open, spacious feeling. Johns Hopkins Hospital Station, Baltimore Metro. DKP Joint Venture.

▼ Example of a high-impact and wear-resistant cladding on platform columns. Los Angeles Metro underground station.

Proven wall cladding systems are granite, stainless steel, heavy-duty porcelain enamel, and porcelain tile.

Although an ASTM No. 4 satin polish is commonly used for transit stations, scratching damage is difficult to repair without changing the finish. Embossed finishes or a hairline polish (also called long grain) provide improved durability. Embossing stainless steel increases its impact strength and reduces both the po-

tential for scratching and the visibility of any scratches. Relatively deep patterns with small, narrow raised areas give the best performance. The Specialty Steel Industry of North America (SSINA) provides information on stainless steel finishes in its brochure *Special Finishes for Stainless Steel,* which is available at www.ssina.com. The Nickel Development Institute (NiDI) publication *Stainless Steel in Architecture, Building and Construction: Guidelines for Maintenance and Cleaning,* is a valuable resource (NiDI 1994).

Woven stainless steel should never be used in coastal areas or where there is exposure to deicing salt. Woven and welded Type 316 may be acceptable because welding seals the crevices created by the overlapping wires.

Glass walls, such as around elevator hoistways, should use heat-strengthened laminated safety glass in accordance with the prevailing codes. The intent is that any broken glass shards will not fall into an opening, but will stay confined within the glass framing system.

Stair and escalator wellway openings through floors should have finishes that are highly impact resistant to compensate for potential vandalism and abuse.

Railing systems should be designed as stainless steel fabrications or laminated glass infill panels.

Precast concrete wall panels, when not required for periodic access, should have the nonexposed face coated with asphalt emulsion to withstand moisture penetration.

Ceilings

Most transit agencies have had poor experiences with suspended ceilings because of their fragile nature and the awk-

wardness in performing routine maintenance. (Suspended ceilings with aluminum frames can collapse in a fire and
block exits, and both aluminum and steel
can fail because of corrosion in some locations. If a suspended ceiling is used,
the best choice is stainless steel, which
provides better high-temperature performance and corrosion resistance than aluminum or carbon steel. Information
comparing the performances of metals in
a fire can be found in the Nickel Development Institute publication *Stainless
Steel For Durability, Fire Resistance and
Safety* (NiDI 1990).

In an underground station, the upper-
most roof structural system is the most
vulnerable to water infiltration and seepage. Avoid placing building services in
areas that tend to act as water conveyors
when roof leakage does occur. Avoid covering the area with suspended ceilings if
possible.

When it is absolutely necessary to sus-
pend a ceiling, use a heavy-duty, impact-
resistant, custom-fabricated stainless steel
system. Design all access panels as integrated hinged doors, subject to regular
access. Design the suspension system to
perform under extreme high-moisture
environmental conditions, subject to extreme positive and negative wind forces.
Ensure that the ceiling suspension system
is attached to a substrate that has an
equal ability to perform under the same
stringent conditions.

Ceiling design should take into consideration the location of all associated
building service elements, such as light
fixtures, ventilation air diffusers, sprinklers, signage and graphic supports, heat
and smoke detectors, exit signs, and the
like. Design all associated elements with
an independent suspension/support sys-

tem if possible, to avoid placing concentrated loads on the ceiling system.

Avoid using heavyweight ceiling panels,
such as concrete, which have a tendency to
sag and/or drop over the long term.

Exterior Exposure

Exterior-quality finishes should be used
for all elements at entrances to underground stations, at-grade stations, and
aerial stations. These elements include all
public features, such as covered stairs and
escalators, and nonpublic structures, such
as ventilation shafts and elevator hoistways.

Finishes are to be suitable for the environment and for use under extreme
conditions. Carefully consider the long-
term performance of the support system,
fasteners, and support substrate and detailing to allow for thermal movement.
Also select veneers and curtain wall products with a proven history of superior
performance under adverse conditions,
including resistance to air pollution.

Exposed concrete walls, columns,
beams, and fascias in colder climates
should incorporate admixtures to with-

▲ *Laminated safety glass,
incorporating artwork in the
interlayer, serves as the train
room wall of Baltimore
Metro's Shot Tower Station.
Water leakage expected
from the slurry wall foundation system dictated the
need for a demountable,
noncorrosive wall finish.
DMJM+Harris.*

▶ *Heavy-duty porcelain enameled metal wall panels enclose an escalator shaft at the South Campus SUNY station in the LRT system of Buffalo, New York. DMJM+Harris.*

stand freeze-thaw cycles. Careful use and application of American Concrete Institute (ACI) committee publications for detailing, specifying, and construction techniques are to be followed.

Likewise, in hotter climates, concrete should be designed to shed water quickly and to use finish coatings to withstand exposure to mildew and the resultant staining.

Walks, plazas, pathways, stairs, ramps, and all other areas leading to a station entrance are vulnerable to severe wear and detrimental service due to weather exposure and deicing salts in colder climates. Positive drainage of all surfaces is essential. Drain inlets at critical transition points are encouraged so that water ponding does not occur. The detailing of surface finishes must consider undersurface drainage to encourage water collection and routing to storm drainage inlets.

Assign locations for cigarette ash containers at station entrances to encourage disposal in an approved manner.

Select floor pavers that have a low moisture-absorption rate and minimal staining.

Select walkway finish materials that can satisfy the stringent ADA requirements for maintaining low slopes and the required coefficient of friction.

SELECTING APPROPRIATE MATERIALS AND SYSTEMS

The following discussion explores a suggested process by which materials and systems can be considered and evaluated for their use.

Determine the Service Conditions

When designing a new station in an existing system or retrofitting an existing station, the architect will need to review the data on materials used in other sta-

◀ Laminated safety glass with a frit interlayer creates the hoistway enclosure at an elevator on the platform. Johns Hopkins Hospital Station, Baltimore Metro. DKP Joint Venture.

tions to gauge their performance. See Chapter 15, "Modernization/Retrofit," for a similar discussion, and consult the transit agency's operations and maintenance staff to understand the history of the materials' performance and the maintenance policy. Visit and observe the stations to judge how the materials perform, and look for weaknesses or opportunities for improved material use or application procedures.

In new stations, in new systems, where design criteria do not exist, initially evaluate the station type by its configuration and exposure to weather (aerial, at-grade, or underground). Evaluate the location of the materials and make basic determinations as to the degree of service expected and/or exposure to elements such as rain, salt, pollution, urine, and freeze-thaw cycles. For a list of points to review, see the sidebar on page 182.

Guidance on evaluating the severity of a site and selecting an appropriate stainless steel can be obtained in the following free publications from the Nickel Development Institute (NiDI) and the International Molybdenum Association (IMOA):

- NiDI publication *Stainless Steel in Architecture Building and Construction: Guidelines for Corrosion Resistance* (NiDI 2001)

- IMOA publication *Which Stainless Steel Should Be Specified for Exterior Applications?* (Houska 2003)

Define the Criteria

Develop a list of criteria that measure the performance of a material, system, or product against a recognized standard such as an ASTM or German Institute for Standardization (DIN). The criteria standards should satisfy the demand

Conditions Review

- Temperature ranges (both inside the station and outside)
- Exposure to moisture (rainwater, groundwater, cleaning materials)
- Locations within 5 to 10 miles of the seacoast or a large saltwater body
- Exposure to ultraviolet rays and potential solar degradation
- Direct exposure to deicing salts or salt mist from busy roads
- Anticipated exposure (light/moderate/heavy) to functions such as walking or touching
- The entire passenger circulation route, including floors, walls, railings, and ceilings
- Industrial and urban pollution levels and the type of industry
- Potential exposure to urine
- Washing and cleaning frequency
- Exposure to airborne steel brake particles resulting from rapid deceleration of trains

placed on it by the exposure identified above and would address such factors as:

- Light and color-fastness
- Coefficient of friction
- Moisture content

Establish the Range of Options

Develop a material evaluation matrix that identifies the full range of systems, locations, uses, and criteria, and identify products that satisfy their requirements.

Use testing standards appropriate to the climate and degree of wear anticipated.

Selection and Application of Materials

The architect should select materials and products with a focus on their long-term performance. This is best achieved by using products that have a proven history, are in as natural a state as they can be, and will facilitate maintenance with the minimum amount of care. Good policy is to use a limited palette of materials and finishes. Select high-performance materials and detail installations using reliable methods. Study the behavior of materials in sheltered areas exposed to the air (canopies, band shells, etc.) and in major exterior public spaces in the area of the station. Determine how well they perform and the level of maintenance they receive. The use of fewer products allows the transit agency to stock fewer replacements. The exposed finishes in a modern transit station, subject to moderate-to-heavy use, may be limited to few materials such as granite, stainless steel, safety glass, and heavy-duty porcelain enamel. Most all finishes or systems are available in this limited range.

Materials that have direct contact with the public are subject to the most wear. This is where materials like granite and stainless steel perform best. Surfaces subject to cleaning abrasives and cleaning machine brushes, such as floors and bases around walls and vertical elements, like elevator hoistways, should be of heavy-duty wear-resistant materials like granite and stainless steel. Station platforms should be designed with the minimum number of objects on them as needed. Avoid columns and objects such as benches or signage pylons that have mul-

MATERIAL EVALUATION MATRIX

SYSTEM / LOCATION OR USE	Flame Spread 0.25	Smoke Developed 0-450	Coefficient of Friction (slip resistance 0.6 or 0.8)	Abrasion Resistance	Light Reflectance	Freeze/Thaw Resistance (in colder climates)	Resistance to Chemical Detergents	Low Moisture Absorption	Color Fastness/UV Resistant	Granite	Stainless Steel	Laminated Glass	Porcelain Enamel	Ceramic Porcelain	Glass Block	Concrete	Cast Iron
Floors																	
Street or entry level		•	0.6	•		•	•	•	•	√	√						
Mezzanine	•	•	0.6	•	•	•	•	•	•	√	√			√			
Platform	•	•	0.6	•	•	•	•	•	•	√	√			√			
Top and bottom stairs	•	•	0.8	•	•	•	•	•	•	√	√						
Stair treads	•	•	0.8	•		•	•	•	•	√	√						
Ramps			0.8	•		•	•	•	•	√	√					√	
Walls																	
Track wall at platform	•	•				•	•		•		√	√	√	√			
Lower track wall at platform	•	•				•	•		•		√	√	√			√	
Walls on platform	•	•		•	•	•	•	•	•	√	√		√				
Wall at mezzanine	•	•		•	•	•	•	•	•	√	√		√				
Exterior walls at entrances	•	•		•		•	•	•	•	√	√		√		√		
Ceilings																	
Platform level above track	•	•				•	•	•	•		√		√				
Platform level above platform	•	•			•	•	•	•	•		√		√				
Mezzanine	•	•			•	•	•	•	•		√		√				
Entrances	•	•			•	•	•	•	•		√		√				
Miscellaneous Surfaces																	
Canopies	•	•				•	•	•	•		√	√	√				
Windscreens	•	•		•	•	•	•	•	•	√	√						
Escalator balustrades	•	•		•		•	•	•	•	√	√						
Elevator cabs	•	•		•		•	•	•	•	√	√						
Railings	•	•		•		•	•	•	•	√							
Security grills at entrances	•					•	•	•	•	√							
Access panels in public floors	•			•		•	•	•	•	√							√
Fan control devices	•						•	•	•	√							
Furniture	•	•					•	•	•	√							
Benches									•	√	√		√				
Trash receptacles							•	•	•		√		√				

tiple support legs. Use closed bases so that cleaning machines can work completely around the objects. Design a floor base a minimum of 12 in. high.

Locations within 5 to 10 miles of an ocean or a saltwater bay are considered coastal areas. Road mists can carry deicing salt hundreds of feet from busy roads. If the site is coastal or exposed to deicing salt, high levels of urban pollution, and/or industrial pollution, Type 316 or 316L stainless steel is usually necessary to avoid corrosion staining. If there is uncertainty about exposure to either source of salt or the corrosiveness of pollutants, a laboratory can determine the type of deposits found on surfaces near the site.

If an application may be subjected to urine and is unlikely to be cleaned frequently, Type 316 will provide better corrosion resistance than Type 304 stainless steel. Regular cleaning should be encouraged when urine is a problem even if it consists of simply hosing down the surfaces.

Specifying smooth finishes and a vertical finish grain orientation will reduce dirt accumulation and the possibility of corrosion. The surface finish roughness should not exceed R_a 20 micro-inches or 0.5 microns. If the wrong stainless steel is selected and it does not provide adequate corrosion resistance, or if there are crevices, a rough finish, or horizontal or sheltered surfaces, then more frequent cleaning will be required.

Avoid certain materials whenever possible, such as:

- Ferrous metals subject to corrosion and requiring painting
- Aluminum, where there is deicing salt or within 5 to 10 miles of the coast (corrosion loss may not be obvious, because of the coloration, but there can be significant structural deterioration)
- Ferrous metal fasteners
- Cementitious products such as plaster or drywall
- Wood, except for platform benches
- Thin floor pavers subject to shear cracks
- Nonlaminated glass

CHAPTER 9
ACOUSTICS AND VIBRATION

This chapter discusses the basic principles along with the practical aspects of good acoustical design for mass transit and railroad stations. The desirable acoustical qualities for public transportation stations have changed over time. Acoustical environments acceptable, or even desirable, 100 years ago may not be acceptable today. For example, the grand, voluminous train stations built in the late nineteenth and early twentieth centuries, such as Grand Central Terminal in New York, Thirtieth Street Station in Philadelphia, or Union Station in Los Angeles, to mention a few, define a golden era of architectural design in public transportation.

The acoustic quality of the arrival halls in these turn-of-the-century train stations is unique and imparts a feeling of spaciousness that reinforces the awe-inspiring volume of the space. Announcements over the public address (PA) system reverberate through the arrival hall, a sound some nostalgically associate with train travel in an earlier era, along with the sound of jointed rails or the swaying motion of passenger coaches. Today's transit stations are smaller, rails are continuously welded, making for a quieter ride, and rail passenger cars are designed to provide stable rides, as exemplified by the modern high-speed trains of Europe and Japan. Transit stations are usually designed to look and feel contemporary, and the acoustical characteristics should reflect this modern approach to design as well.

The three basic issues in the acoustical design of transit stations are reverberation control, general noise control (from both interior and exterior sources), and vibration control. Vibration may result in structure-borne noise as well as perceptible vibration. Although the PA system is not generally thought of as part of the acoustical design, its success is highly dependent on the acoustical properties of spaces in which it is installed. Creative approaches, already tried and found to satisfy the aesthetics of design as well as achieve a desirable acoustical environment, are available. Because of their recent construction, airport terminals often provide good examples of innovative uses of materials and finishes that may be applicable to transit stations.

TERMINOLOGY
The science of acoustics uses specific terminology to describe and quantify the behavior of sound and vibration and quantify their perception by humans. For terms often encountered in dealing with the acoustical design of stations, see page 186.

GENERAL ACOUSTICAL DESIGN CONCEPTS
There are three requirements in the acoustical design of a station:

- Patron comfort
- Intelligibility of PA system announcements
- Patron safety in case of an emergency

The criteria presented here can be used as design goals to meet these requirements. Acoustics is a complex technical subject and requires the involvement of an acoustical consultant experienced in the design of a new station or the retrofit of an existing one. The information presented in this chapter can be used by the

Acoustic Terms

- *Sound* is energy that moves as a wave through the air as a pressure fluctuation, and we hear sound because of this disturbance.

- Sound is usually composed of different *frequencies*, which are much like the tones on a piano, only not as obvious. Frequency is the rate (in cycles/second or Hertz [Hz]) at which the air fluctuates.

- *Noise* is unwanted sound, usually sound that is too loud for a particular situation.

- *Decibel* (denoted by dB) is a logarithmic unit used to quantify the level of sound.

- *A-weighted* decibel (denoted dBA) level accounts for the manner in which humans hear sound, deemphasizing sounds of high and low frequencies.

- When a sound is produced inside an enclosed space, it *reverberates* or bounces around and is absorbed by the material of the room's surfaces; the less absorptive the room's surface materials are, the more energy is allowed to build up, and the noisier it becomes.

- Sound that primarily travels through a building as vibration in the structure is referred to as *structure-borne noise* and can be perceived as reradiated sound within the building at locations distant from the source.

- *Noise criterion* (NC) is a system used for rating the level of HVAC noise in buildings.

- Sound is absorbed when it is reflected from materials on a room's surfaces. The *sound absorption* of porous materials (e.g., fiberglass) is much better than that of hard, smooth surfaces (e.g., marble). Sound absorption is also frequency dependent.

- *Sound absorption coefficient* is a quantitative measure of the efficiency of a specific material to absorb sound; it is frequency, thickness, and application dependent.

- *Noise reduction coefficient* (NRC), for a specific acoustical material, is the average of the sound absorption coefficients, rounded to the nearest multiple of 0.05, at four specific frequencies (250, 500, 1000, and 2000 Hz).

- *Train noise control* is obtained by treating the train room surfaces with a porous material, accounting for the fact that train noise has low-frequency components.

- *Equipment noise control* for mechanical equipment (e.g., fans, pumps, generators), which produces either high- or low-frequency noise, depending on the source, is obtained by the use of barriers and sound absorption.

- *Transmission loss* (TL) is the ability of a building material (e.g., concrete blocks or drywall) to reduce sound that is transmitted through the material.

- *Isolation mounts* obtain vibration control for equipment, which can transmit energy into the building structure and cause structure-borne sound in areas remote from the equipment.

architect as a guide to better understand and appreciate what is necessary to accomplish a design that satisfies functional requirements and is appropriate acoustically. For a more technical discussion than is possible here, the reader can find ample material in Baranek (1971) and Harris (1998).

Adequate acoustical treatment and noise control in a station accomplishes the following objectives:

- Reduction of noise resulting from train operations

- Control of noise generated by patrons walking on hard surfaces and/or talking in enclosed areas

- Control of noise produced by the station's air-handling equipment (i.e., heating, ventilating, and air-conditioning [HVAC] systems and tunnel ventilation fans), vertical circulation equipment, and other mechanical equipment

- Favorable acoustical conditions for speech intelligibility of announcements over the station's PA system

- Reduction of noise from exterior sources (e.g., motor vehicles) for exposed station areas

The primary goal of acoustical design for rooms and spaces within a station is to install a sufficient amount of sound-absorbing material. This will prevent excessive reverberation and aid in controlling interior noise. Its volume, and the surfaces and amount of area, largely drive the acoustical design of a particular space available for treatment with sound-absorbing materials. The surface area of a room does not increase as rapidly as the volume, thus complicating the acoustical treatment of larger spaces.

From an acoustical perspective, a "space" within a station generally implies a definable volume, one that is enclosed (i.e., four walls, floor, and ceiling) or roomlike. However, there are often situations in which a space is not entirely enclosed, and spaces are often acoustically interconnected. In some situations, a space is more open than closed. Aerial transit stations and at-grade stations are often only partially enclosed. When acoustically designing the space within a station, whether the space is enclosed or not and how much of it is open must be taken into account.

The volume of a space is a primary factor in its acoustical design, and it is useful to categorize spaces in terms of their volume. The volume definitions indicated in the table below, although somewhat arbitrary, can serve as a rough guide to the architect.

Major challenges in the acoustical design of stations are often the limitations on the amount of area that can be treated and the surfaces available for treatment. The most efficient use of sound absorption is to evenly distribute acoustical material. However, treating just the ceiling, although far from ideal, may be the only option and is not unusual. The larger a space is, the more difficult it is to incorporate adequate sound absorption. Making the design even more challeng-

VOLUMES OF VARIOUS SPACES		
Size of Space	Example	Volume (cu ft)
Small	Confined ticketing area	50,000 or less
Medium	Waiting room	50,000–150,000
Large	Concourse	150,000–500,000
Very large	Arrival hall	500,000 or greater

ing is the standard practice in station design of using hard floor and wall surface finishes (primarily for ease of maintenance, but also for aesthetic reasons). Unlike some airport terminals, transit stations as a rule do not use carpet (an effective sound absorber) as a floor finish, except possibly in waiting rooms. Thus, for most transit station spaces, the walls and ceiling are the only surfaces available to the acoustician on which to specify sound-absorbing treatment.

The available choices for acoustical materials for station finishes, although not numerous, generally perform adequately when used appropriately. There are five general types of acoustical materials that have been used: fiberglass (or mineral wool), cementitious spray-applied or preformed porous cement material, treated wood fiber composite material, resonant cavity blocks, and propri-

etary materials brought on the market in the last few years. If water intrusion is not an issue (as it would be in a subway station), then material selection can be based on other considerations. Where water may infiltrate, such as on walls and ceilings of subway stations, then the cementitious material is the most durable and should withstand long-term exposure to water. Flammability is another nonacoustical consideration that will affect the choice of materials to be used.

ACOUSTICAL AND NOISE CRITERIA

The acoustical and noise criteria presented herein were developed from experience gained over several years of transit facility design. Most of these criteria have been in use for nearly 30 years; early versions of station acoustical criteria appeared in 1973 and were subsequently

DESIGN CRITERIA FOR STATION ACOUSTICS			
	Train Rooms (platforms)	Concourse and Arrival Hall	Areas Exposed to Street Traffic Noise
Maximum reverberation time* (at 500 Hz)	1.5 seconds	1.2 seconds	1.2 to 1.4 seconds
Treatment			
Minimum wall/ceiling area	35%**	35%**	20–25%
Minimum ceiling only	—	—	70–100%
Treatment Properties			
Minimum absorption coefficient at 500 Hz	0.6***	0.6	0.6
Minimum noise reduction coefficient	0.6***	0.6	0.6

*The acoustical effects of large openings in enclosed spaces should be included for the purpose of calculation.

**Including at least 50% of the ceiling area.

***Under-platform treatment also required with minimum absorption coefficient at 250 Hz is 0.4, and at 500 Hz is 0.65.

incorporated into the 1979 publication of the American Public Transportation Association (APTA) *Guidelines for the Design of Rapid Transit Facilities.* The APTA criteria have been supplemented and expanded over time, based on experience. These criteria are in general use by several major metropolitan transit agencies in the United States for the design of new transit facilities.

Acoustical Criteria

For the design of interior station spaces, acoustical criteria are usually specified in terms of desirable reverberation times and guidelines for the amount and minimum properties of acoustical surface treatments. The table at left is a summary of these general design criteria.

Reverberation time is the most convenient and commonly used measure of a space's acoustical character. It is used to acoustically design spaces where people congregate, and most important, where people go to hear musical performances or public speaking. It is a direct measure of how acoustic energy is absorbed in a room. The less absorption there is, the "livelier" a room or space is and the noisier it can be. As more absorption is added to a room, the sound inside the room will be absorbed more quickly and the room will be quieter as a consequence.

Reverberation time for a room is, by definition, the time (in seconds) it takes for the level of sound to decay by 60 decibels (dB) after the source is turned off. There are several formulas that have been developed to predict reverberation time. The formulas are based on room volume and amount and distribution of sound absorption in the room. The simplest formula, originally developed by Wallace Clement Sabine (1895), assumes uniformly distributed acoustical material with low absorption. Sabine's formula for reverberation time for sound at a specific frequency is:

$$RT_{60} = (0.049 \times V)/(S \times \alpha),$$

where V is the room's volume (cu ft), S is the total surface area (sq ft), α is the average sound absorption coefficient at a particular frequency, and RT_{60} is the reverberation time. The formula is very approximate when conditions are other than stated. It has been included here to allow the architect to determine the approximate effects of volume, surface area, and absorption. There are other reverberation time formulas that are more appropriate for situations typically encountered in station design (e.g., uneven distribution of absorption), but they are beyond the scope of this discussion.

Noise Criteria

The noise generated by trains and buses (both moving and stationary) and the noise generated by the station's HVAC system, also referred to as the environmental control system (ECS), and the emergency ventilation equipment such as a tunnel ventilation fan (TVF), should be considered and adequate noise control included when designing the station. Noise resulting from train and bus operations should be controlled so that it does not annoy patrons waiting on the platform and people in other parts of the station. This can be achieved in part through vehicle noise specifications and track design, but also by incorporating sound absorption in strategic locations. The station's vertical circulation equipment, such as elevators and escalators, should be specified with limits on the maximum allowable noise they emit.

It is important at the inception of a station design project to adopt noise limit criteria. These criteria, if achieved in the finished project, will yield an environment that most patrons will find acceptable. The table below indicates criteria applicable specifically to train noise. In dealing with train noise, there are two train conditions to consider: trains that stop in the station and those that do not (i.e., express trains). The latter obviously produce higher noise levels, but the event does not last as long, which is reflected in the criteria. Buses have different noise characteristics than trains, and there are no specific noise criteria that have been developed for bus stations. The noise criteria in the table below, where applicable (i.e., usually bus transit stations do not have nonstopping express buses), can be used.

The normal sound level of someone talking to another person is in the range of 60–65 dBA at a distance of 2–3 ft apart. Consequently, when train noise levels are as loud as those indicated in the aforementioned table, people talking to each other would either have to raise their voices or contend with some speech interference. To put this in perspective, people would have to strain to talk for a given length of time, so that speech levels would be 70 dBA or more at 2 ft away. The highest noise levels in the table (i.e., 80–85 dBA) are for brief, transient events (e.g., express train movement), which makes them acceptable even though loud enough to momentarily mask speech.

Trains moving in a station generate structure-borne noise. The noise is produced by the vibration energy generated at the wheel-rail interface as the train moves. Faster trains generate higher levels of vibration. This vibration is imparted to the station structure through the track support system. Structure-borne vibration propagates efficiently through concrete structures and is converted to noise when room surfaces in the station vibrate. The primary concern with structure-borne noise arises when there are stacked platforms, whereby the lower platform would experience noise from the tracks above. High-speed trains will result in high levels of structure-borne noise and vibration unless adequate design measures to reduce the vibration are implemented.

Structure-borne noise levels greater than 60 dBA are disturbing to patrons, regardless of where they are in the sta-

DESIGN CRITERIA FOR AIRBORNE TRAIN NOISE		
Station Space	**Source of Train Noise**	**A-wt Noise Level (dBA)**
Platform	Express train passing through station	85
	Stopping train—entering or leaving station	80
	Stopped train, stationary at the platform	70
Concourse	Express train passing through station	75
	All other train conditions	70
Arrival hall	Express train passing through station	65

tion. This is due to the character of structure-borne noise, which has a very low frequency content (i.e., a rumble) much like distant thunder. The design criteria indicated in the bottom table below apply to structure-borne noise in various public spaces in the station. The indicated criteria are for a transient event, for which it is acceptable to have somewhat higher noise levels than for ongoing events.

Equipment used in a station's HVAC system produces noise. Usually this noise is airborne, but it may also be structure-borne. To provide a comfortable environment for the public and the workers in the station, the level of noise must be controlled so that although audible, it is not so loud as to be unpleasant. The appropriate level of noise in different spaces within a station depends on the level of activity of people in the space. In a relatively quiet area such as a lounge, the HVAC noise should be quieter than in a heavily traveled area such as a concourse.

The amount of time people generally spend in a station area affects the level of HVAC noise that is appropriate for that space. As may be expected, when people have a choice, they usually avoid noisy areas of the station while waiting for a train or bus if the wait is going to be longer than 5 or 10 minutes. Station areas where people may spend 15 minutes to one-half hour waiting for a train should be quieter than platforms, where

DESIGN CRITERIA FOR HVAC AIRBORNE NOISE IN PUBLIC SPACES		
Type of Space	Noise Criterion (NC)	A-wt Noise Level (dBA)
VIP lounge	35	40
Ticket sales office	40	45
Waiting areas and lounges	45	50
Retail spaces	45	50
General public areas (excluding platforms)	45	50
Platform/train rooms	50	55

DESIGN CRITERIA FOR STRUCTURE-BORNE TRAIN NOISE	
Type of Public and Ancillary Space	A-wt Noise Level (dBA)
Critical operational spaces (e.g., central train control)	35
Business offices	40
Waiting areas (e.g., lounge)	45
Retail and restaurants	50
Arrival hall	55
Concourse	60
Platform area	60

DESIGN CRITERIA FOR AIRBORNE HVAC NOISE IN OFFICE SPACES

Type of Space	Noise Criterion (NC)	A-wt Noise Level (dBA)
Executive office	30	35
Control room (speech critical)	30	35
Large conference room	30	35
Private office	35	40
Medium-size meeting room	35	40
Open-plan office	40	45
Station agent's booth	40	45
Circulation and lobby	45	50
Computer equipment room	50	55

DESIGN CRITERIA FOR EMERGENCY VENTILATION FAN NOISE IN PUBLIC SPACES

Station Space	A-wt Noise Level (dBA)
Platform, with tunnel or station ventilation system operating in an emergency	70
Concourse or other public area, with tunnel or ventilation system operating in an emergency	65

people typically wait just before boarding a train or bus. Noise levels may affect where people congregate in a station, a consideration that should not be overlooked in the station design.

The HVAC noise criteria in the upper table on page 191 are guidelines used to evaluate projected levels of HVAC noise during the design process and decide on appropriate noise control measures. The noises that are addressed by the criteria in this table are generated by steady-state sources, such as equipment that runs more or less continuously and for long periods.

Some stations, particularly railroad terminals, are large enough to have office space for employees. For those spaces, HVAC noise criteria need to be specified apart from those for public spaces. The upper table above presents design criteria for HVAC noise control for office spaces in stations.

Other stations, such as subway or below-grade stations with approach tunnels, have ventilation fans that may be used in case of an emergency to evacuate smoke from the stations and tunnels when there is a fire. Such fans are by necessity very large in order to move large volumes of air in a short time and are inherently very noisy, but they can be made compatible with the station environment when adequate noise control is used. The criteria are intended to control noise levels in the train room and adjacent tunnels so that patrons trying to leave the station are not frightened and thereby dissuaded from going in the direction of the fans, should that be the best way to evacuate. Even more important for public safety, fan noise levels should be low enough so that PA system announcements are intelligible.

The lower table at left indicates noise criteria to determine specific noise control measures for station areas adjacent to the tunnel emergency fan inlet shafts, which are often located near stations. If noise levels are loud enough to mask PA announcements, patrons in these areas may not be able to clearly understand directions for evacuation during an emergency such as a fire. The criteria allow for a "signal-to-noise" ratio of 10 dBA or more, which is adequate if PA system announcements are at least 80 dBA. Where PA sound levels are less than 80 dBA, the emergency fan noise levels should be less than those indicated in the table.

Noise levels substantially higher than those in the table could potentially lead to a serious public safety situation. If the noise levels exceed 70 dBA over a large area, it will be difficult for patrons to hear PA announcements. There is an exception, however; directly underneath or adjacent to the ventilation shaft opening in the tunnel, levels as high as 75 dBA may be acceptable, if restricted to this immediate area. Some new PA systems automatically boost the loudspeaker output to adjust for higher levels of background noise (referred to as automatic level control). This may allow fan noise levels to be somewhat higher than otherwise.

The noise criteria indicated in the table below are used to determine noise control requirements for ancillary facility equipment where exterior noise emission could be intrusive to the occupants of buildings or outdoor areas adjacent to a station. The most common noise-sensitive receivers are residences, schools, and hospitals. The criteria apply to any point

DESIGN CRITERIA FOR ANCILLARY FACILITY AIRBORNE NOISE		
	MAXIMUM NOISE LEVEL** (DBA)	
Area Category*	Transient	Steady-State
Quiet residential	45	40
Average residential	50	45
Suburban, high-density residential	55	45
Urban residential, Semicommercial	60	50
Primarily commercial	65	55
Industrial or freeway corridor	70	60

*Area category refers to the surrounding land use.

**Criteria apply only to noise sensitive buildings (e.g., residential).

around the facility at a distance of 50 ft away from the noise-emitting area. Where buildings are farther than 50 ft, it may be appropriate to use the property line of the nearest noise-sensitive building as the point of evaluation.

The criteria indicated are in use as systemwide design criteria by several major transit agencies in the United States. Transient noises are those that are intermittent and usually last for a short duration (e.g., several seconds). An example of a transient noise is that of a subway train passing by a vent shaft. A steady-state noise is any noise that lasts for a substantial period of time or for at least 10 minutes in an hour. Examples include the noise from substation transformers or station ventilation fans.

SUBWAY STATION DESIGN

The term *subway station* is used as a generic label for public transit stations with below-grade facilities. Modern subway transit stations typically have two well-defined spaces, the concourse and the train room. The concourse, which usually includes ticketing, is often a large space from an acoustical standpoint, whereas the train room with its platforms may be small in cross section (especially if the two tracks are separated by a dividing wall) but long in order to accommodate the largest train consist (e.g., 10- to 12-car trains) serving the station. Although large (typically 300,000 cu ft or more), the train room behaves more like a small acoustical space.

Experience with station design has shown, and acoustical measurements confirm, that reverberation times for an enclosed platform are shorter than the total volume of the train room may suggest they should be. The reason is that sound propagates away from noise sources in the train room and down the tunnels at both ends, but in an enclosed space it continues to reverberate until absorbed at the room's surfaces. When calculating reverberation time for the train room, the "effective length" to use for the platform should be a fraction of its total length. An effective length comparable to the largest dimension of the train room cross section is usually appropriate.

▶ *Section through an underground side-platform station showing recommended locations for sound-absorbing materials.*

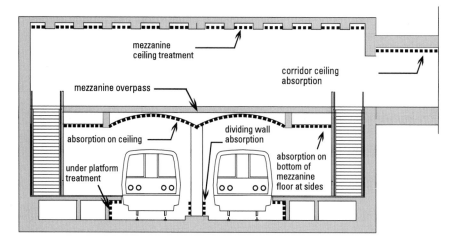

Acoustical Materials

The placement and amount of acoustical material used are important, but the type of material, how it is used, and where in the station it is used are equally important. Some materials are installed with mechanical fasteners, whereas others require on-site application, such as with spray-applied materials. Although the latter may require more labor and care during installation, they have the advantage of requiring little or no maintenance and are much more durable in situations where water intrusion is a possibility.

Acoustical materials are normally mounted on the ceilings of the concourse and train room. In the train room, acoustical material should also be applied under the platform, as shown below at left. Whenever possible, acoustical material on the walls of the concourse and along the platform walls should be included in the design. A uniformly distributed acoustical treatment is preferable to a very localized treatment, unless dealing with a specific noise source that benefits from placing the acoustical material close to it.

ACOUSTICAL MATERIALS

Material Class	Range of Thickness	Mounting Type	Finish Required	Water Damage	Flame Spread[8]	Smoke Density	Examples[6] Manufacturing/ Products
Fiberglass[1]	2"–3"	D or S	Yes	Yes	25	50	Generic
Cementitious spray application[2]	½"–2"	D	No	No	0	0	Pyrok/ Acoustement
Cementitious preformed[3]	2"–3"	D	No	No	Contact manufacturer	Contact manufacturer	CSI/Soundsorb
Composite wood fiber[4]	1"–1½"	D	No	No	Contact manufacturer	Contact manufacturer	Knauf/Fibralith
Resonant cavity blocks[5]	6"–8"	FS	No	No	Yes	Maybe	Soundblox/ Proudfoot
Acoustical ceiling tile	½"–¾"	S	No	Contact manufacturer	25	Contact manufacturer	Armstrong/ mineral fiber
New proprietary	M/D	D or S	M/D	Contact manufacturer	Contact manufacturer	Contact manufacturer	Freudenberg/ Soundtex[7]

D: Direct mounting; S: Suspended ceiling mounting; FS: Freestanding blocks; M/D: Material dependent

Notes:

[1] Still in use, but not advisable because of high probability of water damage in subway applications.

[2] Durable material, but not to be confused with spray-on materials for fire protection.

[3] Likewise a durable material, and may be preformed into wall panels.

[4] Not in wide use in the United States.

[5] Concrete blocks with lined cavity, provide absorption over a limited frequency range.

[6] Manufacturer/trade name.

[7] Soundtex, though not in wide use, has gained some acceptance for ceiling applications.

[8] When tested according to ASTM E84.

Six general types of acoustical materials are available or have been used in subway or other types of transit stations:

- Fiberglass (or mineral wool)
- Cementitious (spray-applied or pre-formed porous cement material)
- Treated wood fiber composite material
- Resonant cavity blocks
- Acoustical ceiling tiles
- New proprietary materials

The last class includes materials that are unique (i.e., generally proprietary) and developed within the last few years. As yet, these newer materials may not have received widespread usage in transit station applications. Although used extensively in the past, fiberglass is not recommended for subway stations because it will deteriorate when wet, and can often hide the spot where water is seeping into the underground portion of the station. Acoustical ceiling tiles would have a similar problem should they get wet in a subway environment.

The primary property an acoustician seeks in a material is its ability to absorb sound, whereas the architect is typically focused on how the material or its finish will look. The common goal of both is to find visually pleasing solutions that adequately absorb and control sound. The table on page 195 presents seven different acoustical materials (cementitious material comes in two forms), their features, and an example of each. The list is by no means exhaustive, but is intended to indicate the range of materials available.

The quantitative measure of a material's acoustical performance is the sound absorption coefficient, which can have a value of 0–1.0. A value of 1.0 implies perfect absorption, indicating that all impinging sound is absorbed. The values at different frequencies are determined in a laboratory test according to the industry standard (American Society for Testing and Materials, ASTM C423). In general terms, the value increases with increasing frequency. If a material is to be used for acoustical purposes, then laboratory test data should be obtained from the manufacturer. Test data that indicate sound absorption coefficients greater than 1.0 are an aberration of the testing method and should be discounted by limiting the value to 1.0 in any acoustical calculations.

The contract specification documents for the station project must include minimum requirements for sound absorption coefficients at six frequencies (125, 250, 500, 1000, 2000, and 4000 Hz). The noise reduction coefficient (NRC) is often used as an indicator of a material's acoustical performance, and although specifying a minimum value is appropriate, the NRC does not indicate a material's ability to absorb low-frequency noise such as produced by trains and some HVAC equipment. For this reason, the six absorption coefficients must be specified individually, particularly the coefficient at 125 Hz, to address this issue.

The manner in which the sound-absorbing material is mounted to the room surface (wall, ceiling) can have an effect on the absorption properties of the installation. If the material is highly porous, providing an air gap behind the material often improves the sound absorption coefficients obtained. This effect is more noticeable at low frequencies. Where mounting is important to the performance of an acoustical material, test data should be obtained. Acoustical material suppliers often have test data available for different mountings, or if not, may be willing to test for a particular nonstandard mounting being considered.

Aside from the absorption properties of an acoustical material, other properties that must be considered in selecting a material are indicated in the table on page 195. The ability of the material to not produce a flame, nor generate smoke in a fire, is obviously extremely important for public safety. Most transit agencies explicitly prohibit the use of materials that allow a flame to spread or produce smoke when subjected to fire.

The industry standard used to test a material's behavior in a fire is ASTM E84. Many materials are rated Class A according to ASTM E84, but this is not a sufficient measure to use alone. Some materials have zero flame spread, but produce smoke, and are still considered Class A. To be considered for use in a transit station, an acoustical material should ideally have zero ("0") flame spread and produce zero ("0") smoke density when tested according to ASTM E84. An unfortunate and tragic example of an inappropriate material used for sound-absorption purposes and implicated in a fire that caused numerous deaths is the highly publicized case in 2003 of the Station, a nightclub in West Warwick, Rhode Island.

Sound-absorption materials are effective because of their porosity and thickness. The more porous a material, the better sound can interact with it and be absorbed. The thickness of a material affects the amount of sound absorption obtainable for that particular material per unit of surface area. This is more important in regard to lower-frequency sound,

which is harder to absorb. The manner in which Soundblox blocks (resonator) and Soundtex (a very thin woven material) absorb sound is more complex than the way a material like fiberglass works and is beyond the scope of this discussion.

Sound absorption is needed for both reverberation control and general noise control. Reverberation control is accomplished with adequate sound absorption in public spaces. When designed properly, the sound absorption treatment will result in appropriate sound levels generated by patrons and reasonably intelligible PA announcements. General noise control refers to train noise and mechanical equipment noise that are not excessive. Noise control is often achieved with sound absorption material, but also requires the isolation of mechanical equipment and the use of silencers or mufflers on very noisy equipment.

Architectural Finishes

Typically, acoustical materials are placed behind an architectural finish, but there are materials that do not require an additional surface finish and can be left either unfinished or given a minor finishing touch. Whether to use a finish is often dependent on the appearance the architect wants to achieve. A spray-on material (such as Pyrok) may require no finish other than a light troweling. Pigment can be added to the material to obtain the desired appearance.

Acoustical materials perform essentially the same with or without finishes as long as there is sufficient "open area" (ratio of area of holes to total area) in the finished material or system. Perforated metal sheeting is the most common fin-

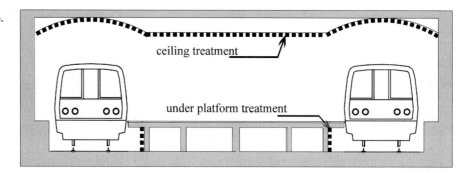

Section through an underground center-platform station depicting location for sound-absorbing materials.

ish material used over acoustical materials. Expanded metal can also be used in the same way. Ceiling systems with metal slats or formed metal with openings are also used.

When perforated metal sheeting is used as the architectural finish, the minimum amount of open area should be 20 percent to avoid significantly affecting the overall acoustical performance.

Perforated metal with very small holes should not be used, because the holes may become clogged with dust, which over time may degrade the overall acoustical performance of the material. The problem of dust accumulation for a porous material cannot be avoided in the train room, where vehicle brake dust is often present, especially at track level. Some materials, such as the cementitious materials, can be washed with high-pressure water spray without damaging them, which would keep them clean and the pores open.

Where architectural finish systems other than perforated metal are used, and which generally meet the aforementioned requirements, it is important that acoustical laboratory test data be obtained from the supplier for the ceiling and absorption material as a complete acoustical system. Most manufacturers who supply quality ceiling systems (with

absorptive material) that are advertised as having acoustical properties should have such data or be willing to conduct tests to obtain the data. For example, an interesting use of an open ceiling baffle system is indicated in the illustration at right.

Reverberation Control

The area percentages in the table on page 188 should be used as guidelines in the preliminary design. After the materials and the areas to be treated are selected, the predicted reverberation time can be calculated for the space. By comparing the reverberation time criteria indicated in the table with the projected reverberation times for the preliminary design, it is possible to determine the amount of additional acoustical material needed for the space.

In the train room, the ceiling above the platform is usually treated, and often the walls. In the concourse, the ceiling is treated and the walls may be too. If the station has an arrival hall, the walls may be glass, which often leaves the ceiling as the only surface that can be acoustically treated.

Noise Control

It is important to control noise produced by train movement and mechanical and electrical equipment. For trains, noise

◀ An open-baffle ceiling system shown in an underground station at a concourse level. Although acoustically effective, it presents challenges for routine maintenance access. (Photo courtesy R.A. Carman.)

control is achieved with absorptive materials applied in the approach tunnel and in the train room. Noise control for station equipment is accomplished with isolation of the noisiest equipment, sound-absorption materials, and special noise control systems.

Noise generated by moving trains is directly related to the speed of the trains, and transit trains are capable of accelerating to substantial speeds before all of the vehicles are out of the station. For example, transit trains are capable of speeds up to 80 mph and can enter or leave the station platform at a speed of 50 mph. Some stations have extra tracks in addition to the platform tracks, which allow express trains to skip a station and maintain high speed. In this situation, additional noise control, such as by using a dividing wall, may be required.

Control of airborne noise from trains is achieved by using sufficient sound-absorbing material. In the train room, the amount and type of material needed for reverberation control may be adequate for reducing the noise from trains. Wolfe (1983) indicates that the "difference between a station with little absorption and stations with a large amount of absorption is 13 dBA—a sufficient reduction to create a dramatic subjective difference."

A train's noise levels are also dependent on the noise emission characteristics of the train. Locomotive noise is louder than the noise emitted by passenger cars. For transit vehicles powered by an electrical traction motor mounted on each car, the movement of the train is usually the loudest source. Each situation must be evaluated using the characteristics of the transit system's vehicle fleet and the design parameters of the train room.

A major source of transit noise is the rolling noise generated at the wheel and rail interface. Consequently, the use of sound absorption under the platform, as shown in the illustration on page 194, is effective for reducing this type of transit train noise. An effective sound-absorption

▶ *Sound-absorbing materials used on a wall across from a platform. Charles de Gaulle International Airport train station. (Photo courtesy R. A. Carman.)*

material in this location should have adequate low-frequency absorption characteristics. Vehicle equipment is often mounted under the car, and sound absorption located under the platform is beneficial in reducing this type of noise. The illustration above shows sound absorption (fibrous boards on a partial dividing wall) at wheel height to control train noise. Wolfe (1983) states that, based on measurements at transit systems in San Francisco, Washington, D.C., and Toronto, "under-platform acoustical treatment is very effective at reducing levels of train noise."

Wolfe (1983) also provides an example of acoustical treatments for a typical subway station in terms of the amount of treatment per foot of station structure. The table at right illustrates a typical treatment for two types of train rooms.

An interesting recent development in train noise control is trackway sound absorption. Porous cement panels manufactured in Germany are available for use on slab track in outdoor applications. The panels are mechanically fastened to the slab between the rails and are sturdy enough to be walked on. Although not yet in use in the United States, such panels might be used in stations as absorptive treatment at track level to effectively control train noise. The data suggest that some of the panels provide as much noise reduction as ballasted track.

Where a station will have express trains passing through it, a full-height dividing wall between the platform and the express tracks is the best way to reduce the direct transmission of airborne noise between the vehicles and the platform. However, noise also propagates well in a concrete tunnel and will enter the platform area from the tunnel entrance to the train room. If possible, noise control material should be applied in the tunnel before and after the station to reduce the level of noise generated by express trains before the sound enters the platform area.

Noise models have been developed to determine platform noise levels produced by moving trains, which is a complex phenomenon involving sound propagation in a long enclosure (i.e., tunnel). Kang (1996), for example, developed a computer model for predicting the temporal and spatial distribution of train noise in underground stations. This model was based on the results of scale model experiments. Carman (2003) developed a theoretically based noise model for moving trains that predicts noise levels in various parts of a station (e.g., platform, concourse, arrival hall).

Noise generated by large mechanical equipment, such as ventilation fans, requires the use of acoustical materials and the use of noise suppression devices at the source. The table on page 202 lists the major types of equipment requiring

noise control. Some of the equipment listed would be found only in a large railroad station or terminal, not in a typical transit station.

Mechanical and electrical equipment are typically located in separate rooms, thereby isolating the equipment and making noise control easier. The room's walls, floor, and ceiling substantially attenuate noise transmitted through them. This acoustical property of the room enclosure is called *transmission loss* (TL). Concrete masonry unit blocks have reasonably high TL, but what is required depends on the noise emission characteristics of the equipment within the room. Incorporating sound absorption within the room that will lessen the TL requirements of the walls and ceiling can also control the noise inside the room. The amount of absorption necessary, as well as the proper amount of TL, must be determined in each case.

ACOUSTICAL TREATMENTS FOR SUBWAY STATIONS

Station Type	Treatment Location	ACOUSTICAL TREATMENT PER LINEAR FT OF STATION STRUCTURE	
		Available Area (sq ft)*	Required Area (sq ft)*
Center platform station	Total**	140	35
	Under-platform	5	5
	Ceiling and walls	80	30
Side platform station	Total**	160	35
	Under-platform	8	8
	Ceiling		
	Coffers	27	27
	Coffer bottoms (beams)	12	—
	Walls	22	—

*Because the station cross sections are relatively uniform, the area for treatment is effectively in terms of the perimeter of the typical cross sections.
**Includes platform and trackway areas.

MECHANICAL AND ELECTRICAL EQUIPMENT NOISE SOURCES

Equipment	Temporal Character	Station Location	Materials	NOISE CONTROL System	Isolation*
Ventilation fans	Continuous	Fan room	—	Silencer	Yes
HVAC ducts	Continuous	Public and office	Duct liner	Sound trap	—
Escalators	Continuous	Public space	—	Mfg. sup.	—
Elevators & equip.	Intermittent	Public space	—	Mfg. sup.	Yes
Transformers	Continuous	Electrical room	Manufacturer supplied room absorption	—	Yes
Chillers	Continuous	Mechanical room	Manufacturer supplied room absorption	—	Yes
Pumps	Continuous	Mechanical room	Manufacturer supplied room absorption	—	Yes
Tunnel ventilation fan	Testing and emergency	Tunnel vent shaft	Plenum absorption	Plenum	—
Emergency generators	Testing and emergency	Generator room	Manufacturer supplied room absorption	Silencer	Yes

Isolation refers to locating equipment within a room.

Platform Screen Doors

A platform screen door (PSD) system, a recent development in passenger control and safety, can also dramatically reduce train noise on platforms. PSD systems are in use in transit in Europe and Asia but have not as yet received acceptance in the United States except at airport terminals with automated people-mover stations. There are PSD systems that serve only as passenger safety devices, with no ceiling above the trackway, allowing some of the train noise to enter the platform and making the PSDs much less effective in controlling noise.

A PSD system can also reduce the noise of a tunnel's emergency ventilation fan at the platform. To be acoustically effective, the PSD system must completely seal off the platform from the trackway.

Public-Address System Design

A good public-address (PA) system design requires an experienced audio engineer and acoustical consultant. More than a cursory review of the subject is beyond the scope of the following discussion. The PA system in a station serves an important function. Patrons rely on clearly hearing train arrival and departure announcements. Although most stations

◀ *Platform screen doors dramatically reduce train noise on platforms. The photo shown here is of an airport people-mover station. (Photo courtesy R.A. Carman.)*

have electronic signage for visual announcements to patrons, the signs do not fully satisfy the requirements of the Americans with Disabilities Act (ADA).

In the design of a PA system, both the *reverberant sound* field and the *direct sound* field must be considered. The best condition for a listener is to be in the direct field, which is typically no more than 10 ft from a speaker. In a large space, PA speakers are often mounted far above the patrons, resulting in patrons being in the reverberant field, which is dependent on the acoustics of the space. Consequently, the volume of a station space presents the greatest challenge to the PA system designer. The smaller the space, the easier it is to locate PA speakers close to patrons. It is common practice to locate speakers on a grid of 20–30 ft on center where the ceiling is low. Where the ceiling is high, larger speakers are normally used and often spaced more than 30 ft apart.

An excellent PA system cannot compensate for bad acoustics in a station. A highly reverberant sound field will make the announcements garbled because of the persistence of sound from earlier spoken words. The quicker sound decays, the easier it is to understand the subsequent words in an announcement. A high level of background noise will make intelligibility more difficult. A quality PA system, which is properly configured and implemented, and properly designed room acoustics should result in acceptable PA announcement intelligibility. The reverberation times indicated in the table on page 188 will result in an acoustical environment in which a good PA system will function properly and announcements should be intelligible, if speakers can be mounted close enough to patrons. Typically, their location at no more than 15 ft from a patron will provide good coverage if the acoustics of the space are favorable.

There are standardized measures of speech intelligibility used to quantify existing spaces and employed as design tools for new spaces. One measure is the Articulation Index (AI), which is based on a subjective measure having a value between 0 and 1.0, as presented in the American National Standards Institute's (ANSI) Standard S3.5. Another is the Speech Transmission Index (STI), as presented in International Electrotechnical Commission (IEC) 60268, which is a mathematically based measure having a value between 0 and 1.0. A modification of the STI is the Rapid Speech Transmission Index (RASTI), for which sound measurement systems are available.

A desirable AI goal of 0.7 implies intelligibility of approximately 88 percent or better. In practical situations this may hard to achieve, and an AI of 0.5 (or about 70 percent intelligibility) may be a more feasible goal. A good design criterion would be an AI of at least 0.5 or, where practical, 0.7. The PA system specification for the station should require testing after installation to confirm that the criterion has been met in a sufficient number of locations throughout the station. Specification of a minimum value for a speech intelligibility measure such as STI is worth considering for inclusion in the station contract documents, but as yet has not received wide acceptance.

Where background noise levels vary, it is advantageous to consider using a PA system that incorporates an automatic level or gain control. An example of where this is appropriate is on the platform, to compensate for higher noise levels when trains are in the station. This will boost the signal-to-noise ratio and usually improve intelligibility.

The most important characteristics of a PA loudspeaker are its power requirement, sound level generated at a distance from the speaker, linearity, lack of distortion, and angle of coverage. The linearity of a loudspeaker refers to the speaker's ability to faithfully reproduce sound over a wide enough frequency range (i.e., frequency response). An example of the high-quality loudspeakers used on the platforms at Charles de Gaulle International Airport train station is shown in

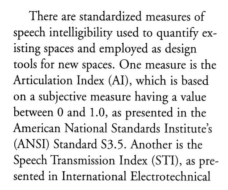

▼ An example of high-quality loudspeakers used on the platforms at Charles de Gaulle International Airport train station. (Photo courtesy R.A. Carman.)

the illustration at left. The typical loud-speakers used in public facilities such as transit stations have low-frequency cut-offs that can affect the intelligibility of PA announcements. The lower the cutoff the better, but the more expensive the speaker will be.

Airborne Noise from Ancillary Facilities

Ancillary facilities for transit systems generate noise that, if not properly controlled, can be an annoyance to the local community, especially where residences or other noise-sensitive buildings are nearby. The most common noise-producing ancillary facilities are fan vents and electrical substations. Vent structures for subways can also emit airborne noise generated by trains operating in the tunnels below. It is possible to acoustically model noise source levels and the amount of attenuation that should occur between the noise source and the opening to the outdoors in the case of sources inside buildings. The acoustical designer, to determine whether the exterior noise from the vent or substation is low enough, based on the initial design, uses the noise criteria in the table on page 193. If this is not the case, then additional noise-reduction measures can be incorporated.

To control noise from vent structures, the acoustical engineer attempts to attenuate the noise, from the ventilation fan or subway train, as much as possible within the vent ducting and structure before it is emitted to the surrounding community. This can be accomplished by using acoustically lined plenums, acoustic absorption treatment in the duct, or acoustical louvers at the opening to the exterior, or with shielding by sound walls

between the exhaust (or intake) opening and the noise-sensitive building.

Substations having large items of electrical equipment can be a source of bothersome noise in a community unless residences, hospitals, and schools are sufficiently far away. What a sufficient distance is often depends on the local ambient noise levels, especially at night. If the substation is adjacent to a freeway, the background noise levels may mask the substation noise, whereas in a quieter suburban or rural area, the noise can be more noticeable because the background noise levels are much lower.

Structure-Borne Noise Control

Where it is not possible to have vibration isolation joints between the track support structure and the rest of the station structure, the structure-borne noise generated by moving trains will propagate into distant parts of the station. If train speeds are high enough, and/or more noise-sensitive station spaces (e.g., waiting rooms) are close enough to the tracks, noise levels can be excessive.

▼ An efficient solution to structure-borne noise is to have adequate vibration isolation between the rails and the track slab.

The most efficient solution to structure-borne noise is to have adequate vibration isolation between the rails and track slab. One such track system is shown on page 205. Noise levels of 55–58 dBA were measured in the restaurant area underneath the tracks, which exceed the recommended criterion of 50 dBA. A similar but improved system (Low Vibration Track) is supplied in the United States by the Sonneville International Corporation. Where special track support systems do not provide sufficient reduction of structure-borne noise, it may be necessary to use a resiliently suspended ceiling system. The design of the ceiling system must include resilient hangers and a ceiling/barrier with a mass great enough to reduce noise radiated from the bottom of the structural floor above. The system must have a sufficiently low natural frequency to avoid transmitting excessive low-frequency noise. Design of the ceiling/barrier is sufficiently complex to require special expertise.

AERIAL STATION DESIGN

Most aerial stations are often only partially enclosed (i.e., ceiling and floor). Walls, if there are any, are usually not full height. In this case, reverberation is not an issue, because the sound is not confined but instead propagates away from the station. However, noise from external sources can be a major problem for aerial transit stations. This is especially true for those constructed in the middle of freeways, a common practice today. This can be a problem for patrons waiting on the platform for trains. PA announcements can also be an issue for the local residential community, particularly at night when ambient noise levels decrease.

Acoustical Treatment

Standard acoustical treatment for aerial stations is used for the ceiling and under-platform areas. Materials that are water and wind resistant are necessary if they are to be exposed to weather. Often, aerial stations are open except for the ceiling. In this case, less absorption may be needed than in an enclosed station, except when the platforms are in the middle of a freeway. In addition to underplatform treatment, ceiling absorption can be beneficial to control train noise and other exterior noise and to provide better acoustics for the PA system.

Noise Control

Most aerial stations need only train noise control. Where the station will be in the middle of a freeway median and the platform is exposed to high levels of noise, it is imperative that a noise wall be used to shield the platform. Otherwise, noise levels can easily exceed 85 dBA (Wolf 1996), which is excessive and will interfere with PA announcements.

Platform areas should be shielded from freeway noise as much as possible, even if only partially. An effective noise barrier will have sufficient mass (at least 4 lb/sq ft) and extend to block line-of-sight with the traffic. Wolf (1996) found that a 10 ft high wall in the middle of the platform and a 6 ft high wall on the end could reduce noise levels by 10 dBA. Patron security is often an issue, and local law enforcement may require that the platform can be seen from the street. In this case, a transparent barrier material may be possible. Sound absorption on the ceiling or underside of the canopy will reduce noise that is reflected off it. Wolf (1996) also discusses the use of 6 by 12 by 4 ft patron shelters as an alternative to building noise barriers between the freeway and the platform.

Public-Address System Design

The PA system design for an aerial station would be much like that for a subway, except that reverberation is not an issue. Often the covered portion of the station does not extend the full length of the platform. Where this is the case, loudspeakers and their spacing must be selected so as to provide adequate coverage. If PA system levels are too loud and residences are nearby, the community may react adversely. This is primarily an issue at night when the general ambient noise levels drop and the announcements are more noticeable; such situations must be investigated on a case-by-case basis.

The designer should determine how loud PA announcement sound levels will be at nearby residences. If they will be louder than the background noise levels in the community, then a special effort may be required to contain sound levels within the station area, using more loudspeakers with lower output levels. If the residential community is on only one side of the station, it may be possible to select loudspeakers and orient them in such a way as to reduce the sound that is transmitted in that direction and still maintain adequate coverage in the station. The use of automatic gain control will also tend to minimize the impact on the surrounding neighborhood. Platform sound levels for PA announcements can be set lower to be consistent with the surrounding ambient noise levels and raised only when trains are in the station.

AT-GRADE STATION DESIGN

At-grade transit stations are often similar to aerial stations, but with the ticketing and concourse areas above the platforms rather than below. Many at-grade stations are, like aerial stations, partially open. Consequently, the acoustical designs of the two types of stations are often similar. Each station must be evaluated with regard to noise control and reverberation control where spaces are sufficiently enclosed.

RAILROAD PASSENGER STATIONS

Railroad passenger stations are typically at-grade stations with a ceiling over the platform. There may be waiting rooms and, in bigger stations, retail space serving train patrons. The primary difference between a railroad passenger station and a mass transit station is the noise characteristic of the vehicles. Railroads often use locomotives, which produce more noise than a typical transit vehicle. More modern, electrified locomotives or individually motorized rail coaches tend to be quieter than the older locomotives. In designing noise control, these issues must be considered; otherwise the acoustical design of the station is much like that of a typical mass transit station.

HIGH-SPEED TRAIN STATIONS

Noise from high-speed express trains is much greater than that of subway trains because of the vast difference in speed. A dividing wall between the platform and express tracks is essential in underground stations with high-speed express trains, and sound-absorption treatment in the approach tunnels is also necessary. For discussion of noise control in underground stations with high-speed trains, one can refer to work by Carman (2003), which found that platform noise levels can exceed 100 dBA for 180 mph express trains unless substantial noise control is implemented. Where the station is at-grade, it may be possible to adequately reduce train noise with partial-height walls and sound-absorption facing the express tracks.

High-speed train stations are also unique in that those with underground platforms can be subjected to a pressure pulse created when the train enters the portal of the approach tunnel. *The Subway Environmental Design Handbook* (1976) discusses the pressure pulse phenomenon as well as the train piston effect (i.e., wind caused by a train moving in the confined space of a tunnel).

AIRPORT PEOPLE MOVER STATIONS

The current design for airport people mover (APM) stations often uses PSDs. The doors open only when the train is in the station. The station, which often consists of a room enclosing the platform, is much like that of any other transit station except for one major difference.

Often APM stations are structurally integrated with the rest of the airport building. Transit stations usually do not have waiting rooms, but airport terminals can have waiting rooms and other similar spaces that may be close to the APM stations. Vibration from the commonly used aerial guideway structure can be transmitted into these spaces. If the vibration is strong enough, occupants of the waiting rooms will feel uncomfortable. To avoid this, it is best to perform an engineering analysis to determine the expected level of vibration and decide whether some form of vibration isolation is needed between the guideway and the airport terminal building.

BUS TRANSIT STATIONS

Bus transit stations should be designed much like any other mass transit station, except for possible differences in noise control for platform areas. The noise emission characteristics of buses are different from those of rail vehicles. A major difference is the presence of low-frequency exhaust noise produced by buses. Consequently, noise control should be designed to address this concern. In general, such noise control requires thicker sound-absorption material.

CHAPTER 10

LIGHTING

The effective illumination of any transportation project is a partnership of technology and design as it strives to integrate the facility's function, its form, and the technical requirements of supporting systems. Good lighting is not just a matter of equipment and light levels, but also of appropriate orchestration of emphasis, movement, transition, color, and intensity.

This chapter explores some of the fundamental aspects of good lighting practice as it pertains to transit facilities. It considers such factors as energy efficiency, passenger comfort and safety, and the ability to respond to evolving technology and future requirements.

DESIGN CONSIDERATIONS
Surface Reflectance

Improving visual perception and passenger comfort is a critical objective. Perceived brightness therefore becomes a primary factor in visibility. Simply put, the lighter the surface, the brighter the eye perceives the surface to be, as the quantity

> Transportation systems in general, and throughways in particular, have replaced the plaza as the most potent single urban design element in a city scheme. Getting around is the most common single experience we all have in cities.
>
> *Franzen and Rudolph 1974*

of reflected light is greater than that of light striking a darker surface.

Certain transportation authorities include within their lighting guidelines recommended percentage reflectance val-

▲ *Indirect lighting used to accent the ceiling and illuminate the overall volume of the Los Angeles Metro Red Line station.*

▶ *Natural lighting over an escalator bank in one of the Jubilee Line stations. (Photo courtesy Alfred Lau.)*

ues for surfaces, reinforcing the importance of material and finish choice as factors in good lighting design. In the interest of providing some measure of guidance, the following material reflectances are suggested:

- Painted surfaces (ceiling planes and walls): 55–70 percent

- Unpainted surfaces (ceilings, walls) 40–60 percent

- Floors (dark) 15–20 percent

- Floors (light) 20–30 percent

To improve acuity and comfort while maximizing lighting system efficiency, the lighting design should be coordinated with the architectural design to assure selection of highly reflective (light-value nonspecular) floor, wall, and ceiling materials whenever architecturally appropriate.

Daylight and Natural Light

The introduction of daylight is a long-standing objective in the design of almost any transit structure. Daylight serves a host of functions: a source of visual refreshment, an energy-saving supplementation for artificial lighting systems, and a means of providing passengers with a sense of connection to the outside world.

A clear distinction must be drawn between direct sunlight and daylight. Sunlight can be defined as direct solar radiation from a visually apparent sun disk (during daytime hours), which is available under clear sky conditions, and from only a specific orientation (i.e., southeast, east, south, southwest, west). The total amount of sunlight that might be expected in any structure would be a result of longitude, latitude, time of day, time of year, local weather conditions, and proximity to adjacent shading elements such as other buildings.

Daylight is the resultant effect of direct solar radiation diffused though the atmosphere (or reflected from the sky) and as such is far less intense and directional than sunlight. It is also less dependent on the presence of clear skies or lack of neighboring obstructions. Given that many transit facilities in urban areas may be shadowed by adjacent taller structures, the potential for the introduction of sunlight is often limited; however, daylight will not necessarily be equally restricted. The introduction of daylight does not in any way replace or preclude the need for artificial light sources, but merely reduces daytime dependence on them. Careful integration and coordination between daylight and artificial lighting systems is always required.

Maintenance and Operations

Maintenance and operations are important concerns for any transit system and should be considered by the lighting designer.

At platform conditions, lighting system components should be located so that they may be easily maintained; that is, no fixtures should be located directly over the trackway. The relationship of luminaires and system components to the platform edge should be determined by the station architecture in conjunction with other system requirements (i.e., coordination with signage; heating, ventilating, and air-conditioning [HVAC] systems; etc.)

The maximum mounting height of luminaires and system components should be determined by the station architecture in conjunction with the feasibility of maintenance of the system components. The average rated life of a light

source must be factored into this assessment.

Luminaires should be located to promote public safety and avert deliberate vandalism or inadvertent damage (e.g., by floor-scrubbing equipment). Tool-less access of lighting fixtures and components reduces maintenance by reducing labor time.

Maintenance of light sources via a group-relamping strategy should be considered. This approach helps to control costs as well as minimize the disruption of any station's normal operations. Group relamping requires scheduling that would be normally based on variables such as the actual lamp life, availability of daylight, hours of peak and off-peak usage, and other operational or programmatic requirements of the particular system.

Facilities with high ceilings should accommodate movable personnel lift equipment. This approach requires adequate storage for such equipment and the appropriate sizing of freight elevators and related conveyances to facilitate access.

Controls

Lighting control systems can offer significant energy savings and can take the form of relays or programmable breakers, integrated with photocells and astronomical time clocks.

Control system approaches include:

- Response to the presence or absence of natural light. Selected luminaires can be deenergized during daylight hours and energized via photocell at sunset.

- Peak/off-peak hours. Selected luminaires may be deenergized only during hours of off-peak ridership.

- Load-shedding at hours of highest power utilization. When energy usage is at its highest in the system overall, cost savings may be realized by deenergization of selected luminaires.

Regardless of the control philosophy, the control system should allow for maintaining minimum light levels at all times.

DESIGN FACTORS

Terminology

The lighting field uses specific terminology to describe various aspects of illumination. For terms often encountered in dealing with the lighting design of any structure or environment, see pages 214–215.

Codes and References

The design of a lighting system for any new or existing transit facility should use the latest editions of all appropriate and applicable reference standards, regulations, and local/state codes of organizations.

Environmental Considerations

Sustainability

The last decade has seen the emergence of credible sustainable design goals, as propagated by Leadership in Energy and Environmental Design (LEED). These address the issues of energy efficiency, indoor environmental quality materials conservation, and water conservation and site management considerations. The following goals have particular relevance for transit station lighting design:

- Energy conservation, via compliance with state or federally mandated energy codes (i.e., IECCC or ASHRAE).

- Daylight integration when used in conjunction with responsive control technology. Natural light may provide sufficient illumination to warrant de-energization of designated electrical lighting, offering potential energy savings.

CODES AND REFERENCES	
Codes	
ADAAG	ADA Accessibility Guidelines
ANSI	American National Standards Institute
BOCA	Unified Building Code
EPACT	Energy Policy Act of 1992
IEEE	Institute of Electrical and Electronic Engineers
NEC	National Electric Code
NEMA	National Equipment Manufacturers Association
NFPA	National Fire Protection Association
IBC	International Building Code
IECCC	International Energy Conservation Construction Code
OSHA	Occupational Safety and Health Administration
TCLP	Toxicity Characteristic Leaching Procedure
UL	Underwriters Laboratories
References	
APTA	American Public Transit Association
ASHRAE	American Society of Heating, Refrigerating, and Air-Conditioning Engineers
IESNA	Illuminating Engineering Society of North America
LEED	Leadership in Energy and Environmental Design

- Reduction in the landfilling of waste materials via use of long-life low-mercury light sources.[1]

Lighting power limits

The establishment of overall lighting power limits (or lighting power density) is normally done by referring to the prevailing energy codes and standards. Depending on the type of transit structure, it is important to determine whether any state energy codes apply. Some states have structured their energy codes to apply to new or modernized air-conditioned, air-tempered structures only. At-grade commuter or light-rail systems may be exempted; consultation with a qualified code consultant on a case-by-case basis is recommended.

Many state energy codes (e.g., IEC-CC) refer to ASHRAE for guidance. In the current ASHRAE Standard 90.1-2001, *Energy Standard for Buildings Except Low-Rise Residential Buildings,* specific reference to a transportation facility may be found. ASHRAE is written to include easily definable building types and spaces and does not describe many of the major spaces found in a transit facility, particularly platforms, mezzanines, and control areas. Some interpretation is required to determine the applicable lighting power density for these areas.

Compliance with ASHRAE is predicated on containing "conditioned" spaces; that is, for areas that are either cooled or heated ASHRAE sets forth two methods to determine the maximum total building/system connected load for lighting, the Space-by-Space Method and the Building Area Method. In the Space-by-Space Method, assignments of watts/square foot lighting power densities (LPDs) for different spaces are given, which must be multiplied by the gross interior floor area to determine the lighting power allowance for each space. The interior lighting power allowance is the sum of the lighting power allowances of all spaces.

In the Building Area Method, the building type is first ascertained. The gross illuminated floor area of the facility must then be determined and multiplied by the LPD listed to arrive at the total installed interior lighting power allowance. The total installed interior lighting power must not exceed the interior lighting power allowance for that building type.

Illumination Criteria

Transportation authorities, for the most part, base their criteria for illumination on a number of sources:

- Information from relevant lighting reference sources (i.e., IESNA and APTA)

---

[1]A major issue confronting any public operating authority involves policies regarding lamp replacement and bulk lamp disposal. Fluorescent and high-intensity discharge (HID) lamps, because they contain mercury, are regulated under the Resource Conservation and Recovery Act (RCRA), which is administered by the U.S. Environmental Protection Agency. RCRA requires generators of such lamps to determine whether their lamp wastes are hazardous. The Toxicity Characteristic Leaching Procedure (TCLP) test determines whether waste is toxic and must be managed as hazardous. Many conventional fluorescent and HID lamps will fail to pass the TCLP test unless they are specifically designed to do so. In order to pass, a lamp must contain a mercury concentration of less than 0.2 mg/L; otherwise, it is classified as hazardous.

Lighting Terms

Accent light. Directional light that emphasizes objects or draws attention to part of the visual field.

Adaptation. The process by which the eye becomes accustomed to more or less light than it was exposed to during an immediately preceding period. It results in a change in the sensitivity to light.

Ambient lighting. See General lighting.

Average rated life. An average rating, in hours, indicating when 50 percent of a large group of lamps have failed, when operated at nominal lamp voltage and current.

Ballast. Electrical device that supplies proper voltage, current, and waveform conditions to start and operate discharge lamps (e.g., fluorescent, metal halide, high-pressure sodium).

Candela (cd). A unit of measurement of luminous intensity in one direction. It is the property of a source of light and is not affected by distance. An ordinary wax candle has a luminous intensity in a horizontal direction of approximately 1 candela.

Candlepower distribution. A curve that represents the variation in luminous intensity (expressed in candelas) in a plane through the light center of a lamp or luminaire; each lamp or lamp/luminaire combination has a unique set of candlepower distributions that indicate how light will be spread.

Color rendering index (CRI). The Color Rendering Index measures the effect of a light source on the perceived color of objects and surfaces. High CRI values make virtually all colors look natural and vibrant. Low CRI causes some colors to appear washed out or take on a completely different hue.

Color temperature (CT). Color temperature, which is measured in kelvins (K), indicates whether a lamp has a warm, midrange, or cool color appearance. "Warm" light sources have a low color temperature (2000–3000 K) and emphasize light in the red/orange/yellow range. Light sources with a higher color temperature (>5000 K) feature more blue light and are referred to as "cool."

Compact fluorescent lamps (CFL). Single-based fluorescent lamps of bent-tube construction, manufactured in ratings 5 to 80 watts (approximately 250 to 3900 initial lumens).

Contrast. The relationship between the brightness (or color) of an object and that of its immediate surroundings.

Direct lighting. Lighting by luminaires distributing 90–100 percent of the emitted light in the general direction of the surface to be illuminated. The term usually refers to light emitted in a downward direction.

Downlight. Lighting fixture that directs light downward. Can be recessed, surface-mounted, or suspended.

Efficacy. The rate at which a lamp is able to convert power (watts) into light (lumens), expressed in lumens per watt (LPW or lm/W).

Efficiency (of luminaires). Luminous efficiency expressed as a ratio of lumen output of fixture to lumen output of lamps alone.

Fluorescent lamp. A low-pressure mercury electric discharge lamp in which a fluorescing coating (phosphor) transforms some of the ultraviolet energy generated by the discharge into light.

Footcandle (fc). The unit by which illuminance is measured. It is equal to the illumination at a point on a surface that is 1 ft from and perpendicular to a uniform point source of 1 candela.

General lighting. Lighting designed to provide a substantially uniform level of illumination throughout an area, exclusive of any provision for special local requirements.

Glare. Harsh, uncomfortably bright light source or reflection that interferes with visual perception.

High-intensity discharge (HID) lamp. An electric discharge lamp in which the light is produced by the passage of electric current through some form of metallic vapor. HID lamps include groups of lamps known as mercury vapor, metal halide, and high-pressure sodium. Lamps can be clear or coated.

Illuminance. Light falling (incident) on a surface. The eye does not perceive illumination, but rather reflected light. (See Luminance.)

Induction lamp. Light generated from this type of lamp is achieved by induction, or the transmission of energy via a magnetic field, combined with a gas discharge. Because such lamps have no electrodes, there are no components to degrade yielding an average rated life of 60,000–100,000 hours.

Incandescent filament lamp. A lamp in which light is produced by a filament heated to incandescence by an electrical current.

Indirect lighting. Lighting achieved by reflection, usually from wall and ceiling surfaces. An example is a space with a high-reflectance ceiling illuminated by an uplight.

Ingress protection (IP). IP ratings provide guidance in categorizing the ability of any luminaire to resist the incursion of foreign elements that could have a negative impact on fixture performance (i.e., dust, water, etc.).

Light. Visually evaluated radiant energy.

Light loss factor (LLF). A factor used in calculating illuminance after a given period of time and under given conditions. It takes into account dirt accumulation on luminaire and room surfaces, lumen depreciation, maintenance procedures, and atmospheric conditions.

Lighting power density (LPD). Watts per a given area, normally expressed as watts/ft2.

Lumen. Unit of light energy used to specify the light output of sources. It is the rate at which light falls on one square foot from a source of one candela.

Lumen Depreciation. The decrease in lumen output of a light source over time; every lamp type has a unique lumen depreciation curve (sometimes called a lumen maintenance curve) depicting the pattern of decreasing light output.

Luminance. Also referred to as brightness or photometric brightness. It is that portion of the lighting experience that the eye actually perceives and is independent of viewing distance. It refers to light reflected off, or transmitted through, a surface in a given direction.

Maintained illumination level. The initial illumination level from luminaires adjusted for depreciation of lamp lumens by aging, effects of dirt accumulation on luminaire surfaces, and other factors.

Point source. Light source that emits its light from a small area relative to the fixture in which it is placed.

Reflectance. Percentage of incident light on a surface that is reradiated. It depends on the angle of incidence as well as other factors.

Reflector. A device used to redirect light from a source.

Refractor. A device used to redirect light (lens). Light rays change direction when passing obliquely from one medium to another (as from air to glass, glass to water, etc.)

Specular. Having the reflective properties of a mirror, where angle of incidence is equal to angle of reflection. Example finishes are polished aluminum, stainless steel, and tin.

Toxicity characteristic leaching procedure (TCLP) test. Federal Environmental Protection Agency (EPA) regulations (Resources Conservation Recovery Act, RCRA, of 1990) have defined a TCLP test to determine whether wastes are to be treated as hazardous or nonhazardous.

Tungsten-halogen (TH) lamp. A gas-filled tungsten incandescent lamp containing a certain proportion of halogens.

Watt. In electric calculations 1 watt is the power produced by a current of 1 ampere across a potential difference of 1 volt.

COMPARATIVE ANALYSIS OF TRANSPORTATION ILLUMINATION CRITERIA (FC)

	IESNA 9th Edition	APTA 1981 Guidelines	NYCT (Current)	Metro North	LIRR	SEPTA	Los Angeles	CTA	Toronto	BART	WMATA	JFK LRS
Street-Level Entrances												
1. Building entrances	3–5	30 day / 10 night	5	10*	50	15	15	10	15	30–40*	NA	10
2. Street-level entrance lobby	3–5	30 day / 10 night	5	10*	50	15	15	10*	15	NA	NA	10
3. Sidewalk cut stairs	3–5	30 day / 10 night	5*	10*	7	NA	NA	10	NA	NA	NA	10
4. Street exterior canopy	3–5	30 day / 10 night	5*	10*	7	NA	NA	10	10	NA	NA	10
Vertical Circulation Elements												
5. Stairs and escalators	3–5	25	10–20	10*	10–20	30	15	20	10–15	30–40	5–10	15
6. Elevators	NA	20	20	15*	20*	20	20	20	10–15	NA	10	20
7. Vertical surfaces	NA	8–10*	NA	NA	NA	NA	NA	NA	NA	NA	NA	NA
Mezzanines												
8. Waiting rooms	NA	30	30	15*	20*	40	30	35	20–25	60–70	5–10*	20
9. Mezzanines	NA	20	20	10	20*	20	15	15	15	30–40*	10	NA
10. Ticket vending machines	NA	30	NA	NA	50	40	30	20–35	20	60–70	10 (V)	NA
11. Passages	3–5	20	10–20	15*	20*	20	15	20	10	30–40	5	15
12. Public toilets	10–30	30	20	15*	20	30	20	35	15	20–30	NA	10
13. Vertical surfaces	NA	8–10*	NA	NA	NA	NA	20 (V)	NA	NA	NA	NA	NA
Platform Areas												
14. Platforms	3–5	15–20	15	15	15	10–15–20	15	25	10	30–40	3–5	25
15. Platform edge	NA	NA	NA	10	7.5	NA	30	15	20	NA	NA	NA
16. Platform seating	NA	NA	NA	NA	NA	NA	NA	20	25	NA	NA	NA
17. Track walls (vertical)	NA	5–8*	NA	NA	NA	10	NA	NA	NA	NA	NA	NA
18. Platform walls (vertical)	NA	5–8*	NA	NA	NA	NA	NA	NA	NA	NA	NA	NA
Nonpublic Areas												
19. Crew quarters	3–5	15	15–35	15*	20–50	20	20	35	15	20–30	3	25
20. Offices	10–50	50	35	10	30	NA	10–50	15	25	40–50	NA	NA
21. Utility spaces	10–30	20	20*	NA	20	5–30	15	35	25	15–40	NA	20–30
Tunnels												
22. Walkway	NA	NA	1	NA	NA	0.5	1	NA	NA	NA	NA	1
23. Vertical surfaces	NA	NA	NA	NA	NA	NA	NA	NA	NA	NA	NA	NA
24. Tunnel station transition zone	NA	NA	NA	NA	NA	NA	NA	NA	NA	NA	NA	NA

*Denotes value most likely to have been applied.

- Information borrowed from other agencies
- Conclusions based on actual individual system experience

Station and terminal areas are normally differentiated by function, which results in criteria developed on an area-by-area basis. In the absence of any existing guidance from the sponsor authority, refer to APTA guidelines (American Public Transportation Association 1981). (See the table at left.) These guidelines should be reviewed with the sponsor authority prior to proceeding with the design.

Although there is no consensus as to what constitutes the optimum illumination criteria, the similarities in illumination levels cited for each portion of a given transit station are surprisingly consistent nationwide. Dropping out the highest and lowest values, a number of trends can be discovered (see the lower table at right).

Emergency Lighting

Emergency lighting is commonly supplied by a percentage of normally energized luminaires, and in the event of a normal power failure should define a path of egress to assist in safe and orderly evacuation. All public areas, including stairs, passageways, and entry concourses, require emergency lighting. In all cases, emergency lighting should conform to the provisions of the applicable local, state, or other governing ordinance code (i.e., NFPA 130/101). Emergency lighting is normally not required for nonpublic areas such as storage rooms, telephone closets, refuse rooms, and similar areas. Emergency lighting for stairs and escalators should emphasize illumination on the top and bottom steps and landings. Electrical and mechanical equipment

RECOMMENDED ILLUMINATION LEVELS (MAINTAINED, AVERAGE FC)	
Passenger Stations	
Platform, subway	10–20
Platform, under canopy, surface and aerial	10–15
Uncovered platform ends, surface	5
Mezzanine	20
Ticketing area—turnstiles	30
Passages	15–20
Stairs and escalators	20–25
Fare collection kiosk	80
Concessions and vending machine areas	30
Elevator (interior)	20
Aboveground entry to subway (day/night)	5/30
Washrooms	10
Service and utility rooms	10–20
Electrical, mechanical, and train control	15–30
Storage areas	10
Bus loading platforms	5
Streetcar loading platforms	5
Bus and streetcar loops	2
Kiss-and-ride areas	5
Parking Areas	
Self-parking	2
Pedestrian walkways	3
Entrance and exit roadways	2
Passenger Vehicles	
Interiors (i.e., train cars)	30

TYPICAL ILLUMINATION LEVELS (FC)	
Street entrances	5–20
Stairs and escalators	10–40
Control areas	20–40
Platforms	10–30
Nonpublic areas	15–30
Crew quarters	15–35
Utility spaces	15–35

rooms should be provided with emergency lighting to enable safe evacuation and troubleshooting.

Exit Sign Lighting

Signs that indicate exits or exit routes should comply with applicable codes (i.e. NFPA). Such signs are normally illuminated internally via light-emitting diode (LED) or compact fluorescent light (CFL) sources. All internally illuminated exit signs should have two sources of power, one normal power and one emergency power.

ADA Provisions

Lighting systems should be designed to comply with all applicable provisions of the *Americans with Disabilities Act Accessibility Guidelines for Buildings and Facilities* (ADAAG). The following sections of the ADAAG are cited for their impact on lighting criteria:

- 4.10.11, Illumination Levels (which refers principally to lighting within elevator cabs)

- 10.3.1.11, Illumination levels in the areas where signage is located

- A.4.30.8, Illumination Levels: Illumination levels on sign surfaces

- 4.28.3, Visual Alarms: Visual alarm signal appliances

Light Loss Factors

Light loss factors (LLFs), sometimes referred to as "maintenance factors", adjust lighting calculations to account for degradation of lighting systems over a period of time. LLFs are input into lighting calculations as modifiers to lamp lumen output, luminaire output, and surface reflectance. Calculations are likely to provide unrealistically high values if not modified by accurate light loss factors. Many factors contribute to the LLFs, among which are Lamp lumen depreciation (LLD), room surface dirt depreciation (RSDD), and luminaire dirt depreciation (LDD).

APTA (1981) recommends that generally an LLF of 0.65 be utilized. In those areas where environmental (dirt) conditions are severe (e.g., underground platforms), a more stringent light loss factor should be considered. For further information regarding the calculation of light loss factors, consult the IESNA handbook.

Light Sources

There is a wide range of light sources capable of delivering the energy economies and proper color attributes necessary to the success of a transportation complex, but it is best from a maintenance point of view to minimize the total number of different light sources (lamps) used. Given the wide range of light source choices available and their unique characteristics, a lighting professional should be consulted.

Parameters for appropriate sources

The selection of a family of light sources that responds to an array of architectural conditions, yet does not pose an inordinate maintenance burden, is important. The following parameters should be considered:

- Correlated color temperatures (CCT) appropriate to the architectural environments

- Good color rendering (CRI) capability (min. range of 65–85)

- High efficacy (lumen-to-watt ratio)

- Long lamp life

COMPARATIVE ANALYSIS OF LAMP TYPES

	Minimum Efficacy (Lumens/watt)	Minimum Color Rendering Index	Color Temperature (degrees Kelvin)	Lamp Life (rated hours)	Applications
Fluorescent					
(T8)	85–95	80	3000–4000	20,000–24,000	Platforms, mezzanines, circulation areas, waiting rooms, utility rooms
(T5)	96–104	82	3000–4100	16,000-20,000	Indirect lighting, task lighting
HO (T5)	83–87	82	3000–4100	16,000	Indirect lighting, task lighting
Compact-fluorescent	65–80	82	2700–4100	10,000–20,000	Stairs, toilets, corridors, utility rooms
HID					
Metal halide (coated or clear)	80–110	65–85	3200–3700	15,000–20,000	Waiting rooms, platforms
High-pressure sodium (standard)	100	22	2200	24,000	Parking, exterior floodlighting, exterior platforms
Incandescent					
Tungsten halogen	20	100	3000–4000	2000	Artwork or special exhibit displays
Induction					
QL	58–63	80	3000–4000	100,000	Site lighting, stairs, and escalators
Icetron	80	80	3500–4100	100,000	Site lighting, stairs, and escalators

- Commercial availability
- TCLP compliance wherever possible

Mercury vapor light sources, because of their poor CRI (44), relatively low efficacies (as compared with other HID sources), and poor lumen output performance should not be considered for any portion of a transit project (except under unique circumstances).

Conventional high-pressure sodium light sources, because of their poor CRI (22), should be considered only for exterior floodlighting or for lighting adjacent roadways, parking areas, or nonpublic area lightings.

Incandescent light sources should not be considered for use as part of any general lighting illumination system. Incandescent and tungsten-halogen (TH) sources offer excellent color rendition, but, as a class, their low efficacy, susceptibility to voltage surge, poor lamp life (2000–4000 hours or less), and limited voltage characteristics (120 V or less) mitigate against widespread use.

The present technology of metal halide sources require a long restrike time, and in light of system operation and passenger safety considerations, no more than 50 percent of the illumination of platforms or other public areas should be based on the use of high intensity discharge (HID) sources.

On the basis of the power limits cited in ASHRAE and other energy guidelines, consideration of direct, direct/indirect fluorescent light sources or principally direct-only HID sources, is generally recommended. For achieving the required illumination levels while staying within these guidelines, consideration of purely indirect strategies as a system-wide approach may not be advisable. In specific localized instances, indirect strategies may be considered when mandated by unique architectural conditions.

Luminaires

Luminaire design considerations
Transit lighting systems must be capable of responding to various conditions. A lighting system integrating multiple services can adapt to a variety of architectural conditions. Total luminaire efficiency and ease of maintenance are important factors in selecting fixtures and fixture systems. Underground and exterior (at-grade or aerial) platforms may be exposed to a range of rigorous environmental factors, including extremes of temperature, wind, driven rain, dirt, steel dust, and vandalism. In such cases the degree of ingress protection (ability to resist the intrusion of dust and moisture) is an important consideration. The appearance of the fixtures and the ability to adapt to a variety of architectural conditions are also important considerations.

Fixture efficiency
Lamp mounting and shielding are factors in understanding total fixture efficiency, expressed as a ratio of lumen output of fixture to lumen output of lamps alone. Both bare lamps and lensed luminaires are commonly found in transit stations. Bare lamp fixtures are suitable for use in transit

▼ *Standard use of fluorescent lighting along the platform edge at the Los Angeles Metro Red Line station.*

environments, with a few caveats: (1) that sockets are protected to prevent steel dust infiltration and to prevent lamps from vibrating loose from their sockets and (2) that the luminaire is designed to minimize the perception of glare (equipped with white reflectors, etc).

Lensed fixtures are also common in the transit environment, for these offer a degree of protection from environmental factors (moisture, steel dust, etc.) and are considered more vandal resistant. Brightness control (shielding) is intrinsic. However, lensed fixtures are inherently less efficient and require more sophisticated fastening, gasketing, and cleaning. These factors must be considered in calculating the impact of energy codes and maintenance procedures.

Integration of system components

Several recent large transit systems (constructed during the last decade) have adopted an integrated systems approach to reduce visual clutter in the station envelope and simplify lamp inventory, ballasts, and related accessories and components. Most lighting systems in use include some of the following components:

- Normal lighting, powered via normal (primary) and reserve (secondary) circuits
- Emergency lighting (designated luminaire on emergency circuit)
- Point source fixtures for use as either general distribution or accent, fixed or adjustable
- Public address
- Wayfinding signage, transilluminated or screened
- Station identification signage, transilluminated or screened

- Dynamic signage, such as variable messaging system (VMS)
- Surveillance (closed-circuit television, CCTV)
- Strobe (fire alert)
- Train annunciation
- Integrated wireway management

In any event, standardization of lamp/fixture and system components is essential to limit the number of elements in the system.

Summary

The principles for luminaire design are as follows:

- Luminaires, whether part of an integrated system or stand-alone, should be durable and suitable for a minimum 20–30-year life cycle. This standard of durability should include the ability of luminaires and components to withstand vibration, moisture, steel dust, and the potential for vandalism.
- Where the predominant lighting is via an artificial lighting system, the system should integrate such components as normal and emergency lighting, wireways and public address, wayfinding and station identification signage, VMS train annunciation, CCTV, and strobe fire alert.
- The elements of luminaires in a lighting system should be standardized and suitable for a wide range of applications, including but not limited to these configurations:
  - Pendant mounted, wherein the wireway integrates associated utility routing

- Recessed ceiling conditions, wherein the wireway is accessible for maintenance although integrated into the ceiling plane
- Cantilevered or supported by structural elements extending from the track wall or other structure
- Individual component units should allow for ease of maintenance and future replacement and expandability.

DESIGN APPROACHES
General Lighting Issues and Opportunities

Lighting systems should allow for maximum design flexibility and architectural expression. This section briefly reviews potential lighting issues and opportunities normally encountered in the design of a transit station. The following key points are instructive.

Fluorescent light sources

The vast majority of systems currently in use rely heavily on the use of linear fluorescent light sources. Most North American systems planned after 1988 have standardized on the use of energy-efficient T8 fluorescent lamps.

Vertical illuminance

Stations that best exemplify a sense of comfort and perceived security do so not only by delivering horizontal lighting levels, but also by illuminating vertical surfaces. Those systems that ignored the illumination of vertical surfaces created environments that are far less inviting or successful visually (Tokyo).

Drama

The most visually exciting station environments are those with systems that accomplish the following:

- Emphasize lighting on a civic scale (London, Washington, D.C.)
- Make efforts to integrate the illumination of public art (Los Angeles, Stockholm, Sweden)

A successful integration of lighting with architectural and/or structural features and elements is the Moscow system.

Systems Integration

Many of the newer transit systems have opted for a system integration approach to coordinate the delivery of lighting with other systems' components such as public address, emergency lighting, signage, and wireway routing.

Platforms

Rail stations can take a variety of forms: urban intermodal rail terminals, suburban commuter stations, aerial rail links to airports, interurban high-speed rail and underground subway stations. These facilities vary in location, size, and program; however, the one physical characteristic they all share is the presence of a platform. Lighting issues for platforms include the following:

- Uniform illumination of the visual field, which assists in leading passengers to and from trains safety and efficiently
- Highlighting of the platform's edge for safety
- Ease of readability of wayfinding and identification signage

- Emphasis at vertical circulation and transition elements (stairs, escalators, and elevator areas)
- Emphasis at platform amenities (e.g., seating areas, information kiosks)
- Integration of lighting systems with other ancillary elements such as:

  Public address

  Wireway routing

  Emergency fire strobe

  CCTV

  Variable message signage

  Wayfinding signage

  Train annunciation

  Emergency lighting

  Public art installations

  Retail installation

  Backlit retail advertising

Concerns for at-grade or aerial station platforms include the following:

- Coordination with windscreen elements
- Integration of lighting with canopy elements
- Coordination of illumination levels and light sources at platform transitions between covered (canopied) and noncovered areas.
- Coordination of illumination levels and light sources at transitions between platform and parking areas

In the case of underground platforms there are some additional concerns:

- Transitional coordination of illumination levels between tunnels and station
- Vertical illumination of platform and track walls
- Integration of lighting systems with platform edge doors

▲ Uplighting of the structure helps to define the overall volume at this London Jubilee Line station. Photo courtesy Alfred Lau.)

Waiting and Ticketing Areas

Most transit station environments contain some form of waiting and ticketing area where fares are purchased and passengers can wait. In smaller-scale suburban station or underground subways these areas are quite often next to or on the platforms themselves. In other cases these areas can be quite substantive. The history of rail terminal architecture is populated with great terminal hall spaces whose primary purpose was to accommodate these functions. Given the vast range of architectural scales and treatments in spaces of this type, the primary concerns are as follows:

- General illumination of the environment to allow for safe and quick traverse
- Emphasis at ticketing transaction points

- Integration with daylighting systems (skylights, clerestories etc.) where feasible, particularly within above-ground terminals
- Emphasis at seating areas
- Focus on civic scale, possibly via indirect or floodlighting techniques
- Illumination of vertical surfaces for spatial definition
- Coordination with and illumination of public art
- Coordination with retail and advertising elements
- Coordination with terminal identification and wayfinding systems

In subways or smaller-scale commuter rail stations, ticketing gives way to fare control areas with either staffed ticket booths or ticket vending machines (TVMs) and turnstiles/fare array elements. The following guidelines should apply:

- General illumination levels higher that those encountered at platforms or passages
- Vertical emphasis at TVMs and perimeter walls
- Horizontal emphasis at turnstiles/fare arrays
- Coordination with wayfinding signage

Vertical Circulation Elements

Vertical circulation elements (VCEs) include stairs, escalators, ramps, and elevators. Lighting should be provided to emphasize changes in grade, transition points, and the VCEs themselves. Key points are:

- Lighting emphasis to make these elements "stand out" from their surroundings and to reinforce passenger movement.
- Bright lighting within elevator cabs to reinforce their transparency and increase perceived security.

▼ Exterior lighting accents the facade of the Tsoying Station on the high-speed rail line in Taiwan. Sinotech; DMJM Architects.

- Different sources with varied color temperatures located directly over VCEs can assist in wayfinding. The use of color to accent station areas may also be considered.

- Providing access for maintenance is a key issue in locating luminaires.

- Lighting within elevator cabs should contribute to passengers' perceived safety.

Entrances

Entrances are critical, as they form a passenger's first impression of the system. Entrances should convey a sense of welcome and enhance the perception of security. These considerations apply:

- Emphasis on the transition between "outside" and "inside"

- Illumination of vertical surfaces (wall washing) to reinforce a sense of clarity and safety and assist in daytime adaptation

- Higher nighttime illumination levels than those encountered outside the entrance

- Coordination with station identification

Retail

Retail storefronts in transit stations are the passengers' first introduction to the merchandise and/or services offered. The proper illumination of retail frontages is paramount to the retailers' success and can contribute to an overall sense of safety and comfort for users. Most transportation authorities hosting retail establishments have developed guidelines for retail frontage zones to optimize the merchandise's visibility. The following standards can be used to

▼ Indirect lighting highlights bus canopies over sawtooth loading areas.

guide the concessionaires' storefronts and displays.

Frontage lighting should be provided in a storefront to enhance the display of merchandise. Consider the following:

- Overhead tungsten-halogen or low-wattage shielded metal halide sources
- Shielded fluorescent sources
- Side-mounted shielded track or spot lighting
- Floor-mounted uplighting

Fixtures should be positioned so as not to direct glare (light above 50 degrees) into the station areas.

Off-hours illumination should be provided to promote an enhanced sense of safety for passengers using the station. This secondary illumination system should be in operation at all times, even when the retail establishment is not open for business.

Newsstands are often located in station areas as free-standing kiosks, integrated under stairs, or recessed into station walls. In these cases the control zone must be compressed to a narrower dimension. The location and design of protective off-hour screens (such as roll-down gates) should be negotiable to allow for some practical degree of off-hours illumination.

Artwork

The integration of public art into the overall architectural fabric of a rail station is a common feature, which adds to the travel experience. Successful lighting for any public art installation can only occur via close collaboration between the artists, the station architect, the engineer, and the lighting designer. To realize this goal, it is critical that clear communication between artist, station architect, and lighting professional is established to explore possible solutions.

The designer must make a strong effort to accommodate the illumination of an art installation with the use of luminaires and lamps common to the transit system. To go outside the basic palette of lighting sources chosen by the operating authority will only serve to increase the maintenance burden.

CHAPTER 11
WAYFINDING

SIGNAGE AND GRAPHICS

Comprehensive information systems, whose key elements include signage and graphics, are intrinsic to the wayfinding success of any transit facility. These elements are most important in the operation of transit systems because of the role they play in conveying vital information needed by the traveling public to successfully comprehend and use any system. The system design, display content, and location of signage and symbols critically affect the passenger's ability to successfully navigate through a transit system. Research conducted throughout the world over the last 20 years supports the need for consistency in the design, development, and implementation of any signage and graphics program. Guidelines to assist in the design and location of passenger information for transit systems must convey concise and accurate information. A comprehensive information system can make transit centers more user-friendly, particularly for new or infrequent users and people with disabilities.

Extreme variations in the content and location of signage and graphics throughout any transit system can, unfortunately, muddle the wayfinding process. Frequently, passengers are bombarded with a variety of signs—some with complicated, confusing, and ambiguous information, which they must decipher quickly at critical decision points. Misleading or ambiguous information adds to visual clutter, preventing passengers from effectively using the system. Transit operators must deal with constantly changing information, security, accessibility, expansion, schedules, and delays on an hourly and daily basis. Through the

consistent use of signage and graphics, and their placement in key locations based on a sound wayfinding analysis, signage specialists (also known as "information architects") can visually instruct passengers, including those with disabilities (particularly those with cognitive and sensory disabilities), on how to effectively navigate the transit facilities.

The impact of the Americans with Disabilities Act (ADA) on signage and graphic systems in transit facilities has been significant. By improving access for individuals with disabilities, we also improve the overall facility access for all individuals. This is particularly applicable for comprehensive transit and intermodal facilities with multiple passenger flows, circulation issues, complicated access, and local and distance destinations. Most transit organizations now have accessibility committees made up of representatives from community organizations who can provide insight through case studies, identification of specific problems, and acceptable solutions and techniques for providing accessible signage and graphics to meet the requirements of the traveling public.

This chapter offers wayfinding and signage design philosophies with recommendations from experienced wayfinding consultants, information architects, engineers, planners, designers, and other governmental and private sources. This information reflects the best practices utilized by transit providers to assist them in providing a wayfinding system and the effective application of signage and graphics for their facilities. In addition, this chapter contains both written and graphic illustrations that demonstrate the design process and signage/graphic standards that must be evaluated in conjunction with the architecture, circulation flows, and passenger requirements of any facility. Utilizing this process will help promote a positive image of the facility to the passenger. It will also greatly improve the level of service to the passenger.

WAYFINDING

The ability to orient oneself and navigate through places is a fundamental human requirement. A sense of security and confidence comes with the ability to recognize routes to safety or where to get help. Without this, people are reluctant to explore an area or to wander far from known locations. Comfort and convenience are heavily dependent on the legibility that information systems provide to users attempting to find their way. For example, knowing the most expeditious route in today's fast-paced society depends on a person's sense of control, competence, anxiety, stress, and awareness. While passengers are determining their route in a transit station, they must be able to recognize their location while evaluating alternative services, activities, and destinations. When this works, they are less fearful because their destination options are clear.

An effective information system for wayfinding provides the following:

- The ability to effectively determine one's location and orient oneself within a facility
- The ability to determine possible destinations and opportunities within a facility
- The ability to confidently establish a plan of action and choose a route to a desired destination

Components of Wayfinding

No single characteristic makes a space legible for wayfinding in a transit station. Instead, all parts of the facility work together (or at odds with each other) to determine the ease or difficulty passengers will have in finding their way around. Signs are actually Band-Aids for the passenger's natural wayfinding ability within a facility. They are located and used to supplement other visual cues in the built environment, to assist in gaining access to or exiting a facility, to define the most efficient use of a facility, and to provide information about the facility when it is too complex to be conveyed by the architecture or when other sources of information in the space are insufficient or unreliable for all potential user groups. Other sources for wayfinding information include the following:

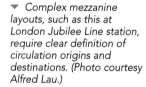

▼ *Complex mezzanine layouts, such as this at London Jubilee Line station, require clear definition of circulation origins and destinations. (Photo courtesy Alfred Lau.)*

- Facility layout
- Visual landmarks
- Terminology and graphics
- Key architectural elements
- Directories
- Maps and brochures
- Directions given by staff

Although signs are important wayfinding tools, signs cannot fix an environment that sends different messages to its users. In fact, in such instances, signs can actually make a facility more confusing to navigate.

SIGNAGE AND GRAPHICS

Signage systems are divided into sign types that display various types of messages. The types are commonly grouped into directional, informational, identification, and regulatory signs. A hierarchy of message importance is developed within each type of sign. The purpose is to logically sort the messages displayed by geographical location, importance of service or a building's functional needs. A standard nomenclature is developed for each of the destinations and services to be accessed by the public. The hierarchical structure of the system is then applied to the architectural program. Consistency and redundancy of display locations, sizes, color, layout of message units, and type style make for an easily read and comprehended information system that complements the experience of the user.

Coordinated systems of signage and graphics are necessary for users to comprehend complex urban environments. Effective signing results in better circulation and traffic control, more efficient use of facilities and services, improved ap-

pearance, and a better public image. The wayfinding knowledge of the public can be augmented through the proper use of interior and exterior graphics on directional, informational, identification, and regulatory signs and by developing directories and guides, color-coding, and other orientation devices. A thorough, successful signage and graphics program will reduce ambiguity, message overload, and visual clutter. It will establish clear paths of movement and facilitate the comprehension of the functions and uses of a space. It will improve legibility and communications while paying careful attention to the cumulative effects of signs and information in the facility. A comprehensive signage and graphics program will prescribe design standards. It will also provide detailed instructions for uniform and consistent application of the various components. Conceptually, wayfinding design must both generally address the facility or system and specifically address unique conditions at specific locations or decision points. Architectural features and the aesthetics of the environment must be taken into consideration when applying a comprehensive signage philosophy. As the designer applies his or her principles of wayfinding, the design process should pay particular attention to the public's natural wayfinding ability.

PLANNING A WAYFINDING SYSTEM
Knowing the Facility
Understanding how a facility works means understanding the design, intent, use, operation, and management of the facility. Elements to consider include such items as architecture, decision points, peak operating hours, exterior accessibility, secondary services, potential

▶▶ *Wayfinding, main level.*

destinations, and the overall aesthetics of the environment.

As compared with many other types of facilities, a transportation facility (with its extensive functions, features, and intermodal complexity) requires a much more elaborate wayfinding analysis and evaluation. Whether the facility is a train station, an airport, a bus terminal, or an intermodal complex, current new designs and remodeling of existing facilities, along with passenger service requirements, have made it much more complicated for the user.

The following example of an intermodal bus facility can help demonstrate the complexity of the wayfinding process.

Facility "X" has a pedestrian count of more than 250,000 people moving through the terminal daily. The heavy pedestrian flows in the morning are reversed in the evening. A typical information system is not capable of addressing the vertical transition changes within the existing static signage. If only 10 percent are novice or first-time users of the terminal, it still means that 25,000 individuals may need to locate, learn to use, and travel from a terminal entry to a bus gate for the first time in this facility. For the first-time or infrequent user it is much more difficult to establish a cognitive map of the facility. Such individuals must depend on proper signage to guide them safely to their destinations, especially in the event of emergency when they have not had an opportunity to establish a cognitive map of the facility to assist them in the evacuation to a safe area or an area of rescue assistance.

User Groups

In the past, transit facilities' signage systems have been designed with a stereo-type user in mind: a physically fit, attentive individual intent on an enjoyable traveling experience within a facility. The reality is quite different. Many users have impairments with respect to perception, cognition, and mobility, which affect their ability to find their way through a facility. Some of the impairments are temporary, some are slight, and some are profound. Motor disabilities, lowered lines of sight, or physical barriers can limit a person's access to the information needed to navigate a space. For a person with sensory disabilities, a whole class of information may be unavailable, such as text, symbols, or audio announcements. Some people may have more than one disability, which compounds their wayfinding problems. Because the users are not a single, homogeneous group, the designer must consider these factors when planning and designing a signage system for a public transportation facility.

The following is an overview of user groups and examples of the major impairments that affect wayfinding. Nine user groups are identified and defined, and eight of the nine are classified as being disabled according to the Americans with Disabilities Act. These user groups are uniquely affected in their ability to obtain, assimilate, and use the information provided by a signage system.

Unimpaired

The category *unimpaired* is difficult to define. For instance, some elderly people who have reduced vision and hearing may be on the borderline of this category. A person who is angry, distraught, or confused may show signs of cognitive impairment. The user who is pushing a baby stroller or carrying luggage may be mobility (situationally) impaired. Thus, anyone

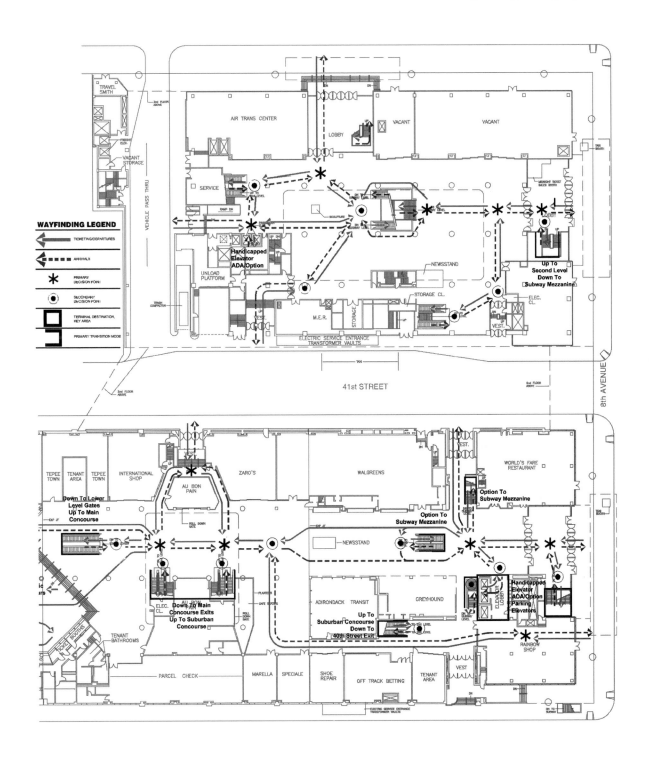

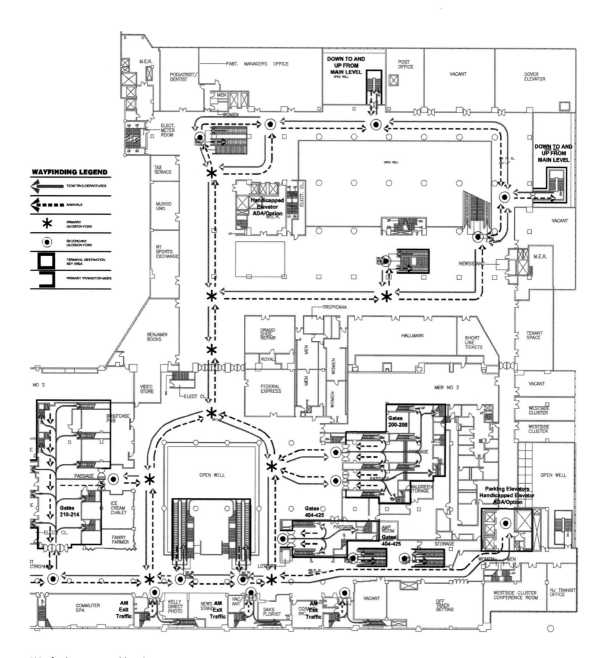

▲ Wayfinding, second level.

may experience a situation in which his or her wayfinding abilities are affected.

Sight impaired

Sight-impaired persons are those who have poor eyesight, partial vision, or an abnormality of vision such as color deficiency or reduced field of vision. Legal blindness is defined as a visual acuity with the best corrective lenses of 20/200 vision or less. A person with 20/200 vision would have to be within 20 ft (or less) of a particular scene to see what a person with normal vision can see at 200 ft away. Tunnel vision is an angle of vision of 20 degrees or less, as compared with the 55 degrees for normally sighted people. Color vision defects are caused by a lack of sensitivity or lack of pigment in certain cone receptors of the eye. There are various levels of color sensitivity in the human eye. As a person passes from higher to lower light levels, blue objects appear brighter than equally pigmented red objects (the reverse is true as the light levels increase).

Blind

Blind persons are without useful vision. Blind travelers have to rely on auditory and tactile cues; only in rare circumstances can they use olfactory or heat perception. All of the senses compensating for sight are generally less informative, less reliable, and less efficient. Nothing replaces sight in gaining a global understanding of the environment or in perceiving distance cues, which are so important for wayfinding.

Hearing impaired

Hearing-impaired persons are those who have a moderate to severe hearing loss and may have to rely on hearing aids.

This category may include persons who have difficulty understanding a conversation without relying on visual support (facial expressions or gestures) and without asking the speaker to repeat what was said. People with hearing impairments have two types of problems in public settings. The first is due to magnetic interference caused by motors or transformers, which can adversely affect hearing aids. The second problem is the difficulty in separating background noise from the desired message.

Deaf

This category includes persons who have profound hearing loss. Those who are deaf may not hear some very loud sounds without the use of a hearing aid. With a hearing aid, some may be able to hear loud sounds; however, deaf people may be able to understand ordinary speech through lip reading, sign language, or written messages. Very few deaf people benefit from a hearing aid at all. The vocabulary of people who are deaf tends to be more action oriented. Abstractions and words describing concepts may not be readily understood.

Cognitively impaired

Cognitive impairment can be situational or developmental. Persons who are situationally impaired are in a temporary state of anger, apprehension, confusion, or distress caused by a particular situation or environment. A person overloaded with information is situationally impaired. Persons who are developmentally impaired are learning disabled, mentally retarded, or mentally disturbed. Elderly persons who have reduced cognitive abilities, people with dyslexia, dyscalculia (inability to count or calculate), inability to write, or an inability to learn left from right are developmentally impaired.

Literacy impaired

Persons who are functionally illiterate in the language in which a message is expressed can be categorized as literacy impaired. A person is considered functionally illiterate if he or she cannot read well enough to fill out a job application.

Mobility impaired (not in wheelchairs)

Persons who have impaired strength, endurance, dexterity, balance, or coordination and those using crutches or other walking aids but not using wheelchairs are in this category. Persons with strollers or carts, persons with heart and other conditions that reduce mobility but are not apparent to others, are also in this category.

Mobility impaired (in wheelchairs)

Persons who are permanently or temporarily restricted to the use of a wheelchair or a scooter are in this category.

THE WAYFINDING DESIGN PROCESS

Two key elements of any design process are (1) system identity and (2) environmental communications through visual and audible programs.

It is critical that the designers of any wayfinding system completely understand the operational and functional goals of the architectural environment. Analysis of pedestrian traffic flow, decision points, destinations, potential problem areas, conflicts, message loads, and nomenclature provide the designer with a basis for programming the sign locations and message types to be applied to each category of sign. The analysis process should highlight functional probabilities of user conflict with the system's environment and provide solutions in the form of message adjustment and sign location. The completion of programming allows the designer to begin to formulate the configuration of the signs and the dimensional relationships to the architectural environment. Close coordination with the architect, interior designer, electrical engineer, lighting designer, electronic information system designer, and other related consultants helps to establish the parameters within which the wayfinding system must function.

The design process has to be developed by the information architect based on a through understanding of the specific transit mode and facility design. There are three basic architectural environments, each of which requires a particular approach to designing a wayfinding system:

- Wayfinding for new/proposed facilities. The wayfinding system is based on concepts, perception, understanding of the architectural design, circulation flows, and visualization of the space (ceiling heights, viewing distances, potential obstructions, etc.).

- Wayfinding for existing facilities. In these facilities it is difficult to use natural signing solutions because the architectural and interior features are in place and often difficult to utilize as part of a total signage system. Existing visual clutter will also impact any proposed signage solution.

- Wayfinding for existing facilities with remodeling/expansion of areas. This scenario requires a much more complex approach to the wayfinding process and signage solutions. The designer may be required to use all or part of any existing signage program, develop a signage program compatible with the existing signage standards, or retrofit the entire facility with a new signage program based on combining the existing wayfinding and circulation flows with the remodeled or expansion program.

The proper design and placement of signage cues is critical for any transit system to be effective. The design process should incorporate the following: system identity; spatial planning (circulation flows, transitions, functions, operation decision points, entries, and exits), environmental communications (visual and interior elements, static and dynamic signage, etc.), content and location (messages based on functions, services, and destinations; locations based proximity to circulation and destinations), and legibility and readability (ease with which information is perceived by the senses and with which information can be understood).

Message Hierarchy

The information designer must know the facility—its architecture, circulation flow, destinations, and passenger needs—before attempting to establish a message hierarchy. A message hierarchy must be based on a solid signage design philosophy that organizes the general information into a functional information system. To ensure a proper hierarchical format, all functions within a transit facility must be identified and listed in the precise order of importance. Interviews with the station operator, information architect, and users can provide valuable insight into a perceived hierarchical order. Key elements to consider include the following:

- Facility entrance
- Fare processing

- Gates to platforms
- Destinations served from the platform
- Transit mode route/destination (during transit)
- Facility name (viewed from transit vehicle)
- Exits to street or transfer points
- Transit schedule information

All new facilities built since the adoption of the federal Americans with Disabilities Act (ADA) must meet the ADA legislation. Accessible routes to each area must be addressed in conjunction with standard routes and in the same order of importance. After all areas of concern have been identified, the functional classification of signs can be applied to determine the various levels of the message hierarchy. The primary functional categories of signs are directional, informational, identification, regulatory, and warning. All primary destination locations must have directional/information signs showing how to locate key areas and identification/information signs telling users that they have arrived at their specific destinations.

▼ *Design studies for the Virginia Railway Express graphics system. DMJM+Harris.*

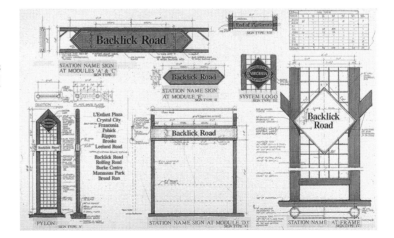

Three Levels of Transit Signs

Primary Signs: Directional/Informational, Guidance, and Identity

- All directional/informational signs
- Entrance identity sign
- Fare processing location sign
- Gate/information location signs
- Platform signs (primary destinations served)
- Platform location signs (station identity)
- Exit signs/emergency evacuation

Secondary Signs: Auxiliary Services and Support Functions

- System maps/directories
- Neighborhood maps/directories
- Fare information
- Schedule information
- Regulatory/warning information
- Restrooms (directional/location signs)
- Telephones (directional/location signs)
- Security/police
- First aid/emergency services
- Facility services and concessions

Tertiary Signs

- Regulatory/warning (federal/state, and local) requirements
- Room numbers
- Equipment (furniture, fixtures, etc.) labeling
- Fire/safety and hazard-related information
- Employee work areas/employment information

Levels of Signs in Transit Facilities

As an information system develops—and all information systems are subject to change based on a myriad of factors—certain primary and secondary messages may switch priority because of a change in passenger flows (i.e., arrival/departure routes). A message that had been indicated on the system as "secondary" in earlier signs may move to the primary level on the approach to a specific area. Gates, platforms, destinations—each of these could become primary messages along the travel route at different wayfinding decision points. Message hierarchy is established to reduce the number of signs, simplify the sign content, and promote a clear and concise presentation of messages in the information system. Secondary and tertiary signs must be coordinated with primary signs.

Trip segments are commonly shown as travel paths (lines of travel that are segmented by intersections, transfers, vertical transitions and turns between a starting point and the destination). There are two different methods of graphically representing segments along the line of travel (decision points): (1) list all decision points along the way to the ultimate destination, creating a need for larger signs and more time to be spent reading and deciphering the messages, and (2) display only that information necessary to get to the next decision point. The second method reduces the message load to a minimum and requires fewer, smaller signs—thus minimizing visual clutter and information overload—and enhances the logical wayfinding process. Both methods can be supported by directories and station maps. A graphic representation of an information system is shown at right for both arriving and departing passengers. The detailed directional information flow and relationship to other transportation modes is demonstrated in the related message/function/component line diagrams on page 238.

Signage Standards

Viewing distances

One of the most important aspects of signing is sign placement. The closer the sign is to the user's natural line of vision, the better. The viewing angle affects the viewing distance. Viewing distance is the straight-line distance between the user's eyes and the center of the sign message. The shortest viewing distance is obtained when the center of the sign message is at eye level. The viewing angle is the angle between the level line of sight and the line of sight to the center of the sign message. A rule of thumb is not to exceed a 10-degree angle from the user's natural line of vision. For example, viewing angles are larger for people in wheelchairs, making it easier for their line of sight to be obstructed. Signs need to be placed where they can be clearly seen by all users. If a person is waiting for a bus and a 12 by 12 in. (305 by 305 mm) bus stop sign is mounted overhead, with an 80 in. (2032 mm) clearance between the bottom of the sign and the ground, the sign should be positioned so a person who is standing can move 8 ft (2.4 m) away to view the sign. A person in a wheelchair must be able to move at least 16 ft (4.8 m) from the sign to keep the sign within the 10-degree viewing angle. Once the viewing angle and viewing distance are determined, the size of the characters can be determined.

Character height/viewing directions

The selection of a typeface is an important element in the design process for viewing and legibility of the message content. However, the height of the characters play an even more important and functional role, because the height has a direct impact on the overall size of the

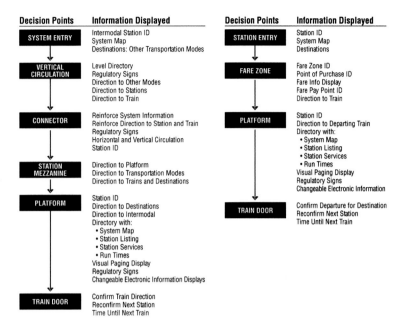

▲ ▼ These diagrams show the typical messages provided along the arrival path of travel from the train to a station exit and the departure path of travel from a station entry to a train.

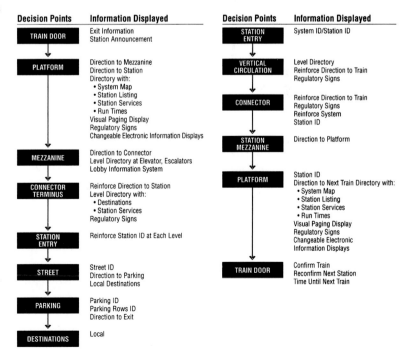

WAYFINDING

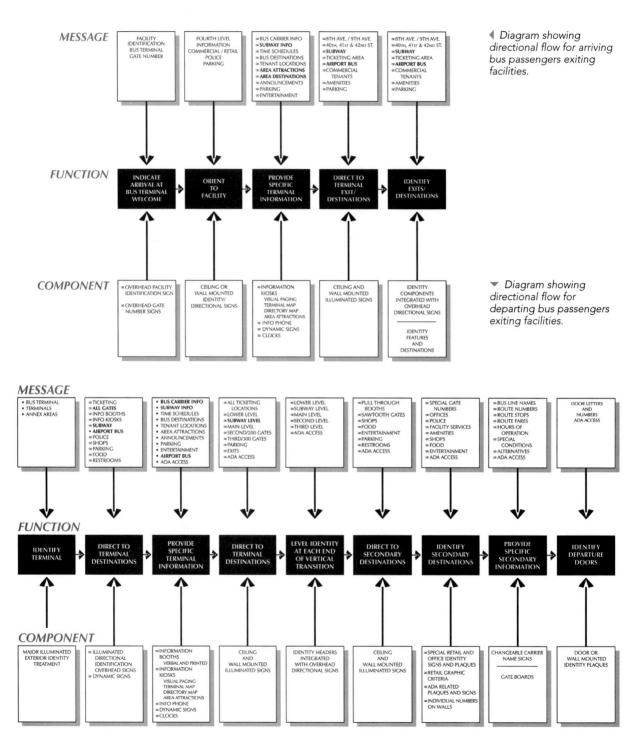

MESSAGE

FACILITY IDENTIFICATION BUS TERMINAL GATE NUMBER	FOURTH LEVEL INFORMATION COMMERCIAL / RETAIL POLICE PARKING	∞ BUS CARRIER INFO ∞ **SUBWAY INFO** ∞ TIME SCHEDULES ∞ BUS DESTINATIONS ∞ TENANT LOCATIONS ∞ **AREA ATTRACTIONS** ∞ **AREA DESTINATIONS** ∞ ANNOUNCEMENTS ∞ PARKING ∞ ENTERTAINMENT	∞ 8TH AVE. / 9TH AVE. ∞ 40TH, 41ST & 42ND ST. ∞ **SUBWAY** ∞ TICKETING AREA ∞ **AIRPORT BUS** ∞ COMMERCIAL TENANTS ∞ AMENITIES ∞ PARKING	∞ 8TH AVE. / 9TH AVE. ∞ 40TH, 41ST & 42ND ST. ∞ **SUBWAY** ∞ TICKETING AREA ∞ **AIRPORT BUS** ∞ COMMERCIAL TENANTS ∞ AMENITIES ∞ PARKING

◀ *Diagram showing directional flow for arriving bus passengers exiting facilities.*

FUNCTION

INDICATE ARRIVAL AT BUS TERMINAL WELCOME	ORIENT TO FACILITY	PROVIDE SPECIFIC TERMINAL INFORMATION	DIRECT TO TERMINAL EXIT/ DESTINATIONS	IDENTIFY EXITS/ DESTINATIONS

COMPONENT

∞ OVERHEAD FACILITY IDENTIFICATION SIGN ∞ OVERHEAD GATE NUMBER SIGNS	CEILING OR WALL MOUNTED IDENTITY/ DIRECTIONAL SIGNS	∞ INFORMATION KIOSKS VISUAL PAGING TERMINAL MAP DIRECTORY MAP AREA ATTRACTIONS ∞ INFO PHONE ∞ DYNAMIC SIGNS ∞ CLOCKS	CEILING AND WALL MOUNTED ILLUMINATED SIGNS	IDENTITY COMPONENTS INTEGRATED WITH OVERHEAD DIRECTIONAL SIGNS IDENTITY FEATURES AND DESTINATIONS

▼ *Diagram showing directional flow for departing bus passengers exiting facilities.*

MESSAGE

• BUS TERMINAL • TERMINALS • ANNEX AREAS	∞ TICKETING ∞ **ALL GATES** ∞ INFO BOOTHS ∞ INFO KIOSKS ∞ **SUBWAY** • **AIRPORT BUS** ∞ POLICE ∞ SHOPS ∞ PARKING ∞ FOOD ∞ RESTROOMS	• **BUS CARRIER INFO** • **SUBWAY INFO** • TIME SCHEDULES • BUS DESTINATIONS • TENANT LOCATIONS • AREA ATTRACTIONS • ANNOUNCEMENTS • PARKING • ENTERTAINMENT • **AIRPORT BUS** • ADA ACCESS	∞ ALL TICKETING LOCATIONS ∞ LOWER LEVEL ∞ **SUBWAY LEVEL** ∞ MAIN LEVEL ∞ SECOND/200 GATES ∞ THIRD/300 GATES ∞ PARKING ∞ EXITS ∞ ADA ACCESS	∞ LOWER LEVEL ∞ SUBWAY LEVEL ∞ MAIN LEVEL ∞ SECOND LEVEL ∞ THIRD LEVEL ∞ ADA ACCESS	∞ PULL THROUGH BOOTHS ∞ SAWTOOTH GATES ∞ SHOPS ∞ FOOD ∞ ENTERTAINMENT ∞ PARKING ∞ RESTROOMS ∞ ADA ACCESS	∞ SPECIAL GATE NUMBERS ∞ OFFICES ∞ POLICE ∞ FACILITY SERVICES ∞ AMENITIES ∞ SHOPS ∞ FOOD ∞ ENTERTAINMENT ∞ ADA ACCESS	∞ BUS LINE NAMES ∞ ROUTE NUMBERS ∞ ROUTE STOPS ∞ ROUTE FARES ∞ HOURS OF OPERATION ∞ SPECIAL CONDITIONS ∞ ALTERNATIVES ∞ ADA ACCESS	DOOR LETTERS AND NUMBERS ADA ACCESS

FUNCTION

IDENTIFY TERMINAL	DIRECT TO TERMINAL DESTINATIONS	PROVIDE SPECIFIC TERMINAL INFORMATION	DIRECT TO TERMINAL DESTINATIONS	LEVEL IDENTITY AT EACH END OF VERTICAL TRANSITION	DIRECT TO SECONDARY DESTINATIONS	IDENTIFY SECONDARY DESTINATIONS	PROVIDE SPECIFIC SECONDARY INFORMATION	IDENTIFY DEPARTURE DOORS

COMPONENT

MAJOR ILLUMINATED EXTERIOR IDENTITY TREATMENT	∞ ILLUMINATED DIRECTIONAL IDENTIFICATION OVERHEAD SIGNS ∞ DYNAMIC SIGNS	∞ INFORMATION BOOTHS VERBAL AND PRINTED ∞ INFORMATION KIOSKS VISUAL PAGING TERMINAL MAP DIRECTORY MAP AREA ATTRACTIONS ∞ INFO PHONE ∞ DYNAMIC SIGNS ∞ CLOCKS	CEILING AND WALL MOUNTED ILLUMINATED SIGNS	IDENTITY HEADERS INTEGRATED WITH OVERHEAD DIRECTIONAL SIGNS	CEILING AND WALL MOUNTED ILLUMINATED SIGNS	∞ SPECIAL RETAIL AND OFFICE IDENTITY SIGNS AND PLAQUES ∞ RETAIL GRAPHIC CRITERIA ∞ ADA RELATED PLAQUES AND SIGNS ∞ INDIVIDUAL NUMBERS ON WALLS	CHANGEABLE CARRIER NAME SIGNS — GATE BOARDS	DOOR OR WALL MOUNTED IDENTITY PLAQUES

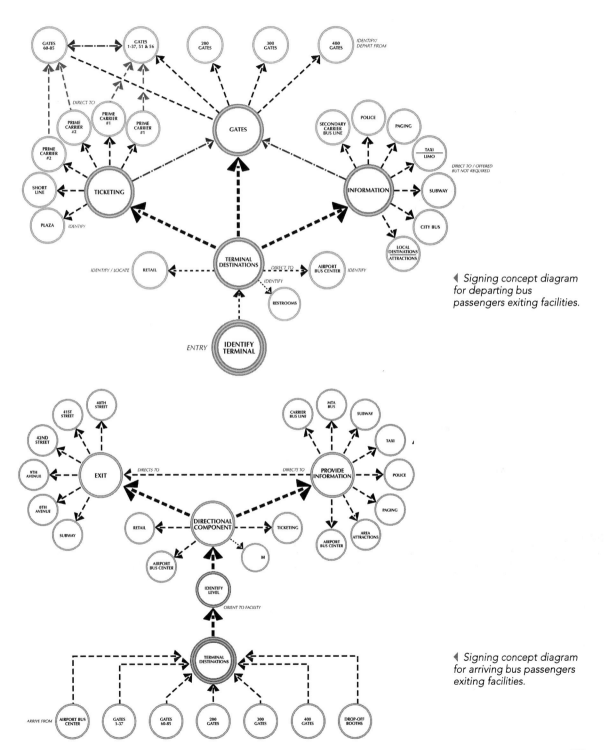

◀ *Signing concept diagram for departing bus passengers exiting facilities.*

◀ *Signing concept diagram for arriving bus passengers exiting facilities.*

239

Character height guidelines.

Viewing Distance (feet)	Normal Sight (inches)	Impaired Sight (inches)
10 (3.1m)	3/8 (10mm)	5/8 (16mm)
15	1/2	3/4
20	5/8	7/8
25 (7.6m)	5/8 (16mm)	1 (25mm)
30	3/4	1-1/8
35	3/4	1-3/8
40	7/8	1-5/8
45	7/8	1-7/8
50 (15.2m)	1 (25mm)	2 (50mm)
55	1	2-1/8
60	1-1/8	2-3/8
65	1-1/4	2-5/8
70	1-3/8	2-7/8
75 (22.9m)	1-1/2 (38mm)	3 (76mm)
80	1-1/2	3-1/8
85	1-5/8	3-3/8
90	1-3/4	3-5/8
95	1-7/8	3-7/8
100 (30.5m)	2 (51mm)	4 (102mm)

signage panels and the expectable distance between signs for continued wayfinding, circulation flow, function identity, setting perception, and confidence in the information system. Each typeface has an upper and lower limit on character height. It is generally accepted that the upper limit provides guidance on the signage for those who are visually impaired, and the lower limit for those who have normal vision. The illustration at left gives direct relationships between character height and viewing distances between 10 ft (3.1 m) and 100 ft (30.5 m).

Contrast and color

Contrast and color are closely associated. Contrast is the degree of difference between the lightest and darkest part of an object. The higher the percentage contrast, the more legible the sign. The minimum acceptable contrast is 70 percent. It should be noted that contrast can never equal 100 percent, because the darker area, no matter how dark, will always reflect some light. The number shown in each box in the illustration at top right is the percent contrast of the two colors; thus, only those colors that have an number of 70 or greater should be used with one another.

Because reflectance is simply the proportion of incident light measured after reflection from a surface, contrast may be conveniently computed from luminance values measured by a light meter, assuming the lighter and darker areas of the sign are uniformly illuminated. Therefore, nonstandard colors should be tested, light reflectance values measured, and percent contrast calculated prior to final selections to ensure that the two colors meet the recommended contrast level.

▼ *Viewing distance, standing.*

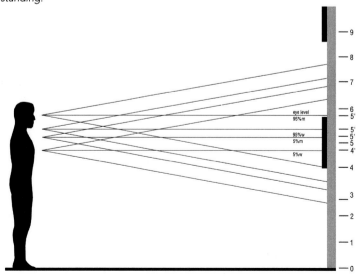

Color contrast is of critical importance to persons with visual impairments. Although maximum contrast is obtained by applying white characters, images, or pictographs to a black background, specific colors are associated with the specific functions of a facility and should be used even though they may not achieve the maximum contrast. When selecting colors for information/guidance and directional signs, care should be taken to select colors that provide adequate contrast between the background and the characters, images, or pictographs.

Color coding and shapes

Colors are used to code different meanings for the signs of the same shape. For example, a yellow triangle means potential hazard or caution, and a red triangle means imminent hazard or danger. Information, guidance, and directional signs can be presented in various colors to direct and identify specific services, lines, or routes within a transit system.

When color coding is used to delineate services, lines, or routes, care must be taken to ensure that the color combinations selected will optimize contrast for all viewers, including those with low vision and those with congenital color vision deficits.

To promote uniformity, the following colors are recommended for specific uses:

- Administrative areas—white image on a dark gray background
- Accessible routes/elements—white image on a blue background
- Services or public areas—white image on a dark blue or blue background
- Recreation or cultural area—white image on a brown background
- Access roadways to transit sites— white image on a green background

	Beige	White	Dark Grey	Black	Brown	Pink	Purple	Green	Orange	Blue	Yellow	Red
Red	78	84	32	38	7	57	28	24	62	13	82	0
Yellow	14	16	73	89	80	58	75	76	52	79	0	
Blue	75	82	21	47	7	50	17	12	56	0		
Orange	44	60	44	76	59	12	47	50	0			
Green	72	80	11	53	18	43	6	0				
Purple	70	79	5	56	22	40	0					
Pink	51	65	37	73	53	0						
Brown	77	84	26	43	0							
Black	89	91	58	0								
Dark Grey	69	78	0									
White	28	0										
Beige	0											

Not Recommended

Minimum Acceptable

▲ Color combinations, contrast.

▼ Viewing distance, in wheelchair.

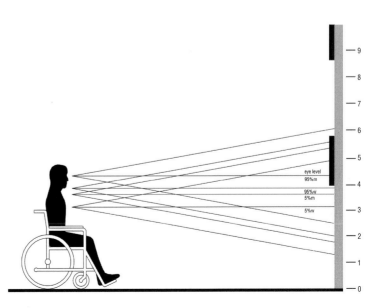

eye level
95%m
95%w
5%m
5%w

**SQUARE:
INFORMATION**

**CIRCLE:
REGULATORY**

**EQUILATERAL TRIANGLE:
WARNING**

 Standard sign shapes.

▼ *Standard colors for common sign categories.*

Certain visual elements must be maintained within a signage program to ensure legibility and recognition of the signs. The basic functional categories for signs are information (rectangle), regulatory (circle), and warning (triangle).

With respect to the three basic shapes of signs and the outside edge of the border of each sign, there is no requirement that the sign panel or signboard be shaped like the border of the sign. The various shapes may be placed on any size or shape of sign panel or signboard. The shape of the border defines the sign.

Characters, images, and color fields

Regulatory/prohibition

Prohibition signs consist of black characters, images, or pictographs located on a white field, circumscribed by a red ring bisected with a 45-degree red slash. The red slash is printed over the black image or pictograph and is oriented from top left to bottom right.

Regulatory/mandatory

Mandatory signs consist of white characters, images, or pictographs on a black circular disc, surrounded by a white border.

Warning/caution

Caution signs consist of black characters, images, or pictographs on a yellow equilateral triangle, surrounded by a black border.

Warning/danger

Danger signs consist of an equilateral triangle surmounted on a rectangle of equal width. The triangle contains the characters, images, or pictographs. The word "Danger" is within the rectangle. The background color of the triangle and the rectangle is red. The image, the text "Danger," and the borders surrounding the triangle and the rectangle are white.

Information/emergency

Emergency signs consist of white characters, images, or pictographs on a green background. The border is white.

Information/guidance and directional

Guidance and directional signs should contain a strong dark/light contrast between the background and the characters and images or pictographs to ensure good legibility. The characters and images or pictographs and the borders

CATEGORY	ELEMENT	COLOR
REGULATORY / PROHIBITION	Field Pictograph / Image Ring Slash Border	White Black Red Red White
REGULATORY / MANDATORY	Field Pictograph / Image Border	Black White White
WARNING / CAUTION	Field Pictograph / Image Border	Yellow Black Black
WARNING / DANGER	Field Pictograph / Image Border	Red White White
INFORMATION / EMERGENCY	Field Pictograph / Image Border	Green White White
INFORMATION / GUIDANCE AND DIRECTIONAL	SPECIFIC USE: Accessible Elements or Routes Recreation or Cultural Construction and Maintenance	Various colors may be used. Recommended colors: Blue Brown Orange

should always be the same, either dark or light colors.

Directional arrows

The arrow is one of the most commonly used symbols in a signage system. Designs for arrows vary greatly, and research shows that many of the presently used designs are confusing and ineffective.

The final arrow of choice for any signage program is an individual decision by the design consultant, based on what is perceived to be appropriate for the specific project. The arrow should be considered in conjunction with the selection of the typeface(s) to be used in the project.

An arrow should be sized in relation to the size of the characters or symbols used on the signboard. Arrow size is defined as the height of the blade. Character size is defined as the height of an uppercase letter *I*.

An arrow should be positioned next to a message so that the arrow always "pulls" the message. The arrow should never "push" the message. For example, an arrow pointing to the left, or up and left, should always be the first symbol on the left side of the signboard, with the message or other symbols following. An arrow pointing to the right, or up and right, should always be the last symbol on the right side of the signboard. Arrows should be placed so that they are centered on the horizontal centerline, or the first line of text of the message, or on the horizontal centerline of the other symbols.

The orientation of an arrow is of equal importance to its design and placement. Because there is no special symbol to convey the message "straight ahead," either the "up" or "down" arrow can be used. This unfortunately causes confusion for the users, who often interpret the directions as "up" or "down" instead of "straight ahead." Arrows should be oriented only in the eight standard positions, which are illustrated below.

Standard symbols

The transportation industry has a subset of standard graphic symbols that are recommended for use in transit facilities. Well-designed symbols will not be effective as communication tools unless they are thoughtfully and carefully applied.

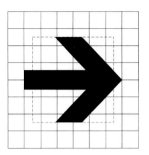

▲ *Standard arrow.*

◀ *Standard arrow directions.*

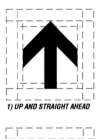

1) UP AND STRAIGHT AHEAD

2) DOWN AND STRAIGHT AHEAD

3) TO THE RIGHT

4) TO THE LEFT

7) UP TO THE LEFT

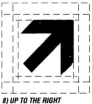

8) UP TO THE RIGHT

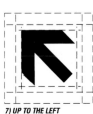

5) DOWN TO THE LEFT   **6) DOWN TO THE RIGHT**

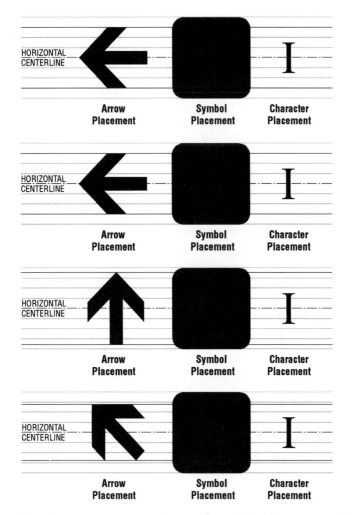

HORIZONTAL CENTERLINE

Arrow Placement   **Symbol Placement**   **Character Placement**

▲ *Sign element alignment.*

- Symbol signs are most effective when they are used to indicate a service or concession that can be represented by an object, such as an auto or service function (e.g., baggage). They are much less effective when used to represent a process or activity, such as ticket purchase.

- To mix messages and symbols for relatively minor or secondary facility functions, activities, or tenants, with essential public messages and main directional information, weakens the overall communications of the entire system.

- It is more confusing to oversign than undersign.

- It is important to note that the use of too many symbols or arrows at any one particular location can be counter-productive. However, when properly used and blended into the overall sign system, symbols can play an important role in facilitating communication and orientation in transit facilities.

To ensure the legibility and recognition of symbols, the following guidelines on visual elements are important:

- The proportional relationship of the figures or elements that define the symbol, to the symbol field, must always be maintained.

- The symbol field should always be square with rounded corners.

- It is recommended that white figures be used on a dark-color field. If white on a dark-color field cannot be used, a strong light/dark contrast should be maintained to achieve the desired 70 percent contrast.

- If a white symbol field is used on a white signboard, the symbol field should be outlined with a dark border.

However, determining *how* to use symbol signs is more easily prescribed than deciding *when* to use them.

The following points are helpful overall guidelines in the use of symbols within any transportation facility:

- Symbol signs are most effective when incorporated as an integral part of the total comprehensive sign system.

- The use of short verbal messages along with symbols is more effective than the use of symbols alone.

- If the symbol field is in color, the color should be light and the symbol should be dark.
- Text that describes the meaning of the symbol should be placed either directly under or adjacent to the symbol field.

The transit industry's standard symbols are grouped by processing, services, regulatory, accessibility, prohibitions, and warning functions. There are three basic rail transportation symbols used for "rapid," "light," and "commuter" rail systems.

Bicycle	Motorcycle	Bus Stop	Bus Bay	Drop-Off / Pick-Up Area
Car Rental	Taxi	Commuter Rail	Light Rail	Rapid Rail
Ferry	Ticketing	Pay Fare		
Elevator	Escalator	Stairs Down	Stairs Up	Exit
First Aid	Information	Lockers	Lost and Found	Telephone
Restrooms	Men	Women	Drinking Fountain	Mail

◀ *Standard symbol categories.*

▶ *Standard signs for various rail transportation.*

▼ *Symbols grouped by category.*

REGULATORY

| Area of Rescue Assistance | Emergency Communication | Fire Extinguisher | Litter | Parking |

| Recycle | Smoking | Pedestrian Crossing | Slippery |

ACCESSIBILITY

| Accessible | Ramp | Text Telephone | Volume Control | Hearing Assistance |

Vision Loss

PROHIBITIONS & WARNINGS

| No Drink | No Food | No Litter | No Parking | No Radio, Food, Drinks, Litter |

| No Radio | No Smoking | Danger - Electricity | Danger - Fire |

ADA AND WAYFINDING

The rules resulting from the requirements of the ADA are very detailed and should be reviewed carefully by facility owners, operators, tenants, and design/engineering consultants. This chapter is intended only to address wayfinding and signage requirements and is not intended to provide legal interpretations of local, state, or federal ordinances or ADA requirements.

WAYFINDING TECHNOLOGIES

There are a variety of static signage media available—computer cut vinyl, screen print overlays, painted supergraphics, embedded fiberglass, etched stainless steel column wraps, illuminated acrylic panels, backlit maps, edge-lit tempered glass, and Lexan pendants—creating a myriad of possible sign types, styles, and usage combinations. However, as information dispersal becomes more complex because of the abundance of information, destination possibilities and the multilingual aspects of the global marketplace, the limitations of static signage are quickly realized. Electronic visual information displays are becoming the keystone to a sound wayfinding system.

The primary purpose of an electronic visual information display system (EVIDS) is to relate information about accurate destination options, clearly identify their location to the passengers, and display a real-time arrivals and departures schedule to transit passengers. In addition, these systems are used to:

- Assist in passenger traffic flow (directional signage)
- Provide accurate and current destination information (identification signage)

- Provide up-to-date information to passengers for operational exceptions to the normal schedule (information signage)
- Provide passenger information for abnormal or emergency conditions (regulatory signage)

Perhaps the greatest advantage of implementing a dynamic electronic signage system is the inherent flexibility it permits and thus the consistency it makes possible. With EVIDS flexibility, not only are regular message changes possible, they can become an important part of a facility's schedule of operations. A local controller or facility manager can administer changes as they are required (e.g., in emergencies) or as part of a pre-programmed loop. Messages can be updated to match monthly, weekly, or daily traffic pattern derivations. Because the EVIDS is, of course, computerized, signage standards such as typography, symbols, character size, spacing, font, and colors are simple to maintain. As consistency is applied throughout the electronic signage system, the passengers' wayfinding comfort level will increase and they will have more confidence in the information system.

Consider how a high-tech EVIDS solution can bolster the wayfinding process in a typical transit facility:

- Add speakers to display screen locations, and visual paging can be supplemented by audio cues.
- Place cameras throughout the facility, creating a monitoring system to protect both passengers and the facility in regard to improving security and identifying theft and false claims.
- Expanding the EVIDS network infrastructure (originally designed only to

carry internal operations information), data pipelines can now be used to distribute additional elements, such as news, weather, and sports.

Of course, the closer the wayfinding system gets to being a fully realized comprehensive electronic signage system, the more essential it is to develop integrity measures to protect the system from hackers and ensure minimal downtime through the use of redundant information channels.

Visual display screens can be further used to abate emergency situations. It becomes an incumbent part of the facility design to make customer service paramount. Passengers must be able to easily determine where they are and relate accurate location information to safety personnel. Well-placed EVIDS signage can assist passengers by helping to create a cognitive map of the facility, often using key architectural features and landmark references to facilitate exiting associations during an emergency evacuation. Passengers require authoritative, clear directions and easily identifiable escape options. By making EVIDS signage part of an intelligent display system, a transit facility can significantly augment the level of service possibilities associated with its dynamic wayfinding package.

However, budgeting constraints inevitably become a key factor in performing a cost-benefit analysis. EVIDS signage is significantly more expensive than static signage, so it is best to evaluate each EVIDS option carefully. A synopsis of many of today's current and emerging dynamic display technologies follows:

Cathode ray tube (CRT). Still prevalent because of its comparatively low screen size cost, CRTs use three-color tubes (red, green, blue) that combine or converge to produce the display image. Encumbered by their size and weight, CRTs are steadily losing their market share to plasmas and liquid crystal displays, as flat-panel display technologies become a more cost-competitive solution. Advantages: low cost, good resolution, virtually unlimited range of color. Disadvantages: deep housing, subject to glare, limited screen size affects possible character size and effective viewing distance.

Light-emitting diode (LED). LEDs are semiconductor devices comprised of component blocks in which each block is a square matrix with flattop cavities for each individual dot of semiconductor material. Available for both indoor and outdoor use, LEDs offer a cost-effective solution for large displays. The driving circuitry, not the technology, itself sets matrix limitations. Advantages: long life expectancy, highly durable design, lower cost than LCDs, capable of extremely large display matrix sizes. Disadvantages: low contrast ratio, limited color, limited viewing angle, subject to glare.

Liquid crystal display (LCD). LCD displays utilize a liquid crystal solution sandwiched between two sheets of polarizing material. An electric current passing through the liquid causes the crystals to align so that light cannot pass through them. Liquid crystal displays consume much less power than LEDs and plasma displays because they work on the principle of shuttering light rather than emitting it. Advantages: long life expectancy, narrow footprint, light weight (typically lighter than similar-sized plasma display panels), good viewing angle as compared with LEDs, very good contrast ratio. Disadvantages: expensive, incompatible with sunlight, longer video response time.

Plasma display panel (PDP). In a PDP display, electricity is used to illuminate a gas sandwiched between two glass plates with transparent electrodes. The resulting electrical discharge produces ultraviolet rays that excite the color phosphors (red, green, blue) painted on the opposite plate of the glass, emitting light through the glass plate to create an image. Advantages: narrow footprint, bright display, vivid colors, wide viewing angle, significantly lighter than similar-sized CRTs. Disadvantages: short life expectancy, expensive, burn-in image problems (visual artifacts), heavy power consumption.

Organic LED (OLED). OLED displays consist of thousands of sub-pixel-sized lightbulbs laid atop a thin-film transistor (the same kind of chip used as a backplane of an LCD). However, unlike CRTs, plasmas, or LCDs, the OLED uses emissive technology. This means that the screen itself emits light and therefore does not require additional hardware for creating light, like tubes or lamps. Advantages: wide viewing angle, better response time than LCDs, bright, thin, extremely lightweight, flexible. Disadvantages: expensive, limited life expectancy due to organic decay, unproven technology.

Electronic paper (electrophoresis, E-ink). Electronic paper is the result of an electromechanical process whereby a slight current is used to arrange electrically sensitive, pixel-like microspeheres into images. The microdots stay put until they are rearranged with another charge. Because the material is reflective, they can be illuminated to readable levels simply by the ambient light that bounces off them. Advantages: inexpensive, thin, extremely lightweight, flexible. Disadvantages: dependent on secondary light source, long response time, limited color performance, unproven technology.

Evaluation criteria for selecting the appropriate type of EVIDS or how to correctly implement a comprehensive signage system composed of different EVIDS subsystems depends on a variety of factors. In the area of technology performance comparison for EVIDS, a number of criteria need to be evaluated, including life expectancy, reliability, contrast ratio, viewing angle, color availability, cost per pixel (manufacturing cost), energy consumption, operating cost, matrix availability (continuous or line-oriented matrix), message and graphics verification (confirmation that the information generated by the controller is actually shown), display modes, maintenance cost, environmental restrictions, and future trends relative to the expected standardization of technology.

As display technology evolves, digital information system solutions will continue to push the concept of what makes a wayfinding signage solution complete. Directional, identification, informational, and regulatory signage must be addressed as part of the whole comprehensive signage system. EVIDS can help guarantee an unprecedented continuity to the flow of wayfinding information.

CHAPTER 12
SAFETY AND SECURITY

This chapter is devoted to the concept that a well-designed station can be a contributing deterrent to crime and terrorism and a moderately safe place in which to move about without danger of tripping or falling. *Safety* in the context of this chapter is defined as the design of physical features that minimize incidents harmful to passengers and employees due to accidents. *Security* is defined as the design of physical features that deter or remove opportunities for criminal or terrorist behavior against passengers or property through planned acts.

Traveling on public transportation has always involved a slight risk of injury due to accidental tripping and a risk of crime, principally due to pickpocketing. Many older transit systems have employed rail police to watch out for criminal behavior and prevent it whenever possible. Statistics would probably demonstrate that a transit passenger's exposure to crime is no greater than that of a person attending a large sporting event or a rock concert. Terrorism, on the other hand, is a recent threat in the United States and has demonstrated its ability to inflict heavy casualties on large numbers of innocent victims. Its primary focus is to cause bodily harm. Transit stations are prime candidates for such harm, particularly in dense urban areas and heavily traveled underground stations. Terrorism has been a fact of life for a long time in many European and Asian countries. Londoners have bolstered themselves against attack on their underground for many years. Their best deterrent is the vigilance of the people; for instance, whenever an empty package is observed, it is immediately reported and removed.

Several studies have recently been prepared to address security issues; much of the material in this chapter is derived from these studies:

- *Transit Security Handbook,* prepared for the Volpe National Transportation Systems Center (Boyd and Maier 1998)

- *Protecting Public Surface Transportation against Terrorism and Serious Crime: Continuing Research on Best Securities Practices,* prepared for Mineta Transportation Institute (Jenkins and Gersten 2001a)

- *Protecting Public Surface Transportation against Terrorism and Serious Crime: An Executive Overview,* prepared for the Mineta Transportation Institute (Jenkins and Gersten 2001b)

Since the World Trade Center attack on September 11, 2001, many transit agencies have been reevaluating their security plans and focusing on eliminating those aspects of the station that might contribute to creating a greater risk of terrorism. Basic precautions, such as removing trash containers that are potential bomb drop-off points, or stopping buses at a greater distance from station entrances, are being implemented. The design procedures identified in this chapter, however, are but one small element of an encompassaing safety and security policy for transit agencies.

SAFETY

The safety of the passenger while in the station area is attributable to three principal elements:

- Good planning techniques
- Regular maintenance along all aspects of the journey, particularly the circulation path
- Monitoring of the passengers' movements

The exposure to risk begins with the initial step off the train onto the platform and ends with the successful connection to another mode of transportation or to the street. If a passenger arrives by automobile and parks on the transit authority property, the journey begins once the passenger drives onto the property. The designer should visualize the entire access path, focus on those elements that have the highest potential for causing an accident, and minimize them as potential risks.

The single greatest safety risk is to those passengers living in the climates subject to moisture and cold temperatures. In these areas when transit systems use at-grade and aerial stations, exposed to the elements, the overhead coverage of passengers along their access path is criti-

cal. Areas of particular concern are waiting zones (such as platforms and bus stops); vertical transitioning such as at stairs, escalators, and ramps; and key decision-making points such as fare purchase machines. In these areas provisions should be made for canopy coverage, high levels of illumination, and maintenance procedures to ensure that walking surfaces are kept free of ice and snow. All walking surfaces should be of a slip-resistant material.

Another safety risk is the failure to design the vertical circulation systems adequately to cover the peak load conditions. In these instances, passengers are forced to compete for access onto vertical circulation elements, causing crowding and the potential for falling. The following approach to avoiding safety risks is based on simulated movement through a station, beginning at a surface parking lot and progressing through the entrance onto a mezzanine and ultimately arriving at the platform. All guidelines suggested here are to be followed in addition to the Americans with Disabilities Act (ADA) requirements for accessibility.

Parking to Street Entrance

After leaving their automobiles, passengers should have a clear view of their destination. The circulation path should be from the parking space to a collection pathway leading directly to the entrance. Avoid crossing major bus circulation driveways when possible. Utilize shrubbery and other vegetation to direct passengers and to prevent them from crossing circulation paths. Illuminate the pathway according to the criteria defined in Chapter 10, "Lighting." The walking path should be level without requiring people to step onto parking islands. Surface drainage should direct

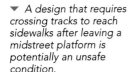
▼ A design that requires crossing tracks to reach sidewalks after leaving a midstreet platform is potentially an unsafe condition.

rainwater away from the pathway and a sufficient number of inlets be employed to ensure that ponding of water does not occur. Automobile and bus circulation patterns should recognize the passengers and give precedent to their movements. Roadway crossings should be well marked.

Street Entrance

- Ensure that the entrance is brightly illuminated.

- Provide canopy coverage over the doorway to allow space for raising umbrellas.

- Use storm water drainage inlets at the entrance to capture any rainfall and prevent it from entering the station. All inlet covers should be designed with narrow ¼ in. slots to prevent shoe heel entrapment. When possible, raise the floor level of the entrance slightly to create positive drainage away from the station.

- Provide gates or vertical coiling grilles to close off the station when not in use.

- See Chapter 6, "Vertical Circulation," for safety considerations in designing and specifying escalators. Consider circulation around escalators when they are being serviced, so that the entrance circulation space is adequate to handle such situations.

- Design 42 in. high guardrails for any floor openings to public spaces below.

- Design all passenger information displays or ticket vending outside the normal circulation path with sufficient queuing spaces that do not overlap.

Mezzanine

- Provide drainage inlets at the bases of the vertical circulation elements

▲ Horizontal railings present a ladder for children to climb on and are discouraged.

(VCEs) to capture rainwater from the stair treads and runnels.

- Use highly wear-resistant material, such as granite, at the floor landing of the VCE banks.

- Use higher levels of illumination at floor landings of VCE banks.

- Use highly slip-resistant floor materials throughout the public areas.

- Do not overlap any queuing of the zones required for ticket purchasing or passing through fare control barriers.

- Design all elevator cabs, doorways, and hoistways with a maximum amount of glass.

Platform Area

- Size the platform to handle the worst-case scenario, such as combined entraining and detraining loads, as described in Chapter 4. This is done to ensure that although passengers are at greatest risk during their time on the platform, sufficient space and adequate VCEs are provided to prevent long queuing times and crowded conditions, which contribute to such risk.

- ADA requires a tactile edge strip. In countries other than the United States, alternative means of providing a visual and tactile platform edge differentiator can be considered.

- The distance from the platform edge to any vertical obstruction, such as a VCE, should be set to the maximum condition the system can afford. "Design Concerns and Process" in Chapter 4 recommends a minimum distance of 8 ft 8 in.

- Do not design the platform to slope from the center to the edge. This can contribute to the possibility of a passenger in a wheelchair accidentally moving toward and over the platform edge.

- In an uncovered exterior platform exposed to the weather, provide platform drainage and slope the platform along its length at approximately 0.4 percent slope to encourage drainage.

- Elevators landing on a platform should have doors facing the length of the platform, not toward the platform edge. This is to prevent passengers who are queuing for the elevator from overlapping with passengers moving along the platform length. It also prevents passengers arriving in wheelchairs from accidentally rolling directly toward the platform edge.

- ADA dictates the dimension from the platform edge to the rail vehicle doorsill. Although the dimension is readily controllable in new construction, the designer is advised, in a retrofit station, to investigate the dimensional variances. Using the range of dimensions from top of rail to vehicle floor for existing rail vehicles and precise survey data of existing platforms, determine what predictable dimensions for edge clearances may be achieved. Consult with the transit agency to obtain its concurrence.

- See Chapters 10 and 11, on lighting and signage, respectively, for relevant discussion on the safety implications of these systems on the platform.

SECURITY AGAINST CRIME

The *system security approach* encompasses the concept that crime can be "designed out" of transit station facilities during the planning phase of the transit life cycle. Failure to recognize and incorporate crime prevention features during system planning may result in higher-than-anticipated crime rates, greater fear on the part of passengers, and expensive system modifications in response to serious criminal incidents.

Note, however, that in a transit environment, the value of architectural design principles is not limited to the system security approach. Older transit systems, such as New York City Transit (NYCT) and Massachusetts Bay Transportation Authority (MBTA), have effectively incorporated crime prevention design to optimize public space, improve passenger flow through stations and corridors, and reduce criminal opportunities. Environmental criminology, focusing on the relationship between physical space design and human behavior, has provided station operators with a valuable crime prevention tool. This section provides a general discussion of the theoretical foundation of the two key approaches used in designing and maintaining transit stations:

- Crime prevention through environmental design (CPTED)
- Situational crime prevention (SCP)

This section also describes effective design and policy solutions used in the transit environment to reduce the incidence of crime and passenger fear.

Foundation of Environmental Crime Prevention

In the United States, crime prevention efforts, particularly for stations, have not always recognized the importance of facility design and maintenance. Traditionally, crime prevention has been based on the assumption that efforts to understand and control crime must begin with the offender. Therefore, through the 1960s, crime prevention strategies consisted primarily of deterrence and rehabilitation of the individual.

During the 1970s, however, new approaches to crime prevention changed these traditional assumptions by focusing not on the individual who committed the crime, but on the *context* in which the crime was committed. This shift removed the burden of trying to predict crimes to provide an opportunity for deterring crimes within the transit environment itself.

Based on this new understanding, crime is now perceived as an activity in which criminals go to work trying to get the most, with the least amount of effort, while subjecting themselves to the least amount of risk. In the transit environment, crime requires the convergence of three elements: a motivated offender, a suitable target, and the absence of a capable guardian.

This understanding avoids speculation regarding the motive of the offender and directs a station's efforts to four distinct classes of crime prevention activities:

- Increasing the difficulty of committing crimes
- Increasing the perceived risks
- Reducing the rewards associated with criminal acts
- Reducing the reasoning that enhances crime (see "Increasing Perceived Effort," points 11, 12, and 13, later in this chapter)

Principles of crime

Crime relies on the following three principles: the participant principle; the behavior settings principle; and the flow principle.

Participant principle

Crime requires three elements: motivated offenders, suitable victims, and the absence of intervening forces to prevent criminal activities. For example, a drug deal in a transit facility is dependent on a buyer, a seller, and the absence of transit or other police to prevent the sale.

Behavior settings principle

Social studies suggest that communities are divided into various behavior settings: time and place where various activities occur, whether legal or illegal, orderly or disorderly. A behavior setting contains three distinct features: time, place, and the activity that occurs there. The transit environment may encompass several behavior settings. For example, a station may consist largely of settings that generate a great deal of social control, such as passenger platforms, stores and vending carts, and

▲ *Large columns on a bus island create hiding places and are discouraged.*

space and time. The order, or flow, within a transit setting is divided into two categories: channeling and chunking.

Channeling provides a distinct advantage in the transit environment by creating more public space and encouraging a smoother flow of people. Chunking divides space into smaller units, creating "nooks and crannies" that provide potential offenders with physical space to commit a crime.

Crime Prevention through Environmental Design and Situational Crime Prevention

The three principles of crime described earlier are central to both *crime prevention through environmental design* (CPTED) and *situational crime prevention* (SCP). For example, CPTED solutions, such as improved access control, better lighting, and architectural structures that effectively move passengers through facilities, do not address other environments that may support crime.

SCP uses CPTED design solutions and integrates them with management policy and legal/prosecution measures. For example, to resolve pay phone fraud at major rail terminals, an SCP solution would involve both surveillance/environmental controls and the provision of "call trace" facilities to private telephone subscribers. CPTED provides a general framework of the design and operation of station facilities, and SCP provides the tools to address specific criminal occurrences.

Both CPTED and SCP create physical and social conditions through environmental design in selected environments aimed at reducing both crime and the fear of crime. SCP typically addresses physical measures, modifies existing op-

information booths. Within this legitimate setting, however, there may be an area that fosters illicit behavior, such as a bathroom or a remote waiting area.

Flow principle

The flow principle applies to crime and disorder within a given behavior setting. Transit stations attract large numbers of people, usually carrying cash and other belongings that can be readily stolen. As people flow from one behavior setting (such as an open public plaza) to another setting (such as a corridor leading to an elevator), a legal behavior setting can exist next to an illegal behavior setting in erating procedures, and addresses the specific nature of crime.

To classify SCP solutions in an easy-to-understand framework, Clarke (1996) and others have developed a matrix to categorize the 16 techniques for SCP. Each of the techniques is discussed in the following paragraphs.

Increasing perceived effort

The four techniques in this category focus on the rationale behind environmental criminology. If an offender perceives that an increased amount of effort must be exerted to commit a particular crime, the crime is unlikely to be committed.

1. *Target hardening.* "Hardening" a target involves using locks, safes, reinforced materials, or other physical barriers to obstruct the potential offender, thus reducing criminal opportunities. Examples include the use of glass or plexiglass screens in token and information booths; cages, covers, and shields to protect public station property (clocks, safety devices, fare card equipment, etc.); graffiti- and vandal-resistant materials; and landscaping and barriers to enhance visibility and direct passenger movement.

2. *Access control.* Controlling access involves using mechanical or electrical systems to exclude potential offenders from designated areas and to prohibit offenders from performing specific crimes. Examples include the use of fare gates or "fare only" areas, access gates to parking lots and garages, standalone lock systems (for employee areas), and magnetic strip cards (for employee areas).

3. *Deflecting offenders.* This is a situational technique applied to "deflect" potential offenders away from crime targets. Examples include closing the station between 1:00 A.M. and 5:00 A.M., eliminating seating in stations/limiting seating on platforms, limiting the number of station entrances and exits, and modifying pay phones (reducing phone card fraud).

4. *Controlling facilitators.* This technique involves placing controls on a range of crime targets, almost eliminating the possibility of the commission of the intended crime. Examples include the use of caller identification (i.e., caller ID), removal of pay phones, and the use of monthly fare tickets.

SIXTEEN CRIME OPPORTUNITY-REDUCING TECHNIQUES			
Increasing Perceived Effort	**Increasing Perceived Risks**	**Reducing Anticipated Rewards**	**Inducing Guilt or Shame**
1. Target hardening	5. Entry/exit screening	9. Target removal	13. Rule setting
2. Access control	6. Formal surveillance	10. Identifying property	14. Stimulating conscience
3. Deflecting offenders	7. Employee surveillance	11. Reducing temptation	15. Controlling disinhibitors
4. Controlling facilitators	8. Natural surveillance	12. Denying benefits	16. Facilitating compliance

Increasing perceived risks

In addition to increasing the effort to commit crime, which places a greater burden on the offender, increasing the perceived risks to the offender also helps to deter criminal activity. There are four techniques in this category.

5. *Entry/exit screening.* Screening methods for entry/exit are employed to increase the likelihood of detection of those who do not comply with station regulations. Examples include introducing exact fare cards and automatic fare gate systems, locating turnstiles directly in front of ticket/information booth agents, and installing locks on train doors and passenger facilities to prevent multiple escape routes.

6. *Formal surveillance.* The technique of formal surveillance includes methods to provide a deterrent threat to potential offenders. Examples include the use of closed-circuit television (CCTV) cameras and recorders linked to fully staffed monitoring facilities; security guards; police patrols; spot checking for fare evasion; intercoms and passenger call buttons linked to monitoring facilities; and passenger telephones, linked to monitoring facilities.

7. *Employee surveillance.* This technique suggests using employees, particularly those with positions involving public contact, to perform surveillance. Examples include security awareness training for transit personnel; two-way radios for transit personnel; the presence of station attendants; and CCTV systems to enable employees to address observed activities.

8. *Natural surveillance.* "Natural" surroundings can be used to enhance vision and surveillance in station facilities, and thus to increase perceived risks. Examples include increased lighting; clear sight lines, open spaces, and high, arched ceilings; and clear doors between train cars.

Reducing anticipated rewards

Removing the reward, or the goal, of the offender also helps to reduce the opportunity for criminal behavior. The following techniques include examples of this category.

9. *Target removal.* This technique requires the recognition and removal of potential criminal targets. Examples include: the use of recessed lightbulbs, scheduling frequent trains, providing off-hours waiting areas, having no pay phones, and providing clear signage, as well as information booths, maps, and schedules.

10. *Identifying property.* This technique encourages marking property or using signs to denote ownership. Examples include the use of photo identification on monthly fare passes and photo identification on employee badges.

11. *Reducing temptation.* This technique requires removing temptations that attract crime. Examples include eliminating corners, nooks, long passageways, and unused space; improving visibility; and improving lighting.

12. *Denying benefits.* This technique requires the denial of any benefits associated with committing a crime. Examples include the rapid removal of graffiti and repair of vandalism and easy invalidation of stolen fare media.

Inducing guilt or shame

This SCP method is designed to associate feelings of guilt and shame with potential criminal activities and the offenders who commit crimes. For example, this category encourages posting signs and advertisements stressing the impact of crime on victims. It includes the following four techniques.

13. *Rule setting.* This technique supports the introduction of new rules or procedures intended to remove any ambiguity concerning acceptable modes of conduct. Examples include the use of drug-free zone markers; regulation signs; and posting penalties for fare evasion, smoking, and the like.

14. *Stimulating conscience.* This technique attempts to stir "second thoughts" in the minds of potential criminals. Examples include the use of "Shoplifting is stealing" signs and advertisement campaigns.

15. *Controlling disinhibitors.* This technique requires the prohibition of substances such as alcohol and drugs that are used to undermine social inhibitions. Examples include the use of anti-alcohol and drug rules and no-loitering rules.

16. *Facilitating compliance.* This technique reduces opportunities for crime by supplying conditions for compliance with rules and regulations. Examples include: clearly marked trash bins; graffiti boards; and community art programs.

Implementing the phases of situational crime prevention

SCP techniques can be used at the following times in a station's life cycle:

- In station design
- In renovation
- In response to specific crimes

▲ *Columns on platforms encourage deviant behavior and can be concealment locations for terrorist devices.*

SCP techniques are best employed when included in the initial design of a station. The design, maintenance, and management of the transit system in Washington, D.C., Washington Metropolitan Transit Authority (WMATA), for instance, provides an excellent example of designing out crime. Documented studies indicate that WMATA's low crime rates, in comparison with those of other transit systems, can be attributed to the station's design. WMATA's entrances, exits, and pathways are designed with the following attributes:

- Clear pathways and stairs to alleviate the problem of criminal activity in dark corners (like those found in many older subway stations)

- Enhanced lighting to remove shadows (which are sometimes responsible for passengers' fear)
- Installation of CCTVs to provide greater visibility, thus deterring criminal activity
- A fare card system that prevents fare evasion
- Training for transit police and personnel in deterring disorderly conduct

WMATA scores high on visibility, and the CCTVs assist this open environment by enabling employees to have a clear view of passenger circulation spaces. The second phase of SCP implementation occurs during station renovation. Though not as cost-effective as SCP methods applied during the time of original construction, major reductions in both crime and passengers' fear may result.

SECURITY BY DESIGN–WMATA

Area Addressed	Preventative Efforts
Supporting columns	Decreased number to reduce cover for criminals
Entrances, exits, and pathways	Designed long and straight pathways, stairways, and escalators
	Eliminated corners to reduce shadows and decrease transient occupation
Lighting and maintenance	Used recessed lighting to reduce shadows and enhance the environment
	Excluded public bathrooms in design to eliminate undesirable activity
	Recessed walls and bars installed in front to discourage graffiti
	Placed litter bins on platforms
	Implemented policy directing the cleaning of graffiti and repairing of vandalism within 24 hours of incident
Security devices	Installed CCTVs on the end of each platform, deterring criminals
	Installed kiosks at entrances to platforms
	Installed passenger-to-operator intercoms
	Installed blue light boxes with emergency phones every 600 ft
WMATA transit police and personnel	Added formal surveillance of facility
	Required to enforce all facility rules
	Trained to report all maintenance problems

SECURITY AGAINST TERRORISM

Planning for terrorism has two goals:

1. *Terrorism mitigation*, which includes the following:

   - SCP techniques, as previously described, focusing on system design and physical security measures to enhance observation and deter criminal activity

   - Deployment techniques, such as police patrol and surveillance, and coordination with operations and maintenance personnel to resolve security threats

   - Coordination with local, state, and federal law enforcement agencies to obtain intelligence on terrorism, training, and technical support

2. *Terrorism response*, which includes the following:

   - Developing plans and procedures to minimize the potential danger to passengers and emergency responders during incidents

   - Maintaining the operation of the transit system while managing a critical incident

Security against terrorism should be a factor in the design whenever new stations are built or old ones remodeled. In the United Kingdom, architectural liaison officers—specially qualified police personnel with knowledge of blast effects on structure, cladding, glazing, fixtures, and street furniture, and an understanding of the principles of emergency evacuation routes and bomb security areas—advise local companies on security issues in design and construction. In France, the removal from rail stations of metal-framed wall signs and other extraneous items, along with combustible materials, has reduced the potential number of casualties resulting from shrapnel, fire, and smoke inhalation.

Good station design includes emphasis on open space, including broad fields of vision, the absence of dark corners and other spaces where criminals might hide or terrorists could place bombs, good lighting, the effective deployment of CCTV, installation of fire doors and blinds, ventilation shafts with reversible fans to provide rapid smoke evacuation, emergency evacuation routes, and bomb security areas.

Fencing and Other Physical Barriers

Public surface transportation must have easy access, which limits the use of physical barriers. However, fences should be built around bus yards, around public parking areas adjacent to stations, and along surface tracks. Gates, CCTV cameras aimed at the drivers of vehicles, and cameras covering the entire parking area can also control public parking areas. Employee and visitor parking in bus yards should be controlled by permit. Power facilities and buildings or rooms containing ventilation systems, electrical power connections and controls, communications systems, switching controls, computers, and other vital systems must remain locked, with access to them controlled and visually monitored.

Access Control and Alarm Systems

The techniques for access control and intrusion detection continue to evolve. Used in conjunction with physical barriers and CCTV, access control systems enable security personnel to monitor and protect vital systems (power facilities, control centers, computers, communications, air-conditioning systems, etc.). This is a major topic in the field of security, with its own extensive literature.

Closed-Circuit Television

Faced with serious terrorist threats, both French and British systems have made extensive use of CCTV to protect public transport. As of 1996, the Paris Metro and RER (commuter rail system) had installed 4000 cameras to monitor entrances and stations to enable drivers to check passengers and to perform other security tasks, and more cameras were being installed. The French video system employs sophisticated hardware that combines the televised image with other types of data input and enables operators to instantly summon the image from any camera.

Standard technical criteria for camera placement have not yet been developed. The physical requirements of installing the cameras and the varying environmental conditions can have a significant impact on their effectiveness.

Limiting Availability of Trash Containers as Receptacles for Explosive Devices

Because bombs are often left in trash containers, a great deal of attention has been devoted to this issue. Removing trash cans entirely and sealing permanent receptacles, sometimes an emergency response following a bombing, are not always useful long-term solutions as they may lead to the creation of piles of rubbish, which (if not maintained), in turn, can provide suitable places for concealing explosive devices and make bomb searches even more difficult.

Trash containers should be removed unless absolutely necessary. Those remaining should be located in prominent,

---

CCTV Camera Locations

In the following station areas:

- On one or both sides of restricted access doors
- In emergency stairwells and on emergency exit doors
- On turnstiles, ticket vending machines, and add-fare machines
- On passenger intercoms and passenger courtesy phones
- At opposite ends of station platforms for full line-of-site view
- In/on elevators
- At the tops and bottoms of escalators/stairs
- On restroom doors
- On train doors and platforms, to assist train operators with door closings

In parking lots and garages:

- On entry/exit lanes
- On attendant booths
- Beside elevators in parking garages
- On courtesy phones/passenger intercoms
- Mounted on high poles or roosts to provide a full view of parking lots
- In parking garage stairwells

In restricted areas:

- On entry and exit doors of administrative facilities
- On one or both sides of restricted doors
- Throughout cash-counting facilities
- Posted on mounts in rail yards

BEST PRACTICES CHECKLIST

Plans	Architect	Public Agency	Transit Agency	Other
Comprehensive security plan		●	●	●
Alert levels with predetermined security measured		●	●	
Emergency response plan		●	●	
Coordinated with local authorities		●	●	
Periodic review		●	●	
Intelligence and Threat Analysis				
Periodic meetings with local, state, and federal authorities			●	
Analysis of local crime patterns		●	●	
Station and Terminal Design				
Target hardening	●		●	
No highly combustible materials or sources of toxic fumes or shrapnel			●	
Reversible fans in underground stations	●		●	
Open spaces	●		●	
Good visibility	●		●	
No hiding or hidden spaces	●		●	
Adequate emergency exits	●		●	
Designated evacuation routes	●		●	
Bomb-secure areas with communications	●		●	
Good lighting	●		●	
Effective CCTV coverage	●		●	
Easy to maintain and well-maintained			●	
Bomb-resistant, well-placed trash containers			●	

well-lit areas within view of CCTV systems and away from sources of interference such as windows, mirrors, or overhead glass. Trash containers should not be located adjacent to obvious terrorist targets such as police stations, post offices, or banks.

A number of blast-resistant trash containers are now commercially available. Transparent trash can liners provide a clear view of their contents.

Emergency Evacuation Routes

Emergency evacuation routes should be preplanned to provide the safest means of egress in a variety of emergency situations. For new facilities, this issue should be addressed in the design phase. Evacuation routes should take people away from the point of danger (e.g., a suspicious object, a source of mysterious fumes) to a safe location at a distance from the facility. The location of the safe area depends on the nature of the threat. For example, passengers being evacuated from a sub-

way in response to a chemical or biological threat or attack should not be allowed to loiter on sidewalk ventilation grates above the station and its tunnels. Evacuation routes should not clog the access routes of emergency responders trying to get to the scene (these access routes should be designated in advance). Alternate routes to bomb shelter areas, to be used when exit is not possible, should be included in the evacuation plan.

Underground stations and subways in tunnels are the most difficult facilities to evacuate. The routes should be broad enough to accommodate a surge of people (e.g., no narrow staircases) and should contain no obvious choke points (e.g., elevators) where impatience and alarm may lead to panic and casualties. Evacuation routes should be able to accommodate stretchers and should be designated clearly by signage as well as easily seen identifiers, such as lighted colored arrows that can be switched on in an emergency.

TRANSIT STATIONS AT AIRPORTS: A CASE STUDY

Robert I. Davidson, Chief Architect of the Port Authority of New York and New Jersey, has built his knowledge of transportation architecture from years of experience as an architect and planner of some of the largest transportation systems in the United States. He is responsible for the development of major public transportation projects that include LaGuardia, John F. Kennedy International, and Newark Liberty International Airports; the PATH Commuter Rail System; the Hudson River crossings, including the Lincoln and Holland Tunnel toll plazas; the Port Authority Bus Terminal, the largest of its kind in the world; and the reborn regional ferry service, with the development of new multioperator ferry terminal prototypes. He recently led the design effort in the reconstruction of the World Trade Center (WTC) temporary PATH station that opened November 2003 and led the development of a transportation master plan for the WTC site and Lower Manhattan that proposes to link PATH with existing subway lines and potential future commuter rail service in the highly congested financial district.

As part of his work related to airport landside access programs that serve the metropolitan area, Davidson has, for several years, been developing light-rail access to Newark International and John F. Kennedy International Airports. In an interview he was asked to describe the planning process and to address the issues facing an architect in planning light-rail service to an airport. This chapter presents a case study, as related by Davidson.

AIRTRAIN GATEWAY STRATEGY

Because of population density and the difficulty of navigating a new transit system through the region, developing a strategy whereby a passenger could travel to the airport via mass transit from the region's core in a seamless fashion could not be realized. Significant issues of environmental impact, community interest, cost, and feasibility had been nearly impossible to resolve. The major breakthrough occurred in the mid-1990s, when we went from attempting to address airport access in the idealized way—the seamless or one-seat ride—to thinking about it in a more pragmatic way, a phased plan that would actually allow a system to be initially constructed without precluding the idealized plan in the future. That approach became what we now call the "gateway strategy."

Essentially, what the gateway idea proposes is to bring the airport environment out to existing regional transportation infrastructure in New York and New Jersey by providing mass transit connections to

▲ AirTrain's system identity and branding began with the development of this symbol.

▼ AirTrain's system identity and branding was carried through to the vehicle design and is incorporated to the gateway terminals at fare zones and pedestrian portals into the system. Coordination of system graphics and wayfinding utilizing the identity in various forms, from signage and information kiosk designs, to pamphlets and advertisements, also plays a large role in the branding strategy.

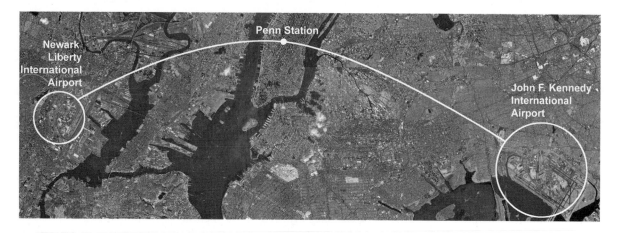

▲ The airport access strategy of the Port Authority of New York and New Jersey links the AirTrain system to existing regional transportation infrastructure through Manhattan, the region's business core. This is accomplished by developing airport gateway terminals that are designed to bring the airport environment out to the existing rail systems at key regional transportation hubs.

John F. Kennedy International Airport (JFK) on the New York side and Newark Liberty International Airport on the New Jersey side. This allows us to take advantage of regional mass transit systems that have been operating successfully for decades by incorporating these systems into our airport access idea. We call the idea AirTrain.

AirTrain, as a branding strategy, allows an airport passenger to think in a different way about using mass transit to get to the airport. For example, in New York, you would be able to access a New York City Transit (NYCT) subway sta-

tion anywhere in New York City, or a Long Island Rail Road (LIRR) station anywhere along the LIRR right-of-way, and take that train to our new airport gateway terminal that incorporates the airport light-rail system and the existing regional transit. At this brand new facility, you would leave that subway or commuter train and seamlessly transfer to another system that is specifically designed as an airport transit system, which transports you to your airline terminal in minutes. The development of these new airport gateways at regional transit hubs is based on the premise that once you arrive at the gateway, you have arrived at the airport. That is the basic AirTrain logic. AirTrain would also target a certain demographic: the individual or paired travelers, business or vacation, not the family of five with baggage who would be better served by a taxi.

Another considerable benefit of AirTrain is guaranteed trip time, which is one of the key branding notions of an airport access system. Barring unforeseen problems within the transit network, AirTrain can ensure that a passenger's trip will always take the same amount of time from origin to destination. In contrast are

▶ AirTrain Newark's system map illustrating its incorporation into the airport's central terminal area (CTA) three-terminal oval master plan. The system alignment leaves the CTA, moving out to the long-term parking zones, then leaves the airport, traveling over state highways, and arrives at the Northeast Corridor rail transit right-of-way where the recently completed Rail Link Terminal establishes AirTrain Newark's gateway strategy.

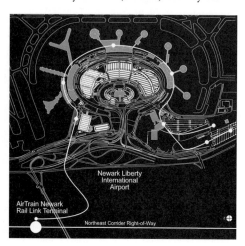

Newark Liberty International Airport

AirTrain Newark Rail Link Terminal

Northeast Corridor Right-of-Way

the uncertainties of the regional roadway network, tunnel crossings, bridge crossings, and how surface transportation is affected by the time of day. Another point in AirTrain's favor is its headway time. With the AirTrain approach, a passenger first travels on the scheduled regional transit service in order to access the gateway terminals—New Jersey Transit, for example, in AirTrain Newark's case. Once there, AirTrain service will be running at 4–5-minute headways during airport peak periods, thereby maximizing the level of service and promoting seamless intermodality. Consider this analogy: When you walk up to an elevator and press the button, you psychologically expect that the elevator will be there in a certain amount of time, and if it is not, your mental clock picks that up. The system has to be that reliable or it will not work.

We began looking at the gateway strategy from a regional perspective starting in the late 1980s when we master-planned what was called the Newark Airport Monorail. The Monorail master plan connected the three Newark terminals and all the remote passenger amenities within the airport such as parking and car rental facilities. We already had an eye toward extending that system off-airport and linking it up with the transportation infrastructure along the Northeast Corridor rail right-of-way, which is a short distance from the airport. That extension, resulting in the first AirTrain Newark Rail Link Terminal, has operated successfully since it opened in October 2002.

AirTrain Newark Rail Link Terminal

The AirTrain Newark Rail Link Terminal, our new facility along the Northeast Corridor, opened in October 2001. Its scope includes two new platforms that

accommodate New Jersey Transit and Amtrak trains, a heated and air-conditioned AirTrain station that is constructed as the terminus of the extended airport monorail system, now part of AirTrain, and an enclosed pedestrian overpass that links the two transit functions. Operating since 2001, this service has enabled airport passengers to take a New Jersey Transit or Amtrak train from New York Penn Station or Newark Penn Station, or get on a train anywhere along the Northeast Corridor and take that

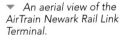 The AirTrain Newark gateway terminal passenger overpass leading into environmentally controlled baggage check-in and AirTrain platform zones.

▼ An aerial view of the AirTrain Newark Rail Link Terminal.

▲ An aerial view of the AirTrain Newark Rail Link Terminal. The terminal was developed as a completely new facility along the Northeast Corridor rail right-of-way, including two New Jersey Transit and Amtrak platforms that provide the regional transit access, and a passenger overpass connection that provides access to the environmentally controlled AirTrain station. In the spirit of bringing the terminal environment out to the airport access gateway, the plan allows passengers to check their baggage in the station and take the AirTrain system to the terminals in minutes.

▼ A view of the passenger overpass and vertical circulation zones that link New Jersey Transit and Amtrak service to the AirTrain station's environmentally controlled baggage check-in and platform zones.

train to the Newark Airport stop, which is the Rail Link Terminal. They can also take PATH, the Port Authority's New York/New Jersey commuter rail service, from New York City to Newark Penn Station and transfer to New Jersey Transit, which enables us to link Lower Manhattan to the airport as well.

When you arrive at the AirTrain Newark Rail Link Terminal, circulation between rail systems is seamless. Passengers circulate from the commuter rail platforms over the Northeast Corridor through the pedestrian overpass. There they move through a fare zone into the AirTrain zone, where they can check their baggage just as they would at any of our airline terminals, and move down to the AirTrain platform. Operating as both an airport and transit environment, the terminal provides the highest level of service from a transit perspective, but it also provides a similar level of service that a passenger would expect when approaching an airline ticketing zone.

Both Amtrak and New Jersey Transit platforms are 1000 ft long. The platform zones adjacent to the vertical circulation that leads passengers up to the pedestrian overpass are canopy covered for weather protection. A heated and air-conditioned passenger waiting zone frames the end of each canopy, promoting an airport environment. The rest of the commuter rail and AirTrain service, all arranged as a unified environment, is easily perceived that way as a passenger arrives at the terminal. This is the key ingredient to the AirTrain experience. As the commuter train pulls into the terminal, the visual connection to the AirTrain station makes it seem as though it is within physical reach of passengers exiting the commuter train; this is the AirTrain idea in practice.

Once airport-bound passengers enter the AirTrain system at the regional gateway, they have entered the airport environment. This is part of a large context that includes the AirTrain terminals, stations, vehicles, and airline terminals.

AirTrain Newark On-Airport Planning and Design

Originally conceived as an elevated guideway, light-rail service, the Newark monorail, as an airport circulator, allows customers to access any of the passenger amenities that exist within the airport precinct. This was the beginning of the second overarching strategy that makes AirTrain unique as an airport access system. Once passengers get on AirTrain, whether on-airport or at the regional gateway, they can seek out any passenger service in the airport—a one-seat ride of a sort. By 2003, this dual-system strategy, airport circulator and airport access as one system, that began with the Newark monorail development, is in full operation at Newark as AirTrain. Through the success of the Newark experience, the dual system service has been implemented at JFK.

AirTrain Newark operates an automated, driverless monorail train that runs at maximum efficiency. Station platforms are glass enclosed with doors that open simultaneously with the train door. It is a system that links together all the terminal buildings and, in turn, the terminals to the passenger amenities that exist outside the central terminal area (CTA), consisting of parking facilities, car rental facilities, remote passenger pick-up/drop-off, and hotel service. Accessing these facilities used to require the passenger to be transported via bus around the airport environs. It also included transferring

▲ The AirTrain Newark Rail Link Terminal platform zone. The operable glass platform screen door system works in tandem with the driverless automated trains, creating a seamless environment between the station and the train. Views from the elevated platform contribute to the sense of passenger safety and security regarding orientation to surrounding airport activity and the ability to see a train coming.

▼ The AirTrain Newark vehicle uses a monorail technology; it operates with maximum seven-car train consists, with each car able to accommodate as many as 20 passengers seated and standing.

▲ The P4 remote area AirTrain station and intermodal parking garage demonstrating AirTrain's ability to influence airport planning. Passengers can self-park or use the valet parking service, circulate up to the station platform, and be at their terminals in minutes.

▼ An airside view of the AirTrain station at Terminal A.

remote locations to develop other types of passenger amenities, for example, parking garages that link to AirTrain stations.

From a surface transportation perspective, particularly private auto, no matter what happens at our airports, airport access will never be the dominant mode of travel. AirTrain is intended to be a viable alternate to surface transportation. A successful airport access program would take about 10 percent of the traffic coming to the airport away from the roadway network, which helps to improve the roadway network. However, there would still be the remaining 90 percent coming via surface transportation, which means that parking will always be needed.

Particularly at an international airport, for passengers and for visitors, there will be different kinds of parking programs based on trip duration. Long-term parking and daily parking are for passengers, whereas short-term or hourly parking is for visitors, either seeing off departing passengers or "meeting and greeting" passengers upon arrival. At an international airport, passengers park in remote long-term areas. Parking within the CTA is usually short-term, with quick turnover times, primarily by people who are seeing passengers off or meeting passengers.

AirTrain provides an opportunity to build intermodal parking garages adjacent to remote stations and terminal stations within the system. The off-airport component of the system that is coming from the gateway terminals can pick up passengers in the long-term parking zones and transport them to the various terminal buildings. Parking flexibility is provided in the CTA by enabling visitors to park in any short-term garage within the CTA and ride AirTrain to their specific terminals.

from terminal to terminal. One of the great benefits of AirTrain is the ability to remove on-airport buses from the airport roadway network. So, in a sense, you are benefiting passengers not only by providing them with a great way to get to the airport, but by providing a great way to get around the airport as well.

AirTrain connects all the terminal buildings in Newark and then goes out to the remote parking areas, which enables the system to provide another benefit beyond just taking buses off the roadways. Because AirTrain provides continuous connectivity, the airport was able to select

Another advantage that AirTrain affords, which is particularly applicable to Newark Airport, has to do with interterminal transfer. Transfer from terminal to terminal is typically the result of arriving on an international flight and, after going through customs, transferring to another flight at another terminal. Prior to the monorail, interterminal transfer occurred via bus. Since the mid-1990s, passengers transfer from one terminal to the other by train in a minute or so. In fact, Newark has developed to the point where airlines have expanded into other terminals, because AirTrain has made that possible. To describe this another way, AirTrain has made the three terminals at Newark into one virtual terminal.

Ancillary benefits

The ancillary benefits have been numerous and have had enormous economic

▲ An aerial view of Newark Liberty International Airport's central terminal area (CTA). The AirTrain Newark system is located on the airside of the oval CTA building plan with a station physically abutting each building, providing direct access into the main public terminal space. The system leaves the airport precinct and connects over to the Northeast Corridor rail right-of-way and into the AirTrain Rail Link Terminal.

City	Airport	Rail Type	Status
AMERICAN AIRPORTS WITH DIRECT RAIL PUBLIC TRANSPORTATION ACCESS			
Atlanta, Ga.	Hartsfield-Atlanta	HR	Open
Baltimore, Md.	Baltimore-Washington	LR	Open
Chicago, Il.	Midway	HR	Open
Chicago, Il.	O'Hare	HR	Open
Cleveland, Ohio	Cleveland-Hopkins	HR	Open
Minneapolis, Minn.	Minneapolis–St. Paul	LR	Construction
New York, N.Y.	Kennedy	AG	Construction
Newark, N.J.	Newark	AG	Open
Philadelphia, Pa.	Philadelphia	CR	Open
Portland, Oreg.	Portland	LR	Open
Saint Louis, Mo.	Lambert–St. Louis	LR	Open
San Francisco, Calif.	San Francisco	HR	Open
South Bend, Ind.	Michiana	CR	Open
Washington, D.C.	Reagan National	HR	Open

AG = automated guideway, HR = heavy rail, LR = light rail, CR = commuter rail
Source: American Public Transportation Association

implications, especially with respect to the airport roadway network. By building the monorail in the mid-1990s, the airport was able to stave off costly capital investment in expanding the roadway network by eliminating the high-occupancy vehicles (HOVs) that traditionally congest the roadways. From a geographical perspective, the closeness of the Northeast Corridor rail right-of-way to Newark's CTA creates the perception of arriving at the edge of the airport precinct. This was a big advantage, because the travel time from the AirTrain Rail Link Terminal to the first airline terminal is just a few minutes. From a planning perspective, the issue of where transfer occurs, geographically, or whether transfer is essential, became clear to us. Systems that claim to have a continuous one-seat connection usually plan that service to arrive at a location within the airport. Typically, the passenger who requires a second movement within the airport transfers from the airport access system to an "on-airport" system for the additional trip. Therefore, the true origin and destination (O&D) trip is not seam-

less. Another misconception regarding the seamless connection concerns transfer between multiple services within the mass transit system that provide access to the airport.

For example, if you access the mass transit system on its "red" line and require transfer to the system's "blue"—the line that goes to the airport—the trip is not seamless. Finally, if the airport access system is a discrete O&D system, it usually requires walking significant distances within the airport for passenger services not geographically related to the O&D system. It also generally requires a second mode of transportation—taxi, for example—once the system arrives at the off-airport location, because it is remote from the central business district.

Our opinion of the "one seat" issue and seamless connectivity was reinforced once we recognized that we would be providing seamless travel from the regional transit connection, transformed into the airport gateway to the airport, by providing access to the system throughout the airport as well. However, the geographical location of the connection within the region, which equates to travel time, was fundamental to the gateway strategy.

AirTrain Newark CTA Service

Newark Airport's terminal master plan, which was developed in the 1960s, had the foresight to provide a transit right-of-way on the airside of the three airline terminals. Anticipating interterminal transfer, the airport planners had envisioned a small people-mover system, dubbed the Inter-Terminal Transit System (ITT), which would circulate between the three terminals. We took advantage of that planning by locating the monorail system within the ITT right-of-way and expand-

▼ An aerial airside view of the AirTrain station at Terminal A. The station is situated directly adjacent to the airport's secure, restricted service road, enabling rampside vehicles to circulate freely between ramp activities, and under the station, to access terminal building operations space. Direct passenger access to the terminal was established early on by the airport master plan of the early 1960s, which provided a vehicular and station right-of-way that could be expanded for future rail access. Terminal stations eliminated the need for interterminal bus operations that moved passengers from one airline to another while clogging the airport CTA roadway network. The system's efficiency regarding elimination of vehicles also precluded the need to build additional roadway capacity.

ing the original station zone to create the terminal stations. This was a substantial design challenge, considering the size of the monorail stations and their potential impacts on airside activity, but an equally great advantage in terms of level of service, because we could circulate passengers directly from the station into each terminal's main space (which is just the opposite at JFK). This also provided spectacular views of the airport's airside as well as its landside, as the system moved from terminal to terminal and eventually out to the remote areas and off-airport.

A prototypical station design was developed that would become the identity for the stations in the terminal and remote areas. The design premise was to create clear connections between the station platform and lobby whereby each is physically and visually connected to the other. This was made possible by establishing a multiheight lobby that enables the lobby ceiling to translate over to the platform zone. Vertical circulation physically connects the two spaces, thereby providing the passenger with a sense of security and orientation, which is essential in an often anxiety-producing airport environment. As on the train, passengers waiting on the platform were treated to spectacular views of the airport airside.

These elevated views were never anticipated in planning an airport. Consequently, the airport had new criteria to consider in future development, and, regarding maintenance of the interior and exterior spaces, never previously viewable within the public realm.

AirTrain Newark Remote Area Service
Planning the remote station locations and design was a much more fluid

▲ AirTrain Newark's remote station lobby, illustrating the multiheight space and ceiling that spans the elevated platform zone, creating one continuous heated and air-conditioned public space. Visual clarity and natural light contribute to the direct paths of travel experienced by passengers circulating throughout the system.

▼ AirTrain Newark's remote station platform zone provides a column-free waiting area.

process. We realized that station locations would be based on elevated guideway alignments that would weave their way through parking areas and roadways. The system's maintenance control facility also required a location that would work efficiently with the guideway. In addition, such remote airport areas are located directly adjacent to state roadways that act as the surface transportation arteries into the airport. This made the presence of the system winding its way through the remote zones a highly visible component of the airport environment. We realized in this case that this public face created an opportunity to develop a "family of structures" that would work in tandem with the system's steel guideway structure, identifying the monorail as a new service within the airport.

▼ A typical remote AirTrain station pick-up/drop-off zone enabling intermodal connections to occur between the system and high-occupancy vehicles such as hotel and car-rental buses that clogged airport roadways before AirTrain.

From a programming perspective, the remote areas offered the kind of flexibility that would enable each station to be functionally different from the others. For example, stations are programmed to handle car rental facilities, long-term and valet parking—at grade or in garages—hotel pick-up/drop-off curbsides, and remote "kiss-and-fly" pick-up/drop-off curbsides for passengers who do not wish to drive into the CTA. All of these amenities were located directly adjacent to the stations. From the passengers' perspective, they were experiencing one big terminal environment linked by the train. Again, this programming removes on-airport buses from the roadways. With their multiheight lobbies connecting to the elevated platforms, the remote stations functionally and visually direct passengers up to the platforms, carrying through the prototypical station design established for the terminal stations that, along with the maintenance control facility, created the monorail, now the AirTrain Newark "family of structures."

AIRTRAIN JFK PLANNING AND DESIGN

AirTrain JFK service differs from Newark service in that it not only links up to an existing regional transportation system, but also connects to multiple existing urban transportation facilities, train stations that have been operating in southeast Queens, New York, for decades. These linkages required AirTrain JFK to go through an extensive approval process on the local and city levels because it was traveling off the airport through adjacent communities. The approval process was far more complex for JFK than for Newark.

AirTrain JFK is based on the same fundamental idea of quality service built on a guaranteed trip time. Whereas the Newark scenario afforded the luxury of building a completely new terminal, Air-Train JFK had to consider the challenge of integrating the airport service within the existing transit facilities by redeveloping the train stations along with AirTrain, thereby establishing the gateway terminal. AirTrain Newark took advantage of the existing right-of-way on the Northeast Corridor and its close proximity to the airport At JFK we had to work through the integration of a new transit system rising out of two active existing conditions. The two off-airport locations also formed the basis for segmenting AirTrain JFK into three distinct services, with the CTA area service linking the other two. The three services work together in regard to the AirTrain objectives of providing airport access and on-airport circulation within the airport precinct.

The two Queens, New York, locations selected for AirTrain JFK terminal gateways were the New York City Transit (NYCT) Howard Beach A Train station, which is the terminus for the AirTrain JFK Howard Beach service, and the LIRR Jamaica station complex, which is the terminus for the AirTrain JFK Jamaica service. Both were chosen because of their close proximity to the airport, as in the case of Newark, and their ability to provide points of transit access throughout the region to the specific train services that run through each station.

The Queens Locations

The NYCT A train Howard Beach subway station is located right at the edge of the airport, adjacent to the remote long-term parking areas. Calling upon our

Newark experience, we recognized that we could develop the most remote long-term parking station with the dual-service approach, a remote parking lot station that is integrated into the gateway terminal. The LIRR Jamaica station complex is the most intricate and diverse of the three AirTrain gateways. At Jamaica, we are not only linking to most of the LIRR system coming from Brooklyn, Long Island, Queens and Manhattan, but also connecting to a significant amount of NYCT service, including the E, J, and Z trains and numerous city buses that service Jamaica station as part of its existing intermodal operation. As with AirTrain Newark's Rail Link Terminal, both of the JFK gateways are being developed under the same guiding principle, with the airport being brought out to the regional transit network.

AirTrain JFK is also similar to Newark in the airport's CTA service. The system alignment follows a loop configuration based upon the terminal arrangement; but that is where the similarity ends. The AirTrain Newark CTA alignment, was relatively straightforward because the airport CTA master plan was developed as the identical three-terminal

◀◀ A typical remote AirTrain station pick-up/drop-off zone enabling intermodal connections between the system and high occupancy vehicles such as hotel and car-rental buses that clogged airport roadways before AirTrain. Interior and exterior remote station environments are developed as public spaces commensurate with the airline terminal experience in order to maintain a consistently safe and secure functional level of service. The AirTrain steel guideway acts as a ribbon, connecting the airport to the region.

▼ AirTrain JFK's system map illustrating the relationship of the 9 miles of the system to its two regional transit points of interface at the New York City Transit A train Howard Beach subway station and the Long Island Rail Road Jamaica Station complex. The John F. Kennedy International Airport central terminal area is on the upper right. The Howard Beach and Jamaica Rail Link Terminals establish the gateway strategy for AirTrain JFK.

▲ An aerial view of John F. Kennedy International Airport's central terminal area (CTA). The AirTrain JFK system is located on the landside of the CTA terminals, integrated into the overall airport landside access. Landside access consists of a fully integrated program composed of the airport roadway network, terminal building pick-up/drop-off zones, structural parking, car rental facilities, and hotel bus operations. AirTrain JFK will complement the landside program by using its plan to organize the other components along unified passenger circulation to and from terminal buildings.

building plan that provided an airside transit right-of-way.

The JFK CTA master plan had its roots in the early 1950s when the airport was called Idlewild.

Airline travel was a special experience then, and airline corporate identity drove the decision-making process. The arrangement of individually expressive airline terminals around a loop roadway network formed the airport's identity. Although rail access into the airport precinct was probably studied in the early master planning for JFK (then known as Idlewild and before that as Major Anderson Field), it probably did not consider the detail of a continuous light-rail system that could provide access to each terminal. In the AirTrain JFK CTA planning, we had to invent the concept of a seamless terminal-by-terminal configuration that was preordained at Newark. The creation of a unified AirTrain environment would have to address a CTA that had been repeatedly redeveloped with new terminals over time that replicated the airport's original master plan premise of individually expressive terminal design.

The loop roadway had been replaced

with a more efficient network in the late 1980s, fortifying the CTA as a purely surface transportation-driven plan. The plan was arranged in a quadrant configuration designed to respond to the individual terminals. The individuality of the terminals not only reflected the building designs, but also included the vehicular pick-up and drop-off zones in front of each terminal and their relationship to the roadways and short-term parking. Each of these zones was linked with pedestrian crosswalks that formed a sequence of landside passenger services in front of each building. Each zone was different from the others, because they were responding to each terminal's unique siting and physical plan.

Because of JFK's CTA plan, AirTrain did not have the luxury of Newark's foresight regarding the airside right-of-way. AirTrain JFK would have to become another layer of the landside access program that would somehow be smoothly interwoven within the existing services without negatively impacting those services. As successful as AirTrain might be in the future, the airport, as mentioned earlier, will still rely on surface transportation; therefore, those roadways, curbsides, parking areas, and crosswalk zones are critical to the operation of the terminal and must remain as customer-efficient as possible.

AIRTRAIN JFK CTA SERVICE

To achieve a balance between elevated AirTrain service and the roadway network in the JFK CTA, we first had to determine where the AirTrain system would be located relative to the terminals on their landside. The natural reaction would have been to locate the system as close to the terminals as possible in order to shorten the passengers' walking distances. That idea was quickly abandoned because of the priority of the multilevel vehicular zones directly in front of each terminal. (The modal split at JFK will remain roughly 90 percent vehicular, 10 percent AirTrain, projected to the airport's maximum air passenger growth. As a matter of fact, that 10 percent projection would place AirTrain JFK at the top of the airport-access-system success stories).

AirTrain's size and scope could never coexist with these vehicular zones, for a number of reasons. The vehicular zones were developed as part of each terminal master plan and were uninterrupted in their interface with the terminals in their own right, as one would expect. AirTrain's stations and guideway require an enormous grade-level scope that could never be accommodated within the vehicular zones and could never be constructed in those active zones without great hardship to the terminal's operation. Another issue concerned the environment beneath the elevated guideway, an area that could never be programmed as a public space. Considering the amount of airport real estate that would sit directly below the guideway, we had to factor that into the equation as well (what could work under the elevated concrete box structures that form the train right-of-way?). We finally recognized that access from the terminals to the AirTrain service had to be along the same path of travel that all passengers and visitors use to access any component of the terminal's landside program.

Upon analyzing the issues, we realized that locating AirTrain in the parking zones, along the existing path of travel from terminal to parking, would enable AirTrain to provide the linkage for all users at grade, and above grade via pedes-

▲ AirTrain JFK central terminal area stations are prototypically developed based on their relationship to the individual terminals and their landside functions. Terminal 1 required a station with a platform zone below the passenger overpass, which physically engages the terminal at a specific elevation. The passenger overpass was also located directly above-grade-level crosswalk zones that integrated terminal pick-up zones and structural parking, enabling all passenger circulation paths to be organized around the AirTrain JFK system.

▲▼ JFK AirTrain terminal.

trian overpasses to whichever landside service would be linked to AirTrain. AirTrain would also link the multilevels of each terminal, in addition to linking the terminals to each other. The same crosswalk that passengers use to move to a curbside vehicular zone, or over to the short-term parking area, would also bring them to AirTrain. This provides the passengers with an option to conveniently use mass transit because it is right there within the seamless landside environment—the AirTrain brand is always in sight.

Defining Boundaries

AirTrain's location in the short-term CTA parking area also enabled the airport landscape plan that defined the boundary between vehicular curbside zones and parking to flourish—you cannot plant under AirTrain, but you can park cars, solving the real estate issue. With the location set, the development of an integrated CTA landside could begin. AirTrain stations, guideway, and parking garages could be planned together, coordinating vertical and horizontal circulation and site development, establishing a dynamic environment that complements the new terminals and has changed the face of JFK.

From a station perspective, AirTrain JFK would follow the Newark program and criteria of safe, secure, visually clear paths of travel with heated and air-conditioned spaces—a family of structures plugging into the terminal buildings and terminal gateways. The individual terminal CTA plan, however, presented another kind of challenge. Individuality usually does not mesh well with a transit system whose nature is to be generally uniform for the sake of efficiency and level of service. We had to devise a way to create a prototypical elevated AirTrain station design that could be adjusted to would work with each of the individually expressive buildings.

Once we had determined the system location within the CTA, including, as stated, the location of each station relative to each terminal's public realm, we were then able to understand the vertical elevation of the guideway, and therefore the station at each location. To state the issue simply, the guideway would adjust its elevation in front of each one of the terminals in order to relate to each specific terminal plan. This meant that the stations and the pedestrian overpasses would exchange vertical positions, based on the site. We called this the "up-and-over, down-and-under" prototype. Passengers would arrive at a station platform zone and then circulate up or down to the pedestrian overpass, depending on the terminal. The only exception in the CTA, Terminal 4, offered an opportunity to incorporate AirTrain within the facility because it was planned in the same time frame. Terminal 4 moved farther landside in its planning to include the AirTrain guideway and develop the station within the terminal envelop.

▼ Like those of AirTrain Newark, AirTrain JFK remote stations are located within long-term parking areas or adjacent to passenger amenities, such as car rental facilities, that also provide pick-up/drop-off zones for hotel buses and other high-occupancy vehicle operations.

The AirTrain JFK Vehicle

The selection for Newark of a system technology significantly smaller than the JFK counterpart would be reflected an early understanding of the impact that a light-rail system would have on the airport and the region. Operations at Newark, from a passenger and business perspective, changed once the system was put in service. The airport, the airlines and the passengers found ways to take advantage of the monorail's flexibility. In fact, that flexibility is still fostering changes today. What was once a series of passenger amenities, spread out over acres of airport space that was connected only by roadways, is now a single interconnected public realm. Just hop on the AirTrain, and minutes later you are at the car rental facility. Passengers departing from one terminal may arrive at another, even though their cars may be at the original terminal—they then just hop on the AirTrain.

A matter of capacity

The most important lesson learned was how successful the monorail was going to be, relative to its limited capacity. As at Newark, AirTrain JFK would be an automated, driverless light-rail system, but with much different technology it would have much greater capacity and be much more operationally flexible for several important reasons.

AirTrain JFK's system technology was required to be adaptable to the NYCT and LIRR rights-of-way in order to allow for future adjustments to the regional transit network. Future planning might develop a hybrid train that could operate in an automated or manually driven mode on all three rights-of-way—AirTrain being the third—thereby creating a seamless or one-seat ride to specific locations within the region, particularly the business core in Manhattan. The big difference at JFK would be its size and the train's level of passenger service. We had a comparatively greater opportunity to

▲ *The AirTrain JFK concrete guideway structure hovering over the Van Wyck Expressway, the New York state highway network that has been the main vehicular artery to JFK from its inception in the early 1950s. AirTrain JFK will circulate from the airport along the Van Wyck over to the Long Island Rail Road Jamaica Station complex.*

▽ *The AirTrain portal structure, the signature component of the AirTrain system under construction. The portal provides the sense of arrival that symbolizes the integration of JFK and regional transit as the overarching AirTrain idea.*

▲ The AirTrain JFK vehicle is a steel wheel, steel rail technology that has been developed as a technology compatible with New York State Metropolitan Transit Authority, Long Island Rail Road commuter rail, and New York City Transit subway train rights-of-way. This far-reaching strategy will enable a future hybrid vehicle to ride on all three rights-of-way, providing for the potential of a "one-seat ride" to the airport from the region's business core. A maximum AirTrain consist contains four vehicles, with each car accommodating as many as 100 passengers seated and standing. Baggage carts and containers are also accommodated within the customized train interior.

brand and customize the JFK train on its exterior and interior as a true airport service. The AirTrain JFK car can accommodate more than 90 passengers and, because of the criteria requiring compatibility with the NYCT and LIRR systems, is a steel wheel, steel rail technology.

The size of the train provides flexibility to do a number of things, aside from just making it compatible with the other transit systems. Its door arrangement and interior seating and space configuration allows passengers to bring baggage carts onto the system. As an airport passenger getting off an NYCT train or an LIRR train at our Howard Beach and Jamaica station gateway terminals, you can pick up a baggage cart and take it with you all the way to your airline ticketing counter. The same service is available when you arrive at the airport—carts at every station. As at Newark, passengers can also check their bags at Jamaica.

HOWARD BEACH RAIL LINK TERMINAL

The Howard Beach service combines the on-airport "airport circulator" remote service with the airport access service in almost the same plan as AirTrain Newark. Once AirTrain leaves the CTA

at either the Newark or the Howard Beach service, it moves to car rental, hotel curbsides, and remote parking areas, where stations are located and programmed to accommodate those passenger amenities. Consequently, the same advantages that Newark is experiencing—the removal of buses from the airport roadways—will occur at JFK. Once the train arrives at the Howard Beach Rail Link Terminal, passengers will see an arrangement of the AirTrain station and the Rail Link Terminal that is very similar to the juxtaposition of AirTrain stations relative to airline terminals in the CTA. The station and pedestrian overpass plug into the Howard Beach Terminal. The concept of terminals and prototypical stations and overpasses, all linked by the AirTrain guideway and trains, is carried through in the gateway strategy. As previously touched upon, the major difference in complexity between Newark's gateway and the Howard Beach and Jamaica gateways is the layering of AirTrain JFK onto the existing transit operations and redevelopment of those facilities to create intermodal gateways that serve all user groups.

The Howard Beach Rail Link Terminal is functionally derived from the NYCT A train platform zone's incorporation into the gateway and is visually derived as a dynamic form that is meant to impart a perceived sense of arrival at the airport. As in a flow diagram, passengers will move from the A train platforms up to an intermodal mezzanine that serves AirTrain and NYCT passengers. Circulation occurs through two vertical circulation buildings that frame the platform environment. These glass-enclosed structures act as armatures for the mezzanine, providing a clear sense of ori-

An aerial view of the AirTrain JFK Howard Beach Rail Link Terminal, one of the two gateway terminals within the AirTrain JFK system. The terminal, in construction, is located over the New York City Transit A train subway station, incorporating the transit station into the idea of airport arrival. The terminal's location at the edge of the airport allows the facility to engage the local community as well as the airport. The terminal's main space is a shared intermodal mezzanine that accommodates subway and AirTrain JFK services. AirTrain passengers arriving via the subway circulate up to the mezzanine before moving over to the AirTrain station, where they can take AirTrain over to the central terminal area in minutes.

▲▲ A model view of the AirTrain JFK Howard Beach Rail Link Terminal, one of the two gateway terminals within the AirTrain JFK system.

▲ ◀▼ Howard Beach terminal.

▲ *Howard Beach terminal.*

totally new facility, the essential premise in creating the overall continuity of the dual regional transit/airport environment at Howard Beach was to design the various interconnected transit spaces, both new and renovated, to be comprehended along with the AirTrain spaces as one architectural entity: the airport gateway. The importance of this notion cannot be underplayed, because the perception of separation between transit and airport would significantly detract from the gateway idea and the AirTrain branding strategy—two transit systems operating as one seamless experience.

Shared Intermodal Zone

The shared intermodal zone has been developed as the main public space that is accessible for NYCT and AirTrain passengers coming from three locations, the A train platforms, a vehicular zone in the Howard Beach community, and the AirTrain station. Constructed at the same level as the AirTrain station, the mezzanine is the space that provides the symbolic and functional point of arrival for AirTrain.

Once they are through the fare zone, AirTrain passengers will move through a pedestrian connector that links up with the prototypical AirTrain station, establishing exactly the same distinct design premise as the AirTrain system's relationship to the corporately distinct airline terminals in the CTA, but with a subtle difference. Whereas the airline terminals and the AirTrain stations are obviously different—planes and trains—the architecturally distinct AirTrain rail link terminals and the intentionally prototypical AirTrain stations must form a clear visual relationship that is embedded in the AirTrain branding strategy, AirTrain's corpo-

entation in terms of the passengers' path of travel. Because the subway station right-of-way is situated between the airport edge and the Howard Beach community, the terminal also required a presence in the community, which was a factor in the local outreach approval process. From the Howard Beach Rail Link Terminal to the first airline terminal is an approximate 8-minute trip, as opposed to the bus trip it will replace, which can range from 15 to 45 minutes, depending on time of day and traffic.

As with the Newark gateway, which had the benefit of being developed as a rate identity that tells passengers that they have arrived at the airport. Customized trains, prototypical stations, and distinctly designed rail link terminals all work together with the regional transit systems and are smoothly incorporated to the extent that the passenger does not perceive the differences between the components of the gateway facility, only the facility as a whole.

AIRTRAIN JFK JAMAICA RAIL LINK TERMINAL

The final piece of the AirTrain story is the evolution of the AirTrain JFK Rail Link Terminal at the LIRR Jamaica station complex. We started this discussion with an overview of how AirTrain evolved into a plan that proposed to utilize the existing transportation infrastructure by developing new facilities that would bring the airport out into the region. For AirTrain JFK, the success of the system was going to rest with the redevelopment of the Long Island Rail Road's key station in southeast Queens. This was the location that would enable us to connect the region, from Manhattan and all the New York City boroughs, to the eastern tip of Long Island. It was a transit facility that was historically developed as a regional intermodal hub, and its redevelopment had the potential to reestablish the Jamaica community, once a bastion of commerce in Queens, as a viable commercial, cultural, and institutional urban center.

To accomplish this goal, the AirTrain system would have to leave the airport and travel down the Van Wyck Expressway, ironically, the heavily used state vehicular artery that would continue to transport the 80–90 percent of the airport's passengers that would not be on

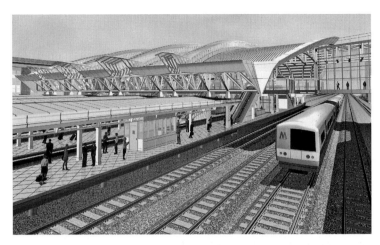

AirTrain. The Van Wyck needed to remain fully operational while the AirTrain guideway was being constructed, a major factor in the city's approval process. An extensive staging and phasing plan took into account issues ranging from minimizing vehicular lane closures, to hours of construction, emergency service vehicle routing, and overall neighborhood safety and protection of property, which were among the many topics that were coordinated with the communities impacted by the project. An extensive beautification of the Van Wyck corridor from the airport to the Jamaica complex was also included as one result of the approval process.

The AirTrain system's integration into the LIRR Jamaica station complex was a rare opportunity to redevelop the Jamaica complex along with the new airport access system into a world-class intermodal transportation hub that would be unprecedented in the New York metropolitan region. Although the Newark and Howard Beach AirTrain gateways were also developed through interagency coordination efforts, the physical plants at Newark and Howard Beach did not

▲ *The AirTrain Rail Link Terminal as viewed from the LIRR platform zone. Rail Road passengers circulate to the multilevel AirTain portal zone, where they access the mezzanine that provides the linkage to the AirTrain ticketing lobby and station. The mezzanine also acts as the main waiting area for LIRR passengers.*

▲▼ *Construction of Jamaica AirTrain terminal.*

have the complexity of scope and size of the Jamaica gateway.

A master plan was required that would encompass public transit zones and system operations spaces discrete to each transportation mode: NYCT subway, LIRR commuter rail, MTA buses, and AirTrain. It would also encompass multiple levels of public space that would have to be smoothly interwoven. The NYCT subway station mezzanine would be expanded and redeveloped below grade with connections up to street, and above the street to an LIRR/AirTrain zone over the LIRR platforms. Existing street-level intermodal zones between rail and surface transportation—bus, taxi, and private auto—would be renovated and expanded. The existing LIRR platform zone would be completely rebuilt and would include a multilevel platform environment that would be programmed to serve LIRR and AirTrain passengers.

Intermodal Mezzanine

As part of the multilevel environment, the intermodal mezzanine would act as the LIRR passenger waiting area and the "umbilical cord" that connects LIRR and NYCT passengers to the AirTrain ticketing and baggage check lobby and AirTrain station. An iconographic weather protection structure—a "portal"—would also provide the visually symbolic airport point of arrival for AirTrain. The portal would also be the most recognizable architectural component of the Jamaica gateway master plan and the AirTrain system.

The mezzanine is the intermodal connection for transit. At the street level, entrances to AirTrain are developed adjacent to street-level intermodal zones that will function in a similar fashion to the LIRR platforms, in that they will be shared between the transit operation and AirTrain. AirTrain passengers will be able to be dropped off beneath the shared LIRR/AirTrain building and circulate to an atrium space that serves as the civic entrance to AirTrain from the Jamaica community. Vertical circulation in the atrium places passengers coming from the street in the AirTrain lobby along with passengers coming from the transit zones through the mezzanine and portal zone. Once they are through the lobby, all passengers move through the AirTrain fare zone onto the station platform, where every 4–5 minutes at peak times a train will travel the 8-minute trip to the airport. As the master plan evolved, the AirTrain lobby was developed as part of a multilevel structure that would also house LIRR operations. It was also designed to accommodate the potential for an air rights program that, along with the overall master plan, could become the catalyst for economic development in Jamaica.

▲ The multilevel AirTrain portal zone as viewed from the Long Island Rail Road platform level. Escalators, stairs, and elevators serve all transit passenger groups that will use the facility, for either daily or airport-specific trips.

▶ The AirTrain JFK Jamaica Rail Link Terminal atrium. The atrium works in tandem with the AirTrain portal, serving as the symbolic street entry to the AirTrain system. A significant street presence was also a major consideration during terminal master planning, with an eye again toward branding the system, but also toward spurring economic development in Jamaica.

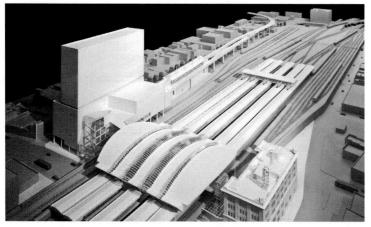

▲ A model view of the AirTrain JFK Jamaica Rail Link Terminal, the most critical of the two gateway terminals within the AirTrain JFK system. Overall master planning of the AirTrain JFK terminal spurred the complete redevelopment of the Long Island Rail Road and New York City Transit zones above and below grade, linking all three rail systems, bus, and vehicular zones at street level. A multilevel intermodal environment at the LIRR platform zone accommodates all passenger circulation paths from the regional transit systems over to the AirTrain terminal, where passengers can check their bags before moving over to the AirTrain station, where they can take AirTrain to the JFK central terminal area in minutes.

▼ The AirTrain JFK Jamaica Rail Link Terminal as seen from the Jamaica Center central business district. A significant street presence was also a major consideration during master planning of the terminal, again with an eye toward branding the system and toward spurring economic development in Jamaica.

AIRTRAIN IN SUMMARY

Several major initiatives define AirTrain. Foremost is the gateway strategy, combined with dual system operation. Connecting to existing regional transit and developing it as part of the AirTrain branding idea enabled AirTrain to be realized. It was a pragmatic plan that was approvable and constructible. Connecting the airport access component to the airport circulator component provided the overall flexibility required to make getting to and around the airport passenger-friendly.

The challenge for the AirTrain planning and design team revolved around the similarities and differences between AirTrain Newark and AirTrain JFK, which led to these conclusions:

- Newark as an airport benefited from a cohesive CTA master plan that accepted the monorail light-rail system in a preordained way. The airline terminals were designed to receive the monorail system on airside greenfield.

- AirTrain Newark airport access benefited from a greenfield site opportunity along the Northeast Corridor to develop a completely new intermodal gateway.

- JFK, in its CTA, required a careful layering of the airport access system over existing, rigorously planned landside access and airline terminal facilities.

- AirTrain JFK airport access required an equally careful layering of its gateways over existing fixed-rail facilities to develop its gateways.

AirTrain's success lies in the plan's ability to develop these different conditions into one cohesive master plan.

CHAPTER 14
CRUISE TERMINALS

Cruise terminals are generally located at deepwater seaports that can accommodate the draft of the luxury cruise ships. They may be located within the industrial operations of a seaport or within mixed-use developments at the waterfront offering both retail and entertainment. In either case, the passengers' experience should be enjoyable and safe. The whole experience—traveling to and from the terminal and through the terminal, as well as the cruise itself—is what the passenger remembers, and these memories dictate the passenger's desire to return.

Historically, deepwater seaports have been transportation nodes for importing and exporting cargo, and as such, seaport businesses did not favor intervention by the public. However, the public has always seen the waterfront as a place for scenic recreation. Mixed-use developments offering retail, entertainment, aquariums, and other attractions have been located at the waterfront and integrated into the urban fabric. Seaports consider their waterfronts as economic generators for their communities and have adjusted their business operations to accommodate and encourage the public and, in particular, the cruise passenger, to visit them.

Cruise lines have developed their markets to suit the needs of their customers. Cruises can be for the day, for an activity such as gambling, or for vacations that last 3–10 days or longer.

CRUISE TERMINAL PLANNING

Cruise terminals can be integrated successfully into mixed-use developments. The passenger who has traveled from a faraway city usually arrives at the terminal several hours before having to board the ship. The passenger's enjoyment at the cruise terminal can be enhanced by other services offered in a mixed-use development; for instance, a passenger can enjoy shopping in the souvenir shops, dining at a restaurant, or visiting an aquarium.

Seaport operations may dictate that cruise terminals be segregated from or integrated with cargo operations. Separation of cruise from cargo facilities requires roadway approaches, signage, and planning of the cruise terminal and cargo terminal to provide clear separation. Seaports may, however, wish to make best use of their limited berth capacity, and as such, may require that cruise terminals and cargo operations occupy the same berths at different times. This may require the cruise terminal to coexist with a transit shed. A transit shed is a waterfront warehouse facility that serves to store cargo under protective cover on a temporary basis; cargo is transported in and out of the shed to either rail or truck. If a cruise terminal must coexist with cargo operations, the terminal needs to accommodate the loading and unloading operations, which are usually done by crane, either on a dock or on a ship and lifted to the apron. The apron is the working area on the wharf between the fender line and the building line.

Cruise terminals may be located at seaports where the itinerary is seasonal or year-round. The arrival and departure of cruise ships may also occur only on certain days of the week, such as Friday, Saturday, Sunday, and Monday. Therefore, the cruise terminal may have to be designed as a multipurpose facility so that it is able to accommodate other uses when not used for cruises, such as exhibit halls and places for public gatherings.

Port-of-Call or Homeport

Cruise ship operations are grouped in two categories, port-of-call and homeport. A port-of-call is a port on the cruise itinerary where the ship berths temporarily for passengers to debark and return after their excursions. A homeport cruise facility is the start and terminus point of the cruise.

A port-of-call facility rarely requires dockside handling of provisions or cargo. It does generate passenger traffic that requires taxi, tour bus, and rental car service. It can be assumed that many of the port-of-call passengers will visit local attractions, such as aquariums and museums, and participate in other activities offered by local entertainment centers.

Homeport operations differ substantially from port-of-call operations. At a homeport, the passenger may arrive at the city by plane from a distant location or travel by local transit or automobile within or near the city. If the passenger is traveling by plane, the connection between the airport and the seaport must appear as a seamless and enjoyable experience, as part of the vacation. The movement of both passenger and baggage must be secure, safe, and efficient so as not to disrupt the passenger's trip. What the passenger sees and experiences during the trip to the cruise terminal is part of his or her resolve to return or not. In general, the cruise ship arrives in the morning hours and departs in the afternoon of the same day.

If the itinerary of a cruise ship includes a foreign port, the passengers and baggage must be cleared by customs upon return to the homeport, at which time provisioning activities begin. This generates a steady stream of trucks onto the apron, where provisions and/or cargo are loaded directly into the ship. Debarking passengers, and their baggage, are cleared through customs and then take ground transportation to their next destination, in most cases to the airport serving the seaport. At some seaports, airlines provide ticketing and baggaage check-in services at the cruise terminal, so as to spare passengers delays at the airport.

The homeport cruise terminal acts as an intermodal facility that allows transfer of passengers and baggage from local transit systems, private automobile, taxi, or bus. Passengers may arrive from a nearby airport by bus furnished by the cruise line, taxi, or shuttle. Buses must be positioned at the terminal for ease of maneuverability and for unloading passengers near the terminal entrance. Where possible, drive-through bus bays are desirable, as opposed to bus bays in which a bus must back up to exit. Buses that back up pose a safety risk for unloading passengers.

Seaports, under their contractual relationships with cruise lines, may wish terminals to be designed for a single cruise line or to be sufficiently flexible to serve multiple cruise lines. Because cruise lines have contracts with fixed durations, seaports desire flexible terminal design to accommodate other cruise lines. Cruise lines have different operations concerning queuing, ticketing, baggage handling, and so on. Since facilities are often provided to cruise lines as part of their lease or contract, the Port (usually being the Owner) does not wish to make major modifications to terminals when cruise line leases expire.

At a port-of-call cruise facility, sight-seeing coaches must load and unload passengers as they debark from or board a ship. This can be accomplished directly on the apron. At a port-of-call, sightseeing coaches will return passengers, and they may board the ship again directly from the apron. A terminal building may not be necessary at a port-of-call, inasmuch as there is only minor handling of baggage. Port-of-call facilities may, however, wish to incorporate shopping and dining to attract tourists prior to boarding. Depending on the country, duty-free shopping may be made available to the passengers and can be incorporated directly into the cruise facility.

Berth Planning

The planning of cruise terminals at a deepwater seaport needs to maximize the berth capacity at the port. Accommodation of the maximum number of passengers at any one time is the ultimate goal, so the number of cruise ships and their passenger capacities need to be maximized. Maximum passenger capacity at a seaport is dependent on the size of the cruise ships and the number of cruise ships that can be berthed at the same time. Cruise ships vary in length from less than 800 ft to more than 1000 ft and must be separated from stern to bow by 50–60 ft. Cruise ships are assisted into berths by tugs or are self-maneuverable. With new improved control systems, new luxury cruise ships maneuver with great ease. Docking a cruise ship is usually performed under the supervision of harbor pilots. Channels and turning basins have to be sized for large cruise ships that allow the harbor pilots to position a ship at either port side or starboard side. Planning for a cruise terminal may need to ac-commodate several cruise lines, with each having its own methods of operation.

CRUISE TERMINAL DESIGN

Cruise terminal design can be viewed as a series of linkages that connect to provide a continuous path for passengers and baggage. In the embarkation process passengers arrive at the cruise terminal and prepare to board the ship. In the debarkation process passengers exit the ship, pick up their baggage, and leave the cruise terminal. The embarkation process starts with passengers arriving at the intermodal zone, where they and their baggage are unloaded from buses and automobiles. Passengers embarking can be waiting in the cruise terminal at the time other passengers are debarking, and the design of the terminal must accommodate both processes without contamination between one and the other. Debarking passengers cannot be allowed to have contact with the public or unauthorized seaport or cruise line personnel. During either process the apron may be occupied only by cleared vehicles or authorized personnel and must be maintained in a sterile condition. An apron is in a sterile condition when all vehicles and personnel within the defined limits of the apron have been cleared to enter.

Cruise terminals may be linked by a continuous boarding concourse, which allows maximum flexibility in accessing different cruise ships. Cross passage of passengers between terminals cannot be permitted, however. Cruise terminals may also be designed in conjunction with sea ferry operations, sightseeing boats, and water taxis.

As the debarkation process is nearing completion, embarkation operations start. Passengers arrive at the terminal via ground transportation, are ticketed, processed, sequestered in a departure lounge, and then boarded when the ship is prepared to receive them.

The design of a cruise terminal requires full compliance with government regulations, and the designer must consult with officials from the U.S. Customs and Border Protection during initial planning. Waterside port operations around the cruise terminal will require review by the U.S. Coast Guard.

Passenger Boarding Bridge

The location and number of the gangways, or passenger boarding bridges, set the framework for the overall terminal design. Height requirements for the passenger boarding bridge will establish either a two- or three-level terminal scheme. Passenger boarding bridges may be of the pivot type, on rails, or mobile. The type of bridge chosen depends on the width of the apron, the height of the passenger opening (pax break) to the ship above apron level, and the ability to maximize passenger access to various pax breaks (passenger doorways to the ship). Passenger boarding bridges must fit on the apron and must also provide sufficiently high clearance for the passage of trucks beneath them on the apron. Bridges may be enclosed, or open with roof cover. Piv-

ot-type bridges are telescoping structures and are similar to airport jetways. This passenger boarding bridge type is fixed at the terminal end and adjustable at the ship end within a limited range. Rail-type bridges travel transversely on train or crane-type rails on the apron. Mobile bridges travel on wheels and are the most flexible type. The apron pavement must be designed for wheel loadings, depending on the type of passenger boarding bridge used. The passenger boarding bridges must comply with the requirements of the Americans with Disabilities Act (ADA) with respect to grab rails, floor slope, floor finish, and level changes.

For mega-cruise ships (approximately 2600 or greater passenger capacity), two passenger boarding bridges are generally needed. The height of the passenger boarding bridge above the apron must provide clearance for trucks, including firefighting equipment.

Window of Accessibility

A cruise terminal must maximize the window of accessibility (WOA) for passengers to enter and leave a ship. Because all ships have different locations for the pax breaks, and these locations differ even from port side to starboard side on the same ship, and because ships are of different lengths, it is critical to allow access to as many pax breaks on the various cruise ships as possible via the passenger boarding bridge(s).

The WOA is defined by both a vertical and a horizontal dimension. The maximum WOA with the greatest range of vertical and horizontal dimension provides access to the largest number of cruise ships in today's fleets and for those of the future. Seaports planning cruise terminals cannot predict long-term use

▼ Vertical window of accessibility.

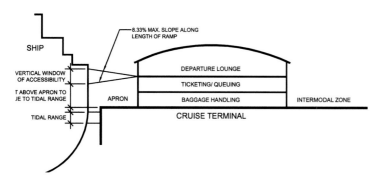

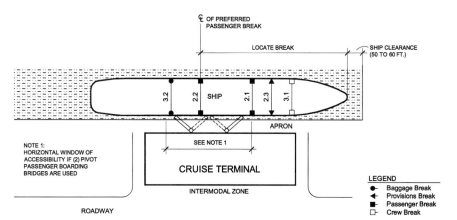

Horizontal window of accessibility for pivot passenger boarding bridges.

(up to 40 years) of a terminal by a particular ship. Therefore, their terminals must be sufficiently flexible to accommodate as many cruise ships that they contract for.

The WOA is also determined by the ramp slope of the boarding bridge, inasmuch as the slope must comply with ADA requirements. The ramp slope must not exceed 1 vertical unit in 12 horizontal units. The WOA is also affected by the tidal range, which determines the vertical height of the pax break above the apron. The passenger bridge provides passenger connection to the ship and must be designed to allow both horizontal and vertical ship movement and be provided with specific safety equipment such as a safety net and devices warning of ship movement.

The Apron

Aprons historically have a width between the bulkhead and the face of a building of 35–100 ft. Aprons have previously served for cargo-handling operations, and the apron widths at seaports have often been determined by the earlier cargo operations. In locating a passenger boarding bridge on an apron, 60 ft width is considered minimum, with a 100 ft

width as ample. The width of the apron, combined with the vertical height requirements of the pax breaks, determines the configuration of the passenger boarding bridge in order for the ramp slope not to exceed 1 in 12.

The apron is also the area used to provision the ship. A cruise ship requires a number of vendors providing multiple supplies. Cruise ships are usually loaded with forklifts delivering supplies into the cargo breaks directly from provisioning trucks (a process called chandlering). This process of loading supplies directly from a truck on the apron has been undergoing scrutiny and change by the U.S. Coast Guard and U.S. Customs since September 11, 2001. Various U.S. deepwater seaports currently have different security regulations covering the screening and clearing of provision trucks prior to loading a ship. At some seaports, provision trucks must unload their goods either in an open paved area or within a cargo warehouse or other structure for examination. Other seaports limit the type and number of trucks that can access the apron at the same time. Once the goods, which are usually palletized, are cleared, forklifts move the

▶ Horizontal window of accessibility for mobile and rail-mounted passenger boarding bridges.

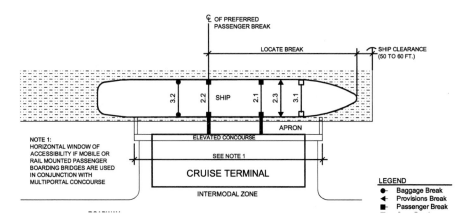

THE EMBARKATION PROCESS

Upon the passengers' arrival at the cruise terminal, the first linkage is the intermodal zone where buses, taxis, shuttles, and private automobiles unload the passengers and their luggage. Passengers arriving by automobile will need a passenger drop-off lane sufficient to accommodate passenger capacity. The roadway system must direct the driver to parking facilities to allow the driver to either park on grade or within structured parking. Because waterfront property is of high value, structured parking for passengers' vehicles may be a necessity. Parking is usually paid for by the passenger to the seaport and is therefore a valuable source of revenue. The number of parking spaces depends on the passengers' original point

palletized goods onto the apron and then onto the ship. This process has to be coordinated with the governmental regulators having jurisdiction at each specific seaport. Berth aprons must be kept as clear as possible of all built-in obstructions, and provisions must be made for temporary closure of a berth to casual traffic during customs clearance of arriving ships. A clear apron is said to be in a sterile condition.

of travel and the percentages of people who are traveling to the cruise facility by plane, bus, and public transportation.

At the intermodal zone luggage must also be removed from the buses and automobiles. Baggage may be moved directly from the intermodal zone into the baggage handling area by porters or placed on conveyors that will move the baggage from the outside to the interior of the terminal. Parking may also be provided at remote locations; however, trams or shuttles would be needed to move passengers to and from the terminal. Some seaports offer valet parking services.

Parking

Generally, a cruise terminal serving several thousand ship passengers may require as many as 750 parking spaces. Any parking structure must accommodate over-height vehicles located on the lower level of the structure or on-grade outside.

Entry

After arriving at the terminal at the intermodal zone, passengers proceed to the point of entry or point of security check-in at the facility. Entry doors should be automatic glass sliding doors because many people will be carrying carry-on luggage. In a cruise terminal, points of entry will not be points of departure, but they must satisfy fire safety requirements for means of egress. At the point of entry, security screening is provided by walk-through magnetometers and baggage-screening equipment. It is preferred to screen all baggage external to the terminal building.

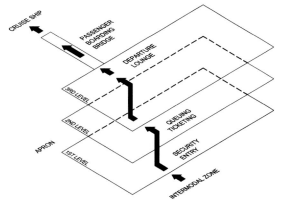

◀ Embarkation passenger flow.

Queuing/Ticketing

Passengers then proceed to queuing and ticketing, where their tickets are processed by the cruise lines. This process is usually accomplished at a series of counters and conducted by cruise line personnel. Because the boarding process may take as long as 3 hours and may need to accommodate more than 3000 passengers, the process needs to handle about 1000 people an hour. Therefore, depending on the cruise line operation, a dozen or more counters may be needed for ticket processing. Sufficient space is needed in front of the counters for passenger queuing. Counters may need to be movable if different cruise lines operate at the same terminal at different times. If movable, they have to be served with communication and data cabling, which is best provided from overhead power and data poles or from a cellular floor deck that allows flexibility in locating power and data outlets.

Departure Lounge

After completing security and ticketing processes, passengers proceed to a lounge area to await boarding. This area is usually at an upper level. The number of stories and the height of each story are dependent on the boarding mechanism or gangway and the individual ship. The departure lounge is fitted with airport-style seating and furnishings to make the wait as comfortable as possible for the passenger. When boarding is called, passengers proceed to the passenger boarding bridge.

THE DEBARKATION PROCESS

Ships returning to the homeport usually arrive in the early morning hours. Passengers have set their luggage outside their staterooms for pick-up by porters. The passengers are called to pax breaks by stateroom number or ship level. They exit the ship by the passenger boarding bridge and are processed through a U.S. Customs and Border Protection station within the cruise terminal. Restrooms provid-

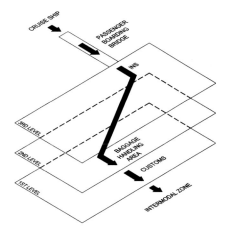

◀ Debarkation passenger flow.

ed for debarking passengers must be separated from restrooms used by embarking passengers and unauthorized personnel. Emergency exit doors accessible by the debarking passengers must be alarmed with special delayed-opening hardware, as permitted by building codes.

Baggage Handling Area

The baggage handling area is located at apron level, with direct access to the apron. Because baggage is usually unloaded from the ship by forklifts at the apron, the baggage handling area must be directly adjacent to the apron, with its longest dimension parallel to the apron. This configuration allows a number of access points for forklifts to enter the baggage area. Baggage may also be unloaded from the ship to the baggage handling area by conveyors. Such conveyors must not block the flow of truck traffic on the apron.

Baggage is delivered and sorted in the baggage handling area by two methods. The lay-down method places the baggage directly on the floor in an organized grid. Through the use of the signage provided, passengers are able to pick up their bags directly from the floor and, with the assistance of porters, take the bags through customs. The other method uses conveyors such as airport carousels that rotate baggage throughout the baggage area for pick-up by the passengers. In both cases, passengers need to identify their bags and accompany them through customs. Customs will select passengers and baggage for scrutiny and may require certain bags to be opened on examination tables. Customs has specific requirements for offices and holding rooms in which to interview selected passengers. It also requires a vegetation disposal system

whereby unwanted plants and vegetables are delivered into the sanitary system via large garbage disposals. Customs is located on the ground floor directly adjacent to the baggage handling area.

The size of the baggage holding area is critical to the overall program requirements of the terminal. The area normally required is between 10 and 15 sq ft per passenger. Sizing the baggage handling area depends on the number of bags per passenger. This varies with the length of the cruise, the climate the cruise ship travels through, and the formality of attire worn on the cruise. To this area must be added the requirements of customs and general circulation. The size of the baggage handling area also depends on whether the lay-down method or the use of carousels is chosen. For vehicles powered by combustion fuels, carbon monoxide detection devices must be present. Even so, it is best to use electrically operated forklifts and tractors for moving baggage carts inside the terminal.

Vertical Transportation

Vertical transportation through the multiple levels of the cruise terminal is by escalator, elevator, and stairs. Cruise terminals normally have two or three levels, depending on the segregation of spaces and the height of the pax break on the cruise ship above the apron level. Typically, entry and baggage handling areas, along with customs, are on the first level. Ticketing and queuing may be on the first or second level, and the departure lounge or concourse is on the second or third level.

Escalators are normally provided for the upward movement of passengers in the embarkation process, as well as for the downward movement of passengers in the debarkation process. Usually, a single escalator is provided for each of the two movement flows (embarkation and debarkation). These escalators, because they must accommodate people carrying carry-on baggage, need to be wide, with the nominal 48 in. width preferable. Escalators should also be of the type in which the first three treads remain level during movement, for safety of elderly persons, children, and those with physical disabilities. Escalators should be keyed for reverse operation.

Elevators, which are needed for ADA compliance, should be sized and configured to accommodate a wheeled stretcher for emergency medical purposes.

Stairs are normally situated adjacent and parallel to the escalator and are straight-run stairs to show passengers the direction of travel. In addition, egress stairs are needed per local building codes.

Restrooms

Restrooms must be located and sized to accommodate passengers in both the embarkation process and the debarkation process. Because passengers cannot cross between the two areas, separate facilities are needed. Restrooms in the debarkation process have to be designed to preclude the concealment of contraband that may be retrievable later. In some instances restrooms will be closed to debarking passengers who have not yet been cleared by customs. Restrooms are also needed for stevedores who work on the apron. These restrooms should have direct access from the apron and be fitted with industrial-type lavatory fixtures.

Concessions, Car Rental, and Airport Ticketing Services

The homeport cruise terminal may need to provide ancillary services. Concessions offering food and refreshments for the passengers can be incorporated into or next to the cruise terminal.

For a seamless relationship between seaport and airport, airlines may choose to establish airline ticket facilities within the cruise terminal. These ticketing services are generally at a counter at the baggage handling level, and once passengers and baggage have cleared customs, they may arrange airline ticketing and check baggage at the airline counter. The airline agent places baggage on a conveyor or carries the baggage to a truck loading dock. The baggage is loaded on a truck, which carries it to the airport. For security reasons, some seaports have not permitted baggage trucks to access the terminal, and baggage therefore travels between airport and seaport by passenger bus.

At homeports, seaports may wish to offer rental car facilities. Rental car offices may be centralized at a location accessible from multiple cruise terminals. Office space is required, and parking and cleaning facilities need to be provided for the vehicles.

Cruise Storage

At homeport terminals, cruise lines must have adequate space to warehouse nonperishable items such as furniture, dry goods, and equipment. These items may be located in a non-air-conditioned warehouse.

Firefighting for Terminal and Ship

As with any building of public assembly, the positioning of a cruise terminal within the roadway network must permit emergency access as required by local officials. In the case of a cruise terminal, emergency vehicles, including firefighting apparatus, must also access cruise ships and be able to pass under the gangways.

Fueling/Water/Waste Removal Services

Seaports may offer utility services to cruise ships. Fuel may be available by bunkering; or fuel is delivered to dockside by underground piping. Fuel may also be delivered to a cruise ship by truck or barge. Potable water is piped to below-apron hydrant connections. Waste removal must meet current standards and environmental regulations. Because of environmental concerns in regard to clean air, attention is being directed to the practice of cruise ships running their engines while berthed at a seaport; therefore, be sure to review local environmental regulations.

MAINTENANCE AND OPERATION

Because cruise terminals are used for relatively short periods, but during these times experience high levels of public use, interior finishes must be durable, sustainable, and easy to maintain. Large spaces should have acoustical controls. In many instances, rubber tile flooring is specified because it is durable, resilient, adds color, and is somewhat soft to foot traffic. Flooring finish in the baggage handling area depends on whether the lay-down method or carousels are used. If the lay-down method is used, the floor must sustain the weight and use of forklifts with attached wagons. If carousels are used, carpeting may be chosen for efficient acoustical control.

Most cruise ports operate cruise ships seasonally or on specific days of the week. One of the largest operating costs is the electric bill. Cruise ship operation lends itself to energy conservation, in particular with ice storage systems; ice can be refrigerated during off-peak periods of electricity demand and then used to generate cool air when the terminal is in use, usually during periods of peak demand, thus effecting major savings. Therefore, it may be wise to consider the use of ice storage systems for energy conservation for terminal operations.

MULTIPURPOSE USE OF A CRUISE TERMINAL

Using a large cruise facility for multiple purposes is warranted where the location can attract other uses, such as multipurpose rooms for public gatherings and exhibition halls. Multipurpose use of a cruise terminal is vital when the terminal is an integral part of a mixed-use development. Even though a cruise terminal may be the portal for entry to a ship, the passengers may wish to dine at restaurants, visit retail shops, and stay at nearby hotels to extend the journey.

Providing a smooth connection between cruise terminal and airport, using light-rail and people-moving technologies, may extend the multiple-purpose nature of the cruise terminal within the urban streetscape environment.

MODERNIZATION AND RETROFIT ISSUES

This chapter addresses issues and problems associated with renovating an existing transit station. An underground station has been selected as an example because of its being a confined structure, its location in a typical urban setting, and the difficulty experienced in bringing the station up to current code standards.

Many transit systems have existing stations built between the late 1800s and the 1930s. These stations were typically shallow in depth, were constructed using cut-and-cover techniques, employed concrete and steel structural systems, and were located below streets in the city-owned property right-of-way. Many of these have been successful in terms of serving communities and have been a force in defining how these communities evolved. Several have been unsuccessful as a result of their initial poor access or the overall negative atmosphere they exude. Communities and transit authorities are now looking to these older established stations as opportunities to revitalize the area and to serve as the new "gateways" to revitalized neighborhoods.

Many of these stations are extremely austere in terms of quality finishes and an inviting architecture. Most were built simply to provide quick and affordable mass transit to and from work. Others, such as the New York City subway, provided elegant entrance kiosks and ceramic murals depicting notable locations or prominent residents, such as the Astor Place station.

Some of the newer transit systems, constructed within the past 30 years, are experiencing maintenance difficulties and changes in operational strategies, resulting in the need for retrofit and modernization programs. The nature of the renovations generally reflects the two time periods in which the stations were built. If a station was constructed in the earlier period (1890s–1930s), then the work has to do with major upgrades such as the following:

- Conformance with requirements of the Americans with Disabilities Act (ADA)

- Remediation of water leakage

- Installation of new lighting

- Replacing finishes

- Introducing new mechanical ventilation systems

- Code compliance

- Installation of new escalators and elevators

Renovations of recently constructed stations (since the 1960s) have more to do with escalator refurbishments, replacement of finishes not selected initially to satisfy weather or service wearing conditions, adding overhead coverage to keep weather elements off escalators, and adding redundant elevators to ensure greater reliability.

CHARACTERISTICS OF AN OLDER STATION

Entrances

Many older stations have prominent entrance locations, close to major street intersections and positioned on sidewalks to facilitate quick access into the station's mezzanine space. Because of the shallowness of construction, mezzanines and fare collection areas were located fairly close to the street surface (16–20 ft), thereby requiring short horizontal runs for stairs. This allowed the stair location to be close to the mezzanine. In many cases the stair entrance occupied a prestigious location on the sidewalk in front of a major building. Generally, the stair does not have an entrance canopy to protect the customer or the stair itself from severe exposure to the weather. Consequently, stair railing enclosures, treads and risers, wall finishes, and railings have been repaired, replaced, and maintained to varying degrees of success. Typically, the stair assembly is not code compliant by today's standards. Dealing with water in a stair has been problematic. Landings are a source of water accumulation during rain. Freeze-thaw cycles in colder climates create a constant safety concern, as well as the potential for deterioration. The use of deicing salts further exacerbates damage to materials. Many stairs include drains and trench inlets, which accumulate debris and have a tendency to clog. Entrances usually have railings or gates to close off the station in nonrevenue hours. These are also subject to weathering and vandalism and often end up chained and padlocked.

Miscellaneous Spaces

Quite often the roofs of the older stations were constructed of steel beams, concrete vaults, and brick and mastic waterproofing. The structural system lent itself to a shallow vertical profile, requiring columns on a frequent center-to-center spacing. This created numerous columns in the main circulation spaces and, consequently, encouraged vandalism or provided safe concealment for deviant behavior. In keeping with the shallow construction methods and the desire for shallow-depth platforms, the distance from the mezzanine to the underside of the roof structure was established as a short vertical dimension. This resulted in a typical space employing many columns on close spacing and low ceiling conditions. Failed waterproofing systems have resulted in spalled concrete surfaces and corroded steel beams. Walls were covered in conventional ceramic tile, providing a hard-surfaced, architecturally negative space that is confining, and at the same time, conveys an image of being an unsafe space to enter. These spaces are typically difficult to handle acoustically and have limited possibilities for creating an architecturally exciting lighting solution. Many of the floor surfaces are exposed structural concrete slabs.

Older stations were planned with a different focus on operations and customer service than is used today. Rooms that existed for a particular purpose have been closed off and rendered obsolete. The result is many closed-off spaces, long, narrow corridors, and doors leading to never-used rooms. The station agent's control booth evolved in many older stations to convey a "defensive" or "bunker" image, not providing the open and welcoming feeling that a modern transit station tries to convey. Environmental support systems for the booth (air-conditioning, for instance) are difficult to introduce into an older station. Quite often the booth was designed for use by one employee but now sees service by two. The booth is too narrow for attendants to sit back-to-back and does not allow those sitting side-by-side free access to doors at both the paid and free sides of the booth.

The fare collection or fare barrier systems are often antiquated and have been renovated over the years in an attempt to compensate for fare evasion. Bars and railings are used to prevent unpaid access, but, unfortunately, create an imprisoned or jailed image. Often new stainless steel turnstiles have been introduced into the older fare barrier without replacing or updating the remaining fixed gates, railings, or, in some instances, the round roto-gates, thus creating a visually disorganized array. Typically, the circulation clearances and queuing distances in front of customer service elements such as ticket vending, control booth, turnstiles, and access onto vertical circulation elements are woefully inadequate.

Platforms

Existing station platforms are often undersized (in width) in relation to the headway and the passenger traffic they experience. Many of the aforementioned problems carry over onto the platform:

- Columns on the platform at a close spacing
- Columns close to platform edge, resulting in non-ADA-compliant clearances
- Low ceiling/underside of structure clearances, resulting in feeling of confinement
- Low overhead clearances, resulting in low-mounted signage and lighting elements, increasing exposure to vandalism; ineffective lighting; and lack of clear viewing sight lines to signage
- Inadequate ventilation, resulting in high ambient temperatures in summer

- Closed-in undersides to stairs, resulting in lack of clear views of the platform and perceived insecurity
- Lack of space needed to accommodate enough vertical circulation required to satisfy National Fire Protection Association (NFPA) Standard 130, which is to unload platforms in 4 minutes
- No clear exit passageways
- Platform height above top of rail not facilitating the creation of ADA-compliant edge clearances

CASE STUDY

DMJM+Harris is part of a team designing improvements to an existing older subway station in Philadelphia. The project typifies many of the renovation programs currently under way with major transit systems that have been operating since the early 1900s. The improvements generally include (1) architectural, structural, mechanical, and electrical upgrades, (2) compliance with current building codes, and (3) ADA conformance. The principal challenges in these older stations are to provide new roof coverage over stairs, introduce elevators, and satisfy modern fire exiting requirements.

Southeastern Pennsylvania Transportation Authority

Principal engineering firm:
Klein + Hoffman
Architects: DMJM+Harris

Focus Points
- Spring Garden Station located in downtown Philadelphia
- Constructed in the 1930s
- Four tracks, two center platforms
- Mezzanine level and fare control barrier

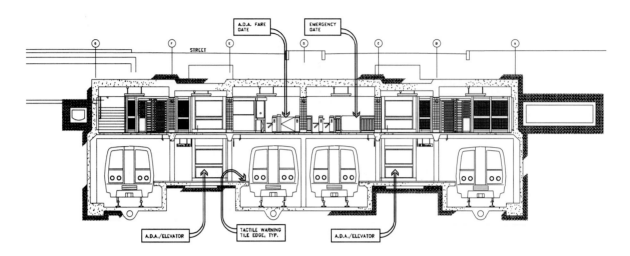

▲ *Cross section plan of south mezzanine of Spring Garden Station, Philadelphia.*

ADA compliance required the following:

- Elevators
- Ramps
- Toilets for employees or personnel
- Tactile warning strip at platform edge
- Platform level raised to meet rail vehicle door sill height
- Additional signage (directional and informational)

Elevators (mezzanine to street)

- To introduce an elevator shaft into the station required construction of a shaft outside the existing station box because of the location of streets above the station and the presence of street utilities.
- As new construction, the hoistway plan dimensions and vertical clearance to accommodate elevator equipment was not a problem.

Elevator (platform to mezzanine)

- To construct the hoistway and provide adequate vertical clearance in the existing structure required removal of a portion of the roof structure. This required street-level excavation and had associated traffic maintenance issues.

- Because of extremely low overhead clearance, the elevator cab height was restricted. This required use of a telescopic cantilevered elevator and special approval from the elevator inspection agency.

- The location of the elevator was based on the availability of space in the mezzanine-level paid area.

- Designing the elevator pit at the platform level was complicated because of the location of column foundations supporting the existing structure. Locating the pit drainage connection source was difficult, considering the thick concrete base slab, the existing track drainage piping not suitable for the added flow, and the desire to keep trains running with minimum downtime to make connections or install piping.

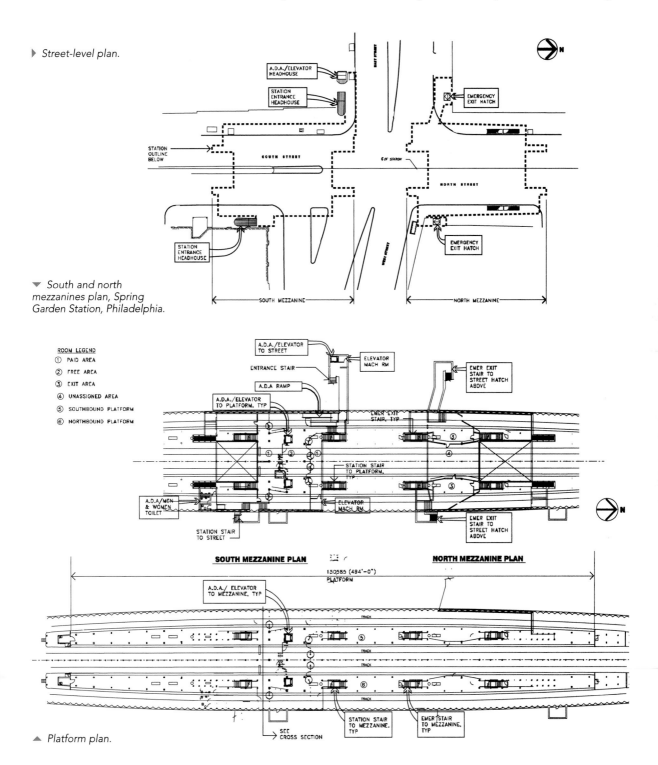

▶ Street-level plan.

▼ South and north mezzanines plan, Spring Garden Station, Philadelphia.

ROOM LEGEND
① PAID AREA
② FREE AREA
③ EXIT AREA
④ UNASSIGNED AREA
⑤ SOUTHBOUND PLATFORM
⑥ NORTHBOUND PLATFORM

▲ Platform plan.

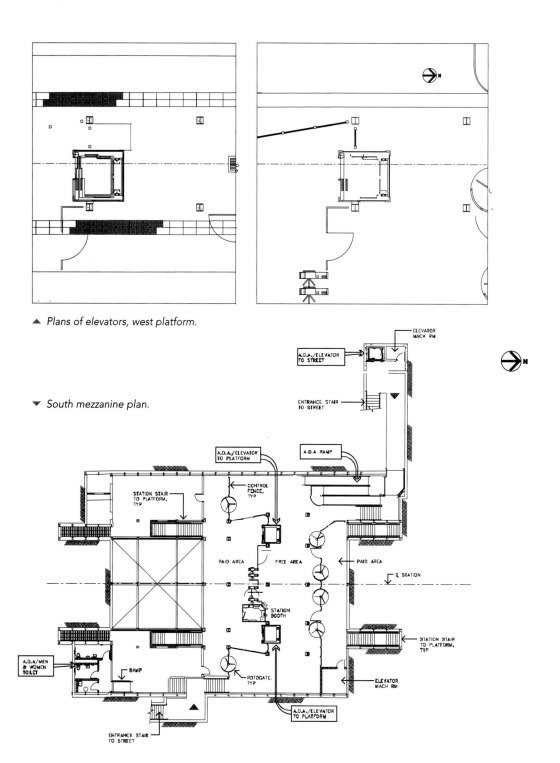

▲ *Plans of elevators, west platform.*

▼ *South mezzanine plan.*

Elevator machine room

The elevator machine room was located at the mezzanine level because of insufficient space at the platform level. The allocation of mezzanine space for a machine room required careful consideration to maximize the distance hydraulic piping could run between the pump and the hoistway.

Ramps

- An ADA ramp was provided between station entrance corridor and the mezzanine level.
- Installation of the ramp required removal of a portion of the station roof structure for minimum headroom clearance.

Toilets

- Existing toilets had to be renovated to meet ADA requirements.
- This renovation required an access ramp to meet the change in the floor level condition.

Platform edge and platform height

- A new 24 in. wide tactile edge strip was provided. This renovation also required extending the edge in order to narrow the distance (maximum 3 in.) between the platform and the vehicle doorsill. In an existing station, defining the edge often requires precise field surveys to establish the track centerline and existing platform location. See "General Design Considerations and Issues" in Chapter 6 for a discussion on track and platform geometry.
- A new topping was designed to raise the platform to match the level of rail vehicles (within $\pm \frac{3}{8}$ in.). Quite often this requires extensive coordination

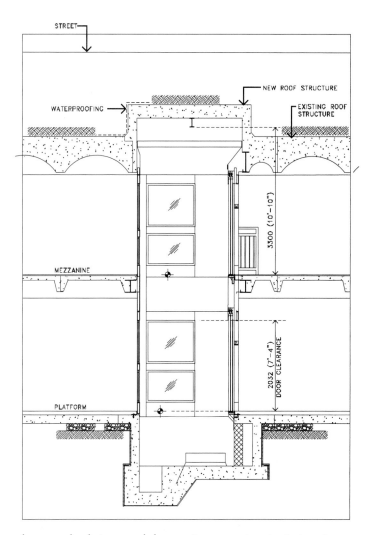

▲ Longitudinal section.

between the designer and the transit authority to arrive at a reliable distance from the top of the rail to the vehicle floor. This is due to the mechanical variables in vehicle suspension systems, particularly in older vehicles, as well as the passenger weight.

Emergency exiting

An exit analysis, per NFPA 130, determined a series of improvements needed to satisfy the 4- and 6-minute rules, such as the following:

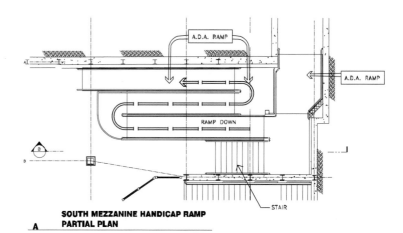

▶ Plan of handicap ramp
on south mezzanine.

SOUTH MEZZANINE HANDICAP RAMP
PARTIAL PLAN

A

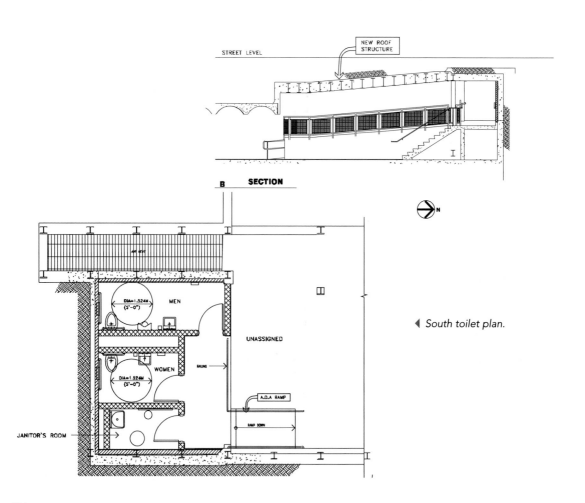

SECTION

B

◀ South toilet plan.

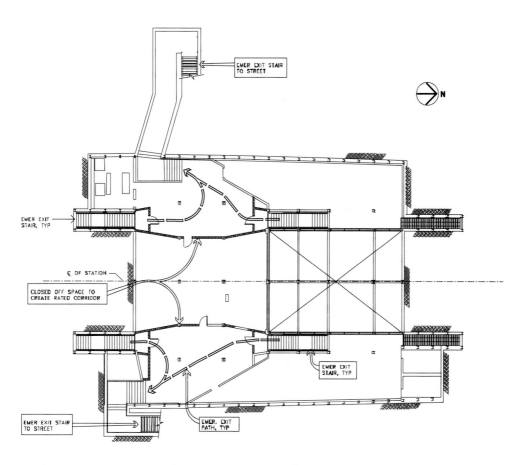

EMER EXIT STAIR
TO STREET

N

EMER EXIT
STAIR, TYP

℄ OF STATION

CLOSED OFF SPACE TO
CREATE RATED CORRIDOR

EMER EXIT
STAIR, TYP

EMER EXIT STAIR
TO STREET

EMER. EXIT
PATH, TYP

▲ North mezzanine plan.

- Provide emergency exit gate in fare control barrier in addition to the roto-gates at the south mezzanine level.
- Renovate the closed north mezzanine level to serve as an emergency exit passageway only.
- Continue the emergency exit passage-way to street level and incorporate egress hatches in the sidewalk.

Finishes
- Stairs were replaced.
- New floor pavers were added to plat-forms.
- Damaged ceramic wall tiles were replaced.

- Ceramic tile joints were regrouted to match existing tile joints.
- Graffiti-resistant coating was applied over repaired tile.
- All walls, floors, and ceilings damaged by demolition work were patched and repaired.
- All exposed concrete ceilings in mezza-nine and platform areas were painted.
- Train walls, doors, columns, and other wall surfaces not covered with ceramic tile were painted.
- All exposed plumbing pipes and elec-trical conduit were painted.

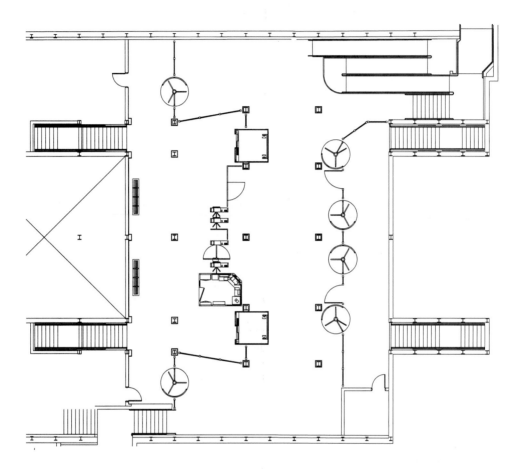

▲ *Plan of south mezzanine control fence.*

Fare barrier renovations

- Barrier rail alarms were added to emergency exit gates.
- A turnstile unit for wheelchair access was added.
- Alarmed swing emergency exit gates were added.
- The control barrier was rearranged to provide maximum clearances within a tightly restricted free and paid area space.

New headhouses

- A transparent glass roof was provided over stairs at station entrances, with gates to allow closing off the station in off-hours.
- Stair treads, walls, and railings were reconstructed; drainage at landings was improved.

STATION OPERATION AND MAINTENANCE

Each transit agency operates its stations in a manner tailored to its specific concerns, but certain fundamental principles are common to most agencies. This chapter can be useful as a reference for new-start systems for which an operational policy has not yet been established. Architects may use it to understand the functional and personnel factors that will assist them in new station planning, particularly in the design of ancillary spaces.

Definitions

The *station command center* is responsible for the operation of all stations in a system. It coordinates all normal day-to-day functions, as well as station emergencies and other unusual events, and dispatches station supervisors and managers to various locations.

The individual station manager is designated as the *customer service agent* (CSA), also known as the *token booth clerk* or *station agent*.

The *security operations command* observes activity in all areas of the stations, including the customers in the public areas via closed-circuit television (CCTV). If unusual activity is observed, the Station Command Center or the police department, as appropriate, is notified.

The base location of the customer service agent in a station is designated as the *station service center* (SSC). Its location and functions are derived from operational needs. Generally, the SSC is located in the fare collection area, along the fare control barrier. The *operations control center* (OCC) train dispatchers monitor the condition of station platforms for crowding. This is supplemented by CCTV viewing, which allows selection of any platform camera at any station.

SUPERVISION OF PASSENGER FLOW

The customer service agent supervises passenger flow through the entrances, free mezzanine, turnstiles, paid mezzanine, stairs, escalators, elevators, and platforms. CCTV viewing from the SSC allows this function through direct observation. The CSA is assisted by "unusual event recognition" intelligence incorporated in the CCTV system.

The Station Command Center has access to any station CCTV camera and can observe any incident that has been brought to its attention, either via CCTV or by other means.

INFORMATION TO PASSENGERS
Audiovisual Information

Information (either live or prerecorded) may be passed to passengers either audibly via a public address (PA) system or visually by a *customer information sign* (CIS) system at each station. PA speakers and customer information signs should be provided throughout all public areas of a station, from entrances to platforms.

Under normal conditions, dedicated announcers at the OCC trigger PA messages.

CIS messages may be initiated by the CSA from a facility in the SSC and by the dedicated announcers at the OCC or automatically from the *automatic train control system* (ATS) to provide train arrival and destination information. Train arrival information is automatically downloaded from the ATS at the OCC. The dedicated announcers at the OCC may select messages from a library and assign them to any combination of signs at any combination of stations.

Signage

Fixed signage is designed for the following purposes:

- Identifying each station
- Directing customers to ticket vending machines and platforms
- Identifying after-hours safe waiting areas on platforms
- Directing customers to station exits and transfers to other lines
- Identifying functions and services available in station entrance areas

Signage requires graphic messages to be of a size needed to comply with the Americans with Disabilities Act (ADA).

PASSENGER INQUIRIES AND ASSISTANCE

Help Points

Customer Help Points are located in both free and paid areas of each station. It is important for the architect to understand their function and to design their placement so that they are out of the mainstream of passenger circulation, yet within view of the public and, preferably, the station agent. Customer Help Points can include provisions for emergency calls and for inquiry calls.

Inquiry calls are routed to the Station Service Center.

Emergency calls are routed to the Security Operations Command (SOC) at the Operations Control Center. Answering an emergency call will automatically activate a CCTV image of the calling Help Point. If emergency services personnel are required, the SOC will make the request. If emergency services personnel are not required, the SOC will advise the Station Command Center, which will dispatch personnel to address the situation. Such personnel may be the local customer service agent.

When the emergency feature at a Help Point is activated, a CCTV image will simultaneously be displayed. If attending emergency services personnel activate the emergency management panel, the Help Point inquiry will be routed directly to the SCC.

Customer Service Agents

Customer service agents respond to direct verbal inquiries from customers. Responses will typically be assistance with the fare vending machines or fare purchase issues, verbal directions, provision of hard-copy literature, or directions to other means of assistance.

For passengers who need directions, customer service agents should provide a printed routing.

Information Kiosks

Information kiosks are unmanned inquiry devices available in each station to direct passengers. A kiosk should display information regarding the transit system and the neighborhood in which the station is located, on a screen and, if requested, provide a printed routing to points of interest. The kiosk may also provide regional travel information.

MONITORING AND CONTROL OF STATION SYSTEMS

Station systems are used to provide for the supervision of station-based devices from one or more locations within each station and from remote locations such as the OCC via a graphical user interface. Examples include monitoring of escalators, elevators, entry/exit turnstiles, fire and security alarms, intrusion and access control, substations, fan plants, station air-conditioning, and pumps.

A station's staff must have access to graphical representations of station floor plans in order to depict the location and basic state of devices.

Monitoring and control may be performed:

- Locally, on or immediately next to the equipment or system
- At each SSC by the customer service agent
- At each emergency management panel, for the use of attending fire and disaster response personnel
- In the OCC by the SCC
- In other remote locations as appropriate (e.g., maintenance workshops, etc.)

Station and Tunnel Ventilation (Underground Stations)

A ventilation fan and damper system is typically provided for each station and section of tunnel. A vent shaft with fans and dampers is usually placed at each end of a station. Other facilities include:

- Monitoring and control for individual vent shafts and adjacent tunnel jet fans at each motor control center
- Monitoring and control for all station and adjacent tunnel ventilation equipment in the motor control center room, typically located near one of the vent shafts
- Status and fault indications, but no controls, at the SSC
- Status indications at the emergency management panel
- Status and fault indications, with controls, at the stations and OCC

Station Air-Conditioning (Warm Climates)

When stations are air-conditioned, chiller plants are provided locally in each station or occasionally consolidated into zone plants, each zone plant providing chilled water to several stations. Typically:

- Monitoring and control for individual chiller plants occur at each chiller plant.
- Status and fault indications, but no controls, are available at the SSC.
- Status and fault indications and system diagnostics may be provided at the OCC.

Elevators

Elevators are monitored as follows:

- Monitoring and control for individual elevators at the SSC
- Status and fault indications, but no controls, at the SSC
- Status indications at the emergency management panel
- Status and fault indications and system diagnostics at the OCC

Escalators

Escalators are monitored as follows:

- Monitoring and control for individual escalators at each escalator control panel.

- Status and fault indications at the SSC. Up/down/stop controls may also be provided at the SSC as necessary.
- Status and fault indications and system diagnostics at the OCC.
- Up/down/stop controls on each escalator.

Traction Power

Supply and traction power substations are monitored as follows:

- Monitoring and control for individual items of substation equipment within each room
- Monitoring and control for all station substation rooms in a station power control room
- In a third-rail traction power system monitoring of the contact rail status indications and contact rail emergency trip controls for the contact rail sections, through the station platform, at the SSC
- Monitoring of contact rail status indications at the emergency management panel and contact rail emergency trip controls at the OCC

Station Electrical System

The electrical system provides each station with low-voltage power distribution, emergency power from uninterruptible power supplies, station lighting, and all other miscellaneous electrical services. The functions include:

- Monitoring and control for individual electrical services at each electrical distribution room
- Station lighting controls at the SSC
- Status and fault indications for certain devices/systems, such as uninterrupt-

ible power supply units, at the Operations Control Center

Fire Hazard Detection and Suppression

Fire hazard detection, alarm, and suppression systems are provided in each station. The system incorporates detection, notification, alarm, and suppression functions, which include:

- Alarm and trouble indications, but no controls, at the SSC
- Alarm and trouble indications and systems controls, including announcements, at the emergency management panel
- Controls, alarm, and trouble indications, and system diagnostics at the OCC

Access Control and Intrusion Detection

An access control and intrusion detection system in each station includes:

- Alarm and trouble indications, but no controls, at the SSC
- Alarm and trouble indications at the OCC
- Intrusion alarms for signaling equipment rooms at the OCC
- Alarm and trouble indications and system diagnostics at the OCC

Public Address/Customer Information Sign

A public address/customer information sign (PA/CIS) system at each station provides audible and visible announcements, including:

- Status and fault indications and announcements control at the SSC

- Announcement control at the emergency management panel
- Announcement controls, status and fault indications, and system diagnostics at the OCC

CCTV

A CCTV system includes:

- Video monitors at the SSC
- Video monitors at the emergency management panel
- Video monitors at the OCC
- Status and fault indications and system diagnostics at the monitoring center at the OCC

Fare Collection

Fare collection system controls include:

- Facilities in the SSC to allow the CSA to analyze tickets to determine their status and value.
- Status and fault indications at the SSC. In addition, if required, the SSC has the ability to set turnstiles in either entry or exit mode.
- Status and fault indications at a magnetic fare cards center, if this particular technology is used.

Money collection and fare media distribution

With the increased use of magnetic fare cards, there is a corresponding reduction in the volume of cash collected at a station. Typically, personnel use armored trucks at street level to collect revenue from fare machines. Empty coin and bill hoppers are brought into the station and full coin and bill hoppers removed directly to the armored truck. Occasionally this is done during off-hours by a rail vehicle. Sometimes full change hoppers are brought into the station and placed directly into the fare machine, and used change hoppers are moved directly to the armored truck. Full or empty coin, bill, or change hoppers are usually stored in stations. Coin, bill, and change hoppers are brought in and out of stations on rubber-tired hand trucks and use station elevators between the street level and the mezzanine level.

Magnetic fare media are delivered to stations from the street level via trucks and installed directly into the machines. Fare media is typically not stored in the stations, as a result of the trend toward eliminating storage of any cash or fare-valued media.

OPENING AND CLOSING OF STATIONS

Station entrances that are not open 24 hours a day or 7 days a week are opened and closed by CSAs.

To close an entrance, a CSA closes gates or coiling grilles at street level, as well as at the platform or mezzanine level, as appropriate. After the gates are closed and locked, the access control monitoring system is set to identify intruders.

To open an entrance, a CSA authorizes the access control system to release the appropriate gates and then secure the gates in the open position.

The status of entrance gates is displayed in the Station Service Center. It is critical for the architect to know the particular requirements for closing off stations so that details for incorporating switches and devices into the gates can be designed and coordinated.

▲ The North Greenwich Station on the London Underground Jubilee Line is closed off, using sliding glass door panels. (Photo courtesy Alfred Lau.)

SECURITY

The reader is advised to refer to Chapter 12, "Safety and Security," for a discussion on elements of a safe environment that depend on electronics. Examples include access controls, formal surveillance, and alarm systems. The following are the two primary groups the designer is looking to protect.

Passengers

Station layouts should avoid minimal recesses and other blind spots. Lighting levels must be maintained at sufficiently high levels to eliminate deep shadows and other dark spots.

Passengers may call for help via a Help Point. Combined with the Help Points, CCTV cameras allow the customer service agents and the Security Operations Command to monitor activity.

The presence of cameras deters crime. In the investigation of a crime, for instance, videotape is often retrieved.

Staff

A customer service agent quite often has a security panic button located in various points throughout the public spaces to alert the Station Command Center.

Access doors to all ancillary spaces must be equipped with an electronic access control system requiring a card reader and an identification control number.

CROWD CONTROL

The disruption of train service can lead to dangerous crowding of station platforms, with the risk that a passenger may fall onto the tracks. Platform edge doors eliminate this concern, even if a station is not designed for overcrowding. Train dispatchers and Security Operations Command operators monitor station platforms for excessive crowding via CCTV. In addition, customer service agents monitor their own stations via direct sight and CCTV to detect excessive crowding. If this occurs, OCC operators direct customer service agents to restrict access to the station platform by locking entry fare gates and stopping inbound escalators. The OCC uses the public address system to warn customers and, if necessary, request them to leave the platform.

Entry fare gates remain locked until the platform is relieved by the passage of trains.

EMERGENCY RESPONSE

In a major emergency, there may be a delay of at least 20 minutes in response time, and the assistance of one or more participating agencies may be required.

In general, the policies governing responses to emergencies should be established with other agencies and described in memos of understanding, defining each party's responsibilities.

Disabled Trains

The decision to evacuate a disabled train in a station is made by the OCC. The train operator then requests customers to leave the train. Dedicated announcers at the OCC advise the customers of the problem and, if the train cannot be moved, advise them of transportation alternatives.

Flooding

If it is associated with the track drainage system, a high water alarm is provided to the CSA in the SSC and to the OCC. The CSA verbally reports the alarm to the OCC to be sure that it is aware of the situation. The OCC confers with the maintenance department to dispatch personnel and suspends or revises the train service, as applicable to each incident.

Power Outages

Ideally, each station has at least two independent sources of power. A power outage therefore occurs only when all sources are lost at the same time. When a power outage occurs, the CSA observes the station lighting system drop to emergency lighting. Loss-of-voltage alarms is reported to the OCC. The station's uninterruptible power supplies maintain power to the station emergency lights and to the signal and communications systems and any other designated essential services.

MAINTENANCE

Operation departments see to the repair and replacement of handrails, lighting fixtures, steps, drains, walls, floors, doors, toilets—virtually anything that breaks down or wears out. Special maintenance teams may perform large-scale jobs such as installing advertising and informational map frames. An architect must be familiar with the maintenance policies of a transit agency so that the design can support the agency's policy.

A consideration of the questions on the checklist below early in the design process will influence planning, particularly in space allocation for cleaning rooms and their relative proximity to the platform.

Maintenance Checklist

- How frequently will the station be cleaned?
- Will light cleaning be performed intermittently with heavy cleaning?
- What kinds of mechanical equipment will be used, and where will it be stored?
- Will special platform edge cleaning machines be used, and where will they be stored?
- Will elevators be used for moving cleaning equipment between floor levels?
- Will fume-emitting, caustic, or abrasive cleaning detergents be used, and where will they be stored?
- Will platforms be hosed down or merely dampened with moisture? Are floor drains required?
- Will platform slope play a role in cleaning procedures?

Air-Conditioning

A heating, ventilating, and air-conditioning (HVAC) engineering group is responsible for maintenance of a station's air-conditioning systems, as well as climate control of the Station Service Center, police and employee facilities, telephone PBX rooms, shops, field offices, crew's quarters, and the OCC. This group typically maintains all boilers, heating plants, air-handling units, self-contained air-conditioning units, unit heaters, hot water circulating pumps, system controls, hot water heaters, and heat distribution systems.

Pumps

An electromechanical group, generally referred to as "hydraulics," maintains all equipment in subway facilities. Hydraulics inspects and repairs emergency ventilation systems, pump plants, deep wells, air compressor plants, and ejector plants. The group also responds to emergencies, such as floods.

The hydraulics group does routine and fault maintenance of pumps. High water alarms and any other available status information relating to pumps are automatically reported to a hydraulics control center at the OCC.

Elevators and Escalators

An elevators-and-escalators group operates, maintains, and repairs elevators and escalators. This group inspects equipment to comply with the safety code for elevators and escalators.

The elevators-and-escalators group does routine and fault maintenance of devices such as status indicators, fault alarms, and equipment diagnostics.

Power

The maintenance-of-way division is responsible for supply power and traction power systems. All status indications and fault alarms are automatically reported to the OCC.

Fire and Hazard Detection and Suppression

Fire detection and alarm system

A fire/life safety alarm system is designed, installed, and maintained to warn of abnormal fire conditions. The system should alert passengers and call for help for occupants to escape and for rescue operations to occur, generally in accordance with the National Fire Protection Association code, NFPA 72.

The requirements consist of the following:

- Maintaining the detectors in accordance with the manufacturers' specifications and the standards of NFPA 72 and other regulators, as applicable.

- Proper testing of the system for full compliance with NFPA 72 and others, as applicable

- Proper location of detectors after installation of equipment or movement of equipment per NFPA 72 and others, as applicable

- Installation of the proper detectors in the correct locations per NFPA 72 and others, as applicable

Fire standpipe system

A fire standpipe system is generally installed throughout tunnels and stations to provide a readily accessible water supply for fire department personnel during a fire. Each station and each tunnel section between adjacent stations has an independent fire standpipe system.

Sprinkler system

Automatic sprinkler systems are provided for stations in accordance with local practice and code. At a minimum, however, sprinklers should protect the areas listed in the sidebar at right.

Gas suppression systems

Gas media fire suppression systems (non-water based) should be provided for electrical/electronic equipment rooms, such as signal relay rooms and communications equipment rooms.

Communications

Typically, a telecommunications maintenance group maintains all communications over phone lines. Members of this group connect with pay telephone and cellular service suppliers as required and maintain transit system communications (i.e., installation, preventive maintenance, remedial maintenance).

Radio base stations and CCTV equipment

A communication equipment repair crew handles field maintenance of all radio base stations and CCTV equipment and responds to trouble calls. Its members are responsible for modifications of existing systems and installation of small systems such as localized CCTV camera installations. They are also responsible for the screening, testing, recharging, and replacement of all radio batteries.

Fare collection

The operations department is responsible for the maintenance of all automated fare card equipment. Operations personnel determine whether any repairs can be done remotely or first hand at the equipment installation.

Areas to Be Protected by a Sprinkler System

- Platform track areas utilizing an under-car deluge system that sprinkler the train vehicle's underside.
- Concession areas
- Storage areas
- Refuse rooms
- Escalator truss areas, per NFPA 130
- Station employee facilities
- Miscellaneous employee facilities

Station finishes

Most systems use a station operations department to maintain a station's finishes.

STATION CLEANING

Cleaning

The station operations department is responsible for maintaining a station in a clean and sanitary condition. The basic responsibilities of a station cleaner are as follows:

- To collect the garbage
- To clean the turnstiles
- To clean, sweep, and wash (including the removal of graffiti) the interior of a station, including platform areas, mezzanine areas, passageways, elevators, stairs, washrooms, toilets, and related rooms and enclosures.

They use cleaning equipment such as vacuums and sweepers and perform light maintenance work on the cleaning equipment.

Mobile wash truck teams can be assigned to perform heavy-duty cleaning and sanitizing at underground stations, using a fleet of trucks. This self-contained equipment allows for operation regardless of the lack of water or power.

Station floors are cleaned with the use of automatic scrubber machines. Special equipment for cleaning tactile platform edge strips is being used in some heavy-traffic stations.

Trash Removal

Refuse collection may be accomplished with the use of refuse trains, or refuse may be collected by station cleaners and stored at the platform or mezzanine level until collected by a refuse truck.

APPENDIX: CASE STUDIES

JR CENTRAL TOWERS
Nagoya, Japan

Situated in Nagoya, Japan's third-largest metropolitan region, this mixed-use station complex contains 4.8 million sq ft of cultural, retail, hotel, office, and transportation facilities. Planned and developed by JR Tokai, Japan Central Railways, JR Central Towers is a commercial project being developed in tandem with a major plan to improve the main regional transportation hub. A multimodal project, JR Central Towers is a station building for the high-speed bullet train—"Shinkansen," the national railway commuter network, city subway, and bus lines. In the future this complex will also serve as a stop for the magnetic levitation train now in development.

The design creates a dynamic sculptural composition of structural forms that relate to the skyline and the low-rise urban fabric. Three vertical building volumes intersect a horizontal podium to generate this dynamic. The 20-story podium is horizontally articulated to further enhance the building's relationship to the ground. A two-story, glass-enclosed sky-street stretches across the top of the podium, providing public circulation between the towers at an upper level. The building design emphasizes the contrast between the horizontal and the vertical, creating a dynamic juxtaposition between building forms.

The 59-story hotel tower is operated by JR Associate Hotels in conjunction with Marriott. The cylindrical form of the hotel allows for 800 guest rooms in a variety of configurations, as well as sweeping views across the city of Nagoya. Both

▲ View of the project from the west side.

the hotel tower and the 55-story office tower are composed of cylindrical and rectilinear forms and are capped by two levels of restaurants and a helipad.

In addition to addressing the challenge of building a large mixed-use structure above a complicated network of transportation tunnels, the building design also guides building users and daily travelers through the project in a clear and orderly fashion. Distinct and separate

paths of circulation were important to the organizational concept of the project.

The JR Central Towers project truly functions as a twenty-first-century gateway into the city of Nagoya.

Client	JR Tokai
Facility	Mixed-use facility
Size	4,800,000 sq ft
Parking for	1700 cars
Status	Completed 2000
Architect	Kohn Pederson Fox
Master Architect	Seizo Sakata
Associate Architect	Taisei Corporation

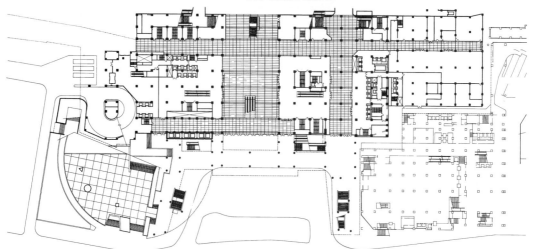

▲ Bird's-eye view of the project from the west side.

▲ Ground floor plan.

▶ Main station concourse.

318

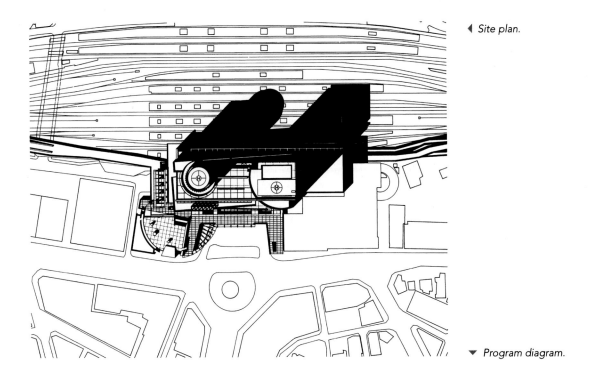

◀ *Site plan.*

▼ *Program diagram.*

North-South Sectional View

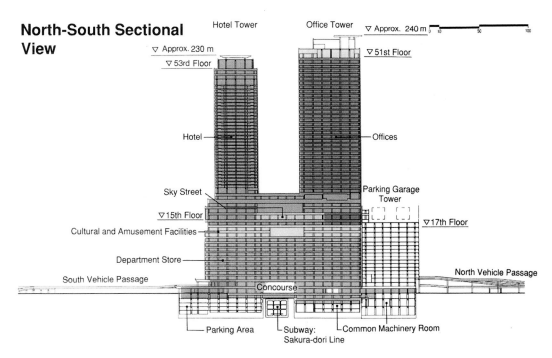

Hotel Tower

Office Tower

▽ Approx. 240 m

▽ Approx. 230 m

▽ 51st Floor

▽ 53rd Floor

Hotel

Offices

Sky Street

Parking Garage Tower

▽ 15th Floor

▽ 17th Floor

Cultural and Amusement Facilities

Department Store

South Vehicle Passage

North Vehicle Passage

Concourse

Parking Area

Subway: Sakura-dori Line

Common Machinery Room

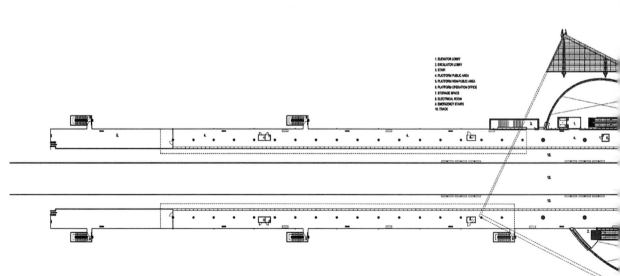

1. ELEVATOR LOBBY
2. ESCALATOR LOBBY
3. STAIR
4. PLATFORM PUBLIC AREA
5. PLATFORM NON-PUBLIC AREA
6. PLATFORM OPERATION OFFICE
7. STORAGE SPACE
8. ELECTRICAL ROOM
9. EMERGENCY STAIRS
10. TRACK

TAIWAN HIGH-SPEED RAIL HSINCHU STATION
Hsinchu, Taiwan

The station is located approximately 75 miles south of Taipei near the city of Hsinchu. Two planned substantial developments adjacent to the station and a new government sponsored Science Park will offset the original concerns about low patronage.

Hsinchu Station is designed to serve as the primary public transportation system for metropolitan Hsinchu. The train station comprises three levels. The first level accommodates the station lobby and concession area, and the upper levels include the mezzanine and the train platforms.

The curving roof, which shelters the railway and the oval volume, is 328 ft long, 229 ft wide, and 85 ft tall.

To reduce sun exposure and minimize the effects of regional wind gusts, the aerodynamic roof is designed with two opposite ends fixed to the ground, and a curved parallelogram supported by additional structures. The roof is left open in the middle to lessen the piston effect caused by the high-speed trains. Inside the station, the architect and artists, to feature themes of tradition and future,

◀ *Side view of station model. Sweeping curved roof contributes to strong station identity.*

▼ *Side elevation of station.*

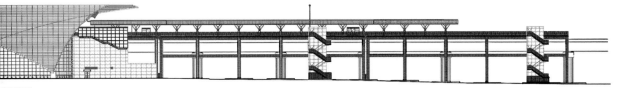

LEVATION

▼ *Upper level platform.*

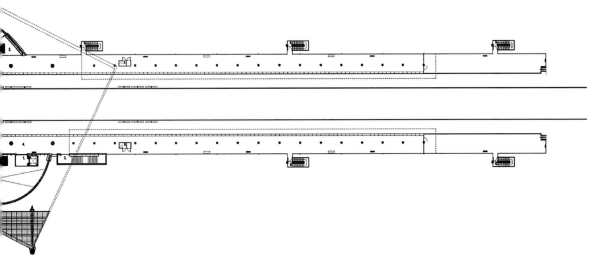

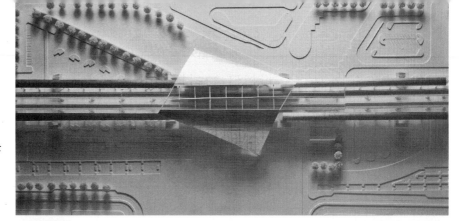

▶ Aerial view of station model. Station location allows passengers clear sight lines into the entrance.

▲ Aerial view of station model. Roof cover is provided over critical core functions.

◥ Aerial view of mezzanine area. The open plan provides clear views for station users.

thus reflecting the character of the area, designed two curved interior walls.

The station will provide more than 1000 parking spaces for a variety of vehicles. Patrons will enter the free area concourse from the east and west façades of the station. Within that space are facilities for ticket sales, information, waiting areas, commercial areas, and two fare arrays. After passing through the fare gates, the patron is in the paid area and can move to the mezzanine level. The mezzanine provides additional seating areas for the general public as well as executive lounges. Platforms are configured to be at the third level over the main station public areas. These spaces are enclosed in an oval form, which is glazed primarily for the full three stories. The patron spaces are covered with a steel truss structure and metal roofing. The interior structures are framed with reinforced concrete. The roof touches down at single points on the east and west sides, offering shade and shelter at the entrances, as well as providing a graceful solution.

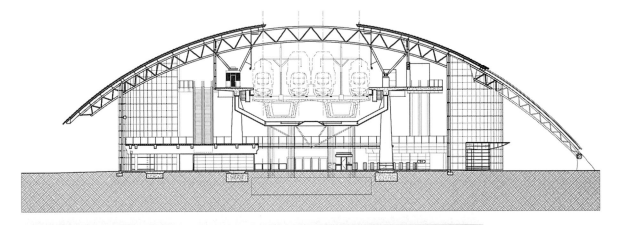

▲ Cross section through station.

◀ View of section model. Illustrates methods through which all systems are interrelated.

The required ancillary spaces are housed separately under the trackway guideways to avoid interference with the riding public.

When completed, the Hsinchu Station will complement the Science Park, as well as the high-speed trains that will use the station.

Client	Taiwan High-Speed Rail Corporation
Facility	Rail station
Size	150,000 sq ft
Status	Under construction
Architect	Artek, in association with DMJM & Harris

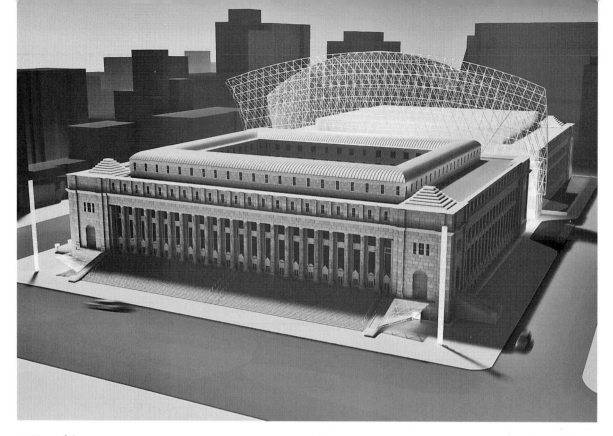

RENOVATION AND ADDITION, PENNSYLVANIA STATION
New York City

Pennsylvania Station is one of America's busiest transportation centers, serving half a million people daily—more passengers than New York's three major airports combined. Because of its size and its failed history as a replacement structure over the original Penn Station, the passenger experience, including ticket purchase and movement down to the platform, is confusing. To remedy this condition, the Pennsylvania Station Redevelopment Corporation was formed to build an expansion to the station utilizing the space in the adjacent James A. Farley Post Office. The post office is a landmarked building designed by McKim, Mead & White in a similar style to that of the original Penn Station. It is immediately west of the original station and above the rail platforms. To convert roughly 30 per-

cent of the original 1.4 million sq ft into a rail station required some modifications to the exterior. New entrances from Eighth Avenue are planned, using lightweight steel and glass canopies to make them recognizable, but without challenging the powerful sweep of the existing stairs leading to the post office. The primary station entrances will be at midblock on Thirty-first and Thirty-third Streets, with covered taxi drop-offs. Above the main entrances rises a 150 ft tall steel and glass shell structure that announces the new station. This structure houses the intermodal hall, which is the primary civic space in the building.

The train room is the next in a series of spaces as one moves from the intermodal hall. Also accessible directly from Eighth Avenue, it occupies the original mail sorting room in the post office. Exposed heavy steel trusses 15 ft deep will be restored and stripped of their com-

◀ View of train hall showing refurbished trusses and new media wall.

mercial cladding and span the 35,000 sq ft space. They will be enclosed by a new glass skylight. The existing floors beneath the skylight will be cut away to yield a tall space with a cascading profile that leads passengers down to the trains. The entire east façade of the room will be a programmable media wall that displays train schedules, weather, news, and entertainment notices. Below this wall will be a glazed area that reveals the activity at platform level and allows a broad band of daylight to reach the tracks, guiding arriving passengers to the new station.

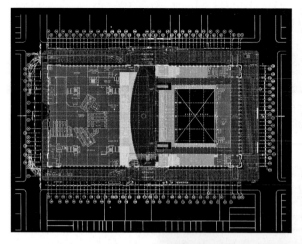

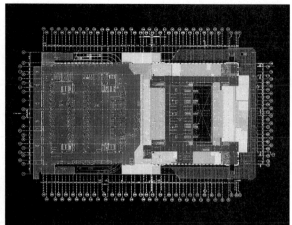

▲ First-floor intermodal hall, with public areas in dark blue and retail in light blue and violet.

◥ Concourse-level plan, with public areas in dark blue and station facilities in light blue and violet.

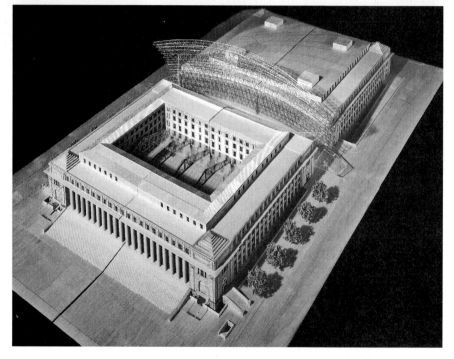

▶ New Penn Station from above, with Eighth Avenue in the foreground.

▶▶ Thirty-third Street entrance.

(Following page)
View of ticketing hall.

Client	Pennsylvania Station Redevelopment Corporation
Facility	Rail station
Size	Approximately 400,000 sq ft
Architect	SOM

327

INTERMODAL TRANSPORTATION FACILITY
South Bend, Indiana

As a result of continued development in downtown South Bend, transit and transportation had become a significant planning issue. Several factors were prominent:

Owner	Transpo/South Bend Transportation Corporation
Building size	24,375 sq ft
Construction Cost	$4.94 million
Architect	DMJM/Troyer Joint Venture

- The existing bus transfer center, located in the center of the central business district, was nearing the end of its lease.

- Amtrak had relocated its passengers to the outskirts of town.
- Transpo was launching a bus circulator system.

◀ Terminal provides an exciting place for transferring passengers and enlivens downtown South Bend.

◀ Canopies sit over extensive passenger loading platforms. The business center has its own entrance through the glazed wall on the left.

▶ *Two-story lobby welcomes the passengers with its balconies, sheer heights, and visibility to the bus transfer areas, creating a safe and dramatic gathering place.*

The new bus circulator system maintained a northbound and a southbound one-way route with a reverse movement at the south terminus adjacent to an existing railroad used by Amtrak on its New York to Chicago route. It was the property near the circulator bus turnaround that offered the best location for an intermodal facility. Transfers were to be made by various modes:

- Intercity bus to intercity bus
- Intercity bus to circulator bus
- Intercity bus to Amtrak
- Automobile to each of the preceding modes

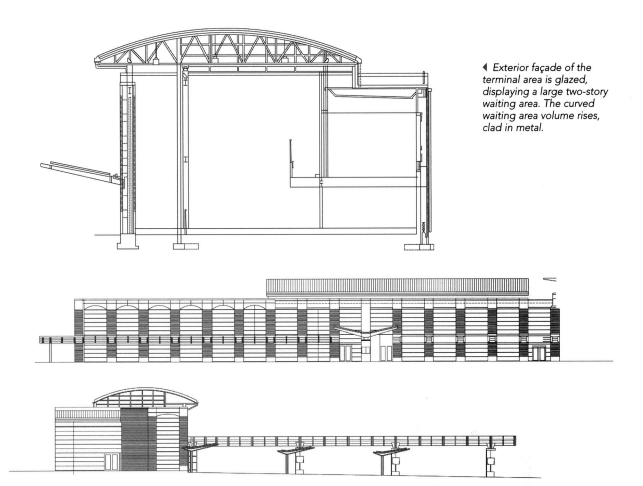

◄ Exterior façade of the terminal area is glazed, displaying a large two-story waiting area. The curved waiting area volume rises, clad in metal.

▲ While the building's rectilinear bases are of traditional brick and limestone, the terminal portion is expressed through a strong curvilinear roof form.

Master Plan

Transpo commissioned DMJM/Troyer to prepare a feasibility study to recommend a phased approach to developing the transfer center. Alternative concepts were developed and analyzed. A recommendation was presented to develop the property as follows:

- Bus transfer center
- 600-car parking structure
- Amtrak station and platform

The bus transfer center was the initial phase for design and construction. The center was to be the hub for all functions and was designed to contain all space needed to serve its growth potential.

Traffic impact analysis demonstrated that the existing one-way northbound street (Michigan) and the southbound street (Main) were functioning at traffic volumes far less than their capacities. The existing street network should therefore accommodate the increase in vehicular traffic at an acceptable level of service, without excessive delay or congestion.

DMJM/Troyer created a three-part master plan that called for (1) the initial

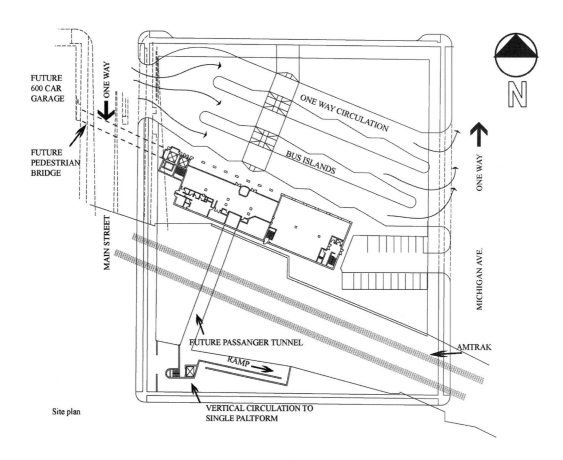

FUTURE
600 CAR
GARAGE

ONE WAY

ONE WAY CIRCULATION

BUS ISLANDS

ONE WAY

FUTURE
PEDESTRIAN
BRIDGE

MAIN STREET

MICHIGAN AVE.

FUTURE PASSANGER TUNNEL

RAMP →

AMTRAK

VERTICAL CIRCULATION TO
SINGLE PALTFORM

Site plan

▲ Site is flanked by one-way streets enabling buses to complete the route around the center city. The south side is bisected by an Amtrak line setting on top of an embankment. Future connections to the platforms require a pedestrian underpass.

construction of the bus transfer center and (2) the construction of a 600-car automobile parking structure across Main Street to the west. This required a future passenger walking bridge over Main Street, connecting the parking to the bus center and (3) a single-platform Amtrak station located on an embankment along the south side of the existing rail lines. This necessitated a passenger tunnel below the tracks, connecting the bus center with vertical circulation, to reach the platform levels.

Bus Transfer Center

Operational requirements were set as follows:

- Use 35 ft long buses.

- Operating hours are to be 5:00 A.M. to 10:00 P.M. on weekdays and 7:00 A.M. to 6:30 P.M. on Saturday. No service on Sunday.

- A minimum of nine bus bays.

- Internal circulation of buses and channelizations should be designed to minimize pedestrians crossing bus paths. One-way internal bus movements are preferred.

- Individual shelters are to be included on the bus islands and are to provide maximum protection to passengers against the winter climate.

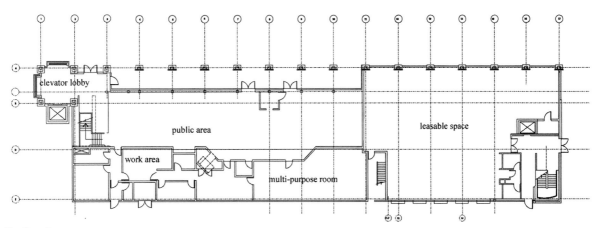

First floor plan

- An interior waiting space is to be provided for use during extreme temperatures and during early and late hours.

- A minimum of 5 parking spaces are to be provided for employees in close proximity to the center.

- An information/ticketing booth is to be included, as well as a lost-and-found kiosk.

A space program was prepared with input from several community groups and Amtrak. It called for space to accommodate the following:

- Public waiting areas for both Transpo and Amtrak passengers

- Counter and ticket sales for both, with a phased approach to Amtrak

- Transpo office space

- Future Amtrak baggage and storage

- Taxi stand

- Tenant office space

Architectural/Urban Planning Goals

The intermodal facility was intended to be a gateway to the city, connecting travelers easily to a variety of existing transportation modes, including trains, local bus service, downtown circulator, taxi, automobile, and bicycle. The facility was to serve as a positive first impression for the people entering South Bend and to offer a welcoming atmosphere that complements the center business district.

The design was to be visually stimulating, require quality construction, and use vandal-resistant materials and design techniques that stress the civic nature of the facility. The design was also to attract complementary businesses, such as retail or commercial, to generate revenue to help pay for the facility, and to encourage the use of the center during nonrevenue bus operating hours.

The Design
Exposing the elements of the structure, the design team created a landmark building reminiscent of the great train depots of major cities. The transportation center connects to the urban fabric, visually and functionally, to become the focal point for urban redevelopment.

▲ Terminal building is a two-story structure comprising public waiting areas and leased tenant space.

Vaulted roofs and lofty structural elements create a sense of grandeur in this compact facility. Structure projecting through the building envelope offers a modern appeal by day and a light-emitting sanctuary by night. Structure and stone combine to convey strength and durability. A series of attractive tapered steel canopies, topped with translucent panels, protect bus passengers from the elements while transmitting light. Canopy details are carried through the building design to integrate the different elements of the facility.

The Elements

The facility incorporates four distinct building elements: the canopies covering the bus islands, the flat-roofed administrative space, the curved-roofed public transfer space, and the two-story stair and clock tower. The design is reminiscent of the rich industrial legacy of South Bend, interpreted in a modern manner. Two story curtain walls create a dramatic effect of light and space at the front and side entries. The clock tower acts as a focal point through all stages of development. The future pedestrian bridge will connect to the tower. The illuminated tower is recognizable from a distance and is a familiar sight to arriving Amtrak passengers.

Exterior materials include brick, limestone, glass, painted steel structure, metal roofing, and granite bases under walls and windows. Materials were selected for their long-standing performance in a transportation environment in the snowbelt zone of Indiana.

GLOSSARY

Accessibility The extent to which facilities are barrier free and useable by persons with disabilities, including wheelchair users.

Advanced design bus See *Bus, advanced design.*

Advanced public transportation systems (APTS) Intelligent vehicle highway systems (IVHS) technology designed to improve transit services through advanced vehicle operations, communications, customer service, and market development.

Aerial tramway An electric system of aerial cables with suspended unpowered passenger vehicles. The vehicles are propelled by separate cables attached to the vehicle suspension system and powered by engines or motors at a central location not on board the vehicle.

Alternative fuels Low-polluting fuels that are used to propel a vehicle instead of high-sulfur diesel or gasoline. Examples include methanol, ethanol, propane and compressed natural gas, liquid natural gas, low-sulfur or "clean" diesel, and electricity.

Amalgamated Transit Union (ATU) A major labor union representing workers in the transit industry; membership is limited to operators, mechanics and other nonsupervisory employees of the transit industry.

American Public Transportation Association (APTA) The nonprofit trade association representing the public transit industry. APTA members include more than 400 public transit systems, as well as state and local departments of transportation and planning agencies, manufacturers and suppliers of transit equipment, consultants, contractors, and universities.

Americans with Disabilities Act of 1990 (ADA) A civil rights law passed by Congress in 1990 that makes it illegal to discriminate against people with disabilities in employment, services provided by state and local governments, public and private transportation, public accommodations, and telecommunications.

Annual element Includes those transportation improvement projects, contained in an area's Transportation Improvement Program (TIP), that are proposed for implementation in the current year. The annual element is submitted to the U.S. Department of Transportation (U.S. DOT) as part of the required planning process.

Arterial street A major thoroughfare, used primarily for through traffic rather than for access to adjacent land, that is characterized by high vehicular capacity and continuity of movement.

Articulated bus See *Bus, articulated*

Authorization Basic, substantive legislation that establishes or continues the legal operation of a federal program or agency, either indefinitely or for a specific period of time, or that sanctions a particular type of obligation or expenditure within a program. An authorization may set appropriation limits. See *Intermodal Surface Transportation Efficiency Act.*

Automated guideway An electric railway operating without vehicle operators or other crew on board the vehicle.

Automatic fare collection system (AFC) A system of controls and equipment that automatically admits passengers upon insertion of the correct fare in coins, tokens, tickets, or fare cards; it may include special equipment for transporting and counting revenues.

Automatic vehicle location system (AVLS) Technology that tracks the current location of fleet vehicles to assist in dispatching, maintaining schedules, answering specific customer inquiries, etc.

Auto restricted zone (ARZ) An area in which normal automobile traffic is prohibited or limited to certain times and vehicular traffic is restricted to public transit, emergency vehicles, taxicabs, and, in some cases, delivery of goods.

Base period The period between the morning and evening peak periods when transit service is generally scheduled on a constant interval. Also known as *off-peak period.*

Base fare The price charged to one adult for one transit ride; excludes transfer charges, zone charges, express service charges, peak period surcharges, and reduced fares.

Bus, advanced design A bus introduced in 1977 that incorporates new styling and design features as compared with previous buses.

Bus, articulated A bus, usually 55 ft or more in length, with two connected passenger compartments that bend at the connecting point when the bus turns a corner.

Bus, charter A bus transporting a group of persons who, pursuant to a common purpose and under a single contract at a fixed price, have acquired the exclusive use of a bus to travel together according to an itinerary.

Bus, circulator A bus serving an area confined to a specific locale, such as a downtown area or suburban neighborhood, with connections to major traffic corridors.

Bus discretionary capital Federal funding granted under Section 3 of the Federal Transit Act (formerly known as the

Urban Mass Transportation Act of 1964). These discretionary funds are used for bus-related construction projects or to replace, rehabilitate, or purchase buses.

Bus, double-deck A bus with two separate passenger compartments, one above the other.

Bus, express A bus that operates a portion of the route without stops or with a limited number of stops.

Bus, feeder A bus service that picks up and delivers passengers to a rapid-transit rail station or express bus stop or terminal.

Bus, intercity A bus with front doors only, high-backed seats, separate luggage compartments, and usually with restroom facilities, for use in high-speed long-distance service.

Bus lane A street or highway lane intended primarily for buses, either all day or during specified periods, but sometimes also used by carpools meeting requirements set forth in the traffic laws.

Bus, medium-size A bus that is 29–34 ft in length.

Bus (motorbus) A rubber-tired, self-propelled, manually steered vehicle with fuel supply carried on board. Types include advanced design, articulated, charter, circulator, double deck, express, feeder, intercity, medium-size, new look, sightseeing, small, standard-size, subscription, suburban, transit, and van.

Bus, new look A bus with the predominant styling and mechanical equipment common to buses manufactured between 1959 and 1978.

Bus shelter A building or other structure constructed near a bus stop to provide seating and protection from the weather for the convenience of waiting passengers.

Bus, sightseeing A bus adapted for sightseeing use, usually with expanded window areas.

Bus, small A bus 28 ft or less in length.

Bus, standard-size A bus that is 35–41 ft in length.

Bus stop A place where passengers can board or alight from a bus, usually identified by a sign.

Bus, subscription A commuter bus express service operated for a guaranteed number of patrons from a given area on a prepaid, reserved-seat basis.

Bus, suburban A bus with front doors only, normally with high-backed seats, and without luggage compartments or restroom facilities, for use in longer-distance service with relatively few stops.

Bus, transit A bus with front and center doors, normally with a rear-mounted engine, low-backed seating, and without luggage compartments or restroom facilities, for use in frequent-stop service.

Bus, trolley An electric, rubber-tired transit vehicle, manually steered, propelled by a motor drawing current through overhead wires from a central power source not on board the vehicle. Also known as *trolley coach* or *trackless trolley*.

Bus, van A 20 ft long or shorter vehicle, usually with an automotive-type engine and limited seating, normally entered directly through a side or rear door rather than from a central aisle, used for demand response, vanpool, and lightly patronized motorbus service.

Busway Exclusive freeway lane for buses and carpools.

Cable car An electric railway operating in mixed street traffic with unpowered, individually controlled transit vehicles propelled by moving cables located below the street surface and powered by engines or motors at a central location not on board the vehicle.

Capital costs Costs of long-term assets of a public transit system, such as property, buildings, vehicles, etc.

Carpool An arrangement whereby two or more people share the use and cost of privately owned automobiles in traveling to and from prearranged destinations together.

Catenary An overhead contact wire system that supplies power from a central power source to an electric vehicle (such as a trolley bus; see *Bus, trolley*).

Central business district (CBD) The downtown retail trade and commercial area of a city or an area of very high land valuation, traffic flow, and concentration of retail business offices, theaters, hotels, and services.

Charter bus See *Bus, charter*.

Circulator bus See *Bus, circulator*.

Clean Air Act Amendments of 1990 (CAAA) The comprehensive federal legislation that establishes criteria for attaining and maintaining the federal standards for allowable concentrations and exposure limits for various air pollutants; the Act also provides emission standards for specific vehicles and fuels.

Commuter A person who travels regularly between home and work or school.

Commuter rail See *Rail, commuter*.

Compressed Natural Gas (CNG) An alternative fuel; compressed natural gas stored under high pressure. CNG vapor is lighter than air.

Conformity The ongoing process that ensures that the planning for highway and transit systems, as a whole and over the long term, is consistent with the state air quality plans for attaining and maintaining health-based air quality standards; conformity is determined by metropolitan planning organizations (MPOs) and the U.S. Department of Transportation (U.S. DOT) and is based on whether transportation plans and programs meet the provisions of a state implementation plan.

Congestion mitigation and air quality (CMAQ) funds Federal funds available for either transit or highway projects that contribute significantly to reducing automobile emissions that cause air pollution.

Contraflow lane Reserved lane for buses in which the direction of bus traffic is opposite to the flow of traffic in other lanes.

Corridor A broad geographical band that follows a general directional flow, connecting major sources of trips that may contain a number of streets, highways, and transit route alignments.

Crosstown Nonradial bus or rail service that does not enter the central business district (CBD).

Deadhead The movement of a transit vehicle without passengers aboard; often to and from a garage or to and from one route to another.

Demand-responsive service Nonfixed-route service utilizing vans or buses, with passengers boarding and alighting at prearranged times at any location within the system's service area. Also called *Dial-a-Ride*.

Department of Transportation (DOT) The cabinet level department of the federal government that is responsible for administration of federal transportation programs, including public transportation, highways, railroads, air transportation, shipping, and the Coast Guard. Each state also has a department of transportation.

Dial-a-Ride See *Demand-responsive service*.

Discretionary spending A federal budgetary term that refers to any funds whose distribution is not automatic.

Discretionary spending encompasses programs controlled by annual appropriations bills and is subject to the constraints imposed by the discretionary spending limits set in the balanced budget law.

Double-deck bus See *Bus, double-deck*.

Downtime A period during which a vehicle is inoperative because of repairs or maintenance.

Downtown People Mover (DPM) A type of automated-guideway transit vehicle operating on a loop or shuttle route within the central business district (CBD) of a city.

Dwell time The scheduled time a vehicle or train is allowed to discharge and take on passengers at a stop, including opening and closing doors.

Elevated (railway) See *Rail, heavy*.

Environmental Impact Statement (EIS) A comprehensive study of likely environmental impacts resulting from major federally assisted projects; statements are required by the National Environmental Policy Act (NEPA).

Equity, federal transit funding A ratio of appropriated dollars between Sections 9 and 18 (Federal Transit Act formula funds) to Section 3 (discretionary funds).

Ethanol An alternative fuel; a liquid alcohol fuel with vapor heavier than air, produced from agricultural products such as corn, other grain, and sugar cane.

Exclusive right-of-way A highway or other facility that can be used only by buses or other transit vehicles.

Express bus See *Bus, express*.

Fare box recovery ratio Measure of the proportion of operating expenses covered by passenger fares; found by dividing fare box revenue by total operating expenses for each mode and/or systemwide.

Fare box revenue Value of cash, tickets, tokens, and pass receipts given by passengers as payment for rides; excludes charter revenue.

Fare elasticity The extent to which ridership responds to fare increases or decreases.

Fare structure The system set up to determine how much is to be paid by various passengers using a transit vehicle at any given time.

Federal Transit Administration (FTA) Formerly known as the Urban Mass Transportation Administration (UMTA); FTA is the agency of the U.S. Department of Transportation that administers the federal program of financial assistance to public transit.

Feeder bus See *Bus, feeder*.

Ferryboat A boat providing fixed-route service across a body of water.

Fiscal year (FY) The yearly accounting period for the federal government, which begins October 1 and ends the following September 30. The fiscal year is designated by the calendar year in which it ends (e.g., FY 94 is from October 1, 1993, to September 30, 1994).

Fixed guideway modernization See *Rail modernization funds*.

Fixed guideway system A system of vehicles that can operate only on its own guideway constructed for that purpose (e.g., rapid rail, light rail). Federal usage in funding legislation also includes exclusive right-of-way bus operations, trolley coaches, and ferryboats as "fixed guideway" transit.

Fixed Route Service provided on a repetitive, fixed-schedule basis along a specific route with vehicles stopping to pick up and deliver passengers to specific locations; each fixed-route trip serves the same origins and destinations, unlike demand-responsive service and taxicabs.

Flexible funds Those federal funds which can be used for highway, transit or other transportation projects, as decided by regional Metropolitan Planning Organizations (MPOs) and state governments. Examples of such funds are the Surface Transportation Program (STP) and the Congestion Mitigation and Air Quality (CMAQ) fund.

Formula funds Funds distributed or apportioned to qualifying recipients on the basis of formulas described in law; e.g., funds in the Section 18 program for Small Urban and Rural Transit Assistance, which are distributed to each state based on the state's percentage of national rural population. See also *Section 9*.

Fringe parking An area for parking usually located outside the central business district (CBD) and most often used by suburban residents who work or shop downtown.

Headway Time interval between vehicles moving in the same direction on a particular route.

Heavy rail See *Rail, heavy.*

High-occupancy vehicle (HOV) A vehicle that can carry two or more persons. Examples of high-occupancy vehicles are a bus, vanpool, and a carpool. These vehicles sometimes have exclusive traffic lanes called *HOV lanes, busways, transitways,* or *commuter lanes.*

High-speed rail See *Rail, high-speed.*

Highway Trust Fund The federal trust fund established by the Highway Revenue Act of 1956; this fund has two accounts, the Highway Account and the Mass Transit Account. Trust fund revenues are derived from federal highway-user taxes and fees such as motor fuel taxes; trust fund uses and expenditures are determined by law.

Inclined plane railway A railway operating over an exclusive right-of-way on

steep grades with unpowered vehicles propelled by moving cables attached to the vehicles and powered by engines or motors at a central location not on board the vehicle.

Intelligent vehicle highway systems (IVHSs) Automated systems of highway transportation designed to improve traffic monitoring and management. IVHSs include advanced public transportation systems (APTSs), automatic vehicle location systems (AVLSs), and "smart vehicles," which assist drivers with planning, perception, analysis, and decision making.

Intercity bus See *Bus, intercity.*

Intermodal Those issues or activities that involve or affect more than one mode of transportation, including transportation connections, choices, and cooperation and coordination of various modes. Also known as *multimodal.*

Intermodal Surface Transportation Efficiency Act (ISTEA) The 1991 law that reauthorized the federal surface transportation program for 6 years. ISTEA heralded a new era in surface transportation because of the emphasis on "intermodalism," the unprecedented increases in authorized spending for transit, the ability to use some highway funds for transit (and vice versa), and the increased reliance on regional planning agencies to weigh transportation options and make decisions utilizing public participation.

Jitney Privately owned small or medium-sized vehicle, usually operated on a fixed route but not on a fixed schedule.

Joint development Ventures undertaken by the public and private sectors for development of land around transit stations or stops.

Kiss-and-ride A place where commuters are driven and dropped off at a station to board a public transportation vehicle.

Layover time Time built into a schedule between arrival at the end of a route and the departure for the return trip, used for the recovery of delays and preparation for the return trip.

Level playing field A balanced approach to federal funding proportions for highway projects and transit projects; may also refer to employee transportation benefits so that the monthly tax-free value of a transit pass is equal to that of a parking space; generally, any situation in which transit and highways receive equal treatment in federal funding and other federal procedures.

Light rail See *Rail, light.*

Liquefied natural gas (LNG) An alternative fuel; a natural gas cooled to below its boiling point of −260°F so that it becomes a liquid; stored in a vacuum-bottle-type container at very low temperatures and under moderate pressure. LNG vapor is lighter than air.

Load factor The ratio of passengers actually carried versus the total passenger capacity of a vehicle.

Magnetic levitation (maglev) A rail transportation system with exclusive right-of-way, which is propelled along a fixed guideway system by the attraction or repulsion of magnets on the rails and under the rail cars.

Managers of mobility Transit systems that expand their role to include services and approaches beyond traditional public transportation to include ride sharing, high-occupancy vehicle programs, public education on transit's benefits and integration of land use, air quality and transportation decisions; the phrase was developed as part of the industry's Transit 2000 policy effort undertaken in the late 1980s and early 1990s.

Mass transit See *Public transportation.*

Mass transit account The federal account, established by the Surface Transportation Assistance Act of 1982, into which a designated portion of the federal Highway Trust Fund revenue from motor fuel taxes is placed (1.5 cents in 1994). This account is used for federal mass transportation assistance.

Mass transportation See *Public transportation.*

Mean distance between failures (MDBF) The average distance in miles that a transit vehicle travels before failure of a vital component forces removal of that vehicle from service.

Medium-size bus See *Bus, medium-size.*

Methanol An alternative fuel; a liquid alcohol fuel with vapor heavier than air; primarily produced from natural gas.

Metropolitan planning organization (MPO) The organization designated by local elected officials as being responsible for carrying out the urban transportation and other planning processes for an area.

Metropolitan railway (metro) See *Rail, heavy.*

Modal split A term that describes how many people use alternative forms of transportation. Frequently used to describe the percentage of people using private automobiles as opposed to the percentage using public transportation.

Model An analytical tool (often mathematical) used by transportation planners to assist in making forecasts of land use, economic activity, and travel activity and their effects on the quality of resources such as land, air, and water.

Monorail An electric railway in which a rail car or train of cars is suspended from or straddles a guideway formed by a single beam or rail. Most monorails are either heavy-rail or automated guideway systems.

National Environmental Policy Act of 1969 (NEPA) A comprehensive federal law requiring analysis of the environ-

mental impacts of federal actions such as the approval of grants; also requiring preparation of an Environmental Impact Statement (EIS) for every major federal action significantly affecting the quality of the human environment.

National Highway System (NHS) A proposed transportation system consisting of approximately 155,000 miles of highway in order to provide an interconnected system of principal arterial routes serving major population centers, major transportation facilities, major travel destinations, and interstate and interregional travel, and meeting national defense requirements. The NHS, defined in the Intermodal Surface Transportation Efficiency Act (ISTEA), is one component of the National Transportation System (NTS).

National Transportation System (NTS) An intermodal system consisting of all forms of transportation in a unified, interconnected manner, intended to reduce energy consumption and air pollution while promoting economic development and supporting the nation's preeminent position in international commerce. The NTS includes the National Highway System (NHS), public transportation, and access to ports and airports.

New look bus See *Bus, new look*

New Start funds Federal funding granted under Section 3(i) of the Federal Transit Act (formerly known as the Urban Mass Transportation Act of 1964). These discretionary funds are made available for construction of a new fixed-guideway system or extension of any existing fixed-guideway system, based on cost-effectiveness, alternatives analysis results, and the degree of local financial commitment.

Nonattainment area Any geographic region of the United States that the U.S. Environmental Protection Agency (EPA) has designated as not attaining

the federal air quality standards for one or more air pollutants, such as ozone and carbon monoxide.

Off-peak period Nonrush periods of the day when travel activity is generally lower and less transit service is scheduled. See *Base period.*

Paratransit Comparable transportation service required by the Americans with Disabilities Act (ADA) of 1990 for individuals with disabilities who are unable to use fixed-route transportation systems.

Park-and-ride lot Designated parking area for automobile drivers, who then board transit vehicles from this location.

Particulate trap A filter that removes a portion of the particulates (solids, soot, etc.) from a vehicle's exhaust stream; generally includes a regenerative unit and associated control system to burn the collected solids.

Passenger miles The total number of miles traveled by passengers on transit vehicles; determined by multiplying the number of unlinked passenger trips by the average length of the trips.

Passenger Transport **(PT)** The weekly newspaper of the transit industry, published by the American Public Transit Association (APTA).

Peak period Morning or afternoon time period when transit riding is heaviest.

Peak/base ratio The number of vehicles operated in passenger service during the peak period divided by the number operated during the base period.

Propane An alternative fuel; a liquid petroleum gas (LPG) that is stored under moderate pressure and with vapor heavier than air; produced as a by-product of natural gas and oil production.

Public transit system An organization that provides transportation services, owned, operated, or subsidized by any municipality, county, regional authority, state, or other governmental agency, including those operated or managed by a private management firm under contract to the government agency owner.

Public transportation Transportation by bus, rail, or other conveyance, either publicly or privately owned, which provides to the public general or special service on a regular and continuing basis. Also known as *mass transportation, mass transit,* and *transit.*

Rail, commuter Railroad local and regional passenger train operations between a central city, its suburbs and/or another central city. It may be either locomotive hauled or self-propelled and is characterized by multitrip tickets, specific station-to-station fares, railroad employment practices, and usually only one or two stations in the central business district. Also known as *suburban rail.*

Rail, heavy An electric railway with the capacity for a heavy volume of traffic and characterized by exclusive rights-of-way, multicar trains, high speed and rapid acceleration, sophisticated signaling, and high platform loading. Also known as *rapid rail, subway, elevated (railway),* or *metropolitan railway (metro).*

Rail, high-speed A rail transportation system with exclusive rights-of-way serves densely traveled corridors at speeds of 124 miles per hour (200 km/h) and greater.

Rail, light An electric railway with a light volume of traffic capacity, as compared with heavy rail. Light rail may use shared or exclusive rights-of-way, high or low platform loading and multicar trains or single cars. Also known as *streetcar, trolley car,* and *tramway.*

Rail modernization funds Federal funding granted under Section 3(h) of the Federal Transit Act (formerly known as the Urban Mass Transportation Act of 1964). These discretionary funds are dis-

tributed by a formula and made available to transit systems for improvements on fixed guideway systems that have been in service for at least seven years. Also known as fixed guideway modernization funds.

Rapid rail See *Rail, heavy.*

Rapid transit Rail or motorbus transit service operating completely separate from all modes of transportation on an exclusive right-of-way.

Reverse commuting Movement in a direction opposite the main flow of traffic, such as from the central city to a suburb during the morning peak period.

Ridership The number of rides taken by people using a public transportation system in a given time period.

Ride sharing A form of transportation, other than public transit, in which two or more persons share the use of a vehicle, such as a van or car, to make a trip. Also known as *carpooling* or *vanpooling.*

Rolling stock The vehicles used in a transit system, including buses and rail cars.

Route miles The total number of miles included in a fixed-route transit system network.

Section 3 The section of the Federal Transit Act (formerly known as the Urban Mass Transportation Act of 1964), as amended, that authorizes discretionary funds for capital public transportation projects.

Section 9 The section of the Federal Transit Act (formerly known as the Urban Mass Transportation Act of 1964), as amended, that authorizes grants to public transportation systems in urbanized areas (population greater than 50,000) for both capital and operating programs based on formulas set forth in statute.

Section 15 The section of the Federal Transit Act (formerly known as the Urban Mass Transportation Act of 1964),

as amended, that authorizes the U.S. Department of Transportation to gather statistical information about the financing and operations of public transportation systems, based on a uniform system of accounts and records.

Section 16 The section of the Federal Transit Act (formerly known as the Urban Mass Transportation Act of 1964), as amended, that declares the national policy to be that elderly persons and persons with disabilities have the same right as other persons to utilize mass transportation facilities and services, and that special efforts must be made in the planning and design of mass transportation facilities and services so that effective utilization by elderly persons and persons with disabilities is ensured.

Section 16(b) The subsection of the Federal Transit Act (formerly known as the Urban Mass Transportation Act of 1964), as amended, that authorizes grants to nonprofit corporations and associations for the specific purpose of assisting them in providing transportation services meeting the special needs of elderly persons and persons with disabilities for whom mass transportation services are unavailable, insufficient, or inappropriate.

Section 18 The section of the Federal Transit Act (formerly known as the Urban Mass Transportation Act of 1964), as amended, that authorizes grants to public transit systems outside urbanized areas, based on formulas set forth in the statute; the funds go initially to the governor of each state.

Shuttle A public or private vehicle that travels back and forth over a particular route, especially a short route or one that provides connections between transportation systems, employment centers, etc.

Sightseeing bus See *Bus, sightseeing.*

Small bus See *Bus, small.*

Standard-size bus See *Bus, standard-size.*

State Implementation Plan (SIP) A state plan mandated by the Clean Air Act Amendments of 1990 (CAAA) that contains procedures to monitor, control, maintain, and enforce compliance with national standards for air quality.

Streetcar See *Rail, light.*

Subscription bus See *Bus, subscription.*

Suburban rail See *Rail, commuter.*

Subway See *Rail, heavy.*

Trackless trolley See *Bus, trolley.*

Tramway See *Rail, light.*

Transfer center A fixed location where passengers interchange from one route or vehicle to another.

Transit See *Public transportation.*

Transit bus See *Bus, transit.*

Transit pass A tax-free employee commuter benefit whereby an employer subsidizes up to $60 per month for an employee's transit fares or vanpool charges. This benefit also applies to military and government employees.

Transit system An organization (public or private) providing local or regional multioccupancy-vehicle passenger service. Organizations that provide service under contract to another agency are generally not counted as separate systems.

Transit 2000 An industry effort undertaken in the late 1980s and early 1990s to develop public policies allowing transit to achieve its greatest potential for the rest for the twentieth century and beyond; recommendations included turning transit systems into managers of mobility, broadening transit's definition to include ride sharing and other high-occupancy vehicle programs, enhancing local decision-making authority, increasing federal funding, and raising the federal gasoline tax.

Transportation Improvement Program (TIP) A program of intermodal transportation projects, to be implemented over several years, growing out of the planning process and designed to improve transportation in a community. This program is required as a condition of a locality's receiving federal transit and highway grants.

Trolley bus See *Bus, trolley.*

Trolley car See *Rail, light.*

Trolley coach See *Bus, trolley.*

Urbanized area (UZA) A U.S. Bureau of Census-designated area of 50,000 or more inhabitants, consisting of a central city or two adjacent cities, plus surrounding densely settled territory, but excluding the rural portion of cities.

Urban Mass Transportation Administration (UMTA) See *Federal Transit Administration (FTA).*

Van See *Bus, van.*

Vanpool An arrangement in which a group of passengers share the use and cost of a van in traveling to and from prearranged destinations together.

Zone fares A system of fares whereby a transit system's service area is divided into zones within which specified rates or fares apply.

BIBLIOGRAPHY AND REFERENCES

Alexander, Edwin P. 1970. *Down at the Depot.* New York: Bramhall House.

American Public Transit Association. 1979. *Guidelines for the Design of Rapid Transit Facilities.* Washington, D.C.: APTA. www.apta.com/research/info

———. 2002. *Heavy-Duty Escalator Design Guidelines.* Washington, D.C.: APTA. www.apta.com/research/info

———. 2004. *Low-Rise Heavy-Duty Elevator Design Guidelines.* Washington, D.C.: APTA. www.apta.com/research/info

Baltimore NRHS Publications. 1981. *What Made All Our Streetcars Go?* Baltimore, Md.: Baltimore NRHS Publications.

Baranek, Leo L., ed. 1971. *Noise and Vibration Control.* McGraw-Hill.

Boyd, M. Annabelle, and Patricia M. Maier. 1998. *Transit Security Handbook.* Washington, D.C.: Federal Transit Administration. DOT no. FTA-MA-90-9007-98-1; Volpe report no. DOT-VNTSC-FTA-98-03; NTIS no. PB98-157761. http://transit-safety.volpe.dot.gov/publications/default.asp

Carman, R. A. 2003. "Noise Control in Stations with High Speed Trains." Paper presented at the 82nd annual meeting of TRB, Washington, D.C., January.

Clarke, Ronald. 1996. *Situational Crime Prevention: Successful Case Studies.* New York: Criminal Justice Press.

Cova, Mustafa. 2002. *Electric Traction Power Supply.* www.trainweb.org

Educational Facilities Laboratories. 1974. *Reusing Railroad Stations.* New York: Educational Facilities Laboratories. Research and writing by Hardy Holzman Pfeiffer Associates.

Franzen, Ulrich, and Paul Rudolph. 1974. *The Evolving City: Urban Design Proposals.* New York: The American Federation of Arts.

Fruin, John J. 1971. *Pedestrian Planning and Design.* New York: Metropolitan Association of Urban Designers and Environmental Planners.

Golay, Michael. 2000. *Railroad Stations, Depots and Roundhouses.* New York: Barnes and Noble Books.

Harris, Cyril M., ed. 1998. *Handbook of Acoustical Measurements and Noise Control.* 3d ed. New York: McGraw-Hill.

Houska, Catherine. 2003. *Which Stainless Steel Should Be Specified for Exterior Applications?* London: International Molybdenum Association. www.imoa.info.; IMOA ABC 00/03

Jane's Urban Transport Systems. 2002–2003. London: Jane's Publications.

Jenkins, Brian M. 2001. *Protecting Public Service Transportation Against Terrorism and Serious Crime: An Executive Overview.* San Jose, Calif.: Mineta Transportation Institute.

Jenkins, Brian M., and Larry N. Gersten. 2001. *Protecting Public Service Transportation Against Terrorism and Serious Crime: Continuing Research on Best Securities Practices*. San José, Calif.: Mineta Transportation Institute.

Kang, J. 1996. "Modeling of Train Noise in Underground Stations." *Journal of Sound and Vibration* 195 (2).

Meeks, Carroll L. V. 1975. *The Railroad Station: An Architectural History*. New Haven, Conn.: Yale University Press.

New Jersey Transit. 1944. *Planning for Transit-Friendly Land Use: A Handbook for New Jersey Communities*. Newark: New Jersey Transit.

Nickel Development Institute (NiDI). 1990. *Stainless Steel for Durability, Fire Resistance and Safety*. Publication no. 10042. www.nidi.org

———. 1994. *Stainless Steel in Architecture, Building and Construction*. Publication no. 11014. www.nidi.org

———. 2001. *Stainless Steel in Architecture, Building and Construction: Guidelines for Corrosion Resistance*. Publication no. 11024. www.nidi.org

Sabine, Wallace Clement. 1922. *Collected Papers on Acoustics*. Cambridge: Harvard University Press.

Schultz, Theodore. 1985. "Acoustical Uses for Perforated Metal." In *Sonderdruck aus den Rundfunktechnischen Mitteilungen*. Available at www.diamondman.com

Specialty Steel Industry of North America. *Special Finishes for Stainless Steel*. www.ssina.com

Subway Environmental Design Handbook. 1976. Vol. 1. 2d ed. Washington, D.C.: Urban Mass Transit Transportation Administration, USDOT.

Triangle Transit Authority. 1995. *Triangle Fixed Guideway Study, Phase II Report*. Research Triangle Park, N.C.: Triangle Transit Authority. www.ridetta.org

———. 1997. *Station Area Development Guidelines for Regional Transit Stations*. Research Triangle Park, N.C.: Triangle Transit Authority. www.ridetta.org

Wolf, Steven. 1996. "Acoustical Guidelines for the Design of Transit Stations in High Noise Level Locations." Paper presented at the APTA Rail Transit Conference, Atlanta, Ga., June.

Wolfe, Steven L. 1983. *Acoustical Treatment for Sound Control in Stations*. Los Angeles: Southern California Rapid Transit District.

INDEX